PRODUCTION AND INVENTORY CONTROL

PRENTICE-HALL, INC.
Englewood Cliffs, N.J.

PRODUCTION AND INVENTORY CONTROL

Principles and Techniques

G. W. PLOSSL

O. W. WIGHT

PRENTICE-HALL INTERNATIONAL, INC., London
PRENTICE-HALL OF AUSTRALIA, PTY. LTD., Sydney
PRENTICE-HALL OF CANADA, LTD., Toronto
PRENTICE-HALL OF INDIA (PRIVATE) LTD., New Delhi
PRENTICE-HALL OF JAPAN, INC., Tokyo

Library of Congress Catalog Card Number 67–10750
Printed in the United States of America

Current printing (last digit):
25

PREFACE

Having both practiced and taught the subject, we have been pleased by the increasing development of the production and inventory control function and the growing interest in a more scientific approach. We decided to write this book to bridge the gap between the scientific techniques and practice, not only to assist the practitioner in doing a better job but also to put the newer techniques in a practical context so that the student of management science will have an appreciation of these techniques from the business manager's viewpoint. Lack of understanding of the practical problems has, in our opinion, tended to hobble progress in the application of scientific techniques in the real world of business. Much of what is between these covers might be called the "knowledge of experience," but we are well satisfied from our own teaching efforts that this experience can be passed on and, in fact, *must* be passed on if business management is to make real progress in understanding and applying modern techniques, particularly now that many companies have computers available to handle the techniques.

In the past, production and inventory control has too often been considered to be a rather loose assortment of techniques such as economic order quantities and machine loading. In fact, all of the elements of a production and inventory control system interrelate, and when one or two techniques are viewed as panaceas, the results are inevitably disappointing. Our objective has been to show the interdependence of all of the elements in a control system and the chapter sequence was chosen to emphasize their logical relationships. Subjects of special interest to the student or special cases have been covered in the appendices so that they would not distract readers from the methodology of production and inventory control.

The development and exposition of many excellent techniques that apply to this field is laudable, but unfortunately, most of these techniques have usually been discussed in a vacuum. PERT, for example, is a real step forward in scheduling but few articles on the subject have bothered to explain the limited applications it has or how it relates to other scheduling techniques. This approach has focussed attention on techniques and frequently obscured the underlying principles. We have tried to relate techniques to one another and to emphasize the principles behind them. In discussing materials control, for example, we have explained the current approaches to order point calculation along with other related techniques while emphasizing where this technique does *not* apply as well as where it does. An underlying principle that has often been ignored, for example, is the effect that work-in-process has on all the elements of production control and control of *all* of the inventories as well as customer service. We have emphasized this basic relationship and the production planning techniques that can be used to get and keep work-in-process under control.

The greatest hope for a broader application of management science techniques and the computer rests with the student of management science who plans to make his career in industry. To make this text more useful to the educator, we have supplied questions and case material. The sheer limitations of space have prohibited us from discussing shop paperwork and manufacturing organization in depth and some students may at first have difficulty becoming accustomed to business terminology. We suggest a plant visit in conjunction with Chapter 1, if the instructor feels his students require more insight into typical shop organization and paperwork. A dictionary of production and inventory control terms is available from the American Production and Inventory Control Society* and would be a useful supplement to this text.

Our own enthusiasm for the new approaches to production and inventory control is easy to discern throughout this book, but we have omitted any mathematics beyond the simplest algebra and mentioned the computer only where necessary to add meaning to the topic under discussion; there is a great deal of excellent literature available on both topics today. Our emphasis is on principles and techniques that apply

---

*American Production and Inventory Control Society, 2600 Virginia Ave., N.W., Washington, D.C. 20037.

whether or not the system is designed for the computer, and our concern has been to explain the techniques as simply as possible—emphasizing where they should or *should not* be used and how they interrelate.

We would like to acknowledge a few of the many friends and associates who contributed to our knowledge and thus to this book. Among these are: C. M. Antisdale of the Bristol Co., W. E. Goddard of the Raybestos Division, Raybestos-Manhattan, Inc.; W. B. Atchison, Jr., R. H. Bartlett, T. T. Gately, and J. D. Harty of The Stanley Works; and L. F. Sargent of H. B. Maynard and Co. The concept of *independent* and *dependent* demand originally suggested by Dr. J. A. Orlicky of the IBM Corporation was of particular help in presenting criteria for the proper application of inventory control techniques. We would also like to acknowledge the kind permission of the American Management Association to use certain illustrations (5–19, 9–1, 9–2, and 9–17) which appeared in their book by Robert E. Finley and Henry R. Ziobro, *The Manufacturing Man and His Job,* (AMA, New York: 1966, pp. 154–174). The objective reviews of Prof. Wallace Richardson, Lehigh University; Dr. Wolter Fabrycky, Virginia Polytechnic Institute; and Prof. Clifton Anderson, North Carolina State University were of immeasurable help in reworking much of this text, as was the constructive criticism and constant encouragement of our editor, Matthew I. Fox, of Prentice-Hall. The greatest thanks of all, however, go to our wives, Marion and Betty, whose patience, encouragement, and practical assistance through many retypings really made this book possible.

G. W. Plossl and O. W. Wight

The Production Control Experts

(with apologies to "*The Blind Men and the Elephant,*"
by John Godfrey Saxe)

It was six men of management
To learning much inclined
Who discoursed on production control
And the answers they did find
—from experience, and the lessons
That reward an inquiring mind.

"Order to mins and maximums,"
The first was heard to say,
"You'll have neither too much nor too little
When production's controlled this way."

"But the answer lies in a forecast,"
Said the second man in line,
"Just anticipate your sales,
And everything will be fine."

"I doubt it" said the third one,
"You've forgotten the EOQ.
With balanced setups and inventories,
What problems can ensue?"

The fourth one said: "Use order points
To get the desired control.
When you order materials soon enough,
You'll never be 'in the hole.'"

"But you really need a computer."
Said the fifth—"P.C. 's a dream
With loads run from last week's payroll cards
And exception reports by the ream."

Said the sixth, "Materials management
Is a concept to which I'm devoted—
Instead of learning production control,
I've escaped by getting promoted!"

So study each book and seminar,
Attend every one you can, sir!
You'll find a thousand experts
—each with PART of the answer.

O. W. Wight

CONTENTS

CHAPTER EIGHT   CONTROLLING PRODUCTION CAPACITY, 220

CHAPTER NINE   CONTROLLING INPUT— SCHEDULING, 241

PERSPECTIVE

The objectives of production and inventory control

Three of the major objectives in most manufacturing firms intent on earning profit are:

1. *Maximum customer service*
2. *Minimum inventory investment*
3. *Efficient (low-cost) plant operation*

The major problem in meeting these objectives is that they are *basically in conflict*. Maximum customer service can be provided if inventories are raised to very high levels and the plant is kept flexible by altering production levels and varying production schedules to meet the customers' changing demands. The second and third objectives thus suffer to meet the first. Efficient plant operation can be maintained if production levels are seldom changed, no overtime is incurred, and if machines are run for long periods once they are set up on a particular product—this results in large inventories and poor customer service while meeting the objective of maximum plant efficiency. Inventories can be kept low if customers are made to wait and if the plant is forced to react rapidly to changes in customer requirements and interruptions in production. In the real-life business world, few companies can afford to work toward one or two of these objectives to the exclusion of the others.

Production and inventory control is basically concerned with providing the information needed for the day-to-day decisions required to reconcile these objectives in plant operations. The fact that these objectives are in basic conflict was readily apparent to the manager who owned his own screw machine parts-making company, for example. He had invested his money in the machines and equipment in his plant, he controlled his own manufacturing schedules and he was his own sales representative. When a customer demanded immediate delivery, his alternatives were clear—either spend money on breaking into machine setups and working overtime or let the customer wait. He also had the alternative of carrying inventory in the future—either finished parts or raw material—so that he would be able to give his customer better service. The basic conflicts among the objectives existed in this one-manager company and they were not easy to resolve, but at least he could see the conflict and weigh the alternatives.

In a large manufacturing company today, the responsibility for customer service rests with one organizational group, the sales department, which seldom recognizes much responsibility for either plant efficiency or for the levels of inventory. On the other hand, manufacturing people usually feel little responsibility for inventories and perhaps little more for customer service. In fact, many plant managers and foremen have probably never thought of their activities from a customer's point of view. Frequently, the performance of these people is measured not on their contribution to overall company objectives but only on their ability to meet their own limited goals. Very few foremen, for example, are rated on their ability to control lead times and keep items in stock, but they know that their careers depend greatly on their ability to get out production and to meet their budget goals. By the same token, very few sales personnel are judged by their contribution to profit, but are rated instead solely on their ability to sell products. One of the overworked clichés in business today is *"It's healthy to have people within a company competing against one another."* There is truth to this statement when managers are competing for the **same goals**—such competition can produce excellent results—but when they start competing for **different goals,** the results can be waste, conflict and frustration.

Reconciling these conflicting objectives in a modern company, where responsibilities have been sharply divided and where managers have been encouraged to suboptimize by their performance measures, becomes a challenging problem; attempting to solve this problem is the prime function of production and inventory control. Working through an information system, planning, measuring actual performance against the plan and then presenting information to line managers who must take corrective action, production and inventory control's function is to reconcile these objectives to meet the overall profit goals of the company.

The evolution of production and inventory control

Production control and inventory control developed separately. In its very beginnings, production control was only one of the many functions performed by the line foreman. He ordered material, set the size of the work force and the level of production by hiring and releasing people, expedited work through his department and controlled customer service through the inventories that resulted from his efforts. As his workload increased, the foreman was assisted by a clerk added to take care of such functions as timekeeping, other miscellaneous record-keeping and answering the telephone in his department. This brought the clerk into frequent contact with the sales department while answering requests for the status of jobs and for delivery promises; he also began reordering material and planning other preparations needed for production in addition to following progress of the work. He was really the beginning of the production control function.

Eventually, as record-keeping activities were transferred into the main office, this clerk developed into a stock chaser. One prominent New England company had a department in the 1890's known as the *"Hurry-up Department"*—it's easy to imagine the responsibilities and activities of these people. While there were a few attempts at a more organized and scientific approach to production control (there was evidently a fairly comprehensive production control system installed at the Watertown Arsenal in the 1880's[1]) general application did not develop prior to World War II.

By World War II, the position of stock-chaser had fallen into disrepute because of its association (in the minds of co-workers) with crises, upsets, pressure and trouble. Henry Kaiser gave his shipbuilding company stock-chasers the name *"expediters"* and, with the aid of a *Reader's Digest* article, popularized the concept of the expediter as an action-oriented go-getter who made a vital contribution to meeting production schedules. By the 1950's, the term *"expediting"* was often used in books defining production control; one practitioner about that time characterized his activities as

[1]Scheele, Evan D., Westerman, William L., and Wimmert, Robert J., *Principles and Design of Production Control Systems,* Prentice-Hall, Englewood Cliffs, New Jersey, 1960, p. 5.

ordering the necessary parts to make an assembly after receiving a customer's order, then, when the customer asked why it wasn't delivered on time, following up to find out where these parts were and putting "RUSH" tags on them. Even today, the expediter is an integral, necessary part of most production control systems.

Inventory control, on the other hand, developed—at least in theory— along more scientific lines. The basic concept of the economic lot size was first published in 1915[1] and the statistical approach to determining order points was presented by R. H. Wilson in 1934[2]. However, these fairly sophisticated techniques of inventory management had very little application. Perhaps this was because the 1930's and 1940's were not years that encouraged scientific management. For most companies during the depression of the 1930's, the most important objective was survival. Much as men in a damaged airplane over the ocean throw food and valuables overboard in order to keep the plane aloft long enough to reach land, long-term profit and growth became subordinate during the Great Depression. During the late 1940's, when pent-up demand provided a ready market for every article that could be produced, the objectives of inventory control—leveling workload or competing on the basis of customer service—were not important in most business operations.

The scientific management movement from the early 1900's to World War II, under Frederick Taylor, Emerson, Gantt, the Gilbreths and others, had helped to provide recognition that the work of planning and controlling production should be a staff activity and, as a result, production and inventory control functions existed as distinct functions in most companies—but were usually very crude. Production control, with the exception of some simple machine-loading techniques, still consisted basically of expediting in most companies, and while inventory control had developed some scientific theories, these had seen very little real application.

Out of World War II came operations research—the application of scientific techniques to solving the problems of war, where the allocation of limited resources was a matter of victory or defeat. These operations research techniques were quite effective in World War II. When the scientists who did this work got back to the problems of a peacetime world, their attention focused on production and inventory control, where elements of the problem can be expressed numerically, where statistical probability theories can be applied and where so many of the decisions are

[1]Harris, F. W., *Operations and Cost* (Factory Management Series), Chapter IV, A. W. Shaw Company, Chicago, 1915.

[2]Wilson, R. H., "A Scientific Routine for Stock Control," *Harvard Business Review*, Vol. 13, No. 1, 1934.

the result of balancing alternative solutions. Some notable results were produced in forecasting, inventory control and mathematical programming, and while operations research has not solved all of the business problems it set out to solve, it has generated new interest in a more rational approach to production and inventory control.

Probably the biggest problem in applying scientific techniques in industry has been the fact that companies were not ready for these techniques because they had not even begun to solve many of their basic problems in controlling manufacturing. Many companies did not even have reasonably accurate lists of the parts that made up their products or route sheets to list the operations sequences; they depended instead upon the memories of the men in the factory who had made the product for years. Before scientific techniques could be applied, basic information had to be readily available and accurate. In addition, the volume of calculations required for applying such techniques as the statistical determination of order points, which was highly developed by operations research, was considerably beyond the capabilities of manual systems.

By the late 1950's, the electronic computer was being widely used in industry, but as with most new technologies, there were as many failures as successes in applying this powerful tool. All the information processed had to be accurate since the personal interference that even a reasonably good clerk could give was no longer available to correct obviously ridiculous errors and compensate for missing information. While the computer offered almost unlimited capacity in computation, it focused attention on the need for disciplines in information-handling that many companies had failed to develop in the past. Efforts to apply the computer were often attempts to install a mechanized system in companies that had never taken manual systems seriously enough to make them work satisfactorily.

Production control today

The production control department is today a recognized part of almost every company. The department manager usually reports to the chief manufacturing executive (plant manager, factory manager, manufacturing vice-president) and is responsible for the system that provides the information enabling other managers to work toward common company goals. He is responsible for seeing that these managers meet customer service and inventory objectives while permitting the plant to be operated profitably. The job is a staff position and provides such a broad picture of overall company operations that it is often the training ground for the chief manufacturing executive, since it requires an understanding of most facets of business, including the financial control systems and the computer. As its usefulness and ability to be of service to higher levels of management have developed, production control has moved up the organizational ladder, and a concept called *"Materials Management"* is now being applied in many companies. A materials manager is usually responsible for traffic, purchasing, production control, receiving, shipping, branch warehouses, storerooms and interplant trucking, although many variations are practiced. In recent years, the materials management concept has been the subject of magazine articles and much animated discussion and competition among purchasing agents, production control managers and materials handling managers, who disagree as to which activity provides the best preparation for the materials manager position—usually overlooking the fact that choosing a man for such a newly-created position will depend a great deal more on his managing talents than upon his technical background.

Materials management offers some solid benefits as a type of organization but, unfortunately, it is rarely the cure-all that some expect it to be. This organization format of itself does not permit use of any systems, procedures, or techniques for controlling that cannot be used without it. The principal benefit to be derived from this form of organization, in which all of the people concerned with the flow of material through the plant report to one man, is that he can direct activities to get the most cooperation and effectiveness from these people working together. If the only way to get the executives responsible for materials handling, traffic, purchasing, and production control to work together effectively is to have them report to the same boss, then the materials management concept offers real potential benefits. In companies grown so large that the span of control is unwieldy for the top level managers to whom the purchasing agent, production control manager, traffic manager, warehouse manager, etc., report, a materials manager is undoubtedly justified.

Should a company adopt the materials management concept? If it has an organizational problem or if a revision in organization will bring more expert talent to help solve some of the problems, materials management should be adopted. If, on the other hand, the real problem lies in the area of systems design, quality and timeliness of information or poorly organized activity within the production control department, an organizational change will not solve these problems, and it would be unfortunate to divert attention or delay action in solving the real problems.

The real challenge in production and inventory control has been in proper application of known tools and techniques that must be used with any organizational concept. New techniques will be developed in the coming years, but the frontier today is in the area of successfully applying the present techniques. The paradox of production control has been that the practitioner knows his company is *"different,"* yet is continually search-ing for a technique someone else has used successfully, hoping it will solve his problem. Such transplanting of techniques all too frequently fails when basic principles are unknown or ignored. As long as the em-phasis remains on techniques, and principles are subsidiary, good techni-ques will be misused.

Professionals have begun to recognize basic principles and to know the useful techniques and apply them to the basic elements that make up any production control system. These elements are:

1. *A forecast*

2. *A plan for:*
   (a) Inventory levels
   (b) Production rates (capacity)

3. *Control—through feedback and corrective action—of:*
   (a) Production rates
   (b) Input—scheduling and loading
   (c) Output—dispatching and follow-up

These are basic elements, some of which comprise all inventory and production control systems. Excepting situations where all work is based on a backlog of orders, every system starts with a forecast. The forecast is then converted into plans for the total inventories needed to support the forecast level of business. These form the base inventory level on which production capacity can be planned. If a plant vacation shutdown is anticipated, for example, inventory should be built-up to cover this period; this inventory will be needed in addition to the base inventory level, and capacity will have to be planned to provide for this buildup.

Once plans are made, control is required to insure that they are met. This requires feedback to report actual status in relation to plan and to show where corrective action is required to get back to the original plan. Input control involves the inventory control system that generates orders on a vendor for purchased items or on the plant for manufactured com-ponents and finished goods. Output control governs the flow from the producing system, whether it be the vendor or the company's own man-ufacturing facilities. Where a company maunfactures for its own inven-tory, this is basically shop floor control. The intimate relationship be-tween input and output control must be recognized in any successful system.

These elements do not all appear in every inventory and production control system. A distributor, for example, is not very concerned with planning manufacturing capacity, since he merely places orders on sup-pliers and depends on their being able to deliver so as to meet his requirements. On the other hand, a make-to-order plant may be able to do little forecasting and may not maintain a finished goods inventory—but even it has raw material and component inventories to maintain. Most of the emphasis in this type of plant, however, will be reaction—*control* of production rates, input and output. Production control in a make-to-stock plant must be deeply concerned with all elements and problems of both inventory and manufacturing control.

Production and inventory control has been developing rapidly as a new management science. Practitioners, whose knowledge in this field has come principally from their own experience, are now learning to distinguish between principles and techniques, and to understand proper application of the latter. It is in this area of application that the real breakthroughs are occurring today. Some of the credit must surely be given to the American Production and Inventory Control Society, founded in 1957, where professional practitioners, educators and other interested individuals are organized to foster education and research in the field of production and inventory control. This group has stimulated development of the trade literature and has provided opportunities for practitioners to compare notes, visit one another's plants and learn from one another's experience rather than having to "reinvent the wheel."

The relationship between inventory control and production control

One common misconception in industry is that production and inventory control are separate functions. This does not recognize the basic truth that inventories in a manufacturing plant are maintained to support production or are themselves the result of production. Only where inventories are purchased and then resold without requiring further work can inventory control have meaning apart from production control.

Much of the literature written on the subject of order quantities and order points, for example, assumes inventory control in a manufacturing plant to be an independent function. However, order points and economic order quantities (EOQ's) can't be used successfully to control finished goods inventory without considering how they affect plant production rates and schedules. By the same token, production scheduling techniques cannot be developed apart from the inventory control system that generates the orders which make up the schedules. The backlogs that build up ahead of operations in the plant are very real inventories and have a real effect on the ordering technique through their effect on lead times. The scheduling system must control these inventories if it is to control production properly.

When inventory control is functionally separated from production control, it is typical for the inventory controller to issue orders to the plant as individual items reach their order points, and then to have the production controller try to expedite these orders through the manufacturing operations, exerting intense pressure on the plant people to work overtime, make extra set-ups, shift the working force, or take other extraordinary—and expensive—action to cope with the peaks and valleys of work that result. In practice, this usually results in backlogs of manufacturing orders and in-process material ahead of the manufacturing facilities as plant operating people strive to keep production going at a level rate. Using backlogs to level the workload, of course, means high inventories, excessive lead times and poor service. In many companies, the inventory control department's reaction to this problem is simply to assert that "*We put the dates on the orders and it's up to Manufacturing to get these orders through on time.*" The major philosophical point of operations research—that people tend to work toward minor goals, or to "suboptimize"—can find no clearer illustration than in these circumstances.

Perhaps the most important result of this division of responsibility and the consequent ineffectiveness of both functions is that production control almost inevitably becomes the whipping boy for most of the ills of the plant. This attitude is prevalent because plant people feel that production control personnel are irresponsible and demanding, that they contribute little or nothing to help operate the plant efficiently, but rather interfere with their efforts and cause upset and confusion.

Effective production control functions have to be intimately tied in with inventory control activities, and both must work together to satisfy all three objectives of production and inventory control; neither can accept responsibility for only one or two of these objectives. It would be pleasant if the control system could be broken into independent elements so that each might handle its own area of responsibility without regard to the others. Unfortunately, the elements of a production and inventory control system are so interrelated that they cannot be isolated from one another in practice without impairing their effectiveness.

Management policy and production control

The activities taking place in the inventory and production control department to meet the goals of customer service, inventory turnover and efficient plant operation should be conducted in accordance with well-defined management policy, but, quite frequently, two breakdowns occur. Management may establish policy without having the facts needed to enable them to make intelligent decisions, or management may fail to set important policies needed to control their operations. The first situation can best be illustrated by policies set by many managements for inventory turnover rates based only on industry averages. Built into the acceptance of an industry average turnover rate as a company's own goal are two basic assumptions—first, that other companies in the industry are managing their operations properly and, second, that such operations are comparable. Both of these are highly questionable assumptions.

On the other hand, when policies are not defined, management yields its decision-making rights to clerical personnel by default. Inventory control clerks or storeroom clerks can establish company policy by the manner in which they place their inventory replenishment orders, for example. These clerks do not have the information required to decide which inventory levels best fit the company's overall requirements. They characteristically react to immediate pressures—increase inventories just when the plant is having the most difficulty meeting its production goals or decrease inventories when the plant is able to produce products at a satisfactory rate.

The absence of intelligent policies relating to inventory levels also leads to a panic reaction to overweight inventories in times of falling business activity. The usual reaction is to issue a decree that inventories must be cut by some specific amount, without regard to the true requirements of the business and without full realization of the impact such cuts may have on the production level. Not only is customer service hurt, but production rate changes caused initially by falling demand are amplified greatly by untimely and excessive inventory reductions. The reverse sequence (with the same amplification effect) occurs when business picks up again and crash programs are initiated to rebuild depleted inventories. Poor inventory management and production planning aggravate the ill effects of the business cycle. Modern society as well as professional management expects better performance from inventory and production control.

In a well-run modern company, the management policies concerning inventories, customer service, and plant hiring and layoff are developed rationally from information supplied by the production control function. The production control manager emphasizes the real alternatives faced by a manager, recognizing that many companies have floundered[1] because their managements did not recognize and face up to the limited, unpleasant alternatives and make the necessary decisions in time to avert crisis.

Once policy has been established, the production control manager develops plans to execute these policies and follows up to see that plans

---

[1]Smith, Richard Austin, *Corporations in Crisis,* Doubleday, Garden City, N.Y., 1963.

are met. He has no direct authority over the foremen in the plant, for example, but guides instead by generating information to show other managers how to meet common objectives. To some extent, he acts as a catalyst, urging others to take proper action in order to satisfy the overall objectives of the company. To do his job, he has no need for the authority to tell a foreman when he must work people overtime or when he must reassign workers to more urgent jobs—this authority must rest with the line personnel, the plant manager, superintendents and department foremen. Perhaps the distinction can be better understood by using the six basic question words of the English language: *"What," "When," "Who," "How," "Where"* and *"Why."* Production control determines **what** items and quantities should be made and **when** they should be made, taking into account the three basic objectives. It's up to the manufacturing people to decide **how** and **where** the product should be made and **who** should make it. When, as is so frequently the case, actual performance does not meet the plan, both production control and manufacturing will have to answer **why**.

Conclusion

Production and inventory control has thus emerged from a long period of clerical status to a position close to the focus of management attention because of management's recognition of the need for a sound function to plan and control plant operations. More and more of the attention of operations researchers and others concerned with the development of scientific management techniques has been focused on production control because it works with quantitative data, with uncertainty, and for conflicting objectives. The advent of the computer has made many useful techniques practical, yet many companies have found that they cannot take full advantage of these because they have not yet learned to handle information in the disciplined manner required by any *real* control system. At the same time, they have found that increasing product complexity and pressures of competition on costs and service have made it impossible to manage their operations while relying upon the memory of experienced workers to maintain the basic information required for manufacturing control.

Production control has, over the years, developed from inventory control and expediting to a fairly well-defined set of techniques applicable to the basic elements of systems required in almost all companies. The modern practitioner avoids grasping at techniques alone to solve his problems: he recognizes that dispatching alone, for example, will not work satisfactorily without some means for planning and controlling total production capacity, he recognizes also that his inventory control system will not function properly unless he has some means of controlling lead times in the plant and, above all, he recognizes that no single technique is a panacea for his troubles. The professional in the field understands the basic techniques, knows where they apply, and relies upon an information system that embraces all the basic elements of production and inventory control to generate the information that he will use to guide other managers in controlling the manufacturing operations.

Production control today is developing as an integrated concept rather than a loose collection of techniques. It is focusing new attention on presenting timely, objective decision alternatives to other managers, and these managers in turn are recognizing a basic truth in a competitive business world: at the heart of any company that is going to take advantage of its marketing opportunities, control its financial investment and run its manufacturing facilities to make a profit is an effective production control system.

Bibliography

1. Broffman, Morton H., "What Management Expects of Production and Inventory Control," *APICS Quarterly Bulletin,* Vol. 2, No. 1, January 1961.

2. Plossl, G. W. and Wight, O. W., "You Can't Eliminate Expediting, But. . . ," *APICS Quarterly Bulletin,* Vol. 5, No. 2, April 1964.

3. Smith, Richard Austin, *Corporations in Crisis,* Doubleday, Garden City, New York, 1963.

FORECASTING

The importance of the forecast

Production control is concerned basically with the future. The past is beyond control—we must start from where we find ourselves now and prepare for the future. To do this, it is necessary to guess, assume, or otherwise estimate what is going to happen from now on. All other things being equal, a company can survive only by preparing itself to meet its customers' needs at least as quickly as its competitors.

Since all of the planning activity in a company deals with the future, much of the organization must work with sales forecasts. Figure 2-1 shows a summary of the various forecasts made by a typical company and their use. Household formations, for example, are used by the marketing department to determine total potential market growth. The plant manager and plant engineering department want to know five-year production requirements, since plans for land acquisition, development of new production processes based on changing volumes and technology, and the procurement of additional manufacturing facilities require long lead times. Figure 2-1 shows only the major requirements; there are many more ways of using the forecasts.

Production control, frequently called the *"planning department,"* is assigned the responsibility for planning the future needs for manufacturing the product. The demand forecast is the vital element in this pre-

Figure 2-1

Types of Forecasts and Their Uses

Forecast:	Required by:
1. Household formations	Marketing — determine total potential market growth
2. Total production required next five years	Production Management — plant expansion program
3. Number of screw machine hours (by machine type) required next two years	Production Management — next year's capital budget
4. Next year's sales	Sales — quotas Finance — expense budgets Production Management — manpower and machine capacities Production Control — seasonal inventory requirements and blanket purchase orders
5. Sales for next quarter	Production Control — manpower capacities, manufacturing and purchasing components
6. Sales for next week	Production Control — assembly schedules and dispatching priorities

paration. Production control uses this forecast as the basis for planning how many components to purchase, how much raw material to buy, what rate to machine or assemble, and, most important, when to order.

There are conflicting requirements for forecasts. The general manager, for example, is concerned with a forecast of shipments since these generate the dollars the company receives from its customers. He may find himself at odds with the marketing manager, who is more concerned with incoming business—since this measures customers' demands on his company requiring servicing. Shipments really represent incoming business filtered out by the company's ability to respond to demand. The sales manager is typically interested in setting optimistic goals as a challenge to his personnel, while the plant manager would rather have a more conservative forecast on which to estimate profits. The production control department wants the forecast in terms that are meaningful to the manufacturing departments (in product groups that go through similar manufacturing facilities, for example). The groups that are meaningful to marketing are those sold in similar channels and are not necessarily the same as manufacturing product groups.

Several forecasts are needed in most companies. These can be classified in many ways, one being the time period involved:

Long-range forecasts: For plant expansion and new machine and equipment acquisition, in order to plan capital investment five years or more in advance.

Intermediate-range forecasts: For procurement of long lead time materials or planning of operating rates, taking into account seasonal or cyclical products one to two years in advance.

Short-range forecasts: To determine the proper order quantities and order timing for purchasing or manufacturing components and to plan the proper manufacturing capacity, taking into consideration the desirability of leveling manload three to six months in advance.

Immediate-future demands: For assembly schedules and finished goods inventory distribution on a weekly or daily basis.

Long-range forecasting involves complex considerations beyond the scope of this book. It requires an understanding of economic factors, competitive and technological influences and capital expansion plans made by top management.

The shorter-range forecast, in general, requires greater accuracy. A forecast of capacity, for example, may indicate a certain number of machining hours required in the milling machine department. When the time comes to use these machining hours, they may be worked on a job that wasn't even considered when the original capacity forecast was made, yet the total requirement forecast for milling machine hours is likely to be quite accurate if there are many items going through the department. On the other hand, this week's assembly forecast establishes a schedule for manufacturing a particular mix of products in the final assembly department. Since these products will determine the specific finished goods inventory available for shipment, it is important that this forecast be as accurate as possible.

The specific forecasts needed by a company depend on the relationship between the length of its manufacturing cycle and the lead time allowed by its customers. This is illustrated in Fig. 2-2. If customers will wait while the company determines what materials are needed, procures these materials, processes them and finally delivers them, there is really no need for any type of forecast. Of course, few customers of any business will wait for their vendor to build or enlarge the plant or to get additional machine tools or other manufacturing facilities, so all companies need long-range forecasts for capital investment.

Figure 2-2

Allowable Lead Time vs. Forecasts Required

Procure material	Manufacture components	Assemble product	Ship	Industry
←————————Allowable lead time————+————————→				Heavy capital goods, ships, locomotives, missiles, etc.
(no product forecast required)				
	←————————Allowable lead time————————→			Special order, job shop.
	(raw material forecast required)			
		←——Allowable lead time——→		Machine tools, electronics, custom assemblies, etc.
	(raw material and component forecast required)			
			Allowable ←—lead time—→	Automotive replace- ment parts, consumer goods, etc. Shipped from stock.
	(raw material, components and product forecast required)			

If a company's competitors can furnish products to the customers in slightly more than the shipping time required, it will be necessary to maintain a finished goods inventory in order to fill orders as rapidly. This means that the company will have to forecast raw material needs, purchase and manufacture parts and schedule production of the necessary finished goods based on forecasts.

Figure 2-2 also indicates components of lead times for some typical industries. Undoubtedly, this picture will change as companies find it to their competitive advantage to ship a product in a shorter lead time, even though this requires them to maintain a higher inventory investment.

Many factors influence the demand for a company's products and services, and it is never possible to identify all of them and measure their impact or predict their effects. It is nevertheless helpful in forecasting to identify broad, major influences and to attempt to predict the changes they are likely to cause.

General business conditions and the state of the nation's economy influence almost every company's customers—and thus affect demand for its products. All long-range forecasts, and many intermediate-range ones, must include some evaluation of the effect of a changing economic climate.

Competitive factors are another major force to be considered. Competition comes indirectly from other demands on the customer's money as well as directly from similar or identical products. No company can afford to neglect an evaluation of what competitors are doing and the probable effects of this on their own business.

Trends in the marketplace, including changing desires of customers, growing demand, styles, fashions, etc., must also be considered as affecting a company's sales. Occasionally, these forces can be influenced to some extent by advertising, but in any case they are most difficult to control.

Finally, a company's plans for advertising, sales promotion, selling effort, pricing and quality improvement can have a major effect in creating or boosting demand. No forecast can be valid without an effort to include these factors.

The evolution of forecasting

In the early days of production control, formal procedures for the preparation of forecasts were not developed. The responsibility was not assigned to any individual or any segment of the organization. A forecast was rarely recognized as a real need. The need was usually filled intuitively by the owner-manager who decided to buy more material because he had confidence that he could process and sell it in the future, by the foreman who decided to hire a man because he believed the work load would continue to stay high and by the stock clerk who wrote out a new order to replenish a dwindling supply of bolts in the stock room.

Some years prior to World War II, many companies began to recognize the potential benefits of preparing forecasts in a formal manner. They set up a separate group responsible for preparing the forecast, outlined the procedures for approval of the forecast by those in the organization who were vitally concerned and frequently restricted distribution of the forecast to those eligible to receive such "confidential" information.

In many cases, large sums of money were spent to develop forecasts using statistical techniques, market research or other sophisticated methods. During this period, the basic assumption seemed to be that forecasting problems could be solved if only enough effort and intelligence were put into making them. This could well be termed the "rose-colored glasses" era of forecasting.

When perfect forecasts were not forthcoming, there set in the inevitable period of disillusionment. Production control systems based upon this premise excused their failures with the explanation that all would have been well "if we only had a good forecast." As a result of this reaction, many companies ceased all organized attempts to forecast and returned to intuitive guesses, stung by the failures and high costs of the "highfalutin' methods" which had let them down. Many companies still have not recovered completely from this reaction. Naive attitudes toward forecasting still abound in industry.

The present trend is to a more rational point of view recognizing that forecasts must and will be made and, therefore, that they might better be made by those most capable; it recognizes the value of using one formal forecast as a basis for all other forecasts rather than having many operating departments making their own guesses about the future. This rational approach also recognizes that forecasts will always be subject to error and that, while there are tools available to improve the art of forecasting, the amount of money and effort put into applying such tools rapidly reaches a point of diminishing return. Beyond this point, it is far more profitable to develop flexibility to cope with forecast inaccuracy instead of trying to improve the forecast. The best solution is to develop an economical forecasting system and a production control system that detects and measures forecast errors and reacts quickly to correct for such errors.

Forecasting principles and examples

The manager of production and inventory control is seldom responsible for the overall forecasts, but he needs to understand forecast characteristics and principles in order to design an effective production control system. He will have the problem of maintaining the thousands of item forecasts that most companies require for their materials control system and he should understand some of the basic forecasting techniques as an aid to interpreting forecasts.

Before discussing the techniques of forecasting, it is important that the general principles of forecasting be understood. The most important of these can be stated briefly:

1. *Forecasts are more accurate for larger groups of items*

2. *Forecasts are more accurate for shorter periods of time*

3. *Every forecast should include an estimate of error*

4. *Before applying any forecasting system, the forecasting method should be tested*

A fundamental statistical observation is that the behavior of individuals in a population is random even where the population as a whole has very stable characteristics. For example, it is extremely difficult to forecast the life expectancy of an individual, but insurance companies predict the average life expectancy of large groups of individuals with great accuracy. Likewise, it is possible to make a forecast for a large family of manufactured products with a fairly high degree of accuracy, although forecasts of individual items are subject to a high degree of error.

Figure 2-3 shows as an example a group of ten items. The individual items were forecast for the 3rd quarter of the year. At the end of that period, the actual sales totals were compared with the forecasts and the percent change from the forecast noted. These forecast errors for the items averaged 19.9%.

Figure 2-3

Forecast Error for Items vs. Group

Third Quarter				
Item	Forecast*	Actual	Difference	% Change from forecast
#7147–Lamp	47,600	42,784	−4816	−10.1
#8014–Tongs	12,800	9125	−3675	−28.7
#8663–File	1505	1157	− 348	−23.1
#8726–Stapler	22,500	28,392	+5892	+26.1
#8933–Screwdriver	10,100	11,934	+1834	+18.1
#9250–Shears	17,450	14,860	−2590	−14.8
#9261–Scissors	28,500	27,733	− 767	− 2.7
#9337–Rake	68,000	68,105	+ 105	+ 0.2
#9604–Hoe	27,200	17,556	−9644	−35.4
#9638–Shovel	3320	4638	+1318	−39.8
		Average forecast error for Items =		19.9
Group totals	238,975	226,284	−12,691	− 5.3

*Forecast made at end of the second quarter

The product group containing all items shows a forecast error of only 5.3%, illustrating the statistical truism that the large group can be forecast far more accurately than the individual item.

Figure 2-4 shows the comparison of a typical item forecast with the actual demand over a long period. This item was originally forecast to sell at 900 units per week and the forecast was not revised over a 50-week period. The cumulative forecast demand is simply the weekly forecast rate extended by the number of weeks, while the cumulative actual demand is the sum of the total actual sales through the number of weeks shown.

Figure 2-4

Forecast Error Over the Forecast Period

Item #9 Forecast = 900 units per week				
Week no.	Cumulative forecast demand	Cumulative actual demand	Approximate deviation from forecast	Deviation as a multiple of weekly forecast
2	1800	2004	200	0.2
5	4500	5230	700	0.8
10	9000	10,224	1200	1.3
15	13,500	15,465	2000	2.2
20	18,000	19,912	1900	2.1
25	22,500	24,472	2000	2.2
30	27,000	28,712	1700	1.9
35	31,500	33,312	1800	2.0
40	36,000	39,120	3100	3.5
45	40,500	46,785	6300	6.9
50	45,000	54,242	9200	10.2

The deviation tends to increase as the forecast is extended. For example, at the end of the second week the actual deviation from forecast is approximately 200 units, representing about $\frac{2}{10}$ of one week's supply, while at the end of the 35th week this has gone up to 1800 units—representing approximately a 2-week supply. At the end of the 50th week, this is increased further to approximately a 10-week supply. In general, forecast error will tend to increase as the length of the forecast period increases. A forecast that is extended over 50 weeks will be far less accurate than a forecast that is extended over only a 5-or 10-week period.

Every forecast should include an estimate of forecast error—the forecaster's expression of *how wrong* he thinks his forecast might be. This estimate can be expressed as a percentage (plus or minus) of the forecast or as a range between a maximum and minimum value. In establishing order points as described in Chapter 5, it is necessary to know both the estimated average usage during the lead time and the maximum anticipated usage during the lead time. The latter, of course, is a function of the accuracy of the demand forecast during the lead time period. Estimates of forecast error provide the basis needed to set up decision rules to determine when to take actions (such as recalculating economic order quantities or changing the production rate of a department). When actual demand falls outside the forecast range, it is probable that more than random influences are present and that action is required.

Although new items reaching the market are the most unpredictable, there are few situations where the estimate of forecast error can be used more profitably than in the new product forecast. The new product may be quite similar to something fairly stable already in the product line. In this case, where the sales department has some similar selling experience and the marketing department has forecast similar products in the past, the anticipated forecast error may be as low as 10%. On the other hand, for an entirely new product in a market where the company has had no experience, the forecast might be off by as much as 300%. Later sections of this book will treat in detail the use of the forecast error in making decisions in production and inventory control.

A good forecasting system will always be in a state of flux as the forecaster learns more about his art. He may develop new techniques and wish to test them against actual company data. If the forecaster wants to determine whether or not a new forecasting technique is effective he does not have to wait for sales to materialize before learning whether this technique is or is not valid. He can pretend that he is making his forecast a year or two earlier and then test the forecasting method against what really happened.

Figure 2-5 shows a simple example. In this case, a seasonal sales index

Figure 2-5

Testing the Forecast Technique

Estimating quarterly sales percentages	
Estimated quarterly sales percentages (based on average of five years actual sales prior to last year)	Actual quarterly sales percentages last year
1st quarter – 21.00%	20.50%
2nd quarter – 29.00%	30.30%
3rd quarter – 29.00%	28.90%
4th quarter – 21.00%	20.30%
Total 100.00%	100.00%

was developed based on the average of five year's actual sales prior to the last year. The last year's actual sales were omitted from this calculation and were used to test the method by comparing the percentage of sales to be anticipated in each quarter based on past history with actual quarterly sales percentages for the test year. While this is not an extensive test, it does indicate that for the past year the forecasting technique for determining quarterly sales percentages would have been reasonably accurate. This technique would not be valid if the test year were one of the five years used to establish the original percentages, since these indices would obviously be very likely to correlate well with the history used in developing them.

The important advantage of testing is that the forecaster is able to make inexpensive mistakes by simulating his forecasting system. If his forecasting system is shown to be good by the testing, then it is likely to be good in practice in the future.

Making a forecast

There are three essential steps in forecasting:

1. *Preparing the data*
2. *Making the forecast (and the estimate of forecast error)*
3. *Tracking the forecast*

For many companies, the basic problem of preparing sound data can often be formidable. Finding sales figures for a long enough period to develop a good forecasting method and test it requires more than a set of sales figures. Without related records, looking at past sales history would not show when strikes, price increases, inventory tax dates, changes in the accounting calendar, special sales promotions and the like may have introduced elements into the data that make them unreliable as a basis for forecasting.

In preparing the data, the forecaster must also determine just what he intends to forecast. A factory that sells most of its goods to customers through branch warehouses must gear its production to warehouse requirements as well as customer requirements, since the warehouses will undoubtedly build some inventory in anticipation of peak customer demands. This will generate requirements on the factory in excess of actual customer sales during such periods. If the forecaster merely predicts the increase in incoming business from customers, the factory will not be ready to produce enough goods at the proper time to fill the distribution pipeline.

The forecaster must determine whether he is going to use the data to forecast shipments or incoming business. Shipments data reflect what the production facility has been able to do in response to incoming business. For example, a product that has been in short supply for four or five months will show a history of low shipments in spite of a high rate of incoming business. The forecaster who bases his estimates of future requirements on past shipments will prolong the shortage period by not reflecting true demand for the product. Very few companies, even with adequate inventories, can respond rapidly enough to sudden surges in demand to keep shipments equal to incoming business. In Fig. 2-6, a

Figure 2-6

Shipments vs. Incoming Orders

Month	Shipments	Incoming orders	Order backlog
Jan.	302	305	31
Feb.	373	372	30
Mar.	465	471	36
Apr.	530	562	68
May	591	681	158
June	626	615	147
July	603	664	208
Aug.	687	675	196
Sept.	731	658	123
Oct.	642	570	51
Nov.	372	340	19
Dec.	254	269	34
Total	6176	6182	

typical example of shipments *vs.* demand, it can be seen that the sudden increase of business in April and May resulted in an increase in the shipping rate, but that the shipping room was not able to overcome the resulting backlog until November. This does not mean that a large number of May orders didn't get shipped until November, but it does show that the delay in customer shipments increased greatly during the peak season. The forecaster who used shipments as a basis for determining seasonal activity would forecast a later and higher peak. As a result, the factory would be manufacturing products too late to meet actual customer demand.

It is also important to separate streams of demand in forecasting. The same factory mentioned above might well be shipping 45% of its goods directly to customers and 55% to them indirectly via warehouses.

This will mean two separate types of forecasts for orders on the factory, one representing actual customer demand directly on the factory and the other representing customer demand on warehouses plus increases or minus decreases in the warehouse inventories.

Many companies have products that are sold to different classes of trade. For example, a company may make a hardware item normally sold to wholesalers in small quantities ordered frequently—but occasionally purchased by an original equipment manufacturer to be used in manufacturing furniture in two lots per year. Twice a year there would be extremely large demands upon the inventory in addition to the great number of small demands from wholesalers, and these two *"streams of demand"* would require different forecasts. The *"average"* demand would be meaningless.

It is extremely important for the forecaster to use the proper forecasting period. Figure 2-7 shows the deceptive picture that "monthly sales" can give to the forecaster. Looking only at this column, it appears that sales in February have dropped substantially from January levels and that sales in March increased over both January and February. When the number of working days per month is taken into account, it can be seen

Figure 2-7

Monthly Sales vs. Daily Sales

Month	Monthly sales	Working days per month	Sales per working day
January	334,000	22	15,200
February	310,000	20	15,500
March	338,000	23	14,700

that the sales per working day actually increased from January to February and were lower in March than in the previous two months.

The next step is making the forecast and estimating the likely error. The forecaster makes the forecast using a technique that he has developed and tested and that he knows to be reliable. Some useful techniques for making forecasts are discussed later in this chapter.

Tracking the forecast means comparing actual sales with the forecast and calculating the actual errors. This is extremely important since it enables the company to react promptly when conditions change from original plans. The comparison of actual demand against the forecast should be made frequently to be most effective and is usually best handled by production and inventory control personnel who must keep these data as part of their regular inventory and production recordkeeping function and who therefore have the means to keep the tracking up-to-date. Giving this responsibility to the marketing department which made the forecast—on the assumption that it is its responsibility to check the forecast's accuracy—results in having duplicate records in marketing and production and inventory control. The marketing department records are usually not kept up-to-date since they are not the department's primary function and this information is not essential to their day-to-day operation. Since tracking the forecast is so important in triggering reaction to change, it is important to place the responsibility with the group planning and controlling the operating information.

Many companies with seasonal products develop special sales programs to allow their customers (usually distributors or wholesalers) to purchase the product before the peak season at a substantial discount. This helps to get inventory off the manufacturer's shelves when he most needs the space, reduces his capital investment in inventories and permits him to level production over the year. Many of these companies believe that such programs also reduce forecasting problems. Unfortunately, distributors and wholesalers seldom have any recognizable forecasting function and usually base their purchases on past sales experience, depending on the manufacturer to respond quickly to unforeseen demands. During the peak season, when actual retail sales are generating heavy demands on his facilities, the manufacturer finds that he must scramble frantically to readjust the product mix on distributors' shelves since past distributor purchases are usually not indicative of the actual retail sales that finally materialize. In order to overcome this problem, some companies recommend stocking levels to their distributors which are based upon their own forecasts of changing product mix.

Many appliance manufacturers include a guarantee postcard with their product which the purchaser must fill out and return to the manufacturer in order to validate the guarantee. This card also contains much information that is of value to the company's marketing department in determining the value of different advertising media and the effectiveness of various distribution systems, but its primary purpose is to give the manufacturer prompt information on actual retail sales. This enables him to react more quickly to correct his production levels as retail sales change (rather than waiting for this change to be relayed through the distribution network, which usually results in far more drastic changes to correct the production level).

Several companies are tying their distributors into a data-collection network and are including punched cards in their packages. As the distributor sells the item, he relays the information back to the manufacturer via the punched card, thereby advising him promptly and accurately of actual consumer activity without having real demand filtered—and usually amplified—through the distribution system.

Forecasts can be classified in many ways, but the most important distinction to make in basic approaches to forecasting is between **judgment forecasts** and **statistical forecasts** (using the term *statistics* in its broadest sense). Forecasts based on judgment, sometimes called "*predictions,*" include those based on the expert opinions of individuals with a "feel for the business," surveys of salesmen to determine the amount of product they think their accounts will be ordering during the coming forecast period, and market surveys in which an interviewer goes out to the marketplace, perhaps with sample products, and either interviews the potential customers directly or the wholesalers or retailers who have close contact with these customers.

There are many pitfalls in the judgment approach to forecasting. While many executives know the marketplace and have the ability to foresee future developments, it is wrong to assume that simply because a man holds an executive position, he is automatically a good sales forecaster. Salesmen, by their very nature, are not oriented toward analytical thinking and generally tend to be either optimistic or pessimistic. For example, salesmen often feel that survey results might be used to increase their quotas, and they then tend to be pessimistic. Getting an objective forecast from a salesman is extremely difficult. Many companies have discarded using this method as their only forecasting technique. Market surveys—whether by mail, telephone, or personal interview—are expensive means of gathering information, and their reliability depends upon the accuracy with which a small sample represents the total market. In some cases, surveys prove unreliable because people do not really do what they tell the interviewer they will. Market surveys on choices in automobiles have shown that people usually state rather conservative desires in styling and horsepower while they actually buy the flashier, higher-powered models. Companies selling consumer products frequently use a test marketing approach, picking a small section of the country thought to be representative and selling their product only in that area in order to determine public reaction. This is a fairly expensive method which has proven highly successful in many instances. As a means of forecasting the whole market, its success depends upon the marketer's ability to pick a representative sample area.

Perhaps the greatest problem with judgment forecasts is the fact that human beings are most intensely affected by recent occurrences. Judgment forecasts normally tend to over-react to immediate circumstances. The human forecaster who uses nothing but judgment can make some very serious mistakes. Figure 2-9, shown later in this chapter, shows a trend line fitted to twelve years of actual sales. An individual making a judgment forecast at the end of Year 5 would be unlikely to recognize the long-range trend and would probably make much-too-low a forecast. A serious practical limitation of judgment forecasts is the relatively small number of forecasts an individual can make as compared to the hundreds of items most companies must handle.

Judgment forecasts are nevertheless invaluable. They are the only means by which human judgment can be brought to bear on the forecasting problem to take known future occurrences into account, such as sales promotions, new product introductions or changing competitive influences. Very few companies use judgment forecasts alone, however, since they are expensive, tend to overreact to recent events and are limited to a few items.

The other basic approach to forecasting—the use of statistical techniques—can involve the use of a product's own demand history to determine a forecast of future sales (using *intrinsic* factors such as averages or historical trends), or it can be based on multiple correlation analysis

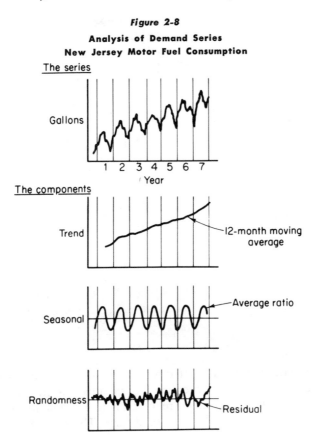

Figure 2-8

Analysis of Demand Series
New Jersey Motor Fuel Consumption

(using *extrinsic* factors such as carloadings, gross national product, housing starts, gasoline consumption and other related activities) to forecast sales.

Statistical forecasting techniques treat the basic elements in a demand series separately—such as the seven-year record of New Jersey motor fuel consumption in Fig. 2–8 which shows that sales are increasing yearly and that there is a definite seasonal pattern. This series can be separated into the three major components of any demand series—*trend, seasonal,* and *randomness*—and each component can be expressed mathematically.

Trend extrapolation is one of the simplest and best-known techniques of forecasting. Figure 2–9 shows twelve years of actual sales data with a

Figure 2-9

Fitting a Trend Line

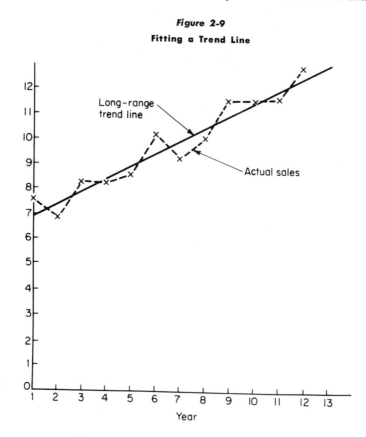

long-range trend line visually fitted to these sales data. Having this long-range trend line helps the forecaster to stabilize his forecasts without over-reacting to short-term occurrences. There are much more accurate methods than visually establishing trend lines. The mathematical technique of "least squares" is described in standard texts on statistics and the individual directly concerned with forecasting should learn this technique since it is an important tool of the forecaster's trade. A 12-month moving average can be used to develop the long-range trend of the series and can be used to project this trend into the future. The seasonal pattern, where consistent year after year, can be represented by ratios of actual monthly sales to average monthly sales.

What remains after the trend and seasonal components have been removed is randomness. There is no way to forecast randomness, but the *range* of randomness can be expressed as an error percentage so that maximum and minimum expected demand can be determined from forecast averages. If this random element is large, then production plans and individual reorder points, for example, will have to include large safety stocks. If, on the other hand, the randomness experienced in the past tends to be small, the forecast can be expected to be more accurate and smaller inventory reserves may be carried in the system.

The one basic assumption of any statistical technique, no matter how sophisticated it may be, is that *the future will be like the past*. The statistical forecast using gasoline consumption as an indicator of automotive replacement tire sales, for example, may be quite reliable until a breakthrough is made and a higher quality, longer-lived tire is developed, at which time this relationship will no longer hold true. Statistical techniques have no way to evaluate such factors; the forecaster must try to determine the important influences in the past and must anticipate how these may change in the future, as well as evaluate the effect of new factors (such as sales promotions, advertising campaigns and new product developments).

Statistical techniques ranging from extremely simple techniques such as simple averages and moving averages to highly complex techniques of mathematical analysis, are used by many companies in forecasting. The most effective forecasting method seems to be to use statistical techniques for routine forecasting of large numbers of items and then to bring in judgment to try to anticipate where the future is likely to differ from the past for families or groups of products, modifying the individual item forecasts accordingly.

One of the advantages of using statistical techniques is reducing the number of factors to which the forecaster must apply his judgment. If he were trying to evaluate past trends, current sales, seasonal swings and the relationship of outside indicators, using judgment alone without the help of statistical techniques would prevent him from giving thorough consideration to these factors as well as to the other factors which definitely require interpretation and judgment (such as competitive climate). By analyzing the data statistically, he quickly develops a base forecast to which he can then apply his judgment, modifying it for the factors he believes important. Used in this way, statistical and judgment forecasts act as checks on each other and eliminate gross errors.

From a manufacturing point of view, the most important requirement is that the forecast be in meaningful terms. Production is usually measured in tons, gallons, feet, hours, pieces, etc. and these terms can be directly related to manload and machine capacity requirements as well as material needs. Dollar forecasts will have to be translated into these terms before they can be used in manufacturing planning, but group (rather than item-by-item) forecasts will usually be sufficient. For example, a paint company must have a forecast of the total number of gallons of paint that will be required. This might also have to be broken down into types of paint produced by individual manufacturing facilities of different types, but will rarely require color or packaging details. Product groupings that are meaningful to manufacturing may not be meaningful to marketing, and close communication and cooperation is required between manufacturing and marketing in order to develop an economic forecasting system that provides the necessary information for both. Usually, the following general organization for making forecasts will be effective in applying forecasting principles to good advantage:

1. Forecasts of intermediate- and long-range demand for groups of products meaningful to the manufacturing organization. *Source: marketing department*

2. Forecasts of short-range demand for individual items that have been in the product line for one year or more. *Source: production control department*

3. Forecasts of short-range demand for new products, promotions, or known-trend items. *Source: marketing department*

In communicating minimum forecast requements to the marketing department (for example), the manufacturing organization should also tell when these forecasts are needed to prepare seasonal production plans.

Marketing should also understand why an estimate of forecast error is essential in order to set policy realistically facing up to the uncertainty inherent in any planning for the future. Supplying this estimate will also tend to focus marketing attention on those forecasts that should be improved. Omitting the estimate of forecast error implies that there will be none.

Many production control people take the attitude that satisfactory performance of their functions requires a perfect forecast. Forecasting is still in its infancy and their complaints about inaccurate forecasts are quite often justified. Reducing forecast errors requires increasing expenditures on forecasting techniques, and there is a point of diminishing return in forecast accuracy. Spending large amounts of money on improved forecasting technique will not produce a perfect forecast. There is usually a lot more to be gained by developing a more flexible production control system that will cope with existing forecasting accuracy instead of spending considerably more money on improved forecasting techniques that will probably result in only a small improvement in the forecasts.

The forecaster is therefore required to manipulate his basic forecasting information into many different configurations to suit different parts of the business. He must understand the requirements of these parts of the business and the implications of his forecast on these business functions. The production control department, for example, can do itself a great service by showing the sales forecaster how forecasts are used to plan production and what the implications of inaccurate forecasts are on hiring, layoffs, excessive inventory buildup, etc. It is more important to improve communications among forecasters and users than to hold rigidly to organizational responsibilities and allow poor forecasting to be an excuse for poor performance in other departments.

The overall business forecast

Before detailed product group forecasts can be made, an *overall business forecast* for the company is necessary. There are many methods of making this type of forecast, including some very useful statistical techniques which will be briefly described. While these techniques are not directly related to control of production and inventory, the production control manager who understands them basically will better know what techniques to investigate if it is necessary for him to do his own forecasting.

Figure 2–10 shows a very useful forecasting technique based on using a leading series. In this case, analysis of past demand has shown that residential housing starts lead the sales of Company "A" products by approximately three months. There are some businesses where this fortunate type of relationship exists. It is important to determine that there is a consistent relationship that can be depended upon in making forecasts and to track continuously so as to detect changes in this relationship. When this type of relationship is available, however, a fairly accurate forecast can be made. Information on activities such as residential housing starts is published regularly in trade magazines. Government agencies (such as the Bureau of Labor Statistics) and private research groups (such as the National Bureau of Economic Research) regularly publish data on many economic series which can form the basis for forecasting various industrial products.

Even if a leading series cannot be found, a company's sales can fre-

Figure 2-10

Forecasting by Means of a Leading Series

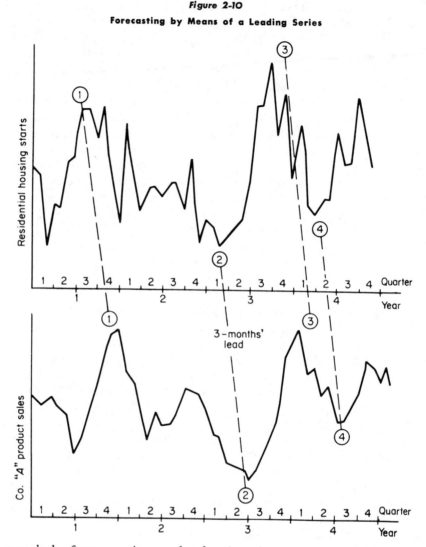

quently be forecast using a related series whose movement is found to coincide or even lag in time, since many other rather sophisticated forecasts of these series are made by government or private research agencies. Earlier in this chapter, an example relating automotive replacement parts to gasoline consumption was noted. A small company in the automotive replacement parts business might not be able to afford much effort in forecasting, but could use forecasts or data on actual sales generated by the larger companies or the American Petroleum Institute. It does not necessarily follow that forecasts will be accurate just because they are made by large companies or prestigious government economists. The user should be prepared to detect significant errors and initiate action to respond to changing demand.

One of the more complex mathematical techniques for forecasting consists of establishing the correlation between a number of extrinsic elements and a company's sales. This type of relationship can be evaluated by *multiple correlation*. The result of this type of analysis is to develop a formula giving relative weights to the various factors included in the development of the forecast. Figure 2–11 shows a simplified example of an extrinsic forecast for packaging material based on retail sales, steel ingot production and carloadings. These figures, available weekly and monthly from many of the business publications, are used to develop

Figure 2-11

Extrinsic Forecast for Packaging Material

Element	Current activity rate	Weight*	Index
Retail sales	$24.3 (billions/mo.)	0.023	0.56
Steel ingot prod.	2700 (tons/week)	0.0001	0.27
Carloadings	62 (thousand cars/day)	0.005	0.31
New index = 1.13			
*Developed by multiple correlation			

weighting factors by means of multiple correlation. Multiplying the weighting factor by the current activity rate of each element establishes a new total index of 1.13, indicating that the forecast for this company's product will now be 13% higher than the base forecast period. Multiple correlation, while beyond the scope of this text, is described in advanced texts on statistical analysis. Computer programs are able to handle multiple correlation rapidly and accurately—this type of forecast will undoubtedly be applied more widely in the future.

The salesman's estimates definitely have a place in making the overall business forecast. They can be extremely valuable if reconciled with a statistical forecast base. For example, statistical techniques could be used to establish a forecast indicating that the total market potential for a company's product should be 10% higher next year. The salesmen could then be polled to determine whether or not the company's market share would remain constant. The salesman, knowing the competitive climate, would be in a position to say whether or not market penetration would be likely to go up or down from the overall trend indicated by the statistical forecast.

Product group forecasts

Once the overall business forecast is made, it must be broken down into more detailed *product group forecasts*. These product group forecasts, as previously mentioned, must be meaningful in terms of manufacturing capacity. A farm implement manufacturer, for example, might make his overall business forecast in dollars, relating it to the government estimate of disposable farm income. He would then need to break the overall dollar total into dollars for each major product line (such as tractors, combines, balers, etc.). He might do this using a percentage based on past experience, modified by any sales department or marketing department knowledge of trends in demand for a particular product line. He might find that there are indicators that relate directly to a particular product, such as the number of acres of wheat under cultivation or a change in the subsidy being awarded for soybeans.

The next step would be to apply known seasonal indices peculiar to the product lines, particularly in a business such as the manufacture of farm implements. Figure 2-12 shows the development of such a seasonal

Figure 2-12

Developing a Seasonal Index for Combines
(Monthly sales as a percent of annual total)

Month	Y-1	Y-2	Y-3	Y-4	Y-5	Average %
January	7.48%	5.46%	6.36%	6.56%	6.54%	6.50
February	8.24	4.70	6.68	7.35	5.78	6.55
March	8.27	7.30	8.84	7.90	8.03	8.05
April	7.95	9.34	9.40	8.79	9.29	8.95
May	9.66	9.65	10.50	11.11	10.44	10.30
June	10.00	11.30	10.60	8.79	9.71	10.10
July	9.06	8.70	7.66	9.01	9.96	8.90
August	9.85	11.10	10.80	10.12	11.00	10.60
September	9.71	9.50	8.15	9.70	7.90	9.00
October	6.65	8.72	8.09	8.78	8.95	8.25
November	7.80	8.08	7.64	7.34	7.72	7.70
December	5.12	6.15	5.13	4.54	4.64	5.10
Total	99.79	100.00	99.85	99.99	99.96	100.00

index for each month, stating it as a percent of the year's sales of combines. In this imaginary case, five years of history have been analyzed, and the monthly sales are shown as a percentage of the annual total. An overall average for each month is calculated, using the data for the five years. A good forecaster would want to have one or two additional years of data which he could use in a simulation to test the validity of the seasonal percentage. Using the annual forecast of sales for this product line, he could apply the average percentages in Fig. 2–12 to each month and thus come up with a monthly forecast. He would probably face a major problem expressing this forecast in terms (like man-hours) meaningful to manufacturing, since it is possible that one specific type of farm implement is built in one manufacturing plant while a second type is built in another. In addition, each plant would need to differentiate between small and large models of this implement if the man-hour requirements varied greatly.

Product group forecasts are used to make production capacity plans; they should not be used to schedule model mix. They are used to determine the manpower and machine capacity requirements for each major production facility. The important purpose of product group forecasts is to establish *production levels*. This application makes use of the principle that group forecasts are more accurate than item forecasts.

Chapter 7 discusses production level planning and control and the use of measures of forecast error to establish decision rules for determining when to change production levels. This is probably the most important use of a forecast and a primary function of production control. There is no chance of providing good service and keeping inventories in balance if the level of production is not planned and controlled effectively.

Item forecasts

Item forecasts are needed for determining order points, materials plans, order quantities and schedules. They are best made using simple statistical techniques based on their own demand history. Contrary to opinion in many production control departments, it is not good practice to have the marketing department make all item forecasts. These should be made by production control. Marketing should be asked to provide information needed to adjust the statistical forecasts for items with significant changes expected because of new market trends, promotions, competitive influences and the like. The sum of individual item forecasts for each group should equal the group forecast prepared by marketing for planning production levels. They usually do not, and will therefore have to be adjusted (as explained later in this chapter) to make these totals equal.

Averages provide a routine way of forecasting many individual items. With data-processing equipment it is now feasible to forecast demand on a weekly basis for many thousands of items, compare these forecasts to actual sales and calculate forecast error. Figure 2–13 shows how averages may be used in forecasting item sales. In this particular example, a forecast based on a weekly average of all of last year's sales (called the *old forecast*) indicated that sales would run at 100 units per week; actual sales the first week of this year amounted to 70 units. Using a straight arithmetical average, a new weekly forecast of 85 units could then be made. This, in effect, gives equal weight to the old forecast and the latest week's sales.

Figure 2-13

The Weighted Average

First week		
	Weight	Weight
Old forecast = 100 (per wk. avg.)	x 0.5 = 50	x 0.9 = 90
Sales = 70 (latest week)	x 0.5 = 35	x 0.1 = 7
New forecast =	85	97
Second week		
Old forecast = 97*		x 0.9 = 87
Sales = 105		x 0.1 = 11
New forecast =		98
General formula:		
New forecast = α x sales + $(1 - \alpha)$ x Old forecast α (Alpha) is the term for the weighting factor		
*This was the "New forecast" last week		

In Figure 2–13 this is shown as 50% (0.5) of the old forecast equal to 50 and 50% (0.5) of the sales equal to 35, giving a new forecast of 85, the same as adding 100 and 70 and dividing by 2. This "equally-weighted" average doesn't seem to be a good method since the old forecast of 100 units per week was based upon 52 weeks of past experience and the latest sales of 70 units is the experience of only one week.

Using the "weighted-average" concept, it would be possible (as shown in the example) to give 90% of the weight to the old forecast and 10% to the actual sales, and thus to calculate a new forecast of 97. In this case, the forecast would decline only slightly because of the drop in sales. Most production control people would recognize this from experience as being more reasonable. Note that the sum of the weighting factors must always equal 1.0 (or 100%).

Figure 2–13 also shows how the forecast for the second week is calculated using the same weighted-average approach. The old forecast is now the 97 pieces forecast for last week, actual sales the second week amounted to 105 and the new forecast is therefore 98. It has gone up slightly since sales increased. This technique is called *"exponential smoothing"* and is based upon the work done by R. G. Brown. [1] It provides a routine method for updating forecasts regularly. With data-processing equipment, a simple program could do this for many thousand items on a regular basis and thus provide information to control inventories far better than an inventory controller could do manually.

The exponential smoothing equation in Fig. 2–13 is called *"first-order smoothing,"* and there are more advanced exponential smoothing formulas which include adjustments for trends and seasonal changes. The first-order smoothing equation can be rearranged to simplify the calculation as follows:

$$\text{New forecast} = \text{old forecast plus } \alpha \text{ (sales} - \text{old forecast)} \qquad (2\text{-}1)$$

This form requires only one multiplication. Using the data for the second week from Fig. 2-13:

$$\text{New forecast} = 97 + 0.1(105 - 97) = 98$$

It can be seen that the result is identical to that obtained using the full exponential smoothing formula. Both of these formulas are classified as "first-order" exponential smoothing. They work very well when dealing with fairly stable items and they will detect trends quite readily, although the forecast will lag actual demand if a definite trend exists. However, where it is believed that a definite trend is likely to exist (when a new product has been introduced, for example), *second-order smoothing* can be used. With second-order smoothing, the forecast is made up of two parts, A and B:

$$A_{new} = \text{old forecast} + \alpha \text{ (sales} - \text{old forecast)} \qquad (2\text{-}2)$$

$$B_{new} = B_{old} + \alpha \, (A_{new} - B_{old}) \qquad (2\text{-}3)$$

The first part, A_{new}, is simple first-order smoothing. The second part, B_{new}, provides a factor to adjust the forecast for a trend in order to eliminate the lagging effect of first-order smoothing.

This correction is made by adjusting the first-order forecast (A_{new}) by the difference between the two factors ($A_{new} - B_{new}$), or:

Given : Starting (OF) = 230 α = .2

[1]Brown, R.G., *Statistical Forecasting for Inventory Control*, McGraw, N.Y., 1959.

Feb. NF = 230 + .2 (250 - 230) = 234

However for next month's forecast, the NF of 234 becomes the old forecast !

$$\text{New forecast} = A_{new} + (A_{new} - B_{new})$$
$$= 2A_{new} - B_{new} \qquad (2\text{--}4)$$

Using the data from Fig. 2-13 and assuming $B_{old} = 99.7$:

$$A_{new} = 97 + 0.1(105 - 97) = 97.8$$
$$B_{new} = 99.7 + 0.1\,(97.8 - 99.7) = 99.5$$
$$\text{New forecast} = (2 \times 97.8) - 99.5 = 96$$

A decision on whether or not second-order smoothing is required can be confirmed by taking real data on a few items and simulating results. In general, it has been found by practitioners that first-order smoothing gives quite satisfactory results for most items—particularly for short range forecasts for order point calculations and scheduling. The exponential smoothing technique has not been too satisfactory where demand is very low or with no demand at all in some forecast periods.

Assuming simulation demonstrates that exponential smoothing will give satisfactory results, the problem is to determine the proper weighting factor (alpha). In Fig. 2-13, a low alpha factor of 0.1 results in the old forecast being the controlling factor in the new forecast and sales exerting little influence.

If a high alpha factor is used, such as 0.3, the forecast will react sharply to changes in sales and will, in fact, be highly erratic if there are sizeable random fluctuations in demand. If, on the other hand, too-low an alpha factor is used, changing trends will not be picked up as quickly as might be desirable. Any alpha factor is a compromise between being too sluggish and too erratic. The proper alpha factor for a given set of data can be determined by simulation, which will show how a particular alpha factor will work as long as demand patterns are the same in the future.

Experience has shown many companies the value of getting started quickly with this highly successful technique without spending a great deal of time trying to determine the proper weighting factor by simulation. It is usually quite satisfactory to use a factor in the range of 0.1 to 0.2 in order to get moving quickly and to let actual experience show those exceptions where a different alpha factor is necessary.

Where a company has been using a moving average of several weeks and wishes to substitute exponential smoothing in order to gain the advantages of storing less data, the following formula can be used to determine the alpha factor which will give results approximately equivalent to the number of weeks in the previously used average:

$$\alpha = 2/(n + 1) \qquad (2\text{--}5)$$

For example, if the previously used forecast were a 12-week moving average, the alpha factor would be:

Exponential Smoothing

$$\alpha = \frac{2}{(N+1)}$$

$$\alpha = \frac{2}{(12 + 1)} = 0.15$$

number of periods

Using this formula, it can be seen that an alpha factor of 0.2 is approximately equivalent to a 9-period moving average and a 0.1 alpha factor approximately equivalent to a 19-period moving average.

Exponential smoothing could also be used for a product group forecast, particularly in conjunction with some type of judgment forecast based on anticipated changes in market penetration, competitive reactions, public acceptance of the product, etc. However, such a product group forecast is unlikely to be exactly the same as the sum of the exponential smoothing forecasts for the individual products within the group. For example, if the market penetration for a product group were expected to increase substantially because of a new pricing policy, this would not show up in the exponential smoothing forecasts, since these are based upon past history. Figure 2-14 shows how the exponential smoothing forecasts for each of 10 items in a product group would be revised due to an increase in the product group forecast. In this particular case, a new total product group forecast has been received from the marketing department, equaling 52,000 units. The individual forecasts totaled only 48,874, and the difference is then prorated across the

Figure 2-14

Reconciling Individual Product Forecasts with a Product Group Forecast

Item	Exponential smoothing forecast		New pro—rated item forecast *
#1	10,450		11,130
#2	4117		4360
#3	6720		7150
#4	1050	New total product	1120
#5	774	group forecast	825
#6	896	from marketing	955
#7	14,140	department:	15,050
#8	2325	52,000	2480
#9	3734		3960
#10	4668		4970
Total	48,874		52,000

* This will be the "Old forecast" in the exponential–smoothing calculation for the first week of the new quarter

10 products, each of them being adjusted upward in proportion to its share of the total so that the sum of forecasts for the individual products equals 52,000. Using a computer, this type of forecast adjustment is very readily made, even for hundreds of items. As indicated by the footnote in Fig. 2-14, the old forecast for Item #1 to be used in calculating the next week's forecast would have been 10,450. This is discarded, and an old forecast of 11,130 will be used in its place.

One common application of exponential smoothing is in conjunction with seasonal indices, when it is necessary to adjust all data "entering" and "leaving" the formula to take seasonality into account.

Assuming that the seasonal indices in Fig. 2-12 apply, some simple examples will illustrate the use of exponential smoothing with seasonal indices:

1. An average month (100% ÷ 12) = 8.33%

2. Assume the old forecast is for average sales of 6000 per month

3. Referring to the indices in Fig. 2-12, it can be seen that this would require the following adjustment if (for example) the June forecast were being prepared:

$$\frac{10.10}{8.33} = \frac{X}{6000} = 7280,$$

since the 6000 forecast is for an average month (8.33%) and June sales are normally 10.10%

4. The June forecast has now been adjusted for seasonality and has increased from 6000 to 7280

5. Assume now that June sales actually *were* 8000, and exponential smoothing were being used. These sales would have to be adjusted to make them equivalent to an average month, as follows:

$$\frac{10.10}{8.33} = \frac{8000}{X} = 6500,$$

which indicates that sales of 8000 in June would be equivalent to sales of 6500 in an average month

6. Assuming an 0.1 alpha, the exponential smoothing calculation to forecast July sales would then be:

New forecast $= 6000 + 0.1(6500 - 6000)$

New forecast $= 6050$

7. But this must also be adjusted seasonally in order to be a proper forecast for July, as follows:

$$\frac{8.90}{8.33} = \frac{X}{6050} = 6460$$

The rationale is that the smoothing must be done with equivalent data in order to average correctly, and thus all data being entered into the formula must be adjusted and all forecasts must be adjusted by their seasonal indices against a common base—in this case, an average month.

Exponential smoothing is in practice an extremely useful technique, since it provides a convenient method for updating forecasts for thousands of items on a routine basis. It requires far less data than a cumulative average and is highly flexible, since a revised marketing forecast can be "plugged in" at any time (the old forecast or the weighting factor alpha can be increased if a quicker response to recent sales is required, for example).

An estimate of forecast error is equally important for individual items and, at times, more important than for total product groups. The estimate of forecast error for individual items determines where the errors will be in the inventory control system or the materials planning system and just how much buffer stock will have to be maintained. The computation of forecast errors for determining reserve stock levels is explained in Chapter 5.

A frequent question is, *"How often should a forecast be revised?"* The answer to this is that a forecast for a given period should be revised only when it has to be: the method for determining when it must be revised is to use the estimate of forecast error to assign control limits and check actual results against these limits regularly, as described for individual items in Chapter 5 and for product groups in Chapter 8.

A particularly challenging type of item to forecast is the product which is custom-assembled from many standard components. An automobile manufacturer, for example, could hardly hope to forecast the number of green convertibles with standard transmission, air conditioning, etc., that he might sell. He can, however, forecast the total number of cars reasonably well and then forecast the percent that will be green, the percent to be convertibles, etc. In essence he is forecasting totals at a lower level than the actual end item and then forecasting individual options as percentages of total production. This general approach with proper allowance for forecast error applies to companies that custom-assemble and can facilitate making a reasonably good forecast for use in the inventory system.

Special forecasts—promotions and new products

Forecasts for promotions and new products are much more difficult to make than those for stable items. Since few new products are truly original, such forecasts can frequently be based upon past experience with a similar product. A television manufacturer, for example, can use his experience with 24″ black-and-white and 21″ color TV sets that he has marketed in the past to estimate sales for a new 24″ color TV. A company manufacturing a new product unlike anything now on the market would probably have to use some type of market survey. Many companies in the toiletries business or manufacturing items such as foods, where personal preference and consumer acceptance are extremely difficult to predict, generally use market surveys or test marketing in order to determine what product acceptance will be before manufacturing on a large scale.

For new products and promotion items, the estimate of forecast error is essential. The management of the company should be shown the effects of planning to meet a forecast of 100,000 units when actual sales could be as low as 20,000 units or as high as 500,000 units. If such wide variations in sales are believed possible when the forecast is made, intelligent planning of high-value items will minimize the risk of excess inventory, while shrewd handling of tooling designs and long lead time components will make it possible for production to respond quickly to increased demands. Such realistic planning will be possible only if an effort is made to estimate the forecast error.

Forecasting demand for promotion items and new products must also consider the "pipeline filling" pattern. When a new program or product is announced to which salesmen react enthusiastically, most salesmen will be able to call their important customers and convince them over the telephone to buy at least a token supply. On their regular sales calls in the following days, their enthusiasm will sell more of this new product.

Back at the factory, an initial surge of orders will be received, followed by a steady influx of orders—all of which merely reflects the demand of the distributor, wholesaler, or other class of customer stocking-up. Most products pass from manufacturer to middleman to ultimate consumer, so that very few initial orders represent actual consumer demand. Once the shelves have been stocked, there is a drop-off in demand until actual consumer sales are felt—these determine what the real demand will be.

A knowledge of this pipeline filling pattern will prevent a forecaster's over-reacting to the surge due to the salesmen's initial enthusiasm, to the sales drop-off when stocking orders are completed and, finally, to the initial consumer response. Steady nerves and this knowledge will help the forecaster to interpret new product sales properly. Exponential smoothing cannot be used for forecasting promotion or new product sales since it is based entirely upon past history, but this technique can be a valuable tool in interpreting actual demand and determining whether or not the original forecast is valid by using it as the old forecast in the exponential smoothing formulas and calculating a new forecast based upon actual sales during intervals of the forecast period. The "pipeline filling" pattern must be considered in tracking such forecasts using exponential smoothing to avoid over-reacting.

It may be desirable to change the total forecast for the product *group* very cautiously; here smoothing can be used to track the sales for the items in the group and by prorating these "forecasts" against the group forecast, product mix can be changed quickly to react to changing sales.

Using the forecast

Production control's most important responsibility is using the forecast intelligently. First this means showing the forecaster the implications of his forecast on the manufacturing activity and on customer service. It means presenting to management the effects of possible forecast errors on inventories, operating costs and customer relations. Continuous communication should be maintained between the originators and the users of the forecast to promote better understanding and insure quick response to changing conditions. This is probably best illustrated in facilities planning, where an engineering group may be given a forecast five years in advance, on which to plan designs for a new manufacturing plant. The property and building sizes are determined by the overall forecast. This information is needed early in the program in order to establish capital requirements, get approval for the project and begin construction. Specific department areas are determined by subgroups of products, as are major pieces of manufacturing equipment, and these breakdowns of the total forecast are needed long after the start of the project, leaving sufficient lead time to have the space and equipment available at start-up. The original forecast upon which the plant was designed will not usually be accurate in terms of product mix since it was made so far in advance. As the time for opening up the new plant draws near, constant communication between the forecasters and the engineers will help to avoid starting up a plant with excess capacity in some areas and inadequate capacity in others. Perhaps more important, manufacturing processing equipment is far more likely to be suitable for the volumes of different items to be turned out—and hence more efficient.

Intelligent use of forecast error data can contribute almost as much to profitable operation as an accurate forecast. Raw material, tooling, and long lead time components can be procured to meet high estimates, so that successful programs are not hamstrung by lack of product. Short lead time parts, or those likely to be redesigned as service experience is obtained, can be held down to the low estimates to minimize the risk of excess and obsolete inventories.

The knottiest question which the production control manager must answer is whether or not more pressure should be put on the marketing department to improve the forecasts, or if the pressure should really be on his department to improve the use of the forecast and the ability to respond to change. The proper answer will give the company the best return on its investment.

In using the forecast, production control should take advantage of forecast characteristics; they should separate the planning of capacity from actual scheduling within the manufacturing cycle, making a long-term commitment only to capacity and making the shortest possible commitment to the actual production schedule. This permits taking advantage of the greater accuracy with which large product groups can be forecast, as compared to the individual items which make up the production schedule. The shorter the scheduling cycle, the better the reaction to actual changes in sales. For example, a company using a monthly schedule of finished goods production cannot react to any abrupt changes in demand between schedules except by expediting. Weekly or daily schedules can reflect the latest information on actual demand while firm schedules far into the future are usually highly inaccurate because forecasts become less accurate when they are extended.

The crux of using the forecast intelligently in the production control department involves recognizing forecast characteristics and designing the production control system to take the fullest advantage of these characteristics.

Forecasting responsibilities

These basic forecasting responsibilities are suggested to develop the maximum effectiveness of the forecasting functions:

1. Make the forecast — *Marketing working with production control*

2. Use the forecast to plan production — *Production control*

3. Track the forecast — *Production control*

4. Report deviations from forecast — *Production control*

5. Interpret deviations and revise the forecast — *Marketing*

6. Revise production plans to reflect the revised forecast — *Production control*

Many companies do not have a formal forecasting function, yet many people in their organizations must have forecasts for budgeting, determining manload and machine capacity, establishing the relative importance of various items (so as to know where to concentrate inventory control efforts), determining the quantities that should be ordered, determining when replenishment orders should be placed and a multitude of other purposes. The absence of a formal program does not eliminate these needs—it only means that a variety of different, uncoordinated forecasts will be made and used by those least able to do such work. While the consensus is that marketing or sales should be responsible for forecasting, production control needs a forecast for each individual item, as well as other types of forecasts discussed earlier in this chapter. In most companies, the sales and marketing departments are too busy selling and developing new promotional efforts to be concerned with regularly updating forecasts for thousands of items.

The solution of this apparent dilemma is for the marketing or sales departments to provide forecasts in meaningful manufacturing terms— but only for *groups* of finished products—together with forecasts for special items (promotion items or new products) where past history would not be a reliable guide for future activity. The production control department should make routine forecasts (using smoothing or other statistical techniques) for run-of-the-mill items that constitute the bulk of the typical inventory investment.

Production control should advise marketing of the groups of products important in planning the level of operation and of the terms meaningful in the manufacturing activities. They should also provide data on past demand history and forecast errors to provide a base for marketing in preparing a new forecast. They should insist on a measure of forecast error—not forcing marketing to admit their forecasts are poor, but simply to get realistic estimates on which to base constructive action. Forecasting *techniques* have frequently been over-emphasized they can contribute a great deal, but the most important contribution to improved forecasting is close cooperation between the marketing and production control departments.

Summary

Forecasting has involved much "muddy" thinking in the past. Many production control men have considered it a panacea. Marketing people have viewed it as an impossible, onerous task to be avoided at all costs. Many saw it as a gift that only few people had—something intuitive, not at all susceptible to science. We now know that forecasting can definitely be improved by using analytical techniques, and that even the use of mediocre forecasts can sometimes give good results through teamwork between the marketing and production control departments.

It is ironic that forecasts made by marketing or sales departments often have greater effects upon customer service than any other manufacturing activity. Forecasts, while they can definitely be improved, will always be wrong. The goal of progressive companies is to improve their forecasting and, simultaneously, to develop sound, flexible production control systems based on forecasting principles and characteristics.

Bibliography

1. Biegel, John E., *Production Control: A Quantitative Approach*, Prentice-Hall, Englewood Cliffs, New Jersey, 1963.

2. Brown, Robert G., *Smoothing, Forecasting, and Prediction of Discrete Time Series*, Prentice-Hall, Englewood Cliffs, New Jersey, 1963.

3. ———, *Statistical Forecasting for Inventory Control*, McGraw, New York, 1959.

4. Kurtz, Thomas, *Basic Statistics*, Prentice-Hall, Englewood Cliffs, New Jersey, 1963.

5. MacLean, Alan and Bourgerie, R. M., "Sales Forecasting With a Computer," *APICS Annual Conference Proceedings*, 1963.

6. MacNiece, E. H., *Production Forecasting, Planning, and Control*, Wiley, New York, 1961.

7. Marshall, B. O., "Sales Forecasting: What It Can Do for Production and Inventory Control," *APICS Annual Conference Proceedings*, 1964.

8. Michell, J. A., "The Preparation and Use of Sales Forecasts," *APICS Quarterly Bulletin*, Vol. 5, No. 3, July 1964.

9. Moroney, M. J., *Facts From Figures*, Penguin Books, London, 1957.

10. Paulis, Robert J., "An Introduction to Sales Forecasting," *APICS Quarterly Bulletin*, Vol. 4, No. 2, April 1963.

11. Reinfeld, Nyles V., *Production Control*, Prentice-Hall, Englewood Cliffs, New Jersey, 1959.

12. Scheele, Evan D., Westerman, William L., and Wimmert, Robert J., *Principles and Design of Production Control Systems*, Prentice-Hall, Englewood Cliffs, New Jersey, 1960.

13. Van DeMark, R. L., "How to Get Along Without a Sales Forecast," *APICS Annual Conference Proceedings*, 1964.

CHAPTER THREE

FUNDAMENTALS OF INVENTORY MANAGEMENT

What is inventory?

Three clichés frequently heard in business are:

1. *"You can't sell from an empty wagon"*
2. *"Inventories are the graveyard of American business"*
3. *"Why don't you make plenty of them—we can always use them"*

These comments illustrate the problems involved in reaching rational inventory decisions. Inventories are the materials that a company carries on hand and that usually represent a sizeable portion of the company's total assets, but few other business topics are subject to the partisan attitudes that exist concerning inventories. The sales department frequently sees inventory as an unlimited resource, and feels that the production control department has failed if any item is not available when an order for it is received. The financial people frequently feel that inventories are a necessary evil that tie up capital which could be used better elsewhere. Factory people have difficulty understanding the costs associated with carrying inventories, and they frequently look upon the effects of inventory control with dismay because of the apparent inefficiency forced on the plant by increased setups. From the factory point of view, inventories are an unlimited resource. Obviously, the problem is simply that inventories are frequently considered from the limited point of view of a particular department rather than from an overall company viewpoint.

What, then, are inventories from the overall company viewpoint? Inventories in a business serve much as the suspension system of an automobile. Ups and downs in sales are absorbed by inventory, just as the car springs absorb bumps in the road. Without inventories, production would have to respond directly to sales if service to customers were not to suffer. Inventories also disengage manufacturing operations which have different production rates. Lot-size inventories make possible fewer machine setups and higher machine utilization.

It was stated earlier that three conflicting objectives in most businesses are customer service, minimum inventory investment and efficient plant operation, and that it is the job of production and inventory control to reconcile these three objectives in the best interests of the company. Inventories are necessary to give good customer service, to run the plant more efficiently by keeping production at a fairly level rate, and to run reasonably-sized manufacturing lots. They are not a necessary evil, but are instead a very useful "shock absorber."

Nevertheless, while some inventory investment is necessary and useful, too much of it may be harmful. In most companies, resources are limited: money that is used for inventories is also needed for plant improvement, for paying dividends to stockholders, for developing new products, and for all the other uses a vigorous business has for capital. Excess inventory serves no purpose and simply ties up capital.

From an overall company point of view, then, it is important to *balance* inventory investment against other demands for capital, considering the costs related to both. This balancing requires decisions that fall into four major categories:

1. *What balance is desired between inventory investment and customer service?* Where effective inventory control exists to execute management policy, there is a definite relationship between the amount of inventory carried and the service that results. The lower the inventory, the more backorders and stockouts; the higher the inventory, the better the service.

2. *What balance is desired between inventory investment and costs associated with changes in the production level?* Excess equipment capacity, overtime, idle time, hiring, training and laying off employees and related costs will be higher if production must fluctuate in response to changing sales rates.

3. *What balance is desired between inventory investment and the cost of placing inventory replenishment orders?* Low inventories can be maintained

by setting-up jobs frequently or by placing a great many purchase orders for small quantities. These practices result in high setup costs, purchasing costs, lost quantity discounts, and other excessive operating expenses.

4. *What balance is desired between inventory investment and transportation costs?* Providing the manpower and materials handling equipment so that jobs in production can be moved hourly, for example, requires a greater expenditure than would be required if jobs were moved daily.

The functions of inventories

Techniques for achieving these balances will be presented in later chapters, but the proper application of these techniques requires an understanding of the functions that inventories serve. There are four basic inventory classes, defined by function as:

1. **Fluctuation**
2. **Anticipation**
3. **Lot-size**
4. **Transportation**

Fluctuation inventories: These are the inventories carried because sales and production times for the product can't always be predicted accurately. Orders may *average* 100 units per week for a given item, but there will be weeks when sales are as high as 300 or 400 units. Material may usually be received in stock three weeks from the time it was ordered from the factory, but it may occasionally not be received for six weeks. These fluctuations in demand and manufacturing lead times are normally covered by *reserve stock* or *safety stock,* the common names for fluctuation inventories. Fluctuation inventories must exist ahead of work centers when the flow of work through these centers cannot be completely balanced. Fluctuation inventories also exist as "stabilization" stock provided in the production plan so that production levels do not have to change in order to meet random variations in demand.

Anticipation inventories: These are inventories which are built-up in advance of a peak selling season, a promotion program or a plant shutdown period. Basically, anticipation inventories store man and machine-hours for a future need.

Lot-size inventories: It is frequently impossible or impractical to manufacture or purchase items at the same rate at which they will be sold. The items are therefore obtained in larger quantities than are needed at the moment; the resulting inventory is the lot-size inventory. *resource*

Transportation inventories: These are inventories that exist because material must be moved from one place to another. Inventory on a truck being delivered to a warehouse may be in transit as long as 10 days. While the inventory is in transit, it cannot serve customers—it exists solely because of transportation time.

eg. As an example, a typical finished-goods item may be manufactured in 12 lots per year of 1000 units apiece. Each month, 1000 units will be received in inventory and used up. On the average, there will be 500 units on hand—the average *lot-size* inventory will be 500 units. To cover fluctuations in demand and lead time, the company may normally carry an extra 250 units as *reserve stock*. This item would therefore have an average inventory (equal to the average lot-size inventory plus the reserve stock) of 750 units. To cover a coming vacation period, another 250 units might be added to the inventory—this would be *anticipation* inventory. If this product were distributed through warehouses, additional *transportation* inventory would exist between the main plant and the warehouses.

Since random demand fluctuations can occur in an entire product line as well as in individual products, it might also be necessary to carry some additional stabilization stock to preclude having to either change *to avoid →*

Table 3-1

To determine:	Balance inventory investment costs against:	Consider also:
Fluctuation inventory	Costs related to the level of customer service and to changing production rates	Number of exposures to stockout, based on lot size. Intangibles related to production rate changes(below)
Anticipation inventory	Costs related to changing production rates	Intangibles—reputation, morale, loss of skills, employment guarantees
Lot-size inventory	Costs related to ordering	Practical limitations on set-ups and inventory; also, quantity discounts
Transportation inventory	Costs related to moving inventory to market	Service rendered by competition, damage in transit

Balance & Justify!

production levels or dip into the reserve stocks as these fluctuations occur. Note that fluctuation inventories in a manufacturing company covers random demands on the individual inventory items and may be required to provide some additional protection against random demands in total product groups, so that it must be balanced against customer service levels and against costs related to changing production rates.

The relationship between the types of inventory, based on the functions performed, and the balancing decisions discussed previously is illustrated in Table 3-I.

Note that there are overlapping functions performed by inventories. Seasonal inventory will provide better customer service while it is on hand, for example, as well as reducing the need to react to minor variations in the total demand rate. Thorough consideration of the interrelationships shared by these inventories is necessary to avoid building too much inventory into the system.   − levelling off −

Classes of inventory

In addition to grouping by functions, inventories can also be classified according to condition during processing:

1. **Raw materials:** these are the steel, flour, wood, cloth, or other materials used to make the components of the finished product.

2. **Components:** these are the parts or subassemblies ready to go into the final assembly of the product.

3. **Work-in-process:** these are the materials and components being worked on or waiting between operations in the factory.

4. **Finished products:** these are finished items carried in inventory in a make-to-stock plant or finished goods sold to a customer against his order in a make-to-order plant.

Inventory levels set intuitively are usually either too high or too low. An analysis of an inventory according to its functions, using techniques to be described in the following chapters, can usually result in very substantial inventory reductions with no reduction in service, or in very substantial increases in customer service with no increase in inventory.

⟶ improvement ...

Costs in inventory

The costs that will result from each specific decision must be determined when deciding how much inventory to carry. The following classes of costs are usually involved in inventory decisions:

1. Ordering costs: The costs of ordering can be either those of placing purchase orders to buy material from a vendor or those associated with ordering a manufactured lot from the plant. When material is purchased, orders must be written, invoices processed to pay the vendor, and the lots received must be inspected and delivered to stores or process areas. When a manufactured lot is ordered from the plant, costs are incurred for paperwork, machine setup, start-up scrap that results from the first production and other one-time costs that are a function of the number of lots ordered or produced. The sum of these is the ordering cost for the lot.

2. Inventory carrying costs: These costs include all expenses incurred by the company because of the volume of inventory carried. The following elements are usually included in inventory carrying cost:

> **a.** *Obsolescence*—these costs are incurred because inventory is no longer saleable due to changing sales patterns and customer desires. This problem is acute in style goods industries.
>
> **b.** *Deterioration*—material carried in inventory may get damp, dried out, dirty from handling or, in many other ways, deteriorate so that it is no longer saleable.
>
> **c.** *Taxes*—many states and municipalities have inventory taxes. Some are based on the inventory investment at the particular time of the year, while others are based on the average inventory investment for the entire year.
>
> **d.** *Insurance*—inventories, like most other assets, are covered by insurance usually carried as a part of other company insurance policies.
>
> **e.** *Storage*—to store inventory requires a storeroom with supervisory and operating personnel, material handling equipment, necessary records, etc. The costs of these facilities

would not be incurred if there were no inventory.

   f. *Capital*—money invested in inventory is not available for use in other areas of the company, and, in fact, may have to be borrowed from banks. The cost of borrowing the money or the cost of "foregone investment opportunity" from using this capital in other areas of the company must be charged against the inventory investment as the cost of capital.

3. Out-of-stock costs: If material is not available to ship when customers order it, sales may be lost or extra costs will probably be incurred. The work of processing a backorder (shipping, invoicing, and perhaps inventory control paperwork and extra time) can be considerable. The cost of backorders results not only from extra paperwork, but also from the time spent by personnel in the various departments who handle the backorder paper, pick and pack the actual shipment and answer customer inquiries. They may include such factors as high freight premiums because of the small quantity of material being shipped.

4. Capacity-associated costs: The costs that are related to capacity include overtime, hiring, training, layoff and idle time costs. These costs are incurred when it is necessary to increase or decrease capacity, or when too much or too little capacity exists temporarily.

Many difficult problems arise in determining and using costs to make inventory decisions. Even when the specific factors to be considered are recognized, the accounting records for most companies will not yield the cost data required in immediately usable and meaningful form. Two basic rules apply to these costs:

1. They should be actual "out-of-pocket" costs, not "standard" accounting costs.

2. They should be costs that are actually affected by the specific decision being made.

Before using cost data in an inventory decision problem, the questions *"Where will the savings come from?,"* and *"How much will be saved?"* must be answered to be certain that the calculation actually represents the real-life situation.

Considering each of the four cost classes in turn, the basic problem with *ordering costs* is in isolating those cost elements which will vary with the number of orders placed. A simple example will illustrate the problem for purchased material:

> A purchasing agent makes $8000 a year in a very small company. He places 2000 purchase orders a year, principally with local merchants like the hardware store in town. No paperwork is involved, he simply turns around and puts a dime in the pay telephone behind him each time he must place an order. Invoices are paid from a cash-box in his desk drawer.
>
> The cost for each purchase order could then be calculated:
>
> Salary of agent = $8000
> Telephone bill =   200
> Total   = $8200 ÷ 2000 = $4.10 per order
>
> Obviously the company will save money by placing fewer purchase orders a year. Suppose larger lots were purchased so that only 1500 purchase orders per year were required. The savings to the company appear to be:
> 2000 − 1500 = 500 × $4.10, or $2050 per year.

From a practical point of view, however, the only saving that will be realized will be the ten-cent phone call since it is highly unlikely that the purchasing agent's salary would be cut or that his time would be used effectively for additional work. In fact, the company would only save $50.00 per year, which is the telephone cost for the 500 orders not placed. In this case, then, a purchase order does not cost $4.10, but only $0.10. Only if *all* purchases could be eliminated (or reduced to such a low level that someone else could handle them at no additional cost to the company, thus eliminating the purchasing agent's job) could a cost of $4.10 be assigned to each purchase order when making inventory decisions.

Similar analyses must be made of setup costs when studying manufactured lot-sizes and ordering costs. Reducing the number of setups by running larger lots through a press department will save the company nothing if the setup man's life is simply made easier because he has less to do. Likewise, overhead portions of production control paperwork charges should not be included unless fewer orders will permit some reductions to be made in these expenses.

The *inventory carrying cost* is a most useful concept (albeit an artificial one) required by the mathematical formulas used in inventory calculations. As listed above, many separate elements are assumed to make up this "cost." Obsolescence is a reality in any inventory, but this cost element in the inventory carrying cost varies widely with time and is not the same for different items in an inventory (it is highest for "style" items). This would indicate that a different carrying cost should be used for each item in the stock-list. This is obviously impractical, and an average figure is usually chosen, either for all products or for each major type of product. The identical reasoning applies to deterioration costs.

Taxes are usually handled more easily, particularly if the tax rate is based on the average value of the inventory. Taxes, at least at the present time, usually represent a very minor part of the total inventory carrying cost.

As shown by the derivation of the economic ordering quantity (EOQ) formula in Appendix III, storage and related handling costs can be handled as a separate element in lot-size decisions. For simplicity and convenience, however, these costs are usually assumed to be part of the inventory carrying cost. The storage charge portion of inventory carrying cost, like other elements, is assumed to vary directly with the size of the inventory. Unless storage space freed up by inventory reductions can be put to use, however, there is no saving. Conversely, unless additional storage space must be purchased by leasing or building more warehouse capacity, there is no increase in storage costs by increasing inventory.

One of the most important and most controversial elements of the inventory carrying cost is the "cost of money" covering the value of capital tied up in inventory. Two alternative choices are common:

1. If inventory has to be increased, money may have to be borrowed from a bank or other source of capital. If existing loans can be reduced by reducing inventory, it would seem reasonable to assume that the interest on such loans would be the proper cost of inventory capital.

2. Many practitioners believe the proper cost to be the return on investment which management expects to realize on the total capital in the business, regardless of whether the source is sale of stock, accrued surplus, or borrowed money.

This second alternative will charge inventory with much higher costs than the first. Its use also raises the question of which return rate to use—the actual rate being earned at present or the rate which the management plans to earn on the net worth.

The proper choice can also vary with time. At one time management may wish to reduce inventories to "raise capital from within" rather than from outside sources or to improve the return on net worth of the company, so that its stock is more attractive to investors or in merger transactions. Expressing such objectives as "a cost" is so difficult as to be hardly worthwhile.

There is considerable support in these difficulties for those who believe that the inventory carrying cost is truly a "management policy variable" which, rather than being a fixed, magic number, is one which should be manipulated to best attain the overall objectives of the company. Additional discussion of this concept and of ways of using it in managing inventories will be covered in Chapter 6.

An equally difficult problem arises when an attempt is made to determine *out-of-stock costs*. Customer dissatisfaction with backorders may be very costly, but it is difficult if not impossible to assign a value to it with any degree of accuracy. One backorder may cause little or no customer inconvenience, while the next may be the reason for the customer to buy elsewhere in the future. The stockout cost, like the inventory carrying cost, is an artificial concept demanded by the mathematical formulas which have been derived to assist in making inventory decisions. We should not, however, be so "beguiled by the mathematical convenience"[1] of having such a number that we lose sight of the real implications of such decisions.

Capacity-associated costs—such as overtime and idle time—can often be calculated by using accounting records, but hiring, training, and layoff costs, like ordering costs, are not all linear. While unemployment compensation taxes, for example, vary visibly with any changes in employment level, other costs associated with hiring, training, and layoff are hidden in the total costs of supervision, personnel department operating costs, etc., and change only when a change in activity is such that it results in reduced clerical labor. These costs are discussed further in Chapter 8.

Distribution by value

"For any given group, a small number of items in the group will account for the bulk of the total value." About 20% of the people in this country have 80% of the wealth; about 20% of the various makes of cars account for 80% of the annual automobile sales; 20% of the items in the family

---

[1]Brown, R. G., *Statistical Forecasting for Inventory Control*, McGraw, New York, 1959, p. 119.

budget account for 80% of the dollar expenditures. This is a very useful concept in business, where it can be applied to inventory control, production control, quality control and many other management problems. This is one of the most applicable and effective, yet least exploited of the basic principles of production control.

When applied to inventories, this concept is called the "ABC" classification. Any inventory can be separated into three distinct parts:

1. **"A" items:** *High value*—those relatively few items whose value accounts for 75–80% of the total value of the inventory. These will usually be from 15–20% of the items.

2. **"B" items:** *Medium value*—a larger number in the middle of the list, usually about 30–40% of the items, whose total value accounts for about 15% of the total.

3. **"C" items:** *Low value*—the bulk of the items, usually about 40–50%, whose total inventory value is almost negligible, accounting for only 5–10% of the value.

The breakdown into A, B, and C items is, of course, an arbitrary one; many companies make further divisions such as adding a D group or breaking down the A group into AAA, AA, and A items. The A group of items, of course, has an ABC distribution within the group. There are some items which justify the production control manager's personal attention just because of the large amount of dollars they represent.

This concept has wide application in many other phases of production control activities:

1. A few customers give a company most of its orders

2. A few departments perform the bulk of the work of the manufacturing operations

3. A few operations produce most of the scrap

4. A few vendors cause most of the delays in procuring purchased materials

5. A few items are holding up most of the backorders for customers

Figure 3-1 shows a typical ABC distribution for a group of items. The horizontal scale represents the percentage of total items while the vertical scale represents the percentage of total annual usage dollars. Note that a very small number of items accounts for the great bulk of the sales dollars. These, of course, are the A items so indicated on the curve. In the B section of the curve, it is typical to find that the percentage of B items is almost equal to the percentage of dollars represented by these B items. The C items occupy the opposite end of the scale—a very large number of items accounts for a very small fraction of the total usage dollars.

Figure 3-1

Distribution of Inventory Dollars

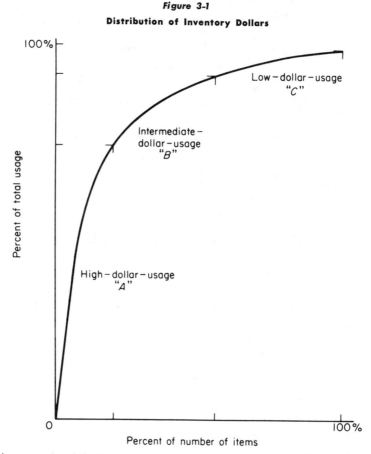

An oversimplified example using only ten items will illustrate how to make an ABC analysis. The first step is to list the items and their annual usage, then multiply the annual usages by the unit costs and assign a number to rank the items in order, starting with the highest dollar value of annual usage. This listing is shown in Table 3-II.

Table 3-II

Item	Annual usage	Unit cost	Annual $ usage	Rank
F-11	40,000	.07	$2,800	5
F-20	195,000	.11	21,450	1
F-31	4,000	.10	400	9
L-45	100,000	.05	5,000	3
L-51	2,000	.14	280	10
L-16	240,000	.07	16,800	2
L-17	16,000	.08	1,280	6
N-8	80,000	.06	4,800	4
N-91	10,000	.07	700	7
N-100	5,000	.09	450	8

Next, these items are listed in ranking order and the cumulative annual usage plus the cumulative percentage calculated. Step two in this ABC analysis is shown in Table 3-III. If it is decided arbitrarily that the A items will be the first 20% of the items, this A group would include the first and second items. The next three in ranking order would be B items and would account for 30% of the total items. The remaining 50% of the items would be designated C items.

Table 3-III

Item	Annual $ usage	Cumulative annual $ usage	Cumulative percentage	Class
F-20	$21,450	$21,450	39.8%	A
L-16	16,800	38,250	71.0%	A
L-45	5,000	43,250	80.2%	B
N-8	4,800	48,050	89.3%	B
F-11	2,800	50,850	94.4%	B
L-17	1,280	52,130	96.7%	C
N-91	700	52,830	97.9%	C
N-100	450	53,280	98.9%	C
F-31	400	53,680	99.6%	C
L-51	280	53,960	100.0%	C

This ABC analysis can be summarized as in Table 3-IV.

If by concentrating maximum efforts on the A items, this inventory could be reduced by 25%, a very substantial reduction in total inventory would result, even if the C item inventory increased by 50% because of reduced attention and looser controls.

Table 3-IV

Classification	% of items	$ per group	% of $
A = F-20, L-16	20%	$38,250	71.0%
B = L-45, N-8, F-11	30%	12,600	23.4%
C = all others	50%	3,110	5.6%
Totals	100%	$53,960	$100.0

There are two general rules to remember about the ABC approach:

1. *Have plenty* of the low value items

2. *Use the control effort saved* to reduce the inventory of high value items

The following examples are typical of the applications of the ABC concept:

1. Degree of control:

    a. *A items*—tightest possible control, including most complete, accurate records, regular review by top-level supervision, blanket orders with frequent deliveries from vendors, close follow-up through the factory to reduce lead time, etc.

    b. *B items*—normal controls involving good records and regular attention.

    c. *C items*—simplest possible controls such as periodic review of physical inventory with no records or only the simplest notations that replenishment stocks have been ordered. Large inventories and order quantities to avoid stockouts. Low priority in scheduling in factory.

2. Types of inventory records:

    a. *A items*—most accurate and complete, with frequent audits of accuracy. Tight control of scrap losses, rejects, etc.

    b. *B items*—normal, good records.

    c. *C items*—no records, or only the simplest.

3. Priority:

a. *A items*—high priority in all activities to reduce lead time and inventory.

b. *B items*—normal processing with high priority only when critical.

c. *C items*—lowest priority.

4. Ordering procedures:

a. *A items*—careful, accurate determination of order quantities and order points. Frequent review to reduce, if possible.

b. *B items*—good analysis for EOQ and order point determination but only reviewed quarterly, or when major changes occur.

c. *C items*—no EOQ or order point calculations. Order one year's supply while there are still plenty on hand.

Further applications of specific techniques to take advantage of the "ABC" relationship are discussed in later chapters. It is the most universally applicable concept in production and inventory control.

How well do we manage inventories ?

The role of industrial inventories in the drama of business cycles has been of great topical interest to economists, politicians and business leaders. While there is little agreement among these on the best solution, there is a common recognition that the problem is *"How to control inventory to minimize or eliminate the amplifying effect on business cycles."*

When sales rates change at the consumer level, production rates must also change. The time interval between these changes depends on:

1. How quickly the new trend is identified as a trend and not as a random fluctuation

2. Whether inventories should increase or decrease

3. How much change in inventory is desired

When sales rates increase, well-controlled inventory levels must generally increase also to maintain the same level of customer service. Production is therefore called on to increase to meet:

1. The increase in sales rate
2. The additional inventory desired

The second factor is, of course, a temporary one existing only until the necessary additional inventory is provided. Because of it, however, a moderate increase in sales can generate a very substantial increase in production, particularly if management moves quickly to maintain customer service. The opposite effect causes production to drop drastically when sales fall off even moderately.

Control over such fluctuations must be established to ease the impact of unemployment and the other economic ills of depression/boom cycles.

Many illustrations such as the following have been given: "... in automotive manufacture, a 5% variation in retail sales may be amplified to a 10% variation at the vehicle assembly plant, to a 20% variation at the first level and to perhaps a 40% variation at the third level. If we compare the retail automotive sales trend with the procurement of steel for automotive use, we find that the sharp increases or decreases in automotive steel procurement are due more to inventory correction than they are to changes in the demand for automobiles. This is not only an automotive problem, because most of American industry works on the same principle."[1]

This is particularly significant since the automobile industry is probably more advanced in control techniques than many other industries. Another article suggests that changes in retail sales will be magnified six to ten times in the effect they have on factory output.[2]

Figure 3-2, The 60-day ordering rule, shows how this type of inventory building and reduction can occur when we use "common sense" inventory control systems. The 60-day ordering rule is a very simple system which can be stated as: *"Each time a reorder is placed, order enough material so that the total on hand and on order is equal to sales for the past sixty days."*

In the example shown, sales increase very substantially through the March to May period and decrease from May through August. The *target inventory,* or the "order up to" level, is always equal to the sales for the previous 2 months. For example, February's target is 120 units,

---

[1] McCoard, Frank G., "Proposed Objectives for Production and Inventory Control," *The Quarterly Technical Bulletin, The American Production and Inventory Control Society,* Vol. 1, No. 1, January 1, 1960.

[2] Sims, E. Ralph Jr., "How Material Control Aids Your Company's Operation," *Materials Handling Engineering,* March 1961.

Figure 3-2

60-Day Ordering Rule

Month	Sales	Target	On hand	Factory order
January	60	120	60	60
February	60	120	60	60
March	80	140	40	100
April	90	170	50	120
May	100	190	70	120
June	90	190	100	90
July	80	170	110	60
August	60	140	110	30

equal to sales for January and February. The amount on hand is the balance from the previous month, plus the receipt of the previous month's factory order, less the current month's sales. The new factory order for the month is arrived at by deducting the amount on hand from the target inventory.

Notice the substantial amplification effect that is built into this "common sense" control system. Sales increase from a minimum of 60 to a maximum of 100 and the factory order increases up to 120. When sales decrease to 60 units in August, the factory order actually decreases to 30 units. This is the type of irrational ordering technique still found to be in use in industry that helps to contribute substantially to serious inventory buildup and reduction problems that amplify business cycles.

There is no question that some inventory increase may be required when business goes up if we are to provide the same service level, but those with only the most elementary knowledge of sound inventory control principles recognize that the increase in inventory should not be proportional to the sales increase.

Moreover, manufactured inventories can seldom be controlled by inventory control techniques alone since the present high cost of changing production rates makes it essential to use inventories to help stabilize production in most companies. The effective use of inventories to help keep costs down and provide competitive customer service without excessive inventory investment requires an understanding of the basic principles of production and inventory control. These principles and the techniques for implementing them will be the subject matter of the following chapters.

Bibliography

1. Austin, Daniel J., "Determining Optimum Inventories," *APICS Annual Conference Proceedings,* 1961.

2. Brown, Robert G., "Dynamic Inventories—Controlling Their New Power," *Modern Materials Handling,* March 1963.

3. Dickie, H. F., "ABC Inventory Analysis Shoots for Dollars," *Factory Management and Maintenance,* July 1951.

4. ———, "Six Steps to Better Inventory Management," *Factory Management and Maintenance,* August 1953.

5. "Do Inventories Make Booms and Busts?," *Business Week,* July 7, 1962.

6. Magee, John F., *Production Planning and Inventory Control,* McGraw, New York, 1958

7. Meal, Harlan G., "Policy Conflicts and Inventory Control," *Financial Executive,* pp. 13-17, December 1963.

8. Van DeMark, R. L., "Hidden Controls for Inventory," *APICS Annual Conference Proceedings,* 1960.

# CHAPTER FOUR

THE ECONOMIC
LOT-SIZE

The value of the economic ordering quantity concept

In inventory and production control analyses, it is usually convenient and practical to study together those items which fall into natural groups. These groups may be made up of parts processed by common manufacturing equipment, purchased items handled by the same buyer, or material ordered from the same vendor. This is particularly true in determining the sizes of lots in which material is procured. Costs, capital requirements, space needs, operating conditions and other factors which must be considered in setting lot sizes are most meaningful when families of related parts are considered.

In the first example of lot-size calculations to be used, five items have been chosen. These items can be imagined as products made on the same manufacturing equipment. Table 4-I shows the present situation, with lot-sizes determined by the rule of thumb "Run once a quarter," representative of the intuitive rules used so frequently.

Four setups or orders per year are being placed for each item, giving a total of twenty orders per year, the resulting average lot-size inventory is $2,430, which is half the total of all lot-sizes. Since each lot is received in total, then used up over a period of time so that the inventory is reduced to zero, the average lot-size inventory will be one-half the lot-

Table 4-I

Item	Annual use	Present orders/yr	Present order quantities
1	$10,000	4	$2,500
2	6,400	4	1,600
3	2,500	4	625
4	400	4	100
5	144	4	36
Totals		20	$4,861

Average lot-size inventory = $2,430

size—assuming the usage rate to be constant over the period. It is apparent that if some of the setups being used on Item 5 were used instead on Item 1, the inventory could be reduced. Even if a year's supply of Item 5 were to be run, it would not affect the inventory investment very much, while each additional setup that could be made on Item 1 would result in a very substantial reduction in inventory. Table 4-II shows a redistribution of the 20 setups made simply by inspection:

Table 4-II

Item	Annual use	Proposed orders/yr.	Proposed order quantities
1	$10,000	10	$1,000
2	6,400	5	1,280
3	2,500	3	833
4	400	1	400
5	144	1	144
Totals		20	$3,657

Average lot-size inventory = $1,828

The result is a very substantial reduction in average inventory from $2,430 to $1,828, without change in the number of orders placed per year.

The principle is very simple: The reduction achieved by cutting in half a large dollar value inventory of an item is far greater than the increase that results from doubling a small dollar value inventory. The use of "inspection" to make this type of analysis is thoroughly practical. A significant improvement can frequently be made in practice using such a common sense approach. While the resulting order quantities are not economic order quantities (since they were arrived at without considering the costs of carrying inventory, setting-up, or ordering) they are more reasonable than the original order quantities. Their use will lower any costs associated with carrying inventory without affecting those costs related to ordering.

In many companies—particularly distributor warehouses that purchase from a manufacturing firm and sell to a retailer—the system of reviewing all products every two or three months and reordering all at the same time and in equivalent time supplies (such as a two-month supply of each item) was common for many years. When a discount for joint purchase of all items was offered, this practice had some justification, but this type of reordering system was more frequently used just because it seemed to make sense. The example given earlier illustrates the fact that this is not an economical approach and that substantial improvements in the use of the company's resources can be made by a redistribution of setup or reordering effort.

Does the example show the best possible distribution of twenty setups per year? Actually, it does not. There is a simple mathematical approach which will result in a better distribution of orders. Before looking at this calculation, however, it is important to understand the concept of the economic ordering quantity.

The basic concept

One of the basic decisions that must be made in inventory management is that of balancing the costs of inventory investment against those of placing inventory replenishment orders. The question to be answered is "*How much should be ordered?*" The right quantity to order is that which best balances the costs related to the *number* of orders placed against the costs related to the *size* of the orders placed. When these costs have been balanced properly, the total cost is minimized, and the resulting ordering quantity is called the *economic lot-size,* or *economic ordering quantity* (EOQ).

The economic ordering quantity concept applies under the following conditions:

1. The item is replenished in lots or batches, either by purchasing or manufacturing, and is not produced continuously

2. Sales or usage rates are uniform and are low compared to the rate at which the item is normally produced so that an inventory results

The economic ordering quantity concept does *not* apply to all items produced for inventory. In a refinery, for example, production is continuous and there are no lot-sizes as such. The bulk of the jobs in a "make-to-order" plant are often made in the lot-sizes ordered by the customer. Nevertheless, the concept has broad application in industry, since most production is not continuous, and individual lots of material are being taken from one inventory, processed, and are then delivered to another inventory.

It is important to distinguish (in a manufacturing organization) between economic manufacturing lot-sizes and movement lot-sizes. Where a large steel blanking press, for example, feeds subsequent piercing and trimming operations, there is no need to wait until the entire EOQ has been blanked before moving part of the lot to the subsequent operations. This portion of the EOQ is the *movement lot-size*. The movement lot-size is usually determined by container sizes or pallet capacities, and may be a small fraction of the total economic lot-size.

It is essential to control manufactured and purchased lot-sizes, because they often represent the largest single segment of the inventory.

Trial and error approach

What are the alternatives available in choosing a lot-size? Assume that a standard stock item is being ordered from the factory by manufacturing orders authorizing them to ₘₐₖₑ the item. One replenishment order per year could be placed for the total annual requirements. This would mean that the factory would only have to setup to manufacture this item once during the year. It would mean also that the average lot-size inventory would be very large, equal to one-half year's requirement.

This average lot-size inventory could be reduced very substantially by ordering fifty times during the year—approximately once a week. This would place a very heavy burden on the factory since the job would have to be setup fifty times to manufacture the annual requirements. These alternatives are shown in Table 4-III.

Table 4-III

ANNUAL REQUIREMENTS = $1,000 WORTH

Replenishment orders per year	Lot-size	Average lot-size inventory
1	$1,000	$500
50	20	10

Table 4-III shows the basic dilemma that must be faced in determining an economic lot-size: Ordering or setup cost can be kept down by ordering infrequently, but the resulting inventory investment will have to be very high; inventory investment can be kept low by ordering frequently, but the resulting ordering costs will be very high. Determining the economic lot-size requires finding the quantity which results in the lowest *total* cost.

For example, assume the cost of placing a replenishment order to be $2.00[1] and the inventory carrying cost to be equal to 10% per year of the average dollar inventory investment. An economic lot-size can be determined by trial and error, as shown in Fig. 4-1. If this item had $1,000 annual usage and were ordered in $50.00 ordering quantities, the average

Figure 4-1

Trial and Error Calculation

	Economic ordering quantity				
Data :-	Ordering cost = $2 Annual usage = $1000 Inventory carrying cost = 10%				
Order quantity	Average inventory	Carrying cost	Orders per year	Order cost	Total cost
$ 50	25	$ 2.50	20	$ 40	$ 42.50
100	50	5.00	10	20	25.00
200	100	10.00	5	10	20.00
250	125	12.50	4	8	20.50
500	250	25.00	2	4	29.00

lot-size inventory would be $25.00; the annual carrying cost at 10% would be $2.50. A total of 20 orders would be placed per year at $2.00 each giving a total ordering cost of $40.00. The total annual cost associated with a $50.00 ordering quantity would be $42.50, equal to the sum of the $40.00 ordering cost and the $2.50 carrying cost.

As the ordering quantity is increased, the average inventory increases and, consequently, the inventory carrying cost increases. With the larger ordering quantity, the number of orders placed per year decreases and the resulting ordering cost decreases. Looking at the far right-hand

---

[1]If "out-of-pocket" costs only were being considered, these costs could be realistic. They are not intended, however, to be representative of industry costs, but are used simply to make the calculations obvious.

column, headed "Total cost," it can be seen that the lowest total cost would result from an ordering quantity of $200.00. This is the ordering quantity that balances the cost of ordering with the cost of carrying inventory, and it is the economic ordering quantity for this item.

Figure 4-2 shows these costs plotted on a graph. As ordering quantities are increased, it can be seen that carrying costs go up and ordering costs go down. The upper curve, the total cost curve, decreases with increasing ordering quantities to a minimum at the $200.00 ordering quantity; from there the total costs increase with larger lot sizes.

Figure 4-2

Order Size vs. Total Cost

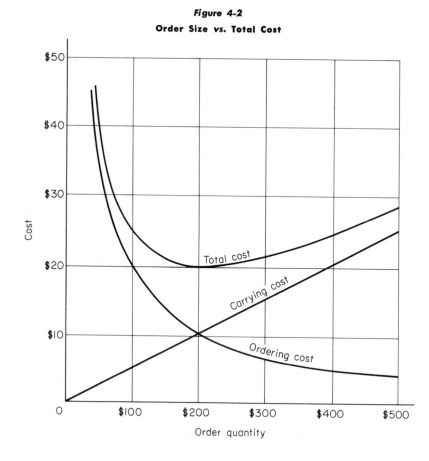

Order quantity

This is an extremely useful concept in inventory control leading to substantial savings over intuitive "guesstimates." Note that the total costs associated with a $200.00 ordering quantity are less than half of those resulting from the $50.00 ordering quantity.

The EOQ formula

In industry, of course, it would not be practical to use this trial and error method to arrive at the economic lot-size for each item in inventory.

Instead, an economic ordering quantity formula is used which calculates the EOQ for any item in one step. One form of this formula is:

$$EOQ = \sqrt{\frac{2AS}{I}} \qquad (4\text{-}1)$$

where: A = the annual *demand* usage, in dollars

S = the setup or ordering cost, in dollars

I = the inventory carrying cost, as a decimal fraction per dollar of average inventory

Substituting the data used in our trial and error tabulation, Fig. 4-1, the economic ordering quantity can be calculated directly from formula (4-1) as follows:

$$EOQ = \sqrt{\frac{2 \times 1,000 \times 2.00}{0.10}}$$
$$EOQ = \sqrt{40,000}$$
$$EOQ = \$200.00$$

Calculations with this formula are greatly simplified by the use of a table of square roots (such as Appendix I) or a square root chart (such as Appendix II). The mathematical derivation of this formula is included in Appendix III. The economic ordering quantity formula is derived by solving the separate equations for inventory carrying cost and ordering cost to find the lowest total cost; in other words, the formula finds the lowest point on the total cost curve of Fig. 4-2—the *zero slope* of this curve.

Use of EOQ when costs are not known precisely

In the simple example shown above, it was assumed that precise values of the ordering cost and inventory carrying cost were known. These are assumed to be available by every formula for EOQ. In actual practice these costs are difficult to determine accurately (for reasons which are discussed later in this chapter). Nevertheless, use of the concept of economic lot-sizes results in practical benefits to production control for two reasons:

1. Ordering quantities set by a consistent, orderly method give far superior results to those determined by rule of thumb or guess.

2. The total cost curve (Fig. 4-2) is flat for a fairly broad range on each side of the economic ordering quantity. This means that reasonably "economic" ordering quantities can be found using cost data which is considerably short of perfection. It also means that adjustments can be made to the ordering quantity arrived at by formula (such as rounding-off a formula EOQ of 1910 units to a more practical figure of 2000 units) without sacrificing significant savings.

The practitioner should not be discouraged from seeking the economies possible through use of EOQ by lack of precise cost data. Improvements over intuitive lot-sizes can almost always be made.

The standard EOQ formula expressed in formula (4-1) contained two cost factors:

$$S = \text{Setup or ordering cost, in dollars}$$

$$I = \text{Inventory carrying cost fraction}$$

For a family of items such as was discussed in the first section of this chapter, the inventory carrying cost is generally assumed to be the same for all items and the setup or ordering cost for the group is often practically the same. If this is true, formula (4-1) can be written as:

$$\text{EOQ} = \sqrt{\frac{2S}{I}} \times \sqrt{A}$$

Once the calculation for the cost constants has been made, the formula becomes:

$$\text{EOQ} = K \times \sqrt{A} \tag{4-2}$$

where:

$$K = \sqrt{\frac{2S}{I}} \tag{4-3}$$

Formula (4-2) points out a very useful relationship: *The most economic lot-sizes are a function of the square root of the annual usages of the items expressed in dollars.*

Returning to the five items whose lot-sizes were studied in Tables 4-I and 4-II, the best possible distribution of the twenty annual setups can now be calculated. The results of the calculation, based on formula (4-2), are shown in Table 4-IV:

Table 4-IV

Item	Annual Use	$\sqrt{A}$	N Present orders/yr	Present O.Q.'s	Calculated orders/yr	Calculated O.Q.'s
1	$10,000	$100	4	$2,500	7.6	$1,310
2	6,400	80	4	1,600	6.2	1,050
3	2,500	50	4	625	3.8	655
4	400	20	4	100	1.5	262
5	144	12	4	36	.9	157
		$262	20	$4,861	20.0	$3,434
Average lot-size inventory				$2,430		$1,717

The value of K used in these calculations for the 20 orders was obtained using the formula:

$$K = \frac{\Sigma \sqrt{A}}{\Sigma N} = \frac{262}{20} = 13.1 \qquad (4\text{-}4)$$

The symbol "sigma" (Σ) is the mathematical notation for "sum." In this formula, the sum of the square roots of the annual usages ($\sqrt{A}$) of all items is divided by the present total of orders (N) per year.

Using formula (4-2), new lot-sizes were then calculated for each item by multiplying 13.1 by the square root of A for each item. These lot sizes are shown in the last column of the table. The average lot-size inventory of $1,717 is the *lowest possible* total lot-size inventory for this group of items when only twenty orders per year are issued. Note that it was obtained *without* knowing specific values of the ordering or inventory carrying costs.

To the practical-minded, the concept of "7.6" orders per year may be somewhat disturbing because seven-tenths of a setup has no real meaning. Nevertheless, the order quantity of $1,310—which would probably be rounded off to $1,300—for Item 1 is a valid one. In an actual factory, it would result in seven orders some years and eight in others. While fractional setups are not real, they are a convenient concept in making lot-size calculations because they make it possible to use the period of one year as a consistent period over which costs can be compared.

This approach could also be used to calculate the lowest total number of orders which could be written for the same average lot-size inventory of $2,430. The resulting lot-sizes are shown in Table 4-V:

Table 4-V

Item	Annual use	$\sqrt{A}$	Present orders/yr	Present O.Q.'s	Calculated orders/yr	Calculated O.Q.'s
1	$10,000	$100	4	$2,500	5.4	$1,855
2	6,400	80	4	1,600	4.4	1,484
3	2,500	50	4	625	2.7	928
4	400	20	4	100	1.1	371
5	144	12	4	36	0.7	223
		$262	20	$4,861	14.3	$4,861
Average lot-size inventory				$2,430		$2,430

These were calculated using the formula:

$$K = \frac{\Sigma \, Q}{\Sigma \, \sqrt{A}} = \frac{4,861}{262} = 18.55 \tag{4-5}$$

Here, the sum of the present order quantities (Q) is divided by the sum of the square roots of the annual usages $(\sqrt{A})$.

Again, using equation (4-2), new lot-sizes were calculated for each item, *without using specific values of the ordering or inventory carrying costs*. For this family, 14.3 orders per year is the fewest that can be written for an average lot-size inventory of $2,430.

Formulas (4-4) and (4-5) for finding the value of K were first suggested by W. Evert Welch and are derived in his book[1]. This approach to EOQ calculations has five significant advantages:

1. For a family of items where setup (or ordering) and inventory carrying costs are the same for all items, it provides a much-simplified method of calculating EOQ's. The value of K is calculated once for all items and is then multiplied by the square root of the annual usage dollars to determine the EOQ for each item. This is illustrated by a sample problem in the next section.

2. If there is a restriction on the number of orders which can be handled by the present organization, this approach can be used to obtain the least total lot-size inventory for the family of items subject to the restriction. This is illustrated by Table 4-IV.

3. If the amount of inventory cannot be increased to the full extent required by EOQ's, the technique can be used to set lot-sizes which result in the least total orders with this restriction and, hence, the lowest ordering cost, as illustrated in Table 4-V.

---

[1] Welch, W. Evert, *Tested Scientific Inventory Control,* Management Publishing Company, Greenwich, Conn., 1956.

4. The approach illustrates a method of obtaining some immediate benefits from applying the EOQ concept where intuitive means have previously been used to set order quantities. As shown in Tables 4-IV and 4-V, inventory can be reduced while keeping ordering costs the same—or ordering costs can be reduced while keeping inventory the same.

5. This calculation illustrates a very important point that is often overlooked: *The application of EOQ's is usually more significant when items are grouped together.*

While it is not necessary to know the specific costs of ordering and carrying inventory to apply this method, the basic assumption must be made that these are the same for all items in the family. In addition, the results may not be "most economical" when *actual* costs are considered, and further improvements might be made if representative cost figures could be obtained.

In actual applications, other limitations may make it impractical to attain the full benefits from EOQ's immediately. Among these are shortage of capital for investment in inventory, restricted space to store inventory, too-few skilled setup men and limited machine capacity available for setting-up.

A technique called LIMIT (*Lot-size Inventory Management Interpolation Technique*) has been developed to make it possible to attain the economies of the EOQ concept within the limits of such restrictions and to study the alternatives available in balancing ordering and inventory carrying costs. This technique will be discussed in detail in Chapter 6, Aggregate Inventory Management.

Economic order quantity formula variations

The use of K in formula (4-2) for simplifying EOQ calculations for groups of items where each item in the group has the same setup or ordering cost and the same inventory carrying cost was discussed briefly in the preceding section. Using formula (4-3), $K = \sqrt{2S/I}$, the constant K is calculated once. Economic ordering quantities are then calculated by using formula (4-2), $EOQ = K \times \sqrt{A}$, multiplying this constant by the square root of the annual usage (in dollars) for each item. Here is a simple example with three items:

		Item 1	Item 2	Item 3
Annual usage (A)	=	\$10,000.00	\$20,000.00	\$30,000.00
Ordering cost (S)	=	5.00	5.00	5.00
Inventory carrying cost (I)	=	0.20	0.20	0.20

We can then calculate:

$$K = \sqrt{2S/I}$$
$$K = \sqrt{2 \times 5.00/.20} = \sqrt{\$50.00} = 7.07$$
$$\text{EOQ} = K \times \sqrt{A}$$
$$\text{EOQ} = 7.07 \times \sqrt{A}$$

For Item 1, EOQ $= 7.07 \times \sqrt{\$10,000} = \$\ 707.00$
For Item 2, EOQ $= 7.07 \times \sqrt{\$20,000} = \$1000.00$
For Item 3, EOQ $= 7.07 \times \sqrt{\$30,000} = \$1225.00$

This type of shortcut can speed-up EOQ calculations very substantially, particularly when square root tables are used or when curves or nomographs are available.[1]

In formula (4-1), the annual usage and the economic order quantities calculated were expressed in dollars. This is sometimes inconvenient, and some practitioners prefer to calculate EOQ's in pieces. The formula for this is as follows:

$$\text{EOQ} = \sqrt{\frac{2US}{IC}} \qquad (4\text{-}6)$$

where: $U =$ Annual usage, pieces
         $S =$ Ordering or setup cost, dollars
         $I =$ Inventory carrying cost, a decimal fraction
               per dollar of average inventory
         $C =$ Unit cost, dollars per piece

Taking the same example used in the preceding section where the annual usage in dollars was \$1000, and assuming that this represents 2000 pieces at 50¢ each, this formula can be used to calculate an answer that will come out in pieces.

$$\text{EOQ} = \sqrt{\frac{2US}{IC}} = \sqrt{\frac{2 \times 2000 \times 2}{.10 \times .50}}$$
$$\sqrt{\frac{80000}{.50}} = \sqrt{160,000} = 400 \ \text{pieces}$$

which is equivalent to a \$200 order quantity of pieces worth 50c each.

---

[1]An excellent reference for developing EOQ nomographs is *Tested Scientific Inventory Control,* by W. Evert Welch, Management Publishing Company, Greenwich, Conn., 1956. *Op. cit.*

This formula can also be used for material ordered in pounds, feet, or other units. The economic order quantity calculated by formula (4-6) will always have the same units as the annual usage *if* the cost, C, is the value of one such unit (either a pound, a foot, or any other).

There are times when the form in which the inventory record has been kept makes it convenient to calculate the economic ordering quantity based upon the monthly usage of the item. The formula for doing this where usage is in dollars is:

$$\text{EOQ} = \sqrt{\frac{24MS}{I}} \qquad (4\text{-}7)$$

where: M = Monthly usage in dollars
          S = Setup or ordering cost, in dollars
          I = Inventory carrying cost, as a decimal fraction per dollar of average inventory

Using the same example, but now expressing the $1,000 annual usage as a monthly dollar usage of $83.30, the same EOQ will result:

$$\text{EOQ} = \sqrt{\frac{24MS}{I}} = \sqrt{\frac{24 \times 83.30 \times 2}{.10}}$$
$$= \sqrt{480 \times 83.30} = \sqrt{40,000}$$
$$= \$200.00$$

This monthly usage formula can also be used where it is more convenient to deal with pieces or other units. In this case, the formula would be expressed as follows:

$$\text{EOQ} = \sqrt{\frac{24MuS}{IC}} \qquad (4\text{-}8)$$

where: Mu = Monthly usage in pieces or other units
          S = Setup or ordering cost, dollars
          I = Inventory carrying cost as a decimal fraction per dollar of average inventory
          C = Unit cost, dollars

Calculating the EOQ once again with the demand for the item now expressed in pieces per month, the same answer results:

$$\text{EOQ} = \sqrt{\frac{24MuS}{IC}} = \sqrt{\frac{24 \times 167 \times 2}{.10 \times .50}}$$
$$= \sqrt{\frac{480 \times 167}{.50}} = \sqrt{160.000}$$
$$= 400 \text{ pieces.}$$

In many companies, the forecasts for individual items are made on a quarterly basis. When forecasts are available by the quarter, the EOQ calculation can be made directly using the formula:

$$EOQ = \sqrt{\frac{8QS}{I}}$$ (4-9)

where: Q = Quarterly usage in dollars
         S = Setup or ordering cost, dollars
         I = Inventory carrying cost as a decimal fraction per dollar of average inventory.

Calculating the EOQ once again, using formula (4-9):

$$EOQ = \sqrt{\frac{8QS}{I}} = \sqrt{\frac{8 \times 250 \times 2}{.10}}$$

$$= \sqrt{\frac{4000}{.10}} = \sqrt{40,000}$$

$$= \$200.00$$

There are many more variations of the EOQ formula to facilitate the use of available data. The bibliography lists references which discuss these formula variations in more depth.

Non-instantaneous receipt

In addition to variations enabling simple EOQ formulas to handle different units, there are other adjustments to the formula that can be made to get more accurate answers in special circumstances. Frequently, for example, the entire lot-size is not received into stock at once. The manufacturing rate may be such that it takes several days or even weeks for the complete lot to be made and delivered to stock. While production is going on, partial deliveries to stock are made, but withdrawals will also be made during this period. Consequently, the average lot-size inventory will not equal one-half the lot-size, as it does where receipt of the lot occurs all at once.

This situation, given the rather formidable name of *noninstantaneous receipt*, can be handled by using the following modification of the basic EOQ formula:

$$EOQ = \sqrt{\frac{2AS}{I(1 - s/p)}}$$ (4-10)

where: A = Annual usage in dollars

S = Setup or ordering cost, dollars
I = Inventory carrying cost as a decimal frac-
    tion per dollar of average inventory
s = Usage rate, same units as production rate
p = Production rate, same units as usage rate

Using the same example, with sales at the rate of $4.00 per day ($1000 annual usage divided by 250 working days) and production assumed to be at the rate of $16.00 per day, the calculation would then be:

$$\text{EOQ} = \sqrt{\frac{2AS}{I(1 - s/p)}} = \sqrt{\frac{2 \times 1000 \times 2}{.10(1 - 4/16)}}$$

$$= \sqrt{\frac{4000}{.075}} = \sqrt{53,400}$$

$$= \$231.00$$

Figure 4-3

Diagram of Lot-Size Inventory

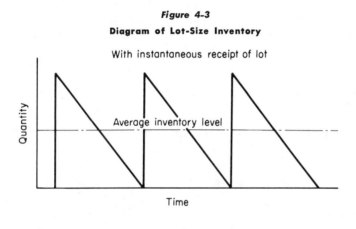

With instantaneous receipt of lot

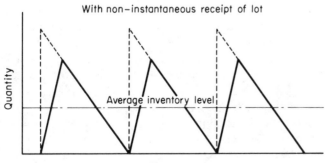

With non-instantaneous receipt of lot

The answer ($231.00) is higher than the $200.00 that was calculated by formula (4-1) in which "instantaneous receipt" is assumed. The size of the manufactured lot is increased by formula (4-10), but the average lot-size inventory is not increased because material will be withdrawn while the balance of the lot is being produced. It can be demonstrated that the $231.00 ordering quantity with noninstantaneous receipt will give an average lot-size inventory of $100.00, the same as that for a $200.00 lot-size received instantaneously.

Figure 4-3 shows a line diagram of the behavior of the lot-size inventory of one item as ordering quantities are received and used up.

When the material is received all at once, the quantity in inventory immediately increases to the total of the lot-size that was ordered. This quantity is then decreased as material is withdrawn over a period of time until a new lot-size is once again received. The resulting diagram in Fig. 4-3 is a right-angle triangle. When the entire lot is not received instantaneously, the highest inventory point is not reached until the complete lot has been delivered, and the "saw-tooth inventory diagram" triangles are no longer right-angle triangles.

Major and minor setup

A situation frequently encountered in industrial applications of EOQ is the so-called "major and minor setup," where it is most economical to run groups of items usually in a definite sequence. When running items through a screw machine, for example, it is often economical to run many similar items consecutively so that only minor changes have to be made in the basic setup to change from one item to the next in the sequence.

Similar parts that can be made with only a minor setup modification in a blanking press can often be grouped together economically. In paper processing industries where it is time-consuming and expensive to clean the equipment, the light colors are run first, followed by darker, and darker still, until the whole process line is shut down, cleaned and changed over.

The basic approach to EOQ may be applied to these situations but will necessitate special handling of the data. Table 4-VI shows a simple example of five items which are made in one major setup. In this example, it is assumed that inventory costs 20% and that annual usage and setup costs for each item are:

Table 4-VI

Item	Annual usage (A)	Setup cost (S)
1	$ 2,000	$2.00
2	4,000	3.00
3	800	3.00
4	10,000	2.00
5	900	2.00
	$17,700	$12.00

There is a major setup cost of $50.00 in addition to the cost S for each item, which represents only the changeover cost for the items within the group. The total setup cost thus equals $62.00.

The standard EOQ formula can be revised to handle this problem by writing it as:

$$\text{EOQ} = \sqrt{\frac{2 \Sigma A \ \Sigma S}{I}} \qquad (4\text{-}11)$$

where: ΣA = the sum of the annual usages for all items.

ΣS = the sum of the setup costs for all items.

Other factors are the same as in formula (4-1). From this:

$$\text{EOQ} = \sqrt{\frac{2 \times 17{,}700 \times 62}{.20}} = \sqrt{10{,}970{,}000} = \$3{,}300$$

Each time a setup is made, $3,300 worth of the group of items should be run. Lot-sizes for each of the items could be calculated individually using formula (4-1), but would have very little practical value. The principal objective is to run a quantity of each item that will equalize the inventory, so that new lots of all will be needed when the major setup is made again. It would be highly undesirable to have the inventory so badly balanced among the items that one was required much sooner than the rest.

Economic order quantities calculated individually would vary as the square root of the usage, and the more active items would run out of stock before the slow-moving ones. The proper solution, then, is to run a quantity of each item which will result in a balanced inventory having an equal number of days' supply of each item. This is known as *equal runout time*.[1]

---

[1] This is assumed to be an equal number of days' supply based on average usage for each item in the examples that follow. A more refined calculation would take into account the probable forecast error to improve the chances of all items "running out" simultaneously.

The present inventory for each item is tabulated as shown in Table 4-VII, together with the average daily usage rate obtained by dividing the annual usage by the number of working days per year.

Table 4-VII

Item	Present inventory	Daily usage rate (250 days/year)
1	$336.00	$ 8.00
2	320.00	16.00
3	100.00	3.20
4	600.00	40.00
5	97.00	3.60
Totals	$1,453.00	$70.80

The procedure for making the proper distribution is to first calculate the total inventory that will result after the new run is added to the present supply.

After running the calculated $3,300 lot-size, the total inventory will be $3,300 + $1,453 = $4,753. If all items were in perfect balance, there would be $4,753/$70.80 = 67 days' supply of each.

Therefore, a quantity of each item should be run to increase the inventory to 67 days' supply of each. This is calculated as shown in Table 4-VIII by subtracting the present inventory from the 67-day total to get the quantity to be run:

Table 4-VIII

Item	67 Days' supply	Present inventory	Run quantity
1	$ 536.00	$336.00	$ 200.00
2	1,072.00	320.00	752.00
3	214.00	100.00	114.00
4	2,690.00	600.00	2,090.00
5	241.00	97.00	144.00
Totals	$4,753.00	$1,453.00	$3,300.00

In this example, the basic EOQ formula (4-11) was used with the annual usages and the setup cost totaled for all items in the group. When a group of items such as this is being run, the production run will usually require a considerable period of time. Because of this, the "noninstantaneous receipt" formula (4-10) would be more applicable. When applied to a group of items, this would be:

$$EOQ = \sqrt{\frac{2\Sigma\, A\; \Sigma\, S}{I(1 - \Sigma\, s/\Sigma\, p)}} \tag{4-12}$$

Based on the production rates and usage rates shown in Table 4-IX for each of the items, a table can be drawn and the calculations made as follows:

Table 4-IX

Item	A	S	Daily usage rate (250 days/year)	Daily production rate
1	$ 2,000	$ 2.00	$ 8.00	$ 60.00
2	4,000	3.00	16.00	80.00
3	800	3.00	3.20	75.00
4	10,000	2.00	40.00	70.00
5	900	2.00	3.60	69.00
Major setup:		50.00		
Totals:	$17,700	$62.00	$70.80	$354.00

$$EOQ = \sqrt{\frac{2 \times 17,700 \times 62.00}{.20(1 - 70.80/354.00)}} = \sqrt{\frac{2,194,000}{.20(1 - .2)}}$$

$$= \sqrt{\frac{2,194,000}{.16}} = \sqrt{13,700,000}$$

$$= \$3,700.$$

Once again, the use of the non-instantaneous receipt adjuster resulted in a larger lot-size. When this group of items is run, the total of the individual lot-sizes should equal $3,700. The individual item lot-sizes should balance the inventory to give an equal number of days' supply in inventory for each item after the new lot is added to the current inventory of the item.

Quantity discounts

When material is purchased, vendors frequently pass along to the buyer some of the advantages of running larger manufacturing lots by offering a discount schedule. The following example shows the EOQ calculation for an item where:

$$\text{Annual usage} = \$10,000$$
$$\text{Ordering cost} = \$5.00$$
$$\text{Inventory carrying cost} = 20\%$$

Using formula (4-1), the EOQ equals $707. If the vendor offered a 1% discount on lots of $2000 or more, the economics of this offer could be shown by setting up a table to determine the total cost of one year's supply in each case:

Table 4-X

Present			With discount
$707	Lot-size ($2000 − 1% =)		$1,980
$353	Average Lot-size inventory		990
$70.60	Inventory carrying cost (20%)		$198
14.1	Number of orders per year		5.0
$70.50	Cost of orders ($5.00 each)		+ 25
	Savings from discount (1% × 10,000 =)		− 100
$141.10	Total cost of 1 year's supply		$123

In this table, the average inventory was determined with and without the discount, and the inventory carrying cost was calculated for each case. The cost of ordering was then determined by calculating the number of orders to be placed in a year and multiplying this by the $5.00 ordering cost to get the total cost of ordering. The "Present" column of the table shows that the total cost for the calculated EOQ is $141.10.

The calculation of these inventory carrying and ordering costs for the discounted quantity shows a total of $223, made up of $198 carrying cost for the higher inventory and only $25 ordering cost since fewer orders have to be placed. On this basis, it would not appear to be economical to order the larger quantity. However, the discount reduces the unit cost of the item, and the cost of a year's requirement would be $100 less if the discount were accepted. This factor is not considered in the standard EOQ formula. It can be seen that it is worthwhile to accept this discount, since the total annual cost would be only $123 instead of $141.10 for the calculated EOQ.

The following are characteristic of discount problems:

1. In order to obtain the discount, a larger quantity will have to be purchased; consequently, the inventory investment will go up and carrying costs will increase (usually by a substantial amount).

2. Ordering in larger quantities reduces the number of orders per year, and the total cost of ordering consequently goes down. This is not usually a large factor in the total.

3. The discount reduces the unit cost of the total annual volume, usually a significant savings.

In order to simplify the discount calculation, the first step of calculating the inventory investment based on the discounted value of the lot-size is often omitted. In the above example, for instance, the lot-size "with discount" would have been shown as $2,000 if this first step had been omitted. This is not significant enough to change the results in most practical instances.

Practical considerations

The various EOQ formulas, in the language of operations research, are very simple "models." It is important to understand the basic concept of EOQ and to be sure that the model used is the best available for the particular circumstances being studied. The EOQ formula contains many assumptions which must be understood by the practitioner if he is to use it properly.

It assumes, for example, that the amount of inventory carried is a direct result of the number of orders placed, and that this inventory will be withdrawn at a fairly uniform rate. It further assumes that the only factors which are significant in the calculation of the most economical lot are those included in the formula, and that costs relating to ordering and to carrying inventory vary uniformly and continuously with the size of the lot ordered. The balance of this section deals with some practical situations where common sense must be used in applying the EOQ formula.

Seasonal production: Many products have a seasonal sales pattern. It is not unusual to see much of the anticipated requirements produced well before the season in order to keep production fairly level throughout the year. During this period of inventory-building, the inventory that is being added is *anticipation inventory, not lot-size inventory*, and the regular EOQ model does not apply. Instead of balancing ordering costs against inventory, the company is now trying to "store man-hours" in inventory most economically. If the peak season occurs suddenly—like Christmas —the sales forecast is the only real information available to the inventory manager, since information about actual sales will come to him too late for him to react. For this reason, many seasonal items are produced in one lot during the year. The question of what lot to run next involves comparing labor *vs.* material costs for all items, ranking them so that the item with the highest ratio of labor to material will be run farthest in advance of the selling season and will therefore be carried in inventory longest. For a product line with less pronounced seasonal demand where anticipation inventory is only built during a brief part of the year, the economic lot-size concept would apply—but during the inventory-building period, some lots could be combined to reduce setups.

Assembly lot-sizes: Another common situation encountered in real-life is the problem of determining lot sizes for assemblies and their components, and once again the extreme situations present the clearest examples. An assembly composed of unique components not used on other assemblies should have its lot-size calculated taking into account all setup costs for the components and the assembly, and most of the components should be manufactured in the same lot sizes as the assembly. Some components with extremely high setup costs could be manufactured in quantities that are multiples of the assembly lot, and a simple calculation of the inventory that would be generated *vs.* setups saved will show the economics of the decision. This type of lot-size calculation is shown for an item with intermittent requirements in Chapter 5. Components used on many items often have usage that is so nearly continuous that the standard EOQ formula can be used.

Die life: Costs associated with limitations, such as the life of a die set used in a blanking press, are seldom included in the EOQ formula. The calculated EOQ for an item might indicate that 20,000 units was the most economical lot-size, whereas the normal die life might be 30,000 units. Because of the high cost of regrinding, refitting, and setting-up a die, it is almost always practical to tie the economic lot-sizes into the die life. In this case, the calculated lot-size would probably be increased to 30,000 units.

Space costs: There is no specific allowance in the simple EOQ formula for the fact that the space cost for different items can be very different indeed. Shipping cartons usually have a low unit value, a very attractive discount schedule and take up great amounts of storage space. On the other hand, electronic components have a very high unit value and take up very little storage space. Using the same inventory carrying cost for both items (where the storage cost is assumed to be included in the inventory carrying cost) would charge the latter more for storage than the former and make little sense. Particularly with bulky items, an estimate of total space requirements resulting from EOQ calculation is essential: storage costs can then be applied to similar groups of items in order to obtain practical results.

Actual runs vs. order quantities: It has been the authors' experience that the ordering quantities indicated on the records and the ordering quantities actually used in the factory can frequently be quite different. In an assembly plant, for example, where components are chronically in short supply, assembly orders may be put out for quantities of two to three thousand units, yet the assembly line may never be set up for quantities of more than five to six hundred units for lack of an adequate supply of components. Any comparisons of new lot-sizes with the present order quantities to determine the effects and economies of change should be based on the actual lot quantity being processed in the plant, not the quantity ordered by the production control department.

Hold-points: Many items are processed through a sequence of operations. The ordering cost must then include the sum of the setup costs for all operations. If setup on one of the early operations is an extremely large proportion of total setup cost, it may be economical to establish an inventory called a *hold-point* beyond this high setup operation, and then do further processing in smaller lots. The decision to have this hold-point should be based on the alternatives of processing the lot through to completion with the resulting inventory of the finished part, or of carrying the inventory as a semi-finished part further back in the process sequence in a less expensive form. Here are a few points to keep in mind regarding this type of calculation:

1. When choosing between alternatives of carrying an item in a semi-finished state or processing it through to completion, *only* that portion of the unit cost actually affected should be used in the calculations. By carrying an item as a finished part rather than in a semi-finished state, only the labor and material of operations beyond the semi-finished point (certainly very little or no overhead) are actually *added* to the inventory investment, although the accounting records will seldom recognize this.

2. The lead time required to replenish the finished item inventory will be reduced and lower inventories can often be carried at this more expensive stage. This is of even greater benefit when several finished items can be made from one semi-finished item. This occurs, for example, where the semi-finished item is unpainted and can be painted one of four different ways to make four different finished items. Note, however, that *total* lead time will

probably increase because larger lots are processed and time will be added moving into and out of the hold point.

3. In general, semi-finished hold points should seldom be established on the basis of differentials in setup alone. Semi-finished inventories are extremely difficult to control and the processing of excessively large lot-sizes through the primary operations often makes mix control to meet changing finished goods needs very difficult. This is especially true when business is increasing and finished goods requirements cannot be satisfied completely from the hold point. The increasing withdrawals from the hold point will generate a large number of replenishment orders that may very well—since the lot-sizes are typically large for these components—create bottlenecks in primary operations that soon cause serious shortages because it becomes impossible to get "some of everything" through.

4. Hold-point inventories will require more control effort, more record keeping and more paperwork. Both their advantages and disadvantages should be clearly recognized when the establishment of hold-points is being considered.

Checking results: One of the best means of checking the reasonableness of calculated economic order quantities is a detailed review by those familiar with the practical situations involved. After the EOQ's have been calculated mechanically (probably using a computer), the production control man familiar with the manufacturing equipment should review them with the foreman responsible for the area in which these lot-sizes apply or with the setup man working on the machine, and round-off the calculated economic order quantities to useable figures. Because of the flatness of the economic order quantity curve, reasonable rounding-off will not result in any serious loss of the economies of EOQ. Such review, however, will insure that practical limitations in applying the lot-sizes have not been overlooked. The experienced practitioner will check each EOQ application to be sure that "the model is valid." With a thorough understanding of the EOQ formula and its applications, the use of the technique can yield large benefits, but if it is applied blindly "by rote," it may result in actual increased costs to the company.

Costs in the EOQ formula

Undoubtedly the most difficult problem to deal with in applying the economic ordering quantity concept is the assumption in the formula that there is a proportional relationship between the amount of inventory carried and the actual out-of-pocket inventory costs, and also between the number of orders placed and the actual total ordering cost. In practice, of course, reducing the number of purchase orders, for example, does not result in a proportional reduction in ordering cost.

The truth is that the relationship between costs and ordering quantities is not directly proportional, but is *stepped*. These steps are controlled by the aggregate effects—such as total number of orders to be placed and total storage space needed—not by the size of individual item lots, hence the need for studying the whole inventory.

Two rules given in Chapter 3 to be used in determining costs in inventory decisions apply specifically to costs used in the economic ordering quantity formulas:

1. They should be actual out-of-pocket costs that will result from the ordering quantities chosen.

2. They should be costs which are actually affected by changes in the size of the ordering quantity.

Unfortunately, the costs shown by the accounting records of most companies are seldom suitable for immediate use in economic lot-size calculations. The unit cost in the EOQ formula is a good example of this type of problem. In many companies, the unit cost of an item is most readily available as a "standard cost" which consists of labor, material, and overhead elements for all manufacturing operations, including some allowance for setup. There are two apparent choices for determining the unit cost to be used in the EOQ formula:

1. Use the standard cost

2. Use only the labor and material portions of the standard cost, plus some overhead which varies with the lot-size

If the full standard cost is used, the two rules regarding costs will be violated (since the overhead portion of the standard cost does not result from and will be affected very little by changes in lot-sizes). An increase in the lot-size inventory, for example, will not actually require any substantial increase in out-of-pocket expense for most of the overhead factors, such as factory clerical expense, supervisory expense, depreciation on equipment, inspection, etc. If the standard cost is used in projecting the dollars that will be spent to increase the inventory, an inflated figure will result since proportionately more will be spent on labor and material but not on overhead. Furthermore, the standard cost usually includes setup, which is a separate cost element in the formulas and should not be included in the unit cost used.

On the other hand, the accounting records will charge overhead to inventory at the rate indicated in the standard costs. Use of only labor, material and the variable portion of overhead costs in the unit cost will mean that total inventory dollar projections based on the EOQ calculations will not agree with the accounting figures. For example, a predicted inventory increase of $100,000 based on costs used in the EOQ formula could result in some real surprises for the manager involved, since the accounting records would probably charge this material to inventory at full standard cost, including all overhead. The "book figures" might then show an inventory increase of $150,000 rather than the predicted $100,000.

Another common problem in using costs occurs on low-volume items. Many companies use the rule of thumb: "*Never run more than a year's supply of anything*" because of high obsolescence risk. This thinking is usually colored by what the accounting records *say* is happening rather than what *is* happening. When one year's supply of a low-volume item with high setup cost is run, it is put into the dollar inventory records at standard cost. If a two-year supply were run on the same machine setup, the inventory value subject to obsolescence risk would undoubtedly be increased, but usually not by the amount indicated by the accounting records. Running an extra year's supply on the same setup would really only result in a proportional increase in cost of material, labor and a portion of the overhead. Sometimes, even labor costs will not be increased proportionately on some semi-automatic equipment. Yet the full standard cost will usually be charged to—and will eventually be written off—the inventory records.

How can this dilemma be handled? Only by speaking two "languages" of cost. One is the real out-of-pocket cost actually affecting our decisions—this should be used in the calculations. The management of the company must also be aware of the effect a given change in inventory will have on the accounting records, since their performance will usually be evaluated based on these records.

Hopefully, the day will come when production control and accounting people can devise mutually satisfactory costing techniques. In the meantime, it is essential for the production control man to:

1. *Understand his company's costing system* and work closely with the company financial people, so that he can use costs intelligently in making his decisions and presenting alternatives to management.

2. *Always make trial applications and predict the results* of EOQ application for the total inventory based on the sample results before using EOQ's on a large scale.

Techniques for taking advantage of the real profits that the economic ordering quantity concept can return and predicting the results of EOQ application will be discussed in more detail in Chapter 6.

Benefits from the use of EOQ

Studies of the applications of the economic ordering quantity[1] find that there has been a surprising lack of application of this concept. Formulas for making these calculations have been available since 1915 and have been well-known in industry since the 1920's. During the depression years and the war years, there was apparently very little interest in economic ordering quantities. This interest was regenerated in the late 1950's with the advent of operations research and with the availability of computers. Since then, interest in the subject has increased greatly.

The foregoing sections pointed out the serious problems in applying this concept as well as the need for common sense and a thorough understanding of the assumptions and limitations of the economic ordering quantity formulas in order to avoid applications that are not profitable. In fact, some applications of the EOQ concept seem to have generated additional expense without coming up with offsetting savings simply because the formulas were not applied properly. It is important to note, however, that application of the economic ordering quantity concept can yield very substantial results. Figure 4-1, in the opening section of this chapter, illustrated that the total cost associated with a "trial and error order quantity" of $50.00 was more than twice the total cost associated with the $200 EOQ. Problems in applying the economic ordering quantity concept result most often because it is applied simply as a *formula*, without a thorough understanding of the *concept*. Properly understood and applied, it is one of the most valuable tools available to the production and inventory control manager.

Bibliography

1. Lander, Jack R., "EOQ: It Can Be Easy," *APICS Quarterly Bulletin,* April 1963.

2. Magee, John F., "Guides to Inventory Policy: I. Functions and Lot Sizes," *Harvard Business Review,* January–February 1956.

---

[1] "Exclusive Survey of Production and Inventory Control," *Factory,* October 1966.

3. ———, *Production Planning and Inventory Control,* McGraw, New York, 1958.

4. Mennell, Roy F., "Early History of Economic Lot Size," *APICS Quarterly Bulletin,* April 1961.

5. Raymond, Fairfield E., *Quantity and Economy in Manufacture,* McGraw, New York, 1931.

6. Scheele, Evan D., Westerman, William L., and Wimmert, Robert J., *Principles and Design of Production Control Systems,* Prentice-Hall, Englewood Cliffs, New Jersey, 1960.

7. Weeks, T. G., "Making Procurement Decisions Based on Contributions to Profits," *APICS Quarterly Bulletin,* October 1960.

8. Welch, W. E., *Tested Scientific Inventory Control,* Management Publishing Company, Greenwich, Connecticut, 1956.

9. Whitin, T. M., *The Theory of Inventory Management,* 2nd Edition, Princeton University Press, Princeton, New Jersey, 1957.

CHAPTER
FIVE

MATERIALS CONTROL

Replenishing a standard
inventory item

The economic ordering quantity concept covered in Chapter 4 provides the answer to the question "How much should be ordered?" each time a replenishment order is placed. In answering this question, the costs associated with ordering are balanced against the costs of carrying inventory to give a minimum total cost. In controlling inventories, the other basic question that must be answered is *"When must the replenishment order be placed?"* In answering this question, inventory investment costs must be balanced against a desired service level. Obviously, if such orders are not placed soon enough, remaining material will be used up before the new lot is received, and customer service will suffer. Conversely, if orders are placed too soon, inventories will be excessively high.

Because the design of the reorder system ultimately determines the level of customer service provided, this decision is usually of far more importance to the production control manager than the lot-size decision. Poor customer service usually comes more frequently and forcefully to management's attention than ordering or inventory costs. In practice, this results in decisions that are often heavily biased toward customer service at the cost of high inventory investment.

Any inventory control system, no matter how humble, has some decision rules built into it. The housewife who shops for groceries once a week makes up her buying list according to intuitive rules that tell her when to reorder. Upon examination, some of these rules are quite sensible. She can probably predict fairly accurately the amount of meat to be used at every meal and will probably be using up the last of last week's meat at the time she prepares to shop again.

Facial tissues, on the other hand, may be subject to a highly erratic demand—depending, perhaps, on whether or not some member of the family comes down with a cold. Our housewife may rule that there should always be an extra box of facial tissues in the linen closet and that, whenever this box is opened, she will buy another on her weekly shopping trip. Vanilla extract is probably only used occasionally and, when the supply of vanilla runs out, she may decide not to purchase any more until the next time she plans to do some baking. Her purchases of salepriced "bargains" are limited by her available funds and also by the storage space of refrigerator, freezer or pantry shelves.

These are simple rules that can be highly effective in practice even though they may not even be applied consistently. In purchasing groceries, the housewife is usually not aware that she is balancing the investment in "inventory" (groceries) against the chance of running out of stock. If she should happen to run out of a staple item, the inconvenience is usually minor since the store is near or a neighbor can lend the item.

This is true of most of the inventory decisions that are made in day-to-day living, and such common reorder systems can be very loose simply because of the short lead time, the small amount of inventory investment and the relatively slight inconvenience of being out of stock. There are many inventories in business—such as office supplies—which can be controlled quite satisfactorily using similar simple decision rules.

There are many others, however, that involve very large inventory investment, an extremely high penalty for being out of stock and very long replenishment lead times. In order to control these inventories properly, efficient reorder systems must be designed. These reorder systems can take many forms, but are usually related to one of the following:

1. **The two-bin system:** A predetermined amount of the stock for a particular item is set aside (frequently in a separate "second bin") and not touched until all of the main stock of this item has been used. When the reserve supply is broken into, notification is then sent

to the production control office and a replenishment order is placed.

2. **Visual review:** The stock level is visually checked periodically and replenishment orders placed after each review to restore the stock level to some predetermined maximum of "on hand" plus "on order".

3. **Order point system** (*Fixed-order quantity—variable-cycle system*): When withdrawals bring the inventory of an item as shown on perpetual inventory records down to a predetermined level, called the "order point," a replenishment order (usually in the amount of the precalculated economic ordering quantity) is placed.

4. **Periodic review system** (*Fixed-cycle—variable-order quantity system*): The inventory records are reviewed periodically, perhaps once a week or once a month, and sufficient material is ordered to restore the total "on hand" plus "on order" to a predetermined maximum level.

5. **The "materials planning" system:** Material is ordered in amounts and on time schedules to meet a preplanned program of production of the item in which the material is used.

All of these systems are closely related in concept. It is apparent, for example, that the two-bin system, although it differs in having no inventory records, is very similar to an order point system where the second bin contains the "order point" quantity. Likewise, the well-known "minimum and maximum" system is merely a variation of the order point system. The minimum is in fact an order point, and the maximum is merely the order point plus the ordering quantity. The order point type system, however, does *not* have universal application in industrial inventory control. In fact, this technique—and the related techniques listed through #4 above—have excellent application for finished goods inventory and repair parts carried in inventory, for example, where demand for the item tends to be fairly continuous and independent of demand for any other inventory item. Replenishing an inventory of components and subassemblies, however, where demands tend to be intermittent and in rather large quantities dependent on a requirement at a higher level of assembly, can usually be handled more effectively with the materials planning method. Each of these reorder systems will be discussed in more detail throughout this chapter. The order point system will be discussed in some depth because it provides the best example of the methods used to cope with uncertainty in reordering systems.

Demand during lead time

Demand is the name given to the total requirement for an item in a given period of time. *Lead time* is the time that elapses from the moment it is determined that a replenishment order must be placed until the material covered by this order has been received into stock and is ready for use. This is the period when an item is most vulnerable to stocking-out, as its inventory is at the lowest point. An *order point* consists of an estimate of demand during lead time, plus some "reserve" stock to protect against the fact that neither demand nor lead time can be predicted with certainty.

The *order point system* is illustrated in Fig. 5-1. This is the familiar sawtooth diagram used so frequently in inventory control discussions. At some point in time, the quantity of the item in inventory is as shown by "A" in Fig. 5-1. As time passes, the inventory is used up, as shown by the heavy downward-sloping line, until it reaches the predetermined level of the order point. A replenishment order for an EOQ is then placed as shown by the dashed line. The inventory continues to drop during the lead time, at the end of which the new supply is received; the inventory is then increased by the EOQ, starting the cycle once again.

The reserve stock is not touched in the first two replenishment cycles shown in Fig. 5-1. In the third cycle, however, the rate of usage increases, as indicated by the steeper line. With this higher demand, the inventory drops into the reserve stock before the new supply is received. Should the demand increase even more, or the lead time become longer, the inventory might drop to zero—resulting in a stockout.

It should be noted with this system that:

1. Order quantities (EOQ) are usually fixed and recalculated only when significant demand changes are expected.
2. In practice, order points are too often fixed and checked only infrequently. Later in this chapter techniques will be presented which can be used to update order points at weekly or longer intervals, to keep them in tune with expected changes in demand or lead time.

Figure 5-1

Order Point System

Fixed Order Quantity—Variable Cycle

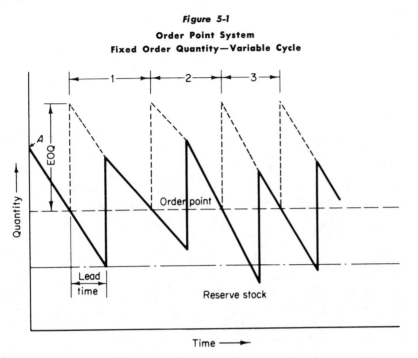

3. Intervals between successive replenishment orders (1-2-3 in Fig. 5-1) are *not* constant but vary inversely as the usage rate: the higher the demand, the shorter the interval between orders.

4. The reserve stock portion of the inventory can be considered to be on hand *on the average* throughout the year.

5. The full order quantity portion of the inventory or cycle stock will only be on hand immediately after it is received. On the average, only one-half of the order quantity will be in inventory throughout the year.

6. The average total inventory will be equal to one-half the order quantity plus the reserve stock.

Unfortunately, in most real inventory situations, the lead time is not definitely known and demand cannot be predicted exactly (as was noted above). Consequently, an order point based simply upon average demand during lead time will not provide enough stock to give even reasonably good protection against running out, since the fluctuating demand will probably *exceed the average half the time*. A major problem, then, is to estimate how much reserve stock will be required in the order point.

In the case of an item with an average demand of 100 units per week and an anticipated lead time of six weeks, it might be found from inspection of past activity as shown on the inventory records that demand during the replenishment period was occasionally as high as 800 units because of lead times being longer than anticipated or demand being higher than expected. If such inspection indicated that demand during the replenishment lead time seldom exceeded 800 units, satisfactory service might be obtained by setting an order point equal to 800 units. In effect, a reserve stock of 200 units has been established to take care of *both* demand and lead time variations.

The order point is the sum of two elements:

Order point = Anticipated demand during lead time + reserve stock

For the example discussed in the preceeding paragraph:

Order point = 600 units + 200 units = 800 units

While the idea of determining order points by inspection is simple and appealing, there is a major problem in practical application. In order to determine order points by observation, a large amount of data must be available, yet in the typical business situation, the farther back the practitioner goes in history to get his data, the less representative it is of what is going on at the present time, even less so of what might be expected to occur in the future.

Determining an order point requires evaluation of both factors comprising it: demand during lead time and reserve stock. Expected demand in a period of time must be determined by some kind of forecast. A method for handling this was discussed in Chapter 2. This demand must then be extended over the lead time period, which usually differs from the forecast period. A technique for doing this is discussed later in this chapter.

The problem of determining the proper reserve stock is a difficult one for which there is no easy solution. Applying rules of thumb will usually result in excess inventory on many items and insufficient inventory on others. The amount of reserve stock required is a function consisting principally of the following elements:

1. The ability to forecast *demand* accurately
2. The length of the lead time
3. The ability to forecast or control *lead time* accurately
4. The size of the order quantity
5. The service level desired

Some statistical techniques—applied with a liberal dose of pragmatism—can be used quite effectively in practice to determine proper reserve stocks. The approaches discussed in the following sections of this chapter have had wide industry application in recent years.

Estimating forecast error

Figure 5-2 shows the 10-week sales history for 2 items, Item T and Item V. The data for Item T shows that, while the forecast is 1000 units per week, sales have been as high as 1400 a week and, on two other occasions, were 1200 units per week. A reasonable order point for Item T might be 1200 units, anticipating that it would occasionally go out of stock when the demand during the one-week replenishment period exceeded 1200 units. The order point would be composed as follows:

Figure 5-2
Ten-Week Sales History

Week	Item T	Item V
1	1200	400
2	1000	600
3	800	1600
4	900	1200
5	1400	200
6	1200	1000
7	1100	1500
8	700	800
9	1000	1400
10	900	1100
Total	10,200	9800

1. Weekly forecast (both items) equals 1000 units
2. Order quantity equals 1000 units
3. Lead time equals one week

Order point = Anticipated demand during lead time + reserve stock

Order point = 1000 + 200 = 1200

If it were desired to keep Item T in stock all the time, the order point would have to be set at 1400. Of course, there is no guarantee that sales would not occasionally exceed 1400 in the future—a ten-week sales history is a fairly small sample.

Item V appears to have a more erratic demand; in fact, if the order point were set at 1200 for Item V, three stockouts would occur since there are three weeks when demand during lead time would exceed the order point quantity. This type of situation occurs frequently in industry; the demand variability is generally higher for low volume items or when fewer customers order the item. Many companies, in addition to selling their products directly to consumers, supply their products with a slightly different configuration to mail-order houses or other large-volume distributors. They usually find that the demand for an item being sold directly to many customers has a more predictable pattern, while the smaller number of large-volume demands tends to be far less predictable. The order point for Item V would obviously have to be higher than that for Item T to maintain the same level of service. Equal reserve stocks for these two items would result in carrying excess inventory of Item T or in giving poorer service on Item V.

The small sample of information available also offers serious problems since there is no assurance that Item V might not occasionally have sales as high as 2200 units or that Item T might have sales as high as 1900 units. Some reasonably reliable, consistent method of determining reserve stocks based on small samples of data is therefore needed in practical applications of the order point concept. A concept that can be very useful in handling this calculation for many items is the so-called *"normal distribution."*

The normal distribution[1] is one of the best known statistical relationships—most people are familiar with the bell-shaped curve. Figure 5-3[2] shows a distribution of the heights of male members of the U. S. population. If the average male height were 5'9", it would be reasonable to expect that a large number of men would be between 5'4" and 6'2", with very few people under 4'6" or over 7'0". As illustrated in Fig. 5-3, plotting the percentage of the total population against the individual heights would form a bell-shaped curve known to statisticians as the "normal distribution". This distribution has some general properties that are of great value in drawing conclusions about the population.

The *"standard deviation"* (sigma) of the distribution, for example, measures the range of heights which contains a certain percentage of the total population, relative to the average. Referring to Fig. 5-3, one standard deviation of male heights is 5", approximately 34% of the males

---

[1] For a detailed discussion, see M. J. Moroney, *Facts from Figures,* Penguin Books, 3rd Ed., London, 1957.

[2] This figure is presented for illustration only and is not intended to be accurate.

Figure 5-3

Distribution of Heights of Male Members of U. S. Population

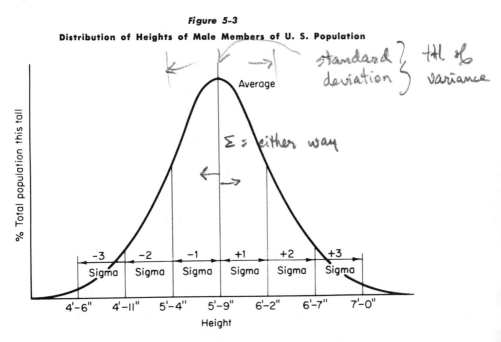

would be expected to be between 5'4" and 5'9", and another 34% would be expected to be between 5'9" and 6'2" tall. In other words, 68% of all males would be within the range of 5'4" to 6'2".

A second standard deviation (±2 sigma) from the average would add approximately 14% more of the population to each side of the average. For example, it could be expected that somewhat less than 14% of males would be between 4'11" and 5'4" or, on the higher side of the average, between 6'2" and 6'7". For a true normal distribution, only about 2% of the population will be outside the range of ±2 standard deviations from the average.

Two characteristics of the normal distribution are of interest in calculating order points:

1. *The mean or average value.* This corresponds to the high point of the bell curve and is the value most likely to occur.

2. *The variation or dispersion of the values about the average, measured by the standard deviation.* This corresponds to the width of the bell curve and measures how closely the individual values cluster around the average.

The conditions that must be met if the normal distribution is to be applied are:

1. *The demand data is unimodal.* This merely means that the demands tend to cluster about the average value. If, for example, demand were likely to be about 500 units per week or approximately 1500 units per week, but not very likely to be any value in between, the demand distribution would have two "modes" or most frequently experienced demands and the normal distribution would not describe the demand data properly.

2. *The demand distribution is assumed to be symmetrical;* in other words, it is just as likely to have a demand that is 200 units less than the forecast as one 200 units more than the forecast. This assumption presents some real problems in calculating order points. If the forecast demand is 20 units per week, for example, it can never be less than zero units yet it can be as much as 100 or 150 units. In other words, there is a floor close to the average but the ceiling is far above it. There are two ways of handling this problem:

   a. When the forecast value is so low that the plus variations are likely to be considerably greater than the minus variations, all minus variations can be ignored, and only plus variations are included in the calculation of the standard or mean absolute deviation.

   b. For certain types of small demand, another special statistical distribution called the *Poisson distribution* frequently gives good results. This is discussed later in this chapter.

3. It is assumed, when using a normal distribution, that the actual average will be the same as the forecasted average (*i.e.,* the forecast is generally accurate). The best safeguard is to use a technique such as exponential smoothing to detect trends, to update the forecast regularly and to use a tracking signal, discussed later in this chapter, to indicate when this forecast is not performing satisfactorily.

Figure 5-4 shows the calculation of the standard deviation of forecast error for Item T, with a weekly forecast of 1000 units and sales as shown in Fig. 5-2. The steps in calculating the standard deviation of forecast error are as follows:

1. Calculate the deviation by subtracting actual sales from the forecast amount for each week.

2. Square each deviation.

3. Add the squares of the deviations.

Figure 5-4
Calculating the Standard Deviation for Estimating Reserve Stock

		Item T		
Week	Forecast	Sales	Deviation	D^2
1	1000	1200	200	40,000
2	1000	1000	---	---
3	1000	800	200	40,000
4	1000	900	100	10,000
5	1000	1400	400	160,000
6	1000	1200	200	40,000
7	1000	1100	100	10,000
8	1000	700	300	90,000
9	1000	1000	---	---
10	1000	900	100	10,000
Total	10,000	10,200	1600	400,000

Average $D^2 = 400,000 \div 10 = 40,000$

Sigma $= \sqrt{40,000} = 200 =$ standard deviation

Alternate Method:

Average $D = 1600 \div 10 = 160 =$ mean absolute deviation (MAD)

Sigma = MAD x 1.25 = 160 x 1.25 = 200

4. Determine the average of the squares of the deviation.[1]

5. Take the square root of the average of the squares of the deviation. This is the standard deviation.

In setting an order point, the practitioner *is not concerned with lead*

---

[1] The precise calculation of the standard deviation would require that the sum of the squares of the deviations be divided by $n - 1$, where n is the number of observations. For simplicity, this has been ignored in this chapter. Further information on the calculation of an "unbiased" standard deviation is available in almost any text on statistics.

time periods when demand is less than average. Reserve stocks are needed to cover only those periods when demand is greater than average. If the forecast is reasonably accurate and is updated frequently, demand will be less-than-average approximately 50% of the time over the long-run and he can expect to give 50% service with *no* reserve stock. If he then adds one standard deviation or 200 units of reserve stock to the forecast average of 1000 (giving an order point of 1200 units), he will have enough inventory during a replenishment period to cover an additional 34% of the demands (1 standard deviation = 34% of occurrences); thus he can expect to give 84% (50% + 34%) service with an order point containing one standard deviation of reserve stock. With an order point of 1200 units, he would experience a stockout during the replenishment period approximately two times out of ten over the long run. Looking at the sales for Item T in Fig. 5-4, this doesn't seem too unreasonable.

If he were now to add two standard deviations or 400 units to his 1000 unit average demand during lead time, his order point would then be 1400 units. The second standard deviation of reserve stock will cover another 14% of the occurrences, giving a total of approximately 98% (84% plus 14%) service. With an order point equal to 1400 units, demand during lead time is likely to exceed it only two times out of one hundred. Again, for the sales data for Item T, this looks reasonable.

The standard deviation, although a very useful measure in inventory control, is a rather tedious one since it involves many calculations. It can be determined in a simpler way via the mean absolute deviation (MAD), as shown on the bottom of Fig. 5-4. The mean absolute deviation is the average (*mean*) of the differences (*deviations*) between the forecast and actual sales, taking no account of plus or minus signs (using *absolute* values). The relationship between the mean absolute deviation and the standard deviation is approximately:

$$\text{Standard Deviation} \quad \text{Sigma} = 1.25 \times \text{MAD}$$

Figure 5-4 illustrates the method of calculating the standard deviation of 200 by first determining the mean absolute deviation to be 160. While this "shortcut" result will not always come out this closely to the results of the direct calculation, it will usually be close enough for most practical inventory control applications. A great deal of computational effort is saved by using MAD. In addition, the mean absolute deviation lends itself to periodic updating which is essential in a good inventory control system. This technique will be described later in the chapter.

Figure 5-5 shows the method for calculating MAD for Item V which, by observation, had a more variable demand. Here, the mean absolute deviation is 400 and the standard deviation is 500—more than double the values for Item T—since demand variability is much greater. For

$$\text{Safety Stock} = K(\text{MAD})$$

Figure 5-5

Calculating the Standard Deviation Using the Mean Absolute Deviation

Weekly forecast = 1000

Week	Sales	Deviation
1	400	600
2	600	400
3	1600	600
4	1200	200
5	200	800
6	1000	---
7	1500	500
8	800	200
9	1400	400
10	1100	100
	9800	3800

MAD = 3800 ÷ 10 = 380 units

Sigma = 380 x 1.25 = 475 units

Item V, an order point for 98% service could be constructed as follows:

Order point = Anticipated demand during lead time + reserve stock

Anticipated demand during lead time = 1000 units forecast

Reserve stock for 98% service = 2 sigma = 2 × 500 = 1000 units

Order point = 1000 + 1000 = 2000 units

Approximately two times out of one hundred, demand is likely to exceed 2000 units in a week, which seems reasonable based on the small sample of data available.

This is a practical technique for calculating reserve stocks that can be tailored to the characteristics of each individual item. Reserve stocks so calculated will be higher for those items that have a greater demand variability and lower for those items that have a more stable demand. This technique assumes that the *actual average demand* and the *forecast demand* are equal, which may not always be true. This problem is illustrated in Fig. 5-6 for Item W, which has a weekly forecast of 1000 units and a mean absolute deviation of 160 units (the same as Item T in Fig. 5-4). Item W sales, however, have been above the forecast most of the time, indicating that the forecast should be increased to about 1100 units. This would reduce the amount of deviation and, consequently, the amount of reserve stock that would have to be carried in the inventory. Knowing only the forecast and the mean absolute deviation for Item W, it might be assumed that this item has the same demand characteristics as Item T, but a "tracking signal" can be calculated which will rapidly

Figure 5-6

Determining the Tracking Signal for Item W

Weekly forecast = 1000

Week	Weekly sales	Deviation	Running sum (Algebraic) of forecast errors
1	1200	-200	-200
2	1000	---	-200
3	1200	-200	-400
4	900	+100	-300
5	1400	-400	-700
6	1200	-200	-900
7	1100	-100	-1000
8	1300	-300	-1300
9	1000	---	-1300
10	900	+100	-1200
	11,200	1600	

MAD = $1600 \div 10 = 160$

Tracking signal = RSFE ÷ MAD

$$= \frac{1200}{160}$$

$$= 7.5$$

flag the fact that the forecast errors are accumulating on one side of the distribution. In this particular case, the forecast is almost always low. By calculating a running sum of the forecast errors algebraically[1] and then dividing the mean absolute deviation into this sum, a measure of this consistent difference between actual and forecast values called the "tracking signal" will be determined. The tracking signal after ten weeks of history for Item W is 7.5, which is very high, indicating that sales are exceeding the forecast consistently[2]. If the forecast errors tend

---

[1] Taking into account the plus and minus signs which are ignored in the absolute deviation.

[2] In an actual inventory system, the forecast would be updated using exponential smoothing and, consequently, the tracking signal would be measuring the effectiveness of this constantly updated forecast. A fixed forecast of 1000 was used in this example to avoid confusing the issue with too many calculations.

to balance each other out (as they would for Item T, for example), the tracking signal would be very low, indicating that the forecast was fairly satisfactory and did not need to be revised.

Acceptable maxima for the tracking signal run between 4 and 8, depending upon how the signal is to be used. A tracking signal of 4 might be used on a high-value item to trigger an early review of the forecast, thus allowing a possible revision without carrying excess inventory or jeopardizing service by waiting too long. For a low-value item, a fairly high tracking signal (perhaps 7 or 8) would be used since forecast errors tend to be higher for low-volume items and since most companies place less emphasis on maintaining good service on the less popular items.

The weighting factor in the exponential smoothing formula for forecasting described in Chapter 2 is a compromise between reacting too slowly to trends and over-reacting to random occurrences—the tracking signal is the same type of tool. A tracking signal set too low would require review of many items for which the system was performing satisfactorily in order to catch those few for which it was not. A tracking signal set too high might delay review and result in poor service or excess inventory. However, having a tracking signal in action does provide an exception technique for indicating that a forecast needs to be reviewed, and it should be part of every complete system.

Calculating the order point

Knowing the general statistical properties of the normal distribution and having calculated the standard deviation or mean absolute deviation of forecast error, the calculation of an order point is straightforward. The fact that adding one standard deviation to the anticipated demand during lead time provides for giving 84% service and that adding two standard deviations increases the service level to 98% was covered in the preceding section of this chapter. The service level is obviously related to the number of standard deviations provided as reserve or safety stock. This number is usually referred to as the *safety factor*. Figure 5-7 shows the table of safety factors for various service levels for the normal distribution using either the standard deviation or the mean absolute deviation. Since the mean absolute deviation is always a smaller number than a standard deviation, a larger number of mean absolute deviations must be used to give the same service level and the safety factor is consequently higher. This does not change the total size of the reserve stock. The table of safety factors is set up so that the mean absolute deviation need not be converted to a standard deviation by multiplying it by 1.25—the adjustment is already built into the table. For example, the 84% service level shown in the table would require one standard deviation, but would require 1.25 mean absolute deviations.

This table allows for the computation of reserve stocks for the entire range of service percentages. Assume, for example, that the following data apply to Item X:

Weekly forecast = 500 units
Lead time = 1 week

Figure 5-7
Table of Safety Factors for Normal Distribution
(Plus Deviations Only)

Service level (% Order cycles w/o stockout)	Safety factor using:	
	Standard deviation	Mean absolute deviation
50.00%	0.00	0.00
75.00%	0.67	0.84
80.00%	0.84	1.05
84.13%	1.00	1.25
85.00%	1.04	1.30
89.44%	1.25	1.56
90.00%	1.28	1.60
93.32%	1.50	1.88
94.00%	1.56	1.95
94.52%	1.60	2.00
95.00%	1.65	2.06
96.00%	1.75	2.19
97.00%	1.88	2.35
97.72%	2.00	2.50
98.00%	2.05	2.56
98.61%	2.20	2.75
99.00%	2.33	2.91
99.18%	2.40	3.00
99.38%	2.50	3.13
99.50%	2.57	3.20
99.60%	2.65	3.31
99.70%	2.75	3.44
99.80%	2.88	3.60
99.86%	3.00	3.75
99.90%	3.09	3.85
99.93%	3.20	4.00
99.99%	4.00	5.00

Mean absolute deviation = 200 units
98% Service desired
Order quantity = 500

Since the weekly demand for this item is 500 units and the lead time is one week, then the demand during lead time is equal to 500 units.

The mean absolute deviation is 200 units. If a 98% service level is desired, Fig. 5-7 indicates a safety factor of 2.56 using the mean absolute deviation.

$$\text{Reserve stock} = \text{Safety factor} \times \text{MAD}$$
$$= 2.56 \times 200 = 512 \text{ units}$$

And:

$$\text{Order point} = \text{Demand during lead time} + \text{reserve stock}$$
$$= 500 + 512 = 1012 \text{ units}$$

This order point (according to this table) should give 98% service level—but what does "service" mean in this calculation? It means the percentage of *replenishment periods* during which demand should not exceed the order point quantity. The order point is designed to cover demand during lead time so that a replenishment order can be placed in time for the material to be delivered into stores before all stock is withdrawn. This replenishment lead time period is the "critical" time when an item can go out of stock. The number of times that an item is *exposed* to going out of stock, then, is equal to the number of times that a replenishment order is placed and this, of course, depends on the size of the order quantity. An item with a large order quantity will require

Figure 5-8

Exposures to Stockout

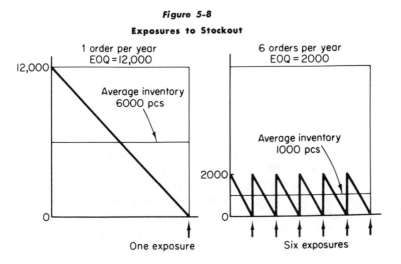

1 order per year	6 orders per year
EOQ = 12,000	EOQ = 2000

12,000

Average inventory 6000 pcs

Average inventory 1000 pcs

2000

One exposure   Six exposures

fewer replenishment orders per year, and hence will be exposed to fewer stockouts than one which is ordered more frequently.

Figure 5-8 shows the difference in the number of exposures of an item with an order quantity equivalent to a one-year supply—in which case there would be one exposure per year *vs.* having an order quantity equivalent to a two-month supply requiring six replenishment orders per year. The smaller order quantity would generate six times as many exposures to stockout during the year as the larger order quantity, and requires more reserve stock to provide a given level of service. Obviously, if one stockout per year were permissible, the larger order quantity would require *no reserve stock.* *There* would be *no* stockout if actual demand during the replenishment period happened to be below the expected average (as it will about half the time).

This relationship between order quantity and reserve stock can be taken into consideration by determining the number of replenishment periods that will occur (the number of exposures to stockout) and then calculating the desired service level as the number of replenishment periods during which no stockouts are desired.

The calculation can be illustrated using the data for Item X in the preceding pages. This item had a weekly forecast of 500 units, one week lead time, MAD $= 200$ units and a 98% desired service level. If this service level were specified instead as "one stockout per year" (roughly equivalent to 98% measured weekly since $1/52 = 1.9\%$), and if the order quantity were 2600 units:

Annual demand $= 500 \times 52 = 26{,}000$ units per year
Exposures per year $= 26{,}000 \div 2600 = 10$ replenishment periods
Required service level for one stockout $= 9/10$ or 90%.
Safety factor for 90% service (from Fig. 5-7) $= 1.60 \times$ MAD
Order point $= 500 + (1.60 \times 200) = 500 + 320 = 820$

This order point for Item X is considerably lower than the previous order point calculated for Item X, where the order quantity was only 500 units. Because the 500 unit order quantity resulted in 52 exposures to stockout, a service factor of 2.56 was required, giving an order point of 1012 units.

The straightforward, independent calculation of order points and EOQ's does not necessarily give the most economical total inventory level because of the interaction between order quantities, exposures to stockout and reserve stock. Further calculations will frequently reveal that an increase in the order quantity will reduce the total inventory investment required for any given service level because it will reduce the number of exposures, and hence the required reserve stock. In some cases, the decrease in reserve stock will be greater than the required increase in the lot size.

This relationship is shown and explained in an example in Appendix IV. This refinement of statistical technique might very well be worthwhile on the highest value A items, but it probably is not worthwhile on items where the resulting savings would be too small for the effort exerted to attain them.

Another problem frequently encountered in practice in calculating statistical reserve stocks arises because the forecast interval is not the same as the lead time period. The many items involved in the usual inventory have widely different lead times, and it would be very awkward to measure forecast error over each of the lead times for the different items in order to determine variations in demand during the lead time and to calculate reserve stocks. Some other method for adjusting forecast error to compensate for different lead times must be used.

If Item X had a lead time of four weeks, the demand during lead time would be: 4×500 units per week $= 2,000$ units. It would be reasonable to expect that there would be a good chance of having more than one week with demand considerably above average so that the reserve stock based on one week's demand would have to be increased to give an equivalent level of protection during the longer lead time.

On the other hand, it is equally apparent that the reserve stock for a one-week lead time cannot simply be multiplied by four to determine the reserve stock needed for a four-week lead time since it is extremely unlikely that demand would be very high four weeks in succession. It is apparent that the reserve stock must increase as lead time increases, but that the increase *is not directly proportional to the increase in lead time.* Some adjustment factor is necessary when the forecast interval is different from the lead time interval, as is so frequently the case in practice.

Figure 5-9 gives a table of factors for adjusting the mean absolute deviation when lead time is not equal to the forecast interval. This table gives factors for multiplying the mean absolute deviation for the forecast interval to determine an equivalent deviation for the longer lead time interval to be used in calculating reserve stock. The formula by which these factors were determined is:

$$\text{Adjusted MAD} = \text{MAD}\left(\frac{LT}{F}\right)^{\beta} \tag{5-1}$$

where: Adjusted MAD $=$ MAD for lead time interval

              MAD $=$ MAD for forecast interval

                  $LT =$ Lead time interval

                    $F =$ Forecast interval

                    $\beta =$ A constant (*beta factor*) depending on the demand patterns of the particular business

Figure 5-9

Table of Factors* (For adjusting deviation when lead time does not equal forecast interval.)

When forecast interval = 1 and lead time interval is:	Standard deviation or mean absolute deviation should be multiplied by:
2	1.63
3	2.16
4	2.64
5	3.09
6	3.51
7	3.91
8	4.29
9	4.66
10	5.01
11	5.36
12	5.69
13	6.02
14	6.34
15	6.66
16	6.96
17	7.27
18	7.56
19	7.86
20	8.14

*Assumes beta = 0.7

The particular exponent to be used for adjusting a specific company's data should theoretically be determined by simulation, using actual data. In practice, it has been found that a beta factor of 0.7 gives reasonably good results. In fact, a great deal of simulation would be needed to determine a more accurate factor to fit the company's actual demand patterns. The multipliers shown in Fig. 5-9 are based on a beta factor of 0.7 and are used as follows:

1. Express the lead time interval as a multiple of the forecast interval
2. Find the resulting ratio in the first column of the table in Fig. 5-9
3. Multiply the forecast interval mean absolute deviation by the corresponding value in the second column to convert it to the lead time mean absolute deviation

Using the data for Item X, and Fig. 5-9, the order point would be calculated as follows:

1. Assume lead time for Item X is four weeks (4 times the one-week forecast interval)
2. When the lead time interval is four times the forecast interval, the adjustment factor from Fig. 5-9 is 2.64
3. The mean absolute deviation for a one-week lead time was 200 units

$$\text{Adjusted MAD} = 2.64 \times 200 = 528 \text{ units}$$
$$\text{Reserve stock required} = 1.60 \times 528 = 845 \text{ units}$$
$$(\text{for OQ} = 2600 \text{ units and 1 stockout 1 year})$$
$$\text{Order point} = (4 \times 500) + 845 = 2845$$

For most items, this type of approximation will be accurate enough. For high value items, however, results using this table should probably be checked by simulation to determine a more precise adjusting factor, or the forecast error should actually be calculated over the lead time interval.

Putting the techniques to work

One of the most pressing problems facing the production control manager is finding the means for routine updating of the forecast demand during lead time and recalculating reserve stock requirements. Figure 5-10 shows thirteen weeks of actual demand for Item X, the item discussed in previous examples. The exponential smoothing technique explained in Chapter 2 provides a method for regular forecast updating and Fig. 5-11 shows a new forecast being made each week using this technique and the data in Fig. 5-10. In this case, the starting forecast was 500 units per week, and the exponential smoothing calculation has caused this

Figure 5-10

13-Week Demand History For Item X

Forecast weekly demand = 500 units	
Week	Actual demand
1	464
2	330
3	474
4	847
5	618
6	772
7	573
8	432
9	938
10	642
11	750
12	294
13	672
	7806
Average weekly demand = 600	

Figure 5-10

13-Week Demand History For Item X

forecast to dip somewhat and then to pick up to 526 units for the 6th week. Figure 5-10 shows that the demand for the thirteen weeks averaged 600 units and the exponential smoothing calculation, although lagging somewhat, is a much better forecast than the original figure of 500 units per week. This demonstrates the usefulness of the technique in correcting a forecast that was obviously too low and making it more responsive to actual sales.

Figure 5-12 shows the same data used both to calculate and *to update the mean absolute deviation.* The updating uses the same calculation as regular exponential smoothing, substituting "MAD" for "forecast" and "deviation" for "demand." In Fig. 5-12, for example, the starting mean absolute deviation is 200. Using the exponential smoothing formula, the old mean absolute deviation is multiplied by 0.9, the new deviation is multiplied by 0.1 and the new mean absolute deviation is the sum of the two, as shown in Fig. 5-12. In practice, the calculations in Figs. 5-11 and 5-12 would go on simultaneously and the order point could be recalculated each week. Even for thousands of items, the modern computer can easily handle these calculations.

The full computation of an order point using the techniques covered in this chapter is as follows:

1. Determine the permissible number of "stockouts" per year (replenishment periods when stock may be exhausted before the order quantity is received). This is a *management policy decision,* not a calculation.

2. Calculate the number of replenishment orders to be placed (or "exposures") per year by dividing the order quantity into the annual demand forecast.

3. Calculate the "service fraction," expressed as a percentage. This is

Figure 5-11

Calculating a Routine Forecast with Exponential Smoothing

	New forecast = α x actual demand + $(1-\alpha)$ x old forecast where : $\alpha = 0.1$ $(1-\alpha) = 0.9$				
Week	Old forecast	$(1-\alpha)$ x Old forecast	Actual demand	α x actual demand	New forecast
1	500	450.0	464	46.4	496
2	496	446.4	330	33.0	479
3	479	431.1	474	47.4	479
4	479	431.1	847	84.7	516
5	516	464.4	618	61.8	526
6	526	473.4	772	77.2	551
7	551	495.9	573	57.3	553
8	553	497.7	432	43.2	541
9	541	486.9	938	93.8	580
10	580	522.0	642	64.2	586
11	586	527.4	750	75.0	602
12	602	541.8	294	29.4	571
13	571	513.9	672	67.2	581

Figure 5-12

Calculating Deviation from Forecast and MAD

	New MAD = α x deviation + $(1-\alpha)$ old MAD where $\alpha = 0.1$ $(1-\alpha) = 0.9$						
Week	Forecast	Sales	Deviation	α x deviation	Old MAD	$(1-\alpha)$ x MAD	New MAD
1	500	464	36	3.6	200	180.0	184
2	496	330	166	16.6	184	165.6	182
3	479	474	5	0.5	182	163.8	164
4	479	847	368	36.8	164	147.6	184
5	516	618	102	10.2	184	165.6	176
6	526	etc.					

the ratio of the number of replenishment periods during which *no stockout* is desired (total exposures minus the number of permissible stockouts) to the total number of replenishment periods.

4. Using this percentage, find (in Fig. 5-7) the safety factor, *i.e.*, the number of deviations (Std. or MAD) that must be included in the reserve stock.

5. Calculate the standard or mean absolute deviation as shown in Fig. 5-4 or 5-5.

6. Calculate the adjusted deviations (Std. or MAD) to account for any difference between the forecast interval and the lead time interval, using the table in Fig. 5-9.

7. Multiply the adjusted deviation by the safety factor to calculate the total reserve stock required.

8. Add this reserve stock to the forecast demand over the lead time to get the total order point.

Here is an example using the data for Item X:

$$\text{Annual demand} = 26,000 \text{ units}$$
$$\text{Order quantity} = 500 \text{ units}$$
$$\text{Lead time} = 4 \text{ weeks}$$
$$\text{Mean absolute deviation} = 200 \text{ units}$$

Then: 1. Tolerable number of stockouts per year has been set by management at *one*

2. Number of exposures per year $= 26,000 \div 500 = 52$
3. Service fraction $= (52 - 1) \div 52 = 98\%$
4. From Fig. 5-7, safety factor $= 2.56$ (using MAD)
5. MAD $= 200$ units.
6. Adjusted MAD $= 2.64 \times 200 = 528$ units
7. Reserve stock $= 2.56 \times 528 = 1352$ units
8. Order point $= \text{DLT} + \text{reserve}$
$$= (4 \times 500) + 1352$$
$$= 3352 \text{ units.}$$

The techniques discussed here provide a simple method for generating a revised order point as frequently as once a week. These approaches have had considerable application in industry in the past few years and have proven to be very satisfactory. The advantages come not only from measuring forecast error and determining realistically what the reserve stock level should be, but also from having a means for forecasting the demand for thousands of items regularly and for updating both the forecasts and the estimates of forecast error on routine bases.

These statistical techniques must be used with caution based on an understanding of the underlying assumptions and a knowledge of their limitations. All statistical techniques assume that the future will be like the past. Fortunately, this is a reasonably valid assumption in most situations, but there will always be changes. Use of techniques such as exponential smoothing, forecast tracking signals and regularly updated measures of forecast error can help to detect these changes promptly and make appropriate corrections.

For the sake of simplicity in the previous calculations, only the forecast error has been calculated, and it has been assumed that a constant lead time—usually called the "longest normal" lead time—will be used. If it is desirable to also include lead time variations, these variations *must not* be added directly to the demand variations since the longest lead times are not likely to occur simultaneously with the maximum demand. There are really *two* statistical distributions working together, and the calculation of their combined effect is made as follows:

$$\text{Total error} = \sqrt{(SDF)^2 + (SDLT)^2} \qquad (5\text{-}2)$$

where:
$$SDF = \text{Standard deviation of forecast error}$$
$$SDLT = \text{Standard deviation of lead time error}$$

In using this formula, it is imperative that both terms be *expressed in common units* (such as weeks) if the results are to be meaningful.

The techniques of statistics have great value even where applied with some license. Like any other so-called "scientific" tool, the normal distribution should be used with judgment. If the answers that result do not make sense, the calculations should be reviewed with someone well-versed in statistics (the quality control manager, for example) and checked for reasonableness by the practitioner before being applied. Such concepts merely try to describe mathematically the real events that occur in business. It is more important that the practitioner understand their limitations and implications than that he understand all the mathematical and statistical theory used in their derivation.

Using the Poisson distribution

The Poisson distribution is convenient for order point calculations for certain types of demand because it has the property that the standard deviation is always equal to the square root of the average value. The Poisson distribution has had its principal applications in quality control and in studies involving random arrivals of customers at supermarket checkout counters or of automobiles at turnpike toll booths. In inventory control, the Poisson distribution has not had wide application although it has been known to practitioners for many years.[1] It best fits small, infrequent demands where the quantity of items per order is fairly constant.

To be used properly in calculating order points, the demand history must be expressed in the number of *orders* received as well as the number of items per order. For example, demand during lead time for an item might be equal to 4,000 units; to use the Poisson distribution, further examination of these 4000 units of demand would be necessary to determine that they actually amounted to 40 orders averaging 100 units each.

The formula for order point calculation using the Poisson distribution is:[2]

$$\text{O.P.} = u\left(a + f\sqrt{a}\,\right) \tag{5-3}$$

where: O.P. = the order point in number of units
           u = the average demand per order in units
           a = the average number of orders arriving during the lead time period
           f = the service factor (equivalent to the number of standard deviations used with a normal distribution)

Using the above data, an order point could be calculated for this item:

$$\begin{aligned}
\text{O.P.} &= 100\,(40 + 2.1\sqrt{40}) \\
&= 100\,(40 + 13.23) \\
&= 4000 + 1323 = 5323
\end{aligned}$$

The factor of 2.1 was chosen from Fig. 5-13 which gives the required values for corresponding service levels using the Poisson distribution. A service factor of 2.1 with the Poisson distribution will give 98% service. This calculation shows that a reserve stock of 1323 pieces will be required to give 98% service for this particular item.

If there were another item with the same total number of units demanded during lead time, but this item were sold to a very small number of

Figure 5-13

Poisson Distribution Service Factor f

Min % demand to be met	Max % back orders permitted	f
75	25	0.7
80	20	0.8
85	15	1.0
90	10	1.3
95	5	1.7
98	2	2.1
99	1	2.3
99.9	0.10	3.1

---

[1] See R. H. Wilson, "A Scientific Routine for Stock Control," *Harvard Business Review,* Vol. 13, No. 1, 1934.

[2] For further information on the Poisson distribution and its proper application, refer to: G.W. Plossl and O.W. Wight, "Determining Order Points Using the Poisson Distribution," *APICS Quarterly Bulletin,* Vol. 4, No. 2, April 1963.

distributors who ordered infrequently and in large quantities, the answer would be quite different. If the average order size were 1000 units and there were only 4 orders received during the lead time period, the calculation would be as follows:

$$O.P. = 1000 (4 + 2.1\sqrt{4})$$
$$= 4000 + 4200 = 8200$$

With this more erratic type of demand, a reserve stock of 4200 pieces would be required to give the same degree of customer service as was attained with 1323 pieces in the first example.

The Poisson distribution has been suggested by many authors as a means for calculating order points. It is important to remember one thing: *The Poisson distribution CANNOT be used to describe the total number of units of demand during the lead time. It CAN be used to approximate the number of individual orders that will be received during the lead time.*

The accuracy of the results obtained using the Poisson distribution depends directly on how accurately the average quantity of the item included on the orders can be determined. The Poisson distribution predicts accurately the random arrival of orders, but not the total unit demand.

Summarizing the limiting assumptions which must be remembered when using the Poisson distribution for calculating order points:

1. Order arrivals fit the Poisson frequency distribution curve. The fit is generally better when the number of arrivals per lead time period is relatively small.

2. Order arrivals are random and independent. This would not be true of customer orders filtered through a sales office which accumulates orders for like items over a period of time and releases them in batches.

3. Accurate forecasts can be made of mean order size. Errors in its determination will cause corresponding errors in the order point and reserve stock.

4. Order quantities do not vary widely from the mean. Some research is needed to determine what variation can be tolerated, but it is known that results are poor when the variation is large.

5. Finally, remember the basic assumption of all

such statistical methods—the future will resemble the past.

Used in the correct manner, the Poisson formula for calculating order points has two distinct advantages:

1. It gives consistent, useful results, far superior to some popular rules of thumb, (such as setting reserve stocks equal to "one month's supply" or "10% of the demand during lead time").

2. It does not require the preparation and analysis of a large amount of statistical data. More refined methods of order point calculation will give more accurate results but will require expensive and detailed analyses of data.

The concept of service

The measure of service used in the previous discussions—the number of stockouts per year—is a fairly simple one to handle statistically, and one that is easy to relate to real business situations. If there are 52 deliveries of stock per year because the order quantity is a one-week supply, then a service level of one stockout per year would require a delivery ratio of $\frac{51}{52}$, or 98%. If the order quantity were a four-week supply giving 13 exposures to stockout during the year, then the service level of one stockout per year would require a delivery ratio of $\frac{12}{13}$, or 92%. This is merely expressing statistically the obvious fact that the more frequently stock is received and the more frequently the inventory is depleted to the reserve level, the greater the chance of running out of stock.

How would this service measure be used in practice? Stockouts per year do not measure the *amount* of the stockout or its *duration*. Nevertheless, this measure is meaningful and can be used quite readily. If a product group containing a fairly large number of individual items is checked each week and the number of items out of stock is counted, the result can be correlated fairly well with the statistical concept of stockouts per year per item. Each week, the number of items out of stock could be counted, and each of these occurrences would then constitute one stockout.

If, for example, there are 120 items in this product group and 52 weeks during the year, the worst that could possibly happen would be to have every item out of stock every week. This would be 120×52, or 6240 stockouts. The assumption made here is that once a stockout occurs, it will not last longer than one week. A stockout that occurred and lasted through two weeks would actually be counted as two stockouts using this method.

Another statistical measure of customer service that can be used specifies the desired percentage of total pieces of demand that will be filled from goods on the shelf. For example, if total demand for the year is expected to be 26,000 units and it is desired to backorder only 1000 units, the service percentage is then $\frac{25}{26} = 96\%$. This measure of customer service is as valid as the number of stockouts per year. It must usually be set considerably higher than the service measure percentage using stockouts per year in order to provide enough reserve stocks to generate a comparable level of service[1]. This service measure based on pieces does not measure the duration of a stockout period nor does it measure the frequency of the stockouts to be experienced.

Before applying new measures or changing existing measures of customer service, the following should be observed:

1. Simulate the actual functioning of the inventory to be controlled to determine how well the proposed statistical measure of service correlates with whatever measure of service is currently being used. No statistical measure of service will correlate perfectly, and the statistical service level *should always be set somewhat higher than the service level actually desired* in order to attain the latter in actual day-to-day inventory situations. This simulation can be made manually, but most practical applications will require a computer.

2. The service level that actually results is usually somewhat lower than the statistical service level because:

a. Statistical measures of service usually measure only one characteristic, like total quantity backordered or number of stockouts. There are several other characteristics that contribute to poor customer service (such as the duration of the stockout) not all of which can be included in any one practical service measure.

3. Using the statistical service level proposed, start using the control system and reduce reserve stocks as experience shows that fewer reserves are required.

4. Once established and operating, the real power of statistical service measures can be employed to show the economics of changing from one service level to another. This will be covered in detail in Chapter 6.

---

[1] Further information on this measure of service is available in IBM's *General Information Manual, IMPACT,* 1962, and *Statistical Forecasting for Inventory Control,* R. G. Brown, McGraw, New York, 1959.

5. Statistical measures of customer service deal only with variations in demand over *normal* lead times—they *do not* consider machine breakdowns, strikes, quality problems, etc.—which effect replenishment lead times drastically. Conversely, since normal lead time is usually assumed in the statistical concept of service, a good foreman can often make his department perform far better than the statistics indicate it should because he reacts very quickly to changes in customer demand and he controls lead times.

The value of the statistical approach

While statistical calculation of order points is simple in concept, it requires the application of considerably more effort than intuitive methods. Is it worth the effort? Emphatically yes, because statistical techniques actually distribute the reserve stock where it is needed most rather than applying it uniformly across the entire inventory.

Figure 5-14 shows an example of intuitive distribution of reserve stocks where the reserve level is set at one week's supply for Items P, Y, and Z, each of which has the same average weekly demand. Item P is

Figure 5-14

Intuition vs. Statistics in Setting Reserve Stocks

	Intuitive reserve = 1-wk supply						
Item	Weekly demand forecast	Order quantity	Standard deviation	1-wk reserve	No. std. deviation	Delvy.* service Ratio	No. stock-outs
P	500 pcs.	500 pcs.	261 pcs.	500 pcs.	1.92	97.2	2
Y	500 pcs.	500 pcs.	551 pcs.	500 pcs.	0.91	81.9	9
Z	500 pcs.	6500 pcs.	261 pcs.	500 pcs.	1.92	97.2	0
Totals				1500 pcs.			11

	Statistical reserves required for 2 stockouts per yr					
Item	Orders per yr	Delvy. service ratio	No. std.* deviations	Standard deviation	Reserve required	No. stock-outs
P	52	50/52 = 96%	1.75	261 pcs.	460	2
Y	52	50/52 = 96%	1.75	551 pcs.	965	2
Z	4	2/4 = 50%	0	261 pcs.	0	2
Totals					1425	6

*From figure 5-7, table of safety factors

a stock item sold to many customers; its sales history yields a standard deviation of 261 units. Item Y has the same forecast of average weekly demand but is purchased by a small number of customers and, consequently, its demand is more erratic. Its standard deviation is found to be 551 units. Item Z has the same weekly demand forecast as Items P and Y and the same type of demand variation as P, with a standard deviation of 261 units also. It is a low-value item made on a punch press, for which setup costs are high and, consequently, the order quantity is large, 6500 units. All items are assumed to require one week lead time for replenishment.

Setting the reserve stock level at one week's supply for all of these items would result in approximately 11 stockouts per year, as shown in Fig. 5-14. Calculating statistical reserve stocks for these items would reduce this to approximately 6 stockouts per year, at the same time actually reducing the total reserve to 1425 units. The reserve requirements are different for each item because:

1. Item P has a very small order quantity and, consequently, many exposures to stockout (52 per year).

2. Item Y requires a higher reserve stock because its demands are much more erratic. This greater variation results in the larger standard deviation.

3. Item Z has an order quantity of 6500 units; thus there are only 4 exposures to stockout during the year. In fact, *no* reserve stock need be added to the anticipated demand during lead time for Item Z in order to stay within the desired number of stockouts per year.

This example illustrates how worthwhile the difficulty and expense of using statistical approaches to inventory control actually are. It is not uncommon for improvements from these techniques to result in inventory reductions of one-third or more with no increase in the number of stockouts or to yield reductions in stockouts to one-third the previous level with no increase in inventory as a result of better distribution of reserve stocks.

The reason for the better results is simply that intuitive techniques cannot take all of the factors into account:

1. *Forecast error*
2. *Lead time*
3. *Order quantity size*
4. *Desired service level*

These are the factors that affect the size of the reserve stock.

Many practitioners are awed by the computations required by the statistical approach to order point calculation. These computations, however, are quite routine once they have been established and can be handled by a reasonably intelligent clerk on a periodic basis such as once a month. In companies where computers are available, the computations can be handled routinely for thousands of items.

Statistics and common sense

While statistical ordering techniques can generate substantial improvements in companies where intuitive techniques have previously been used, they should be applied with discretion and common sense, always keeping in mind the principles of ABC inventory classification. The high value items should receive the closest attention, and it is sometimes practical to segregate even the A items into "Top A" items which will receive the frequent personal attention of the production control manager. These items should probably have "floating" order points calculated using statistical techniques and, in some cases, it may be worthwhile to employ even more sophisticated techniques to obtain the greatest economy in control of their inventories. On the other hand, statistical techniques would probably not be used to control low-value items unless a computer were available so that this could be done economically.

Statistical concepts not only help the practitioner to reduce inventories, but an understanding of these concepts can give him a better grasp of the day-to-day workings of inventory systems. One of the problems that constantly faces most production and inventory control people is the ever-increasing number of items that must be kept in inventory. Better knowledge of inventory behavior characteristics is certainly not going to eliminate this trend, but better knowledge of the functioning of the inventory system can help the practitioner to cope with it. A simple example will illustrate the point:

It seems to be a characteristic of demand in most businesses that the more active items will have more stable demand and the less active items will have more variable demand. Looking at almost any stock record will show that the item which averages ten units of demand per month typically has few months during which demand is very close to ten units—it is quite as likely to be zero or thirty as it is to be ten, even though the total demand for the year averages ten units per month.

Popular items, on the other hand, tend to have a more stable demand. If demand averages two thousand units per month, there will probably be very few months when demand will exceed three or, at most, four thousand units. For the popular item, demand will rarely be more than twice as much as the average demand, while the demand for the low-activity item may frequently be three to four times the average demand.

When it is decided to add more items to the inventory, this phenomenon almost always makes it necessary to increase the total inventory level. This point is not readily understood by people unfamiliar with inventory control, and they frequently ask: "If we sold 1000 red widgets a month for the last year, and we are now going to make them in red, white and blue, but still only sell a total of 1000 a month, why should your inventory have to increase?" The actual inventory situation might look like this:

One inventory item	Lead time demand	Reserve stock
Red widgets	1000 units	300 units

Inventory split into three items	Lead time demand	Reserve stock
Red widgets	160 units	100 units
White widgets	420 units	200 units
Blue widgets	420 units	200 units
Totals	1000 units	500 units

In this hypothetical example, splitting one product up into three products requires an increase in reserve stock to provide the same service level because the lower volume for each of the three products will result in greater demand variability.

One group of authors[1] notes that if a company adds branch warehouses—an excellent example of inventory splitting—the inventory reserve will vary with the square root of the number of distribution points involved. If a company were using a reserve stock of 300 units, for example, and added two warehouses (each assumed to supply an equivalent part of the demand) the reserve required to give the same service level as before would be:

$$\text{Reserve (each distribution point)} = \frac{\text{Reserve for 1 distribution point}}{\sqrt{\text{Number of distribution points}}}$$

$$= \frac{300}{\sqrt{3}} = 173$$

and 173 × 3 distribution points equals a total of 519 units of reserve stock that will now be required.

Increases in the number of items in the product line also aggravate the lot-size problem. Doubling the number of items going through

[1]Putnam, Arnold O., Barlow, E. Robert, Stilian, Gabriel N., *Unified Operations Management,* McGraw, New York, 1963, pp. 212–213.

a department means either running lot-sizes that are twice as big, doubling the number of setup hours, or some compromise between these two alternatives.

These are typical examples of the problems that face the production and inventory control practitioner every day. With the knowledge of the behavior characteristics of inventory, he can at least understand what is likely to happen and, if he is ingenious enough in applying statistical concepts, he can show management the available alternatives in each case. They can make their decisions knowing *all* of the resulting effects rather than learning about these effects after they happen, or assuming that the resulting increase in inventory was due to poor production control.

The most important point to remember about any type of ordering system is that *it should make sense*. Statistics can provide useful tools for the practitioner, but the results will depend on his good sense and judgment in applying the tools.

Practical precautions in determining order points

When first applying statistical techniques, the practitioner is advised to try them on a sample before applying them across the entire product line, in order to gain familiarity with the concepts and the limitations of the techniques. From there, he may want to extend the statistical calculation of order points to all A items before applying it to the B class. Use with C items should be approached with caution—in fact, it might never be worthwhile to go to this amount of effort for the low-value inventory items.

Periodic recalculation of order points using exponential smoothing to forecast the demand during lead time and using updated standard deviations to determine the reserve stock is manually feasible, but requires a great amount of tedious, detailed calculation which makes it questionable that it can be done economically. Even the simplest data-processing equipment can be of tremendous assistance to this type of application. Electronic computers are being used extensively in industry to keep order points updated for thousands of items, frequently on a weekly basis. Computer manufacturers make available programs that can be used readily by the practitioner to experiment with these techniques and to determine how well they apply in his own company. These same "canned" programs can then be used to form the nucleus of his own computer programs for operation. This reduces to a minimum the work of programming the computer and the time required to get useful results.

Periodic review system

Another major inventory control system is the periodic review system, frequently called the "fixed-cycle" system. In this system, the inventory records are reviewed periodically and replenishment orders are placed

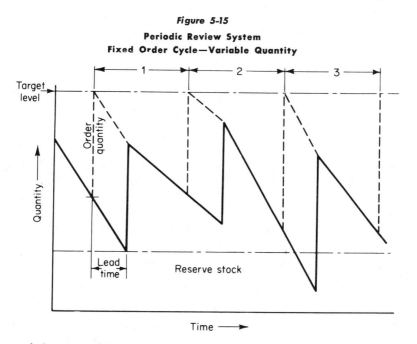

Figure 5-15

Periodic Review System
Fixed Order Cycle—Variable Quantity

for each item at each review. The review period may be one week, two weeks or a month, whichever is best for the situation. When ordering, enough stock is ordered to bring the total "on hand" and "on order" up to a predetermined "target" level. Figure 5-15 shows how this system would work over a period of time for one item.

This should be contrasted with the other major system—the order point system—where the inventory records are reviewed each time entry is made and a replenishment order placed when the balance "on hand" and "on order" reaches a predetermined "order point." In the order point system, the order quantity is fixed *and is usually* the economic order quantity.

The periodic review system finds application where:

1. There are many small issues of items from inventory, so that posting records for each issue is impractical. Retail stores, particularly food supermarkets, automobile parts supply houses and similar retail businesses fit in this category.

2. Ordering costs are relatively small. This occurs where purchase orders are placed for many different items from one source, or orders transferring many items of stock from a central to a branch warehouse are written.

3. It is desirable to order many items at one time to make up a production schedule, for example, so that equipment setups for the family of items can be combined, or to obtain a discount from a vendor by means of a combined order, or to reduce freight costs by shipping full carload quantities at regular intervals.

The "target" is the sum of the following:

1. Anticipated demand during the lead time
2. Anticipated demand during the review period
3. Reserve stock

Obviously, if the inventory record is not to be reviewed again for two weeks, anticipated usage during this period *must be added to the lead time demand,* since this lead time cannot begin until two weeks have passed. Reserve stocks for this system are calculated by the same means discussed earlier in this chapter for the order point system.

A simple example of a target inventory calculation is as follows:

Lead time $= 1$ week
Forecast demand during lead time $= 20$ units
Review period $= 2$ weeks (thus, average order quantity $= 2$ weeks' supply)
Forecast demand during review period $= 40$ units
Reserve stock $= 30$ units
Target inventory level $= DLT + DRP + R = 20 + 40 + 30 = 90$ units

Using this inventory target, the stock would be reviewed every two weeks and ordered up to a total of 90 units. The total inventory on hand and on order, for example, might equal 70 units at the first review; 20 more units would then be ordered. During the next two weeks, demand might total 45 units, and this would be the quantity ordered at the second review, since 45 units would be needed to restore the total to the target level of 90 units. A few important points about periodic review systems should be noted:

1. The total lead time is actually equal to the delivery lead time plus the review period.

2. Lengthening the review period is equivalent to lengthening the lead time and will require carrying greater amounts of reserve stock.

3. The ordering quantity is equal to demand during the review period.

4. The average inventory level is equal to one-half the demand during the review period plus reserve stock.

Two simple ordering systems

For the many low annual value items that are usually found in industrial inventories, it is often not worthwhile to post inventory records (as was discussed in Chapter 3). There are two general methods mentioned earlier that are used for controlling these low-value items without records: the two-bin system and the visual review system. These are worth reviewing.

The two-bin system: An amount of stock equivalent to the order point is physically segregated either into a second bin or into a container, and this is then sealed. When all of the open stock has been used up, the second bin or reserve container is broken into, and the production control office is notified to order more stock. This is a practical method for keeping control of low-value items. The most common problems that arise in its application are:

1. When the responsibility for breaking into the second bin and notifying the production control office is not clearly assigned to an individual, this type of system will deteriorate very quickly. Personnel who do not understand the system will use up the reserve stock without notifying the production control office. Material will be received and not properly segregated into an open stock and reserve stock.

2. After being set up, the quantity to be carried in the second bin is never reviewed. As demand changes for the item, this quantity is no longer adequate or may be far too large.

A two-bin system works best in a controlled stockroom where the responsibility for replenishing stock and maintaining the inventory can be assigned to one man, such as the head storekeeper.

Visual review system: Stock is periodically checked (perhaps once a week or once every two weeks) and each item is ordered to a preestablished stock level. This technique is far more satisfactory than the two-bin system when the responsibility for storekeeping cannot be assigned an individual, or when there are too many small transactions on a large number of items to make the keeping of inventory records economical or practical. It works particularly well where lead times are short and vendors "ship or cancel" (the backorders), thus eliminating the need for any record of material previously ordered. It is, of course, the principal technique employed by many retail stores—especially large food supermarkets. There are three principal problems involved in using this system:

1. The necessary periodic reviews of the stock level are overlooked or forgotten.

2. Because of poor housekeeping, stock is not put in its proper location and the stock clerk does not find all of the inventory actually on hand when making his review.

3. Ordering targets are not reviewed frequently and become outdated and useless as demand changes.

Low-value item control systems involving a minimum of record-keeping can be used very successfully if the following points are kept in mind:

1. The ABC concept of inventory classification is based on carrying high levels of inventory of low value items and on exerting a minimum of effort in controlling them. Nevertheless, it must be remembered that an assembly line can be shut down for lack of a cotter pin as surely as for lack of a major casting. It must never be forgotten that the basic rule for controlling low value stocks is to "*have plenty.*"

2. No good has been accomplished if tighter controls of high-value stocks do not more than offset the inventory increase resulting from looser controls of the low-value stocks. Time saved by the latter should be devoted to reducing high-value inventories.

3. Visual controls are frequently associated with loose controls, and perpetual records are associated with tight controls: neither is necessarily so. A common industry case is the example of rivets in the aircraft industry. These are low *unit* value items, but their tremendously large annual usage makes them A items. Control of such items using visual techniques will save a great deal of record-posting time, but the inventory levels can and should be controlled very closely.

4. It is not always best that all items having low annual dollar usage are controlled using visual review techniques. This can result in having a casting which is used in an assembly once a year checked visually every week rather than having the withdrawal posted once during the year. The inventory level for this casting should be set fairly high, and a large order quantity should be used.

Materials planning

The concept of a reorder point assumes a fairly uniform rate of continuous demand on the inventory so that protection can be given by safety stocks against "normal" fluctuations in demand, and also assumes that inventories should be replenished *immediately* when depleted. For most items carried in a finished goods inventory, for example, these are valid assumptions and the order point is an excellent technique for controlling such inventories. The normal demand on the inventory is *independent* of activities of the manufacturer and no specific events are known to generate large demands; in fact, demand comes from many customer orders received pretty much at random.

There are other inventories, however, on which demand is not uniform or continuous, but is instead intermittent: demand comes in occasional large quantities and immediate replenishment may not be necessary or desirable. This intermittent type of demand exists for components of an assembly which are required only when the assembly is being made. Since assemblies are usually made in lot quantities, demand for the components will occur in lumps at intervals. For example, components used on an assembly that is made twice a year would experience two demands for six-month's needs, compared to small weekly demands made by customers for the finished assembly. It is apparent that use of an order point to replenish this inventory would result in components lying in the storeroom for long periods of time with no real requirements fot them. More important to the practitioner in many instances is the fact that the reorder point used to replenish this type of inventory generates many orders that are not really needed, and around which needed items must be expedited through the factory.

Requirements for this type of component can be based on anticipated release of manufacturing lot quantities for the assembly on which it is used. Figure 5-16 shows an example of both continuous and intermittent demand patterns. In the former, the finished goods inventory item has a steady rate of depletion, demand during lead time can be predicted using a technique like exponential smoothing and reserve stock can be calculated using the concepts explained earlier in this chapter. The component inventory item, although subject to intermittent demands, is also assumed in Fig. 5-16 to be controlled by an order point and the result is that it is usually carried in stock for some time before actually being required. A more economical approach to ordering would involve predicting when the finished goods inventory item would need to be

Figure 5-16

Continuous vs. Intermittent Demand Patterns

Finished product item – many small <u>independent</u> demands from customers

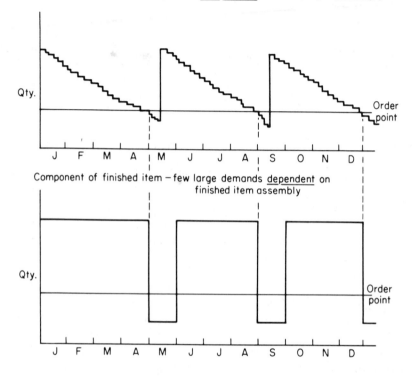

Component of finished item – few large demands <u>dependent</u> on finished item assembly

assembled and then placing component manufacturing or purchase orders to bring these into stock in time for the assembly date. Such an inventory control system for *dependent demand* items requires a parts list, or *bill of materials,* so that assembly requirements can be translated into requirements for components.

Simple bill of materials

Figure 5-17 shows a bill of materials for a simple wall lamp listing the component number, its description, the quantity required per assembly and indicating whether these parts are manufactured or purchased. With this bill of materials, a planner can order components in the quantity required for the next assembly lot. For example, if 2000 #9 wall lamps were to be assembled, he would place purchase requisitions for

Figure 5-17

Bill of Materials

#9 Wall Lamp

Mfg. code 1010218			Date 8/10/66 Approved AES		
Component		Quantity required	Source	Remarks	
Number	Description				
X18	Switch	1	Purch.		
Y2L	Socket	1	Purch.		
9W	Shade	1	Mfg.		
414	Hanger	2	Mfg.		
4107	Cord set	1	Purch.		

Figure 5-18

Bill of Materials

#9 Pin-up Lamp

Mfg. code 1020314			Date 8/10/66 Approved AES		
Component		Quantity required	Source	Remarks	
Number	Description				
X18	Switch	1	Purch.		
Y2L	Socket	1	Purch.		
9P	Shade	1	Mfg.		
414	Hanger	2	Mfg.		
4107	Cord set	1	Purch.		

2000 each of the X18 switch, the Y2L socket and the 4107 cord set; and manufacturing orders for 2000 9W shades and 4000 #414 hangers.

This extremely simple example illustrates none of the usual complications that make the job of controlling component inventories extremely complex in many companies. One of the most common complications is that components are used on more than one assembly. Figure 5-18 shows a second lamp, in this case a #9 pin-up lamp, which differs from the #9 wall lamp only in having a different shade. It's apparent that a great many economies and efficiencies can be gained by combining requirements for common components. For example, it would be more economical to purchase the cord set in larger quantities. Therefore, before placing an order, the planner should know all requirements for this cord set. Also, it is important to combine requirements for components being scheduled through the plant so that setups, dispatching and expediting can be reduced to a minimum.

The explosion chart

Of the many ways of combining requirements, the simplest is the explosion chart. Figure 5-19 shows an explosion chart, really just a series of bills of material listed together with assemblies down the left side and components across the top. The "X" in the box in the matrix shows the components *not* used in the assembly shown in the corresponding row. The bills of material for the #9 wall lamp and #9 pin-up lamp were used with the bills of material for all other lamps in this product line to make up this explosion chart. A planner determining his requirements for the next thirteen weeks of assembly, for example, would insert the expected required quantity of each finished lamp in the explosion chart in the second column and then extend that quantity across all components indicated by the open boxes in the matrix, multiplying it by the figure in the upper left-hand corner of the box (which indicates if more than one piece is required per assembly). For example, the #414 hanger is used in pairs on the #9 wall lamp and, therefore, a small 2 appears in the matrix.

Once the requirements have been totaled for each component by adding the figures in the columns, they can be compared with the total quantity of each item available in inventory. Figure 5-20 shows the inventory record for the #9P lamp shade. As the explosion chart indicated, there is at the present time a need for 1256 shades to take care of the manufacturing requirements in the second quarter, so an order for 1300 is written and will be released to the factory when required.

During the quarter, the explosion chart will be used weekly to deter-

Figure 5-19
Explosion Chart
Product Line—Lamps

Assembly	Required Qty	X18 Switch	X27 Switch	Y2L Socket	Shade #7W	Shade #7D	Shade #9W	Shade #9D	Shade #9P	Shade #11D	Shade #11P	414 Hanger	418 Hanger	VT Base	UP Base	#4107 Cord Set
#7 Wall	2000															
#7 Desk	2000															
#9 Wall	2000	2000		2000			2000					2×4000				2000
#9 Desk	2500	2500		2500												
#9 Pin–up	2500								2500			2×5000				2500
#11 Desk	2000		2000	2000												
#11 Pin–up	2000		2000								2000	2	2×4000			2000
Total required	6500	4500	2000	6500			2000		2500		2000	9000	4000			6500
Total available		7105	15,423	7002			4595		1244		4715	29,531	11,648			6400
To obtain	✓	✓	✓	✓			✓		(1300)		✓	✓	✓			(100)

Figure 5-20

Inventory record card #9P shade						
Date	Rec'd	Withdrawn	Available on hand	On order	Required	Available to plan
3/12	400	---	1844	-----	600	1244
3/14	----	600	1244	-----	------	1244
3/23	----	----	1244	-----	2500	−1256
3/23	----	----	1244	1300	2500	44

mine whether or not components for the next few weeks are coming through on schedule to meet assembly requirements. In this case, the quantity that will be posted in the *total available* row at the bottom of the explosion chart will be taken from the *available on hand* column on the inventory record card rather than the *available to plan* column.

This type of simple "requirements planning" technique has been used for many years. While its users often feel that it is superior to an order point system for ordering components, its use often results in excess inventory unless it is refined substantially. The explosion sheet (Fig. 5-19, for example) can only show the total quantity required over a period of time, and this period must be long enough to cover the longest manufacturing or purchase lead time of any component. Many companies do their planning on a quarterly basis, and must plan more than one quarter ahead, showing "firm requirements" for the current quarter and "anticipated requirements" for the following quarter. This is necessary because any component requiring more than a week or two to manufacture could well be in short supply at the beginning of the next quarter if not planned for.

Further problems occur because the planning period is so long. Planning "firm requirements" for a thirteen-week period requires a forecast of anticipated requirements for each end item; the farther out into the future this forecast is extended the less accurate it will become. In such a "quarterly planning" system[1], the planner typically finds that as he begins each quarter, many components are in short supply or in excess simply because of the forecast errors. A cardinal rule to remember in any requirements planning system is:

---

[1]For a more detailed discussion of the quarterly ordering system, see Chapter 7.

Figure 5-21
Time Series Ordering Assembly Requirements

#9 pin-up lamp
(master schedule)

	Past due	14	15	16	17	18	19	Week 20	21	22	23	24	25	26
	---	---	---	500	---	---	500	---	---	500	---	---	500	---

#9P shade
Materials plan

Lead time: 4 weeks

	Past due	14	15	16	17	18	19	Week 20	21	22	23	24	25	26
Projected usage	---	---	---	500	---	---	500	---	---	500	---	---	500	---
On hand	---	1244	1244	744	744	744	244	244	244	---	---	---	---	---
Scheduled receipts	---	---	---	---	---	---	---	---	---	256	---	---	500	---
Planned order release	---	---	---	---	---	256	---	---	500	---	---	---	---	---

Requirements must be recalculated frequently to reflect changing demand and revised forecasts

Shortening the time period for planning requires considerable refinement of the simple techniques described so far. Merely showing (as in Fig. 5-19) that 2500 units will be required during the second quarter does not pinpoint *when* in the quarter these components will be required and in what quantities. Some manual approaches take the planned assembly requirements and, using the bill of materials, post the "required" date on the component record and calculate the start date based on standard lead times. This approach does not lend itself readily to combining requirements or recalculating component schedule dates as requirements change. This is why, in practice, the manual requirements planning approach is frequently no more effective than the order point system. Figure 5-21 is a time series planning chart showing the projected assembly schedule for the #9 pin-up lamp by week for the second quarter. This type of assembly plan is usually called a *master schedule*.

A master schedule might very well be based upon an estimate of when the assembled end product would be reaching its reorder point. The intermittent demands shown in weeks #16, #19, #22, and #25 of Fig. 5-21 are actually economic order quantities for the end item.

Below the master schedule are shown the projected requirements for the #9P shade, based upon the assembly schedule for the #9 pin-up lamp. This ordering technique specifies in which week components will be required and, based upon the lead time for the component, shows when manufacturing or purchase orders must be released. It can be seen, for example, that the #9P shade inventory will be reduced by 500 units in week #16, when 500 pin-up lamps are assembled, and that it will be necessary to order another 256 shades in week #18—in order to have them arrive in week #22, so that another 500 pin-up lamps can be assembled as scheduled.

Figure 5-21 shows only the projected assembly requirements for the #9 pin-up lamp, and this is perfectly satisfactory for determining requirements for the #9P shade which is used only on that lamp. A materials plan for a component common to two or more assemblies would have to be based on the sum of the requirements for all assemblies broken into their proper time periods. This type of ordering is quite complicated and extremely difficult to do manually.

There are some general principles to remember about time series planning:

> 1. *The materials plan must extend over a long enough period to cover the longest lead time of any component.*

2. *The materials plan must be revised frequently in order to react to changes in requirements.*

3. *The smaller the time period used, the more effective the materials plan will be.* For example, a plan in weekly periods revised every week would be far more effective than one in monthly periods revised only once a month.

Multilevel bills of material

The lamps used as examples in the earlier sections of this chapter had a very simple bill of materials with very few parts required and with no subassemblies. In more complex assemblies, the planner must frequently plan the manufacture of subassemblies as well as components

Figure 5-22
Multilevel Bill of Materials
#9 Pin-up Lamp

		Date		
		8/15/66		
Mfg. Code		Approved		
1020314		AES		

Component				
Number	Description	Quantity required	Source	Remarks
X18	Switch	1	Purch	
Y2L	Socket assembly	1	Mfg.	
10314	Switch	1	Purch.	
Y2L–S	Shell	1	Mfg.	
Y2L–B	Base	1	Mfg.	
Y2L–SI	Shell insulator	1	Purch.	
Y2L–BI	Base insulator	1	Purch.	
Y2L–XI	Screw stem	1	Mfg.	
9P	Shade	1	Mfg.	
414	Hanger	2	Mfg.	
4107	Cord set	1	Purch.	

Figure 5-23

Indented Bill of Materials

#9 Pin-up Lamp

						Date
						8/18/66
Mfg. Code						Approved
1020314						AES

1st level component number	2nd level component number	Description	Quantity required	Source	Remarks
X18		Switch	1	Purch.	
Y2L		Socket	1	Mfg.	
	10314	Switch	1	Purch.	
	Y2L-S	Shell	1	Mfg.	
	Y2L-B	Base	1	Mfg.	
	Y2L-SI	Shell insulator	1	Purch.	
	Y2L-BI	Base insulator	1	Purch.	
	Y2L-XI	Screw stem	1	Mfg.	
9P		Shade	1	Mfg.	
414		Hanger	2	Mfg.	
4107		Cord set	1	Purch.	

and final assemblies. If, for example, a lamp manufacturer decided to make the Y2L socket himself instead of buying it, his bills of material would then have to show the components required to put this subassembly together as well as showing the other components going into the final assembly.

Figure 5-22 shows this more complex bill of materials, but it does nothing to indicate that the #10314 switch, for example, is part of the Y2L socket subassembly. Some notation is usually made on the bill of materials to indicate this relationship, such as showing by an asterisk all items used in subassemblies, but if these subassemblies in turn have subassemblies, the asterisk technique gets very awkward.

A more common approach is to show the bill of materials in "indented" form as illustrated in Fig. 5-23. Here all the components going into the Y2L socket, the so-called "2nd level" parts, are indented to the right to indicate that they are components used in a subassembly.

Recalling that the Y2L socket is used in every lamp, it can be seen in Fig. 5-23 that any change in this socket or any of its components will require that *every* bill of materials be remade. A slightly different form of bill of materials which lends itself better to maintenance and updating can simplify this work. For example, if the bill of materials shown in Fig. 5-18 were used, but the Y2L socket were noted (by an asterisk or some other notation) as a manufactured subassembly, a separate bill of materials (such as Fig. 5-24) could be maintained for that subassembly. Any change in the subassembly would then require changing only one bill of materials—each of the higher level bills would be unaffected as long as the Y2L socket continued to be used in the final assembly.

Figure 5-24

Bill of Materials

Y2L Socket

		Date		
		8/20/66		
Mfg code		Approved		
1030418		AES		
	(Used on: #7W, #7D, #9W, #9D, #9P, #11D, #11P)			

Component		Quantity required	Source	Remarks
Number	Description			
10314	Switch	1	Purch.	
Y2L–S	Shell	1	Mfg.	
Y2L–B	Base	1	Mfg.	
Y2L–SI	Shell insulator	1	Purch.	
Y2L–BI	Base insulator	1	Purch.	
Y2L–XI	Screw stem	1	Mfg.	

" Gross " and " Net " requirements

An accurate calculation of component inventory requirements involves determining inventory requirements for each level of subassemblies and components and then checking these requirements against the inventory at that level in order to determine requirements at the next level of inventory. If, for example, a planner simply took the bill of materials in Fig. 5-23 and determined his requirements, he would order all the components as well as the subassemblies in which they were used. This would result in "pyramiding" the inventory, generating inventory for components when subassemblies are already in inventory. Assuming that there are 1500 Y2L sockets already in inventory, the planner should make the following computation:

Y2L Gross requirements = 2500 pieces
Y2L Available to plan = 1500 pieces
Y2L Net requirements = 1000 pieces

This calculation of gross and net requirements must be made at each level of inventory. If, for example, the #10314 switch were now manufactured by this lamp company, it would become another subassembly level going into the Y2L socket subassembly—a further calculation of net requirements for components going into that switch would be necessary, taking assembled switches into consideration.

This calculation of net requirements avoids duplicating inventories and helps keep balance among the items. In most manufacturing companies, inventories tend to get out of balance with shortages or excess quantities of subassemblies and components resulting from engineering changes, scrap, producing parts in different-sized economic lots and the like. Net requirements calculations will help to avoid getting more of excess parts and speed overcoming shortages.

It is usually desirable to have some reserves built into a time-series plan, but these reserves usually do not take the form of quantity—they take instead the form of extra time. If, for example, a component will be required in week #25, it can be ordered to be delivered in week #23. Extra quantity is, of course, added for scrap allowances, spare parts and similar demand over and above assembly requirements. The following points should be kept in mind in setting up reserves for a time-series planning system:

1. The same general principles apply to forecasting for a time-series plan as for any other ordering system: the farther out the forecast is extended, the less accurate it becomes. Consequently, time reserves built into the time series plan should be greater for long lead time items and,

in fact, as the delivery date for the item gets closer, the required date should be reviewed and revised since it can now be predicted more accurately.

2. Because of this forecasting relationship, some companies revising their materials plan base tolerances on the period between review and required delivery, with tighter tolerances for shorter periods. For example, if the original required delivery date for a component was forecast as week #25 by a materials plan made in week #13, a review in week #14 indicating that the delivery date should be week #24 would cause no change in the order for the component. However, if the materials plan were being reviewed in week #19 and the requirement for the component showed up in week #24 as opposed to the original week #25, a change to the new date would be made in the component schedule since more reliance is placed on this later revision.

3. The component should be scheduled to be *delivered* earlier than required rather than only scheduled to be *started* earlier. Having it in production does not provide a real reserve or buffer, will tend to increase work in process and, consequently, will also increase the job of controlling work out on the factory floor.

4. Reserves may be held in the form of "semi-finished" components inventories which can be completed quickly to meet unexpected demand. This is most appropriate if such semi-finished parts are processed differently for various finished assemblies.

The entire success of any materials planning system will be directly related to the accuracy of the bills of material on which it relies. An explosion chart drawn from inaccurate bills of material will inevitably result in overordering some or failing to order other components. Particularly if there are complex products requiring hundreds of components with many different levels and frequent engineering changes, the job of maintaining bills of materials up-to-date can be staggering, but nevertheless essential to good materials control.

In a manual system, the planner will usually keep himself informed about the major engineering changes and other important factors affecting the bills of material, and will often develop side records to help himself. As his explosion charts become less and less accurate, he can temporarily "outsmart" them by using these devices, but lack of proper record maintenance inevitably causes deterioration of the whole production control system. Maintaining the basic information upon which the company's customer service, inventory investment, efficient plant operation and its cost control system depend somehow seems less important to many managers than making an immediate cost reduction by laying off a clerk. Such savings are invariably consumed many times over by the massive effort required to get this information corrected once again. Installing a computerized system generally forces recognition of this maintenance problem because of the inability of the computer to "outsmart" the system: inaccuracies will show up right away rather than being postponed.

The most common information maintenance problem probably exists in the area of part-numbering. The part-numbering system used in the lamp examples in this chapter is a very simple one, typical of the type of part-numbering system used in small companies, combining numbers and letters without significance or reason. As the company grows and its product line expands, the numbering system begins to get incredibly complicated, so that even simple filing systems start to bog down. Typically, a program is then begun to develop a more reasonable part-numbering system—usually with a great many digits, each having some significance (describing the material the product is made from, the basic method by which it is made, whether it is manufactured or purchased)—and this part-numbering system is introduced. For some components, it also becomes extremely cumbersome to keep each digit significant, so a non-significant part-numbering system is finally introduced. It is not uncommon, in a deficient production and inventory control system, to find three different part-numbering systems in simultaneous use. Few managers seem to recognize the connection between the lack of a good part-numbering system and lack of results from production and inventory control.

One further complication in using bills of materials is the common occurrence of a component used in different levels of different assemblies. If, for example, the #10314 switch were used both in a Y2L socket and in the base of a model lamp, it would be part of a subassembly in one use and part of a final assembly in the other. Because of this, the problem of accumulating total requirements would be compounded. A simple explosion sheet for the product would no longer be satisfactory since it would show only the requirement for the base switches used in final assembly. The planner would need some cross-reference notation to show that he should first determine net requirements for the Y2L socket and add the latter figure to final assembly net requirements to get gross requirements for the #10314 switch before checking his inventory of the switch and reordering.

This is done by a technique known as *low-level coding* in a computer system. Low-level coding consists of assigning a code number to each "break back" or indentation in the bill of materials which indicates another level of subassembly or component. For example, the #9 pin-up lamp assembly would have a level code of 0, the Y2L socket would be assigned level code 1   (since it is a subassembly) and the #10314 switch would have level code 2. The computer inventory record for the #10314 switch would carry this code 2 identification and, in making each explosion, the computer would add gross requirements for this switch without checking against available inventory to get its net requirements until it had reached the second level usage (in the Y2L socket, in this example) and knew it had accumulated requirements for both final assembly and subassembly needs.

Economic ordering quantities with time-series planning

The basic concept of the economic order quantity[1] assumes that demands will be fairly continuous rather than intermittent. If demand tends to be fairly uniform even in a time series planning system—where there are weekly demands for the component—the standard economic ordering quantity formula can be used. When requirements come in large lots at irregular periods, however, the effect is to increase the average inventory carried. A slightly different approach embodying the same general principles can be used to determine the economic ordering quantity with intermittent demands. The basic idea of this "time-series EOQ" calculation is the same as that behind the standard calculation of EOQ: balancing the costs associated with ordering the item against those connected with carrying it in inventory to get the minimum total cost.

Figure 5-25 shows a calculation of the time series ordering quantity, using an inventory carrying cost of 20% per year ($\frac{4}{10}$ of 1% per week), an item unit cost of 80¢ and a setup cost of $18.00. The known requirements fall in weeks #15, #21, #32 and #40, and the question is how many of these requirements it will be economical to combine. If each requirement is manufactured separately, 4 setups will be required in the plant, but very little inventory will be carried because components will be withdrawn immediately after they arrive in stock to be used at the assembly operation. If the $400 requirement for week #15 is combined with the $560 needed in week #21, this will save one setup but will result in carrying $560 of excess inventory in stock for 6 weeks before it is required. The calculation of extra inventory cost is shown in Fig. 5-25 along with the savings that would result by avoiding one setup. It would be economical to combine the requirements for week #15 and week #21 into one manufacturing lot.

---

[1] Cf. Chapter 4 and Appendix III.

Figure 5-25

Time Series EOQ

Part #17321
Inv. cost = 20% or 0.4% per week
Unit cost = $0.80
Setup cost = $18.00

Quantity		Week required	Cum. lot size	Excess inventory	Weeks in stock	Setups saved
Pcs.	$					
500	$400	15	$ 400	----	----	----
700	$560	21	$ 960	$560	6	1
1000	$800	32	$1760	$800	17	2
400	$320	40	$2080	$320	25	3

A. Combine week 15 and week 21:

   1. Order $960 to be delivered Week 15

   2. $560 excess will be carried in stock 6 weeks

   3. One setup will be saved

Thus:

$$\text{Additional inventory costs} = \$560 \times 6 \times 0.004 = \$13.44$$
$$\text{Setup savings} = 1 \times \$18.00 \qquad\qquad = \$18.00$$

B. Combine week 15, 21 and 32.

   1. Order $1760 to be delivered week 15

   2. $560 excess will be carried in stock 6 weeks

   3. $800 excess will be carried in stock 17 weeks

   4. Two setups will be saved

Thus:

$$\text{Additional inventory costs} = \$560 \times 6 \times 0.004 = \$13.44$$
$$\phantom{\text{Additional inventory costs} = } \$800 \times 17 \times 0.004 = \underline{\$54.40}$$
$$\text{Total} = \$67.84$$
$$\text{Setup savings} = 2 \times \$18.00 \qquad\qquad = \$36.00$$

Section B of Fig. 5-25 shows the economics of combining the requirements for weeks #15, #21 and #32 into one manufactured lot. In this case, the $800 of material required for week #32 will be carried in stock 17 weeks before it is used and, as Fig. 5-25 shows, the extra inventory cost would far offset the savings in setup.

This technique for calculating economic lot sizes with the materials plan involves a trial-and-error calculation which adds to the basic complexity of materials planning.

Designing an effective reordering system

Using exponential smoothing to update forecasts and using the MAD to measure and update forecast error can result in a substantial improvement over intuitively developed reorder points, but this technique is usually not the best one to use for *dependent* demand items. Referring to Fig. 5-21, it can be seen that exponential smoothing used to project usage for the #9P shade could generate some very unsatisfactory results. In week #14, the forecast would drop because actual demand would be zero, and it would be very low by week #16—just when the actual demand occurs! The 500-unit demand in week #16 would then increase the forecast just as demand dropped to zero once again in week #17. It is easy to picture how weekly recalculation of forecast error would merely compound this misapplication of an excellent technique.

One other advantage of the materials planning approach in controlling component inventories is that it is usually more effective in projecting anticipated increases in requirements, while the order point technique—as it is usually applied—will not react to changes until *after* they occur, since the order point is based on history.

These techniques can be combined in practice. In a small company without data-processing equipment, for example, time-series planning can be used for high value ("A") components only, order point control can be used on the medium value ("B") items, and visual control methods used on the low value ("C") items. Some companies take a slightly different approach, using order points for the longest lead time components (trying to keep some in stock at all times) and using time series planning on the shorter lead time components. This takes advantage of the fact that a typical product contains only a few very long lead time components but many with shorter lead times. The extra inventory investment required to keep the long lead time components on hand insures a much quicker reaction to increasing customer requirements.

A make-to-stock company assembling an electrical product with many interchangeable components would probably want to keep components "uncommitted" to any particular assembly as long as possible. Order points used on the finished stock of assemblies would be used, not only to reorder the assembly, but also as a basis for the "master schedule" used in the materials plan for components. The following example shows this relationship:

Situation as of week #21:

a. Order point for finished assembly = 3 weeks
b. Current stock on hand and on order = 7 weeks
c. Order quantity equivalent to: 10 weeks
d. Component requirements are therefore anticipated in week #25 (when stock reaches order point), #35 (because order quantity will last about 10 weeks), #45, etc.

The order point would probably be recalculated regularly, using exponential smoothing and MAD, and the accuracy of the individual component requirement forecast date would be a function of the MAD for the assembly adjusted for the length of time over which the requirement is projected.

In like manner, the anticipated requirements for other components can be combined to make up the master schedule, and the technique presented in Fig. 5-25 would be used to calculate the best lot-sizes.

A similar application of these principles and techniques would be made in a company making a one-piece hardware item. The product really represents a "reverse explosion" since one semi-finished item can be plated differently to make it into a dozen or more end items. The finished goods inventory would typically be controlled using order points, the semi-finished stock would be controlled using order point for semi-finished items that have a continuous demand, while semi-finished items experiencing an intermittent demand would be ordered based on the next anticipated requirements of the end items.[1]

Order point techniques and materials planning are complementary techniques, and the successful practitioner will want to use each where it best applies rather than adopting one or the other as the "correct" method.

---

[1]Note that this would require the equivalent to bills of material in a "where used" sequence where the semi-finished stock identity is the same as an "assembly" and the end items are its "components."

Bibliography

1. Brinkman, Victor, "Periodic Ordering Systems—The Orphans of Inventory Control," *APICS Quarterly Bulletin,* Vol. 3, No. 1, January 1962.

2. Brown, R. G., *Smoothing, Forecasting, and Prediction of Discrete Time Series,* Prentice-Hall, Englewood Cliffs, New Jersey, 1963.

3. ———, *Statistical Forecasting for Inventory Control,* McGraw, New York, 1959.

4. *IMPACT General Information Manual,* IBM Publication No. E20–8105.

5. Lander, Jack R., *A Basic Training Program in Production and Inventory Control,* American Production and Inventory Control Society, Chicago, Illinois, 1964.

6. Moroney, M. J., *Facts from Figures,* Penguin Books, London, 1957.

7. Neter, J., and Wasserman, W., *Fundamental Statistics for Business and Economics,* Allyn and Bacon, Boston, 1956.

8. Plossl, G. W., and Wight, O. W., "Determining Order Points Using the Poisson Distribution," *APICS Quarterly Bulletin,* Vol. 4, No. 2, April 1963.

9. Whitin, T. M., *Theory of Inventory Management,* Princeton University Press, Princeton, New Jersey, 1957.

10. Wilson, R. H., "A Scientific Routine for Stock Control," *Harvard Business Review,* Vol. 13, No. 1, pp. 116–128, 1934.

# CHAPTER SIX

AGGREGATE
INVENTORY MANAGEMENT

The need for aggregate inventory
management

Today, the typical production and inventory control manager operates in an awkward situation. He seldom has the necessary information to show the true inventory alternatives to his management, in order to assist them in making policy. Since the total inventory investment is of vital concern to higher management, they have typically set some arbitrary inventory policies, such as: "total inventory must not exceed four million dollars." These policies are probably not the best from an overall point of view. More often than not, the financial vice-president, for example, will set the inventory policy without ever recognizing the effect that it will have on customer service. The sales vice-president is even less likely to recognize the balance that must be struck between customer service and inventory investment.

A more rational approach to inventory would require that the production control executive spell out how much lot-size inventory investment would be required in aggregate, and what the setup and ordering costs corresponding to that inventory investment would be. He could also point out the extra inventory that would be required if it were desired to reduce the setup costs. He should also be able to show the inventory required to give any desired level of customer service, the work in process level required to maintain a steady flow of work without excessive downtime and the amount of "anticipation" or seasonal inventory required *vs.* the alternative capacity change, cost of hiring, layoff, overtime, etc.

The present state of the art of production control is such that few executives in this field can do a very good job of pointing out these alternatives. Moreover, many systems in operation today leave so much to be desired that it is unrealistic to say that a particular inventory level is required to meet a customer service level objective, when improved systems could probably both reduce inventory *and* improve service.

Nevertheless, as systems improve and business executives demand more substantial information on which to base their policies, the need for aggregate inventory management information will become more pressing. In some areas—such as the EOQ or lot-size decision—calculations that are not done in aggregate are unrealistic. Techniques for making aggregate lot-size calculations are available today. In other areas, such as work-in-process inventory, very little has been done to calculate the *correct* levels and, as a result, most—if not all—companies carry far too much. This chapter, then, will deal with two areas of aggregate inventory management in some detail, and will discuss the logic behind other aggregate inventory calculations.

The total lot-size inventory

In Chapter 4, some of the problems arising in the application of EOQ's were discussed. These centered around the costs used in the formulas, and the basic assumptions in the derivation of these formulas that these costs are proportional to the lot-size selected.

Even more important reasons for the surprising lack of application of this potentially powerful concept, however, are the problems arising because practitioners must deal with *total* inventories and with *changes* in operations.

EOQ formulas apply to individual items and indicate a desired optimum condition for each item based on some definite assumptions regarding costs. They do not indicate the total results in either inventory or operating conditions (setups needed, number of orders to be handled, etc.) which can be expected, and neither do they give any consideration to the changes in these from the present situation.

Intuitive order quantities are seldom economical. If set by manufacturing people concerned with the costs involved in setting up machines, they will be too large and, conversely, they will be too small if established by individuals more concerned with the costs associated with inventory.

Introduction of EOQ's in such cases may not really improve the actual situation, and can probably have an upsetting effect. The larger number of orders generated in a period of time by EOQ's that turn out to be smaller than the present lots may be beyond the capacity of those employed in setting-up. They may even be beyond the capacity of the equipment, if time cannot be spared from production for setup and changeover. If present order quantities are too small, EOQ's will cause substantial increases in the lot-size inventory and may strain financial resources or overcrowd available space. To prevent such unpleasant surprises, EOQ's should not be introduced (or changed substantially) without studying the total inventory and the changes in operating conditions which will result.

When inventories are reduced by the introduction of EOQ's, whether or not the savings resulting from reduction in invested capital, lower obsolescence and deterioration, lower taxes, etc. can actually be pinpointed, the inventory reduction should be of real value wherever capital so released can be put to work promptly in other areas. When EOQ's produce fewer orders, however, savings may never be realized. Unless *fewer* buyers or setup men are actually employed, larger order quantities (and correspondingly fewer orders to handle) will only increase inventory costs without achieving the offsetting savings in operating costs.

Obviously, to prevent increasing total costs by applying economical order quantities, all effects on total inventory and total operating conditions must be investigated.

Inventory carrying cost—a policy variable

A basically different approach to EOQ determination is needed. Based on the standard EOQ equation, formula (4-1):

$$\text{EOQ} = \sqrt{\frac{2AS}{I}} \qquad (4\text{-}1)$$

it is evident that the EOQ *and the total lot-size inventory* can be increased if a lower value of the carrying cost I is used, and can be reduced if a larger I is employed. R. L. Van DeMark[1] suggested this in 1960.

In 1961, R. G. Brown[2] suggested that I should be considered a

---

[1] Van DeMark, R. L., "Hidden Controls for Inventory," *Proceedings of the 1960 APICS Annual Conference,* Detroit, Michigan.

[2] Brown, R. G., "Use of the Carrying Charge to Control Cycle Stocks," *APICS Quarterly Bulletin,* July 1961.

management "policy variable" to control the cycle stock or lot-size inventory. This interpretation of the real meaning of I holds the key to the true function and application of EOQ's in the management of lot-size inventories.

This concept now has many adherents among practitioners who consider that the inventory carrying cost, while it is a very real business expense, cannot be identified as a single "magic" number any more than the "cost of a stockout"—an equally real business expense—can be expressed as a specific dollar value. While these two "costs" are needed concepts for the derivation of useful mathematical formulas, the search for fixed, "true" numbers to be used in their place can be a frustrating experience and should not obscure the real-life factors which determine the economies.

How can the advantages of using the EOQ concept be realized without having a precise value of I to use in the formula? Some simple examples of the use of inspection to redistribute the number of orders among a family of items to get a lower inventory investment were discussed in Chapter 4. A simple technique to calculate individual order quantities to obtain the lowest total lot-size inventory for a family of items without changing the number of orders written was also described in Chapter 4. It was shown that total inventory could be held constant, and that a reduction could be obtained in the number of orders written by a variation of the same technique.

While this oversimplified technique was developed principally as a teaching tool, it does give some insight into the type of approach that can be used when applying EOQ in the real business world, where constraints are almost always present. Some of the limitations in real-life which must be considered when applying the EOQ concept are:

1. A limit on the space available for storage

2. A limit on the number of orders the clerical force can process

3. A limit on the number of setups the labor force can make

4. A limit on the time productive equipment can remain idle while it is being set up and still produce the total requirements

5. A limit on the amount of money that can be invested in inventory

A technique for handling EOQ's in aggregate and dealing with problems of constraints on the EOQ calculation was developed as part of a special project for the American Production and Inventory Control Society[1]. The following section will describe this technique in detail.

The LIMIT technique

LIMIT (Lot-size Inventory Management Interpolation Technique) is designed to handle a family of items which passes over common manufacturing facilities. All the parts that pass through a screw machine department or a milling machine department or all parts purchased by one buyer would be logical groups to be handled with LIMIT.

The LIMIT calculations can be made manually or on a computer. These calculations are simple and straightforward—even if a computer is available, they should be made manually on a sample number of items by the practitioner to insure complete understanding of the concept. For large numbers of items, a computer program is the practical day-to-day way to apply this technique.

LIMIT is a two-phase technique: in the first phase, trial economic lot-sizes are calculated for each item in the chosen group using the standard EOQ equation, such as formula (4-1). The total setup hours required for these "economic" lot-sizes is then compared with the total setup hours required for the present lot-sizes. New "LIMIT" order quantities are then calculated which result in a total of setup hours equal to the present total. The result is usually to reduce the total lot-size inventory very substantially without changing total setup hours. Thus, benefits from reduced inventory investment are obtained with no change in operating conditions.

In the second phase, a series of alternatives is presented for the family of items, showing the effect on the lot-size inventory of changing the present ordering conditions. It reveals what happens to inventory when more orders are placed or more time is spent on setting-up machines. The number of alternatives can be varied to suit the existing conditions. This phase of the program presents for study the alternatives available if it is desired to move in controlled steps from present conditions toward operations which result in lower total costs.

LIMIT manual technique

For purposes of illustration, an example will be used involving 10 parts. These are all of the items machined on a group of 4 milling machines

---

[1] *Management of Lot-Size Inventories,* American Production and Inventory Control Society, Chicago, 1963.

Figure 6-1

Lot-Size Inventory Management Interpolation Technique
LIMIT Calculations

| | | 0.20 | Inventory carrying charge | | | | | | |
| | | $2.80 | Setup cost per hour | | | | | | |
(1) Item no.	(2) Annual usage	(3) Setup hrs. per ord.	(4) Unit cost	(5) Pres. order qty.	(6) Yearly setup hrs. pres.	(7) Trial order qty.	(8) Yearly setup hrs. trial	(9) Limit order qty.	(10) Yearly setup hrs. LIMIT
1 A	3000	5.5	6.12	600	27.5	274	60.0	391	42.3
2 B	2000	6.0	2.85	350	34.3	343	35.0	490	24.4
3 C	8000	7.0	0.56	1500	37.4	1673	33.6	2389	23.4
4 D	1100	4.0	2.26	400	11.0	233	18.9	333	13.2
5 E	600	4.0	4.08	300	8.0	128	18.8	183	13.1
6 F	1200	2.0	0.91	950	2.5	271	8.9	387	6.2
7 G	300	4.0	3.09	150	8.0	104	11.6	149	8.1
8 H	2000	2.0	0.42	1000	4.0	516	7.7	737	5.4
9 I	275	8.0	2.05	275	8.0	173	12.7	247	8.9
10 J	615	6.0	0.79	310	11.8	361	10.2	516	7.2
Total	19,090	---	----	5835	152.5	4076	217.4	5822	152.2

in a factory. The following data is required for each item in order to perform the LIMIT calculations:

1. Annual usage in units
2. Unit cost
3. Present order quantity
4. Setup hours per order
5. Setup cost per hour, including paperwork costs

Figure 6-1 shows the data for the 10 items that have been chosen for this example. In addition, a setup cost of $2.80 per hour is assumed to be the same for all 10 items. The first series of calculations is then made to determine the present annual setup requirement for each part and the total setup for all 10 items. These are determined by dividing the annual usages by the present order quantities to find the number of setups, and then multiplying by the setup hours per order, as follows:

$$\text{Yearly setup} = \frac{\text{Annual usage}}{\text{Present order quantity}} \times \text{Setup hours per order}$$

For example, the calculation for Item 1A is:

$$\frac{3000}{600} \times 5.5 = 27.5 \text{ hours yearly}$$

Figure 6-1 shows the annual setup hours for each item calculated in this manner and the total for the family under the heading "Yearly setup hrs. pres."

The next step in the LIMIT analysis is to calculate trial order quantities. This is done using the standard EOQ formula and the data from Fig. 6-1:

$$EOQ = \sqrt{\frac{2US}{IC}} \qquad (4\text{--}6)$$

where: $U = $ Annual usage, pieces

$S = $ Setup cost per setup (setup hours per order $\times$ setup cost per hour)

$I = $ Inventory carrying cost expressed as a decimal fraction

$C = $ Unit cost

Some reasonable value of the inventory carrying cost should be used in the formula to calculate the trial order quantity. The specific value of the inventory carrying cost used in this first calculation is not of great significance because the order quantities eventually obtained as LIMIT order quantities will be the same regardless of the value selected. Using a reasonable value of I, however, shows what would result if the standard approach to EOQ calculations were adopted and the trial order quantities were used directly.

For Item 1A, the following answer would be obtained for the trial order quantity using the EOQ formula and a carrying cost, I, equal to 0.20:

$$T. O. Q. = \sqrt{\frac{2(3000) \times (5.5 \times 2.80)}{(.20) \times (6.12)}} = 274$$

Similarly, an order quantity is calculated for each item and is entered in the "Trial order quantity" column, as shown in Fig. 6-1.

The yearly setup hours resulting from the use of the trial order quantities are then determined in the same manner used to calculate the yearly setup for the present order quantities. Item 1A is calculated as follows:

$$\frac{3000}{274} \times 5.5 = 60.0$$

This trial setup is calculated for each item and entered in the column headed: "Yearly setup hours, trial." The column is then totaled, as in Fig. 6-1. Note that the order quantities calculated using an inventory carrying cost of 20% would give a 30% decrease in the total order quantity, but would cause a 43% increase in setup hours over the present order quantities.

The next step is to determine the order quantities which will result in the same total annual setup hours as the present order quantities. Having calculated the total setup hours that would result from the present order quantity ($152\frac{1}{2}$ hours), and the total yearly setup hours that result from the trial order quantities (217.4), the LIMIT formulas can now be applied to calculate LIMIT order quantities. The derivation of these formulas is shown in Appendix V.[1]

$$\text{LIMIT formula } \#1: \quad I_L = I_T \left(\frac{H_L}{H_T}\right)^2 \qquad (6\text{-}1)$$

and:

$$\text{LIMIT formula } \#2: \quad M = \left(\frac{H_T}{H_L}\right) \qquad (6\text{-}2)$$

where: H_L = Total setup hours resulting from present order quantities, which will be equal to the total for the LIMIT order quantities, since this is the *limiting* factor

H_T = Total setup hours resulting from trial order quantities

I_T = Inventory carrying cost used to calculate trial order quantities

I_L = The implied inventory carrying cost used in calculating the LIMIT order quantities

LIMIT Formula #1 is used to determine the implied inventory carrying cost that would be used in the EOQ formula to calculate LIMIT order quantities so that the total setup hours associated with these lot sizes will be approximately equal to those resulting from present lot sizes. LIMIT formula #2 provides a multiplying factor M to convert trial order quantities simply and directly to LIMIT order quantities, eliminating the need to recalculate these using the square-root formula with the implied inventory carrying cost. LIMIT order quantities will be identical in both cases and will be the most economical lot sizes that can be used while staying within the present setup hour limitation.

The following illustrates the calculations of the LIMIT order quantities and the resulting yearly setup hours in Fig. 6-1. Using LIMIT formula #1 and LIMIT formula #2, the implied inventory carrying cost and the multiplier factor are determined as:

---

[1]LIMIT formula #1 is equation (15) and formula #2 is equation (19) in Appendix V. Subscript "*a*" becomes "*T*" and subscript "*b*" becomes "*L*" in these formulas to convert from the general derivation to mnemonic subscripts for clarity in practical applications.

$$I_L = .20 \left(\frac{152.5}{217.4}\right)^2 = .098$$

$$M = \left(\frac{217.4}{152.5}\right) = 1.428$$

Using the multiplier factor, the LIMIT order quantity for Item 1A is calculated as follows:

Trial order quantity $\times$ multiplier factor $=$ LIMIT order quantity

$$274 \times 1.428 = 391$$

Similarly, the order quantity is calculated for each item and entered in the table as shown in Fig. 6-1.

The yearly setup hours resulting from the use of the LIMIT order quantities are calculated as before. For Item 1A, for example, the calculation would be:

$$\tfrac{3000}{391} \times 5.5 = 42.3$$

This setup hour calculation is then made for each item and entered in the column headed "Yearly setup hours, LIMIT" and this column is totaled. Note that the total yearly setups are equal for both the present and LIMIT order quantities, which was the desired result. There is apparently no reduction made in the total number of pieces in the order quantities by the LIMIT calculations. Extending these ordering quantities by the unit costs, however, will show that there has been a substantial reduction in the total value of the average lot-size inventory.

A comparison of the three sets of order quantities is shown in Fig. 6-2 for both pieces and dollars. The average lot-size inventory (one-half

Figure 6-2

Average Lot-Size Inventory Value

	Pieces				Dollars		
No.	Present	Trial	LIMIT	Unit cost	Present	Trial	LIMIT
1A	600	274	391	$6.12	$3672	$1677	$2393
2B	350	343	490	2.85	998	977	1396
3C	1500	1673	2389	0.56	840	937	1338
4D	400	233	333	2.26	904	527	753
5E	300	128	183	4.08	1224	522	747
6F	950	271	387	0.91	864	246	352
7G	150	104	149	3.09	464	321	460
8H	1000	516	737	0.42	420	217	309
9I	275	173	247	2.05	564	354	506
10J	310	361	516	0.79	245	285	407
Total	5835	4076	5822		$10,195	$6063	$8661

Figure 6-3

Implied inventory cost (%)	Total setup hours	Total setup cost (at $2.80 per hour)	Total avg. order qty. inv. ($)	Mult. factor
(Present)	152.50	$ 427	$ 5097.50	— — —
4.2 %	100.00	$ 280	$ 6660.00	2.2
9.5 %	150.00	$ 420	$ 4550.00	1.5
9.8 % (LIMIT)	152.20	$ 426	$ 4330.50	1.4
17.0 %	200.00	$ 560	$ 3340.00	1.1
20.0 % (Trial)	217.40	$ 609	$ 3031.50	1.0
26.5 %	250.00	$ 700	$ 2730.00	0.9
38.0 %	300.00	$ 840	$ 2120.00	0.7
52.0 %	350.00	$ 980	$ 1820.00	0.6
68.0 %	400.00	$ 1120	$ 1515.00	0.5

the total order quantity) for the LIMIT order quantities is actually $767 less than it was with the present order quantities. This is a reduction of 15% in inventory investment with *no* increase in operating expense. In the preceding steps, the LIMIT order quantities were calculated to obtain the most economical order quantities possible within the present setup limitation.

Illustrating the second phase of the LIMIT calculations, Fig. 6-3 shows the total lot-size inventories that will result from various alternative setup limitations calculated using LIMIT formula #2. For example, if management wanted to know what the minimum average lot-size inventory would be for this family of items using only 250 hours of setup time, it would be determined as follows:

$$M = \frac{217.4}{250} = 0.87 \quad (\text{or } 0.9)$$

The corresponding value of the total trial order quantity in dollars (from Fig. 6-2) is $6063. The total lot-size inventory for a 250-hour setup limitation would therefore be:

$$\$6063 \times 0.9 = \$5460$$

and the average lot-size inventory would be:

$$\frac{\$5460}{2} = \$2730$$

Figure 6-3 shows the average order quantity inventory for various alternative setup levels for this family of items. It also shows the data for present conditions and for the trial and LIMIT calculations. As stated previously, it is possible to reduce the present inventory level without increasing the setup cost. Inspection of Fig. 6-3 shows it is also possible to reduce the total setup requirement without increasing the average inventory level. A setup total somewhere between 100 and 150 hours will yield the same total average order quantity inventory as the present $5097.50. Both of these result in savings with no offsetting increases in cost.

The data in Fig. 6-3 can also be presented as a curve, such as is shown in Fig. 6-4. The present condition is shown as point "A" and the LIMIT situation is point "B". Holding inventory constant and reducing setup costs is illustrated by point "C." The trial order situation is represented by point "D." The curve shows the lowest total average order quantity inventory which can be obtained by operating with the setup hours shown.

Figure 6-4

Curve of Lot-Size Inventory vs. Setup

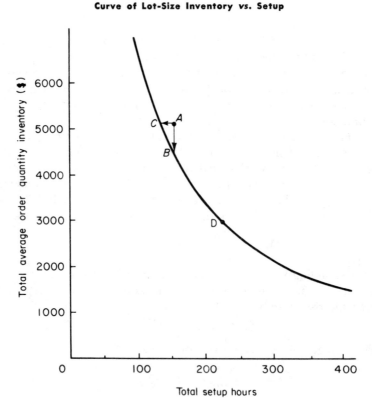

Total setup hours

The example used here involved a family of items having a setup limitation. The technique can be used equally well to solve a problem for purchased parts where the limitation is based on the number of orders. In this case, the items would be grouped according to vendors or buyers. When worthwhile discount schedules are involved, the LIMIT-discount program covered later in this Chapter should be used.

Advantages of LIMIT

The standard approach to economic ordering quantities assumes that a precise value for the inventory carrying cost can be determined. The LIMIT concept makes it possible to realize substantial savings through the use of lot quantities obtained by applying the EOQ principles without the need for determining a precise value for the inventory carrying cost.

In addition, it has the following advantages:

1. It is simple to understand and easy to apply.

2. It points the way to immediate gains—either decreased inventory investment or lower ordering costs, without any offsetting increases.

3. It shows the real-life economies of EOQ as they apply to a specific situation and what action must be taken to attain these economies.

4. LIMIT presents information on *total* inventories, *total* ordering costs and *total* inventory investment costs, and is not restricted to individual item considerations.

5. LIMIT is on management's "wavelength." It shows the alternative of increasing investment *vs.* reducing operating costs in the familiar terms that management needs to manage the lot-size inventory.

Applications of LIMIT

One of the first applications of LIMIT was in a large screw machine department. Standard EOQ calculations had been used to generate lot-sizes and, as a result, far more setup time was required than could be provided by the available manpower in the department. There were no additional trained setup men to be hired in the area, and training operators to be setup men would have required a very long time. The economic ordering quantities generated by the formula were, as a consequence, not at all economical. In fact, the company had to purchase screw machine parts from outside sources because their machine utilization decreased substantially as a result of the additional setups required by the economic ordering quantities. The LIMIT formulas were used to recalculate lot-sizes for all the parts made in the screw machine department, so that setups stayed within the setup hour limitation that existed—these were the *most* economical lot-sizes for the existing circumstances. LIMIT also showed the management of this company the overall economics of the application of EOQ's and how to reduce the lot-size inventory by increasing setup hours as more trained setup men were added.

Plant management people whose experience has been primarily in manufacturing are frequently disturbed by the amount of setup time that is needed. They feel that too many setup hours are being generated to allow the most economical operation of the plant. Use of the LIMIT program shows what the total setup hour requirement should be with the present lot-sizes and what the lot-sizes would be using whatever inventory carrying cost is considered appropriate by the company, and it shows the range of alternate decisions. After reviewing these alternatives in one plant, management personnel who were previously concerned about having too much setup time decided to increase the amount of setup. The fact that LIMIT shows them the inventory costs implied by their decisions aids them in establishing more rational policies that can better balance the real alternatives in lot-size inventory management. The LIMIT calculations show the total lot-size inventory *vs.* total setup cost decision in terms familiar to management, which is accustomed to making decisions when additional investment must be balanced against decreased operating cost.

While the LIMIT concept was developed around the philosophy of varying the inventory carrying cost to suit management policy, it can be used as a simulator even if management has a known inventory carrying cost which they believe to be correct for their circumstances. One of the two possible results of the application of economic ordering quantities is to increase the lot-size inventory. Using the LIMIT calculations, the amount of this increase can be predicted and even planned in practical steps. Plans can then be made to have the necessary cash and space available to handle this increase. Since the corresponding reduction in setup hours is also shown, definite plans can be made to realize the setup savings that should result from increases in the lot-size inventory.

With the standard approach to economic ordering quantities, these savings are seldom known definitely in advance and are therefore seldom achieved. A reduction in setup hours of 15% or 20% among a group of set up men would rarely result in a proportional savings to the company, unless management knew about this reduction ahead of time and had made specific arrangements to capture these savings. This is also true of reductions in clerical costs associated with preparing purchase or manufacturing orders.

LIMIT is also of great value to the production control manager when the addition of automatic equipment is being considered. Most companies today are constantly exploring applications of equipment which is complex and usually requires long and expensive setups. This results in larger lot-sizes and very substantial increases in the lot-size inventories of the parts made on the equipment. The LIMIT technique can be used to show the increased inventory investment and space requirements with the new equipment in comparison with the present situation. The result will be a far more practical and satisfactory application of automated equipment, since *all* related factors will have been considered.

The idea of using the inventory carrying cost as a management policy variable rather than a fixed-cost factor enables the practitioner to cope with changing real-life conditions in industry. It frees him from dependence on faith in a formula and provides him with some valuable tools in managing the lot-size inventory.

LIMIT-discount

The standard EOQ calculation or the LIMIT program can be used to arrive at the optimum ordering quantities for manufactured parts. When material is purchased, however, there is frequently a discount schedule offering a reduction in unit price for larger purchases.

The normal method for handling discounts was covered in Chapter 4. Basically, calculations are made to determine whether the added inventory carried because of the larger lot-size will cost more or less than will be saved by taking advantage of the discount. Once again, the entire decision hinges upon the inventory carrying cost used to determine what the added inventory will cost. This cost is then balanced against the total savings from the discount and from the fewer number of orders being placed.

One of the most serious problems for the practitioner arises because practically every discount appears attractive. If every discount were taken, however, the inventory could be increased beyond the financial capacity or beyond the available storage space. It is not a novelty for a production control manager to wonder where to store material ordered to obtain savings from an attractive discount schedule.

The standard method for handling discounts is very much like an individual going to a stockbroker and asking him what he recommends as an attractive rate of return on an investment in common stocks. The broker indicates that $5\frac{1}{2}$–6% is a good figure and recommends several stocks presently earning at this level. It is obvious that the investor is limited as to the number of shares of stock he can buy by the capital he has to invest, regardless of how many attractive opportunities are available. An investor begins by determining how much capital he has to invest and then picks the investments which he hopes will yield him the greatest return. Discounts should be handled in the same way, recognizing that funds and space are limited, rather than basing all investment decisions solely upon an inventory carrying cost that is, at best, only an approximation, and which ignores the fact that some discounts yield higher returns than others.

How can this be done? LIMIT-discount is a technique for evaluating many discounts simultaneously. Using LIMIT-discount, the amount of money saved by the discount and the reduction in orders (because of larger order quantities when the discount is accepted) is expressed as a percentage of the required increase in the lot-size inventory level. This percentage is called the *discount preference ratio,* and is really an expression of the rate of return on investment that each discount opportunity will yield. Using the discount preference ratio, each possible discount (there are often several available for a given item) is ranked according to its rate of return on investment. This shows the manager the most preferable discounts, listed in order of their attractiveness, and also shows him the added investment required in order to obtain the discount. He can now set a limitation on the amount of extra money that will be put into inventory, and he can be sure that he is realizing the maximum savings within that limitation.

The steps in LIMIT-discount are:

1. Choose a group of purchased items (these may be product, vendor, or buyer groupings).
2. Calculate economic order quantities for each item.
3. Obtain the discount schedule for each item from the vendors.
4. For each possible discount, calculate what will be saved by the discount, what will be saved by placing fewer purchase orders per year and the added investment that will be required in order to attain this saving.

5. Express the savings as a percentage of the added investment to obtain the "discount preference ratio."
6. Rank each available discount according to the discount preference ratio, with the highest ratio item first.
7. List all available discounts showing savings for each *vs.* investment and cumulative discount savings *vs.* cumulative inventory investment.

The following example will illustrate the technique. Figure 6-5 shows the basic data concerning economic ordering quantities before considering discounts for 10 items. All of the annual figures and lot-sizes are expressed in dollars for simplicity of calculation. Figure 6-6 lists the available discount schedule. All of the percentages are the amount to be saved by going to the first discount order quantity. For example, Item 1342 has a present lot-size of $1720, a 2% discount is available if Item 1342 is ordered in lots of $10,000. A further 1.6% discount is available (this 1.6% is a percentage that can be saved on the *already* discounted price used with the previous lot-size) if Item 1342 is ordered in lots of $20,000 each. *Each discount is handled as if it were a separate item* (and, in fact, in the final ranking the two available discounts for Item 1342 rank in positions 5 and 9, respectively).

Figure 6-5

LIMIT—discount

Economic Ordering Quantities Before Considering Discounts

Item #	Annual forecast	EOQ ($)	Orders per year
1342	$ 18,350	$ 1720	10.7
1343	5700	920	6.2
1434	4480	825	5.4
1460	2480	775	3.2
1469	2450	775	3.2
1471	1090	408	2.7
1620	926	368	2.5
1633	840	362	2.3
1635	565	296	1.9
1701	485	272	1.8
Totals		$ 6721	39.9
Average total lot-size inventory	$ 3360		

Figure 6-6

LIMIT—discount

The Discount Schedule

Item #	First discount at minimum % order qty.		Second discount at minimum % order qty.	
1342	2.0 %	$10,000	1.6%	$20,000
1343	12.0 %	$10,000		
1434	11.0 %	$5000	10.0%	$10,000
1460	7.0 %	$5000		
1469		None available		
1471	7.0 %	$3000		
1620		None available		
1633	5.0 %	$1000	3.0%	$2000
1635		None available		
1701	5.0 %	$1000		

Figure 6-7 shows the calculation of the discount preference ratio. The first five columns are taken from Figs. 6-5 and 6-6. The suffixes 1D and 2D refer to first and second discounts. The annual discount is calculated by multiplying the discount percentage rate by the annual forecast and represents the amount of money to be saved annually because of the lower unit cost. Note that the annual forecast for the second discount for Item 1342 is different from that for the first. This is because the LIMIT-discount program assumes that the first discount has already been taken or the second one would not even be under consideration.

The *discounted annual usage* is the total annual forecast minus the value of the annual discounts taken. It is the net cost of one year's supply at the discount price.

The eighth column in Fig. 6-7 shows the number of orders per year that would be placed if each discount were accepted. The ninth column shows the number of orders per year saved by taking each discount, and is obtained by subtracting the figure in the eighth column from that in the fourth. To keep this example simple, it has been assumed that the cost of placing orders is negligible and no annual savings is included because of the reduction in number of orders placed.

The tenth column lists the discounted order quantities and the eleventh shows the average added inventory resulting from accepting the discount. This calculation is made by subtracting the order quantity before discount from the discount order quantity, and dividing the answer

Figure 6-7
LIMIT—discount
Calculating the Discount Preference Ratio

(1) Item	(2) Amount forecast $	(3) O. Q. before disc.	(4) Ord. per year	(5) Disc. %	(6) Ann. disc.	(7) Disc. annual usage $	(8) Disc. ord. per year	(9) Ord. saved per year	(10) Disc. O.Q. $	(11) Avg. added inv.	(12) Disc. pref. ratio	(13) Rank
1342–1D	$ 18,350	$ 1720	10.7	2.0 %	$ 367	$ 17,983	1.8	8.9	$ 10,000	$ 4140	8.9	5
1342–2D	17,983	10,000	1.8	1.6	286	17,697	0.9	0.9	20,000	5000	5.7	9
1343	5700	920	6.2	12.0	685	5015	0.5	5.7	10,000	4540	15.1	3
1434–1D	4480	825	5.4	11.0	494	3986	0.8	4.6	5000	2087	23.6	1
1434–2D	3986	5000	0.8	10.0	399	3587	0.4	0.4	10,000	2500	15.9	2
1460	2480	775	3.2	7.0	174	2306	0.5	2.7	5000	2113	8.2	6
1471	1090	408	2.7	7.0	76	1014	0.3	2.4	3000	1296	5.9	8
1633–1D	840	362	2.3	5.0	42	798	0.8	1.5	1000	319	13.2	4
1633–2D	798	1000	0.8	3.0	24	774	0.4	0.4	2000	500	4.8	10
1701	485	272	1.8	5.0	24	461	0.5	1.3	1000	364	6.6	7

by two to determine the *average* extra inventory investment. Here is an example for Item 1342-ID:

Discount order quantity = $10,000
Order quantity before discount = $1720
Increase in order quantity = $8280
Increase in average lot-size inventory = $4140

The *discount preference ratio* is now calculated by expressing the annual discount savings (column 6) as a percentage of the average added inventory investment (column 11). An example for Item 1342-ID is shown:

Annual discount = $367
Average added inventory = $4140

$$\frac{\$367}{\$4140} = 8.9\% \text{ discount preference ratio}$$

The items under consideration are next ranked in order of their discount preference ratio, the highest one first.

Figure 6-8 is then drawn up showing the discount *vs.* investment situation in perspective. Some important points should be noted:

1. Before the discounts were considered, there were 39.9 orders placed per year and the

Figure 6-8

LIMIT—discount

Discount vs. Investment

				No. of orders					Average lot-size inv.
Present totals				39.9					$ 3360
Item	Disc. pref. ratio	Orders/ year saved	Cum. orders saved	No. of orders left	Disc.	Cum. disc.	Added inv.	Cum. added inv.	
1434-1D	23.6	4.6	4.6	35.3	$494	$494	$2087	$2087	
1434-2D	15.9	0.4	5.0	34.9	399	893	2500	4587	
1343	15.1	5.7	10.7	29.2	685	1578	4540	9127	
1633-1D	13.2	1.5	12.2	27.7	42	1620	319	9446	
1342-1D	8.9	8.9	21.1	18.8	367	1987	4140	13,586	
1460	8.2	2.7	23.8	16.1	174	2161	2113	15,699	
1701	6.6	1.3	25.1	14.8	24	2185	364	16,063	
1471	5.9	2.4	27.5	12.4	76	2261	1296	17,359	
1342-2D	5.7	0.9	28.4	11.5	286	2547	5000	22,359	
1633-2D	4.8	0.4	28.8	11.1	24	2571	500	22,859	

average lot-size inventory was $3360. (See Fig. 6-5.)

2. If all of the available discounts were taken, the number of orders would be reduced to 11.1 orders per year, but the inventory would have been increased by $22,859 to a new average lot-size inventory of $26,219. The savings resulting from a reduced number of orders was neglected in this example. The cumulative discount of $2571 would require an increased inventory investment of $22,859.

3. A good manager would undoubtedly move very slowly in considering a total investment increase of this magnitude for these few items. Using LIMIT-discount, he can go back over the individual discounts offered him and determine which ones he wants to accept. For example, Item 1434-ID has a first discount which is quite attractive at $494 and would require an additional inventory investment of only $2087. He can now go through item-by-item, determine how much he wants to invest and see what the corresponding savings will be.

LIMIT-discount can be done manually (as illustrated in the previous example). It is a fairly simple computer program to set up and is, of course, far more practical on the computer for a large number of items. The basic calculations can be varied to suit a particular company's situation. For example, if it were wished to attribute a cost of $5.00 for each purchase order placed, the savings from placing fewer orders could be added to the discount savings in calculating the discount preference ratio.

The basic advantage of LIMIT-discount is that it presents the results of ordering quantity decisions in terms that are familiar to management. The manager can see how much extra money he must invest and what savings will result from this investment. If he chooses to take all of the savings possible, he will know how much extra investment will have to be made, and he will also have a basis for estimating the amount of extra space required.

Unless funds and space are unlimited, the standard approach to discounts presents many problems to the practitioner. The LIMIT-discount approach removes such risks.

Using decision information to manage lot-size inventories

The techniques discussed in this chapter can be very helpful in calculating lot-sizes. They certainly will not solve all production and inventory control problems, but they do represent a more realistic approach than the standard EOQ and discount calculations. They must be used with judgment because they do not take into consideration all of the possible variables that enter into such decisions.[1]

Before using lot-sizes calculated by LIMIT or any other method, it is recommended that they be reviewed by manufacturing *and* production control personnel most closely associated with the manufacturing area that will produce the pieces, to be sure the lot-sizes are *reasonable*. In the LIMIT computer program, lot-sizes are not rounded-off, but are printed exactly as calculated. This is done deliberately so that the lot-sizes will be reviewed for reasonableness and then rounded-off as part of this review.

The man reviewing the lot-sizes should adjust them to take into consideration spoilage, deterioration, exceptional bulk or other factors not included in the calculations. Reference to Fig. 4-2 in Chapter 4 will show that total cost increases only slightly as the lot-size varies from the EOQ—particularly for *larger* lot-sizes. The minor loss of economy due to slight variations in the lot-sizes is more theoretical than real. The value of having lot-sizes that make sense is very tangible.

The standard LIMIT program works best where there is one major machine group (such as a screw machine or punch press department) under consideration. When an item goes through a sequence of operations, the decision information presented by LIMIT is not as clear-cut as it is when there is only one major machine group that is being set up. If, for example, an item goes through six different operations in sequence, LIMIT would handle all of these as one operation. The program can still be useful under these circumstances if the following suggestions are considered:

1. Run the LIMIT program first treating each major machine group as a separate operation. This will show what the desired lot-sizes would be if each operation were run separately.

2. Run the LIMIT program again, adding all of

---

[1] One point to remember is that reductions in order quantity generate more re-order periods and thus more frequent exposure to stockout. Consequently, the total inventory will not be reduced in direct proportion since reserve stock will increase. Appendix IV shows an example of this phenomenon.

the setup times together for all operations and treating the group of operations as if it were one machine group.

3. Compare the lot-sizes that result from these calculations to determine the most practical lot-sizes. It may be desirable to break up the operation sequence with an inventory of parts held in semi-finished condition. A detailed treatment of all the possible alternatives is beyond the scope of this book.

Even in circumstances where LIMIT must be run as a simulation program in order to study different lot-sizes, it definitely helps the practitioner to avoid the pitfalls of the standard EOQ approach by showing him where setup hours will have to be increased or where the inventory will increase as a result of economic lot-size decisions.

A computer and the LIMIT program can be of great value even if the calculated LIMIT lot-sizes are not used because the program focuses attention on inventory and setup totals. To use the LIMIT program this way, the lot-sizes that have been determined by some desired means are entered into the LIMIT card format as *present lot-sizes,* and the LIMIT program then makes the balance of the calculations as discussed above.

There are other effects of the lot-size decision that often must be considered. If, for example, there is only one machine to perform a particular type of work, the portion of its capacity occupied in producing the total parts required in a year may leave very little time for set-up, and lot-sizes will consequently be very large. These lot-sizes will not be chosen from the point of view of the economics of balancing setups *vs.* inventory, but to meet the setup restrictions on the equipment.

The effect they will have upon reserve stock due to the cycling problem must also be considered. Large lot-sizes will require long running times, and higher order points (including extra reserve stocks) will have to be set for each item to cover the additional lead time each item will undergo while waiting to be processed. It is almost certain that some jobs will be in the machine or waiting for it when the order for another item is generated. This item will then have to wait for the current backlog of orders to be completed before it can be run. This waiting time can be many times the normal processing time and will increase inventories because it requires higher levels of reserve stock.

This is typical of the situations met in real-life, where production and inventory control decisions are highly complex. No single calculation can take into account all of the variables encountered in manufacturing situations. Formulas, techniques and programs discussed in this chapter can be a great aid to good judgment, but should be used with discretion and with the realization that they alone do not solve all of the problems.

These techniques attempt to deal with the total lot-size inventory and to show the real-life implications of the mathematical calculations. Other techniques can be used to deal with other segments of the inventory in aggregate. The following sections deal with the reserve stock *vs.* customer service inventory decision.

The concept of customer service vs. inventory investment

The balance between customer service and inventory investment is seldom the result of a well thought-out policy in most businesses today. It is not always recognized by management that there is a basic relationship between inventory levels and customer service and that these are not independent variables. The better the desired service to customers, the higher the finished goods inventory must be in a business using effective inventory control systems.

In Chapter 5, the method for computing statistical reserve stocks was presented using a mean absolute deviation computed from the demand data for a particular item. An item designated "Item M" will be used below to illustrate the calculation of the service *vs.* inventory investment relationship over a range of service levels. The pertinent data needed to make the calculations are:

> Annual forecast $= 26{,}000$ units
> Order quantity $= 2000$ units
> Mean absolute deviation $= 209$ units
> Unit cost $= \$1.35$

The reserve stock required for each service level can be calculated using the method shown in Chapter 5. A typical calculation for one such level is as follows:

1. Tolerable number of stockouts per year $= 4$
2. Number of exposures per year $=$ Annual forecast divided by order quantity $= 26{,}000/2000 = 13$
3. Service fraction $= (13 - 4)/13 = \frac{9}{13}$
4. Service ratio $= \frac{9}{13} = 69.2\%$
5. Required number of mean absolute deviations (from Fig. 5-7) $= 0.75$
6. Reserve stock required $= 0.75 \times$ the mean absolute deviation $= 0.75 \times 209 = 157$

Figure 6-9

Service vs. Reserve Stock Tabulation
Item M

Data:
Mean absolute deviation = 209
Order quantity = 2000
Annual forecast = 26,000
Unit cost = $1.35

SO/Year	Exposures	Service fraction	Service ratio	Required #MAD	Reserve
4	13/Year	9/13	69.2%	0.75	157
2	13/Year	11/13	84.5%	1.29	268
1	13/Year	12/13	92.4%	1.80	376
One in 2	26	25/26	96.1%	2.20	460
One in 3	39	38/39	97.4%	2.40	501
One in 4	52	51/52	98.1%	2.60	544
One in 5	65	64/65	98.5%	2.70	565
One in 10	130	129/130	99.2%	3.00	626
Never	---	---	100%	5.00	1044

Figure 6-10

Service vs. Reserve Stock Curve
Item M

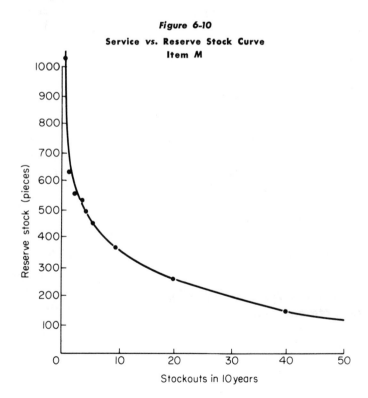

Similarly, the required level of reserve stock inventory can be calculated for different service levels. Figure 6-9 shows this calculation for Item M at nine different service levels. The amount of reserve stock inventory required for theoretically perfect service (never out of stock) is almost seven times the amount that would be required if four stockouts per year could be tolerated.

This relationship is plotted on a curve in Fig. 6-10, which shows the reserve stock inventory (in pieces) required for various levels of service. Here, the number of stockouts per year has been expressed as *stockouts in 10 years,* in order to have a uniform scale for all conditions included on the curve. This curve clearly illustrates the rapid increase in reserve stock as the required level of customer service is increased. Using such a curve, a reasonable level of customer service can be selected, and the required reserve stock can be determined to attain that service level.

In most real-life situations where reserve stock inventory has previously been determined intuitively, this statistical solution will provide an immediate improvement in the relationship between inventory and customer service. The most important aspect of this curve, however, is that it puts the conflict between customer service and inventory investment into perspective, showing production control and other management personnel the levels of finished goods inventory required to give corresponding levels of service to customers. This type of curve is a very useful management tool.

The number of items held in inventory ranges in the thousands in most businesses, and it would not be practical or significant to develop and analyze data and curves like this for each item. Production control must determine the required reserve stock for each item in order to establish order points, but these should be set after management has decided on the specific level of service to be provided. Furthermore to make its decision on service level, management needs service *vs.* investment data not on individual items, but on the total inventory of all items. The individual inventory items are significant to the inventory controller, but at higher levels of management, the concern is with the aggregate inventory investment.

Preparing total service vs. investment data

The same general method used to plot a service *vs.* investment curve for one item can be extended to a group of items, and the inventory investment required for an entire product line can be shown in relation

Figure 6-11. Service vs. Investment Calculations—Four Items

Item	No. Exp.	Serv. Fract.	Serv. Ratio	#MAD	1/2 Reserve	O.Q.	Avg. Inv. Units	Unit Cost	Avg. Inv. $
	For 8 Stockouts per year (2 per item):								
M	13	11/13	84.5%	1.29	268	1000	1268	1.35	$1710
N	12	10/12	83.4	1.20	1920	4000	5920	0.70	4140
O	6	4/6	66.7	0.54	146	1000	1146	0.90	1030
P	4	2/4	50.0	0	0	750	750	0.85	638
									$7518
	For 4 Stockouts per year (1 per item):								
M	13	12/13	92.4	1.80	376	1000	1376	1.35	$1860
N	12	11/12	91.6	1.75	2800	4000	6800	0.70	4760
O	6	5/6	83.3	1.20	325	1000	1325	0.90	1192
P	4	3/4	75.0	0.84	202	750	952	0.85	810
									$8622
	For 2 Stockouts per year (1 every other year per item)								
M	26	25/26	96.1	2.20	460	1000	1460	1.35	$1970
N	24	23/24	95.8	2.16	3460	4000	7460	0.70	5220
O	12	11/12	91.6	1.75	474	1000	1474	0.90	1325
P	8	7/8	87.5	1.45	348	750	1098	0.85	932
									$9447
	For 1 Stockout per year (1 every 4 years per item)								
M	52	51/52	98.1	2.60	544	1000	1544	1.35	$ 2085
N	48	47/48	98.0	2.56	4100	4000	8100	0.70	5660
O	24	23/24	95.8	2.16	585	1000	1585	0.90	1428
P	16	15/16	93.7	1.92	461	750	1211	0.85	1030
									$ 10,203
	For 1 Stockout every two years (1 every 8 years per item)								
M	104	103/104	99.1	2.95	616	1000	1616	1.35	$ 2181
N	96	95/96	99.0	2.91	4660	4000	8660	0.70	6060
O	48	47/48	98.0	2.56	694	1000	1694	0.90	1525
P	32	31/32	96.9	2.33	560	750	1310	0.85	1113
									$ 10,879
	For 1 Stockout every three years (1 every 12 years per item)								
M	156	155/156	99.4	3.14	656	1000	1656	1.35	$ 2219
N	144	143/144	99.3	3.10	4960	4000	8960	0.70	6260
O	72	71/72	98.6	2.75	745	1000	1745	0.90	1571
P	48	47/48	98.0	2.56	615	750	1365	0.85	1160
									$11,210
	For "Never"(99.9%)								
M	---	---	99.9	4	835	1000	1835	1.35	$ 2480
N	---	---	99.9	4	6400	4000	10,400	0.70	7270
O	---	---	99.9	4	1083	1000	2083	0.90	1878
P	---	---	99.9	4	960	750	1710	0.85	1452
									$ 13,080

to the customer service that will be provided.

In the following example, a service *vs.* investment curve will be calculated for a family of four items, Item M (used in the previous example), Item N, Item O, and Item P. Assume the following data:

Items	Annual usage	Order quantity	Unit cost	Mean absolute deviation
M	26,000	2000	1.35	209
N	96,000	8000	0.70	1600
O	12,000	2000	0.90	271
P	6,000	1500	0.85	240

Choosing a lowest service level of eight stockouts per year for the entire group of items (equivalent to two stockouts per item per year), the reserve stock calculations are made for the other items in the group in the same way as for Item M.

This calculation is shown for each of the four items in the top section of Fig. 6-11, where the required reserve stock for each item is shown in the column headed "Reserve." The next column shows the average cycle stock equal to one-half the order quantity for each item. The following column shows the total of the reserve stock plus one-half the order quantity (this is the average inventory in units). In order to express these inventories for the whole group in common terms, the average inventory is then extended by the unit cost for each item, and the total average inventory is expressed in dollars in the last column.

Figure 6-11 shows that a total average inventory of $7,518 would be required in order to provide a service level of eight stockouts per year for this group of items or two stockouts per year per item. Figure 6-11 also shows similar calculations for a total of four stockouts per year for the group of items and for subsequent increasingly higher service levels.

Figure 6-12 shows the total relationship of service *vs.* investment for this group of four items. It is a summary of the preceding tables with all the data expressed in dollars. In Fig. 6-13, these data are plotted as two curves, the lower curve showing the reserve stock portion and the upper curve showing the total inventory investment required for various service levels.

Most important from a practical point of view is the fact that in almost every real situation where the statistical computation replaces intuitive approaches to order points, a substantial improvement in the service *vs.* investment relationship can be attained immediately. It might be found,

Figure 6-12
Total Service vs. Investment Data
Four Items

No. of Stockouts Group service level		1/2 O.Q. $	$ R	Total average inventory
1–Yr. base	10–Yr. base			
8	80	$ 5687	$ 1831	$ 7518
4	40	5687	2935	8622
2	20	5687	3760	9447
1	10	5687	4516	10,203
1/2	5	5687	5192	10,879
1/3	3.3	5687	5523	11,210
"Never"	0	5687	7393	13,080

for example, that the current inventory investment equals $11,000 for the items shown in Fig. 6-13, and that approximately ten stockouts were occurring in ten years for the group. Using statistical methods to redistribute the reserve stocks, the curve shows that $11,000 worth of inventory investment should result in only four stockouts in ten years for this group. This is the same kind of improvement that was attained in Chapter 4 when lot-sizes were calculated using the square root relationship of the EOQ concept instead of intuitive methods. An immediate improvement was available to the practitioner, and other alternatives leading to even greater economies were shown.

In making this particular group of calculations, it was assumed that the number of stockouts should be kept equal for all items in the group. That is, if the total number of stockouts desired for the group equaled eight, then it should be spread out evenly across the items in the groups so that each item would have two stockouts per year. This is not always the case, and it might sometimes be desirable to have more frequent stockouts on some items than on others. This could be done by allocating the number of stockouts as desired among the items in the group, and then calculating the appropriate reserve stocks.

Showing management total service vs. investment charts

Looking at the curve in Fig. 6-13, it can be seen that the total investment in reserve stock needs to be increased almost fourfold as the service requirement is increased from two stockouts per item per year to *never*

Figure 6-13

Total Service vs. Investment Curve
Four Items

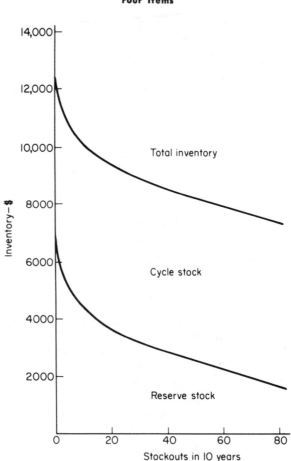

out of stock. Using such a curve, management can see the service *vs.* investment alternatives that are available, and it can—with the help of production control— determine a reasonable level of inventory for any group of items. The basic conflict between those who feel that inventory turnover rates are by themselves a good indicator of business efficiency and those who feel that customer service is the only measure of the effectiveness of inventory control can thus be quantified using statistical approaches to reserve stock determination.

This is the type of information with which management personnel are used to dealing. The calculations certainly do not give them the final answer directly. If, for example, the cost of a stockout were known, a formula could be developed to balance this cost against that of carrying the necessary inventory, and there would be very little need for management judgment. Unfortunately, neither of these costs can be determined accurately in most real-life business situations. In most businesses, they are recognized as real, yet highly nebulous costs that are not susceptible to being captured and expressed in specific numbers.

Experienced management personnel are accustomed to making decisions where all of the desired information is not available. They are constantly called on to use their experience and judgment in such situations. Nevertheless, production control personnel cannot merely collect information, express it in a form usable by management and then depend upon management to make a decision. Considerable help and guidance should be provided by production control personnel, who are in a position to recognize the implications of any decision regarding inventory level or desired customer service level.

With this type of approach, a far more rational decision on inventory investment can be made. Significant improvements can usually be made in the relationship between inventory investment and customer service. Once production control has presented this decision information and a particular inventory and customer service goal has been set, it becomes production control's job to operate the inventory control system so that these goals are met. This is done by setting up the reserve stock levels and order points that correspond to the service *vs.* investment level chosen and operating the inventory system using these order points.

Applications

While many others have suggested that a service *vs.* investment curve could be made for an individual item, the first application of a total service *vs.* investment curve for an entire product line known to the authors was made in 1959. This application was made for a group of 80 different items that constituted one "family" of purchased parts. Economic order quantities were calculated for each item and reserve stocks were computed as described in the beginning of Chapter 5. Both the cycle stock and reserve stock are included in the inventory figures shown in this curve, expressed in dollars of total inventory.

The curve developed for this family of 80 items is shown in Fig. 6-14. It can be seen that zero stockouts per year would require approximately $24,000 worth of inventory for the group. If it were decided to operate with $18,000 worth of inventory, there would be approximately 15 stockouts per year distributed among all of the items in the group (equivalent to approximately 1 stockout in 5 years for each item). The

Figure 6-14

Total Service vs. Investment Curve

Eighty Items

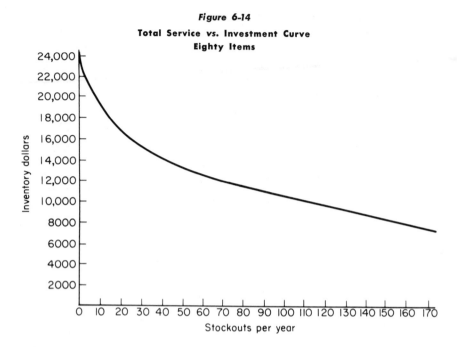

Stockouts per year

curve also shows that a further reduction from $18,000 to $12,000, for example, would result in a drastic increase in the number of stockouts per year to approximately seventy, or very close to 1 stockout per item per year, thus illustrating the relationship between customer service and inventory investment.

When this statistical inventory control system was first set up, the total inventory level for this group of items was equal to approximately $30,000 and the stockouts ran between 80 and 100 per year. The statistical calculations indicated that a substantial improvement in this relationship was possible and it was determined to try to keep the inventory level at approximately $18,000 and the stockouts at approximately 15 per year. In practice, the system worked very well: the inventory level seldom went above $21,000 or below $16,000, and there were 22 stockouts during the first year of operation.

One of the reasons for the fact that actual stockouts exceeded the level indicated by the statistical calculations was the method for counting stockouts. Statistically, a stockout is defined as a delivery period for an item when stock is not available to meet the total demand. There is no attempt made to measure the duration of this stockout. In practice, it was more practical to count the number of items out of stock each week and consider each occurrence as a stockout. Thus it was possible for one item to go out of stock and remain out for three weeks, in which case the number of stockouts would be counted as three rather than one.

After running the system for a short period of time, it was possible to correlate the statistical measure of service with the method of measuring actual customer service and to set the statistical measure of service somewhat higher than the level desired in order to attain the latter in practice. Interestingly enough, although the number of stockouts was actually half again as much as the number predicted by the statistics, the improvement in service had been so dramatic that this minor discrepancy caused no great concern. Management appreciated the "near-miss" as far better performance than the blind shooting which had preceded it.

One of the problems brought into focus by this approach to inventory control was that of lead time. The vendor for this group of purchased items, like so many other manufacturers, usually experienced an increase in lead time when his business was good and a decrease in lead time when his business was dropping. When he shipped in shorter-than-planned lead time, the result was a higher inventory, and when his lead time was extended the inventory level dropped and customer service suffered as a result. It became necessary to watch delivery performance very closely in order to keep the total inventory investment under control.

In operation, this was a highly successful inventory management system. It represented a substantial improvement in the service *vs.* investment relationship. Management personnel were pleased that they were at last able to determine the total inventory investment for this product line and choose the levels of inventory and customer service that they desired. Production control personnel had a challenging job in attaining the service and investment levels that they had predicted, yet these levels were not as difficult to attain in practice as had been anticipated. Overall, everyone concerned was highly satisfied that they were at last able to manage the total inventory investment directly rather than through a lot of individual decisions whose total effect could not be foreseen.

This particular application was based on manual calculations. These required constant revision, updating for changes in the forecast and demand variations. Because of the experimental nature of this first service *vs.* investment calculation, it was applied to a low-dollar-value product group. Eventually, after being in use for approximately two years, it had to be abandoned because of the excessive amount of manual effort involved in its upkeep.

Since that time, computers have become available to many production and inventory control people. Many companies use them to obtain periodic stock status reports, using exponential smoothing to forecast the demand for individual items and calculate the mean absolute deviation of forecast error on a regular basis. The reserve stock is then determined and incorporated with the updated item forecast into a floating order point for each item.

With this type of information regularly available, the maintenance required for a total inventory management system of the type presented in this chapter is reduced to manageable proportions. Figure 6-15 shows a total service *vs.* investment curve for a product group involving 125 items. This service *vs.* investment chart was calculated using the technique described in this chapter. Various levels of service for the entire product group were simulated and the group curve developed as a result of these simulations. Using the computer, these simulations take a very small amount of time, and the use of statistical concepts to develop a service *vs.* investment chart becomes thoroughly practical.

Figure 6-15

Total Service vs. Investment Curve
125 Items

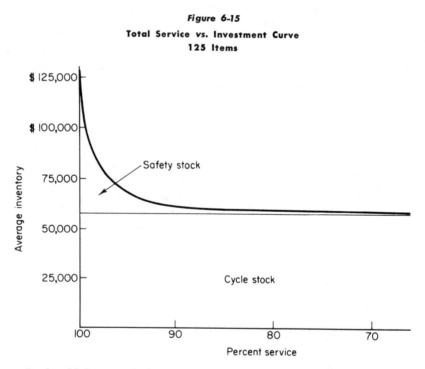

It should be noted that the horizontal scale in Fig. 6-15 is labeled *Percent service* rather than *Number of stockouts per year,* as in Fig. 6-14. The number of stockouts per year can be converted to a percentage of service quite easily as follows:

1. Total number of items in the group $= 125$

2. Total number of selling weeks in the year
= 52

3. Total number of stockouts possible = 125
× 52 = 6500

4. If during the year there are 650 stockouts
(number of items out of stock each week
totaled for the year), this is equivalent to
90% service.

This expression of customer service is frequently a desirable one to use. It is important to remember that the statistical measure of service does not describe the duration of stockouts. If items out of stock are counted each week, an item that stays out for two weeks will be counted as two stockouts. Therefore, it is necessary to set the statistical level of service somewhat higher than the actual level of service required. As described in Chapter 5, there are other statistical measures of customer service that can be used. There may be some situations where these are more appropriate to the particular application. In general, however, *any statistical measure of customer service must be correlated with the actual customer service, and the statistical measure will usually need to be set higher than the actual level of service desired.*

Getting started

The steps involved in using the statistical order point method for determining a service *vs.* investment chart are:

1. Calculate a mean absolute deviation for each item in the product group and develop a system for updating it regularly. This system will probably involve the use of exponential smoothing to forecast demand during lead time and may involve an adjustment (as in Fig. 5-9) if the forecast interval and the lead time interval are not identical.

2. Run a sample calculation to develop the total service *vs.* investment curve, including the cycle stock inventory (sum of one-half the order quantities) and the reserve stock in the total. In setting targets to which the inventory will be reduced at stated times in the future, do not forget to include any slow-moving stock. The best regulated inventory control systems cannot avoid having some slow-moving stock. It is not reasonable to compare the present inventory level with a theoretical inventory level, and assume that the reduction can be made immediately, since some "dead stock" items in it will not move for a number of years.

3. Compare the present levels of inventory required for present

customer service and show the improvement possible using statistical inventory control techniques. If the calculations do not indicate an improvement, the implication is that reserve stock is now distributed very equitably across the items in inventory. This is a highly improbable result using intuitive methods, and it would indicate that the calculations should be checked.

4. Show management the present service *vs.* investment relationship, the improvement possible using statistical techniques, and then help management to choose the "best" inventory level.

5. Set the order points at the agreed level and run the inventory control system.

There are some practical hints of value to the production and inventory control man starting this type of system:

1. When setting up a system of this type, the inventory almost invariably increases very quickly when the system is first started. This occurs because items that are *below* the new order points are ordered all at once. There are many other items for which the inventory is too high, and the only way to eliminate these is to wait for them to be worked off. Consequently, an upward bulge in the inventory level can normally be expected. A sample check will indicate the amount to be expected, and management *should be warned* that it will occur.

2. These techniques alone should only be used for purchased items. Later chapters will describe how the inventory control and production control systems dovetail to control manufactured items.

3. Use weekly sales history in developing demand data whenever possible. Monthly sales figures are usually more difficult to use since they must be adjusted to compensate for the different number of selling days in each month.

4. It is well to try the system manually for a small number of items in order to understand it thoroughly. This can be done using a desk calculator or a slide rule.

5. *A computer is not necessary*; this type of calculation can easily be done manually for a small number of items. Once it has been proven for a low-value inventory (where mistakes will not be as serious), a manual system could then be used for the highest dollar value items (the "A" items). Simple tabulating equipment can be a big help. There are actually quite a few companies using far more sophisticated systems than those described in this chapter with nothing more than a calculating punch.

6. When computers are available, however, the statistical approach

to inventory control is simplified considerably. Most computer manufacturers make program decks available to the practitioner. While these computer programs are not always identical with the techniques described in the past few chapters, they are basically designed around the same principles. A thorough understanding of the principles in these chapters is necessary if the practitioner is to use these programs effectively.

7. Service *vs.* investment charts need only be made periodically. For those companies that do not have computers, service bureaus offer a convenient method for obtaining this help. Nearby companies owning computers have been known to permit their use by friends for periodic analyses of this type, often at no cost. Computer manufacturers can sometimes arrange this type of help.

8. It is important to remember, when starting any new system, to insure that it does *at least* as good a job as the old, even in the beginning. A company's reputation for service can be damaged for a long time by one brief lapse in the service level. The practitioner who risks this reputation while he tries out new systems, no matter what their potential, is not acting in the best interests of his company.

Other aggregate inventory calculations

The concept of aggregate inventory management is so significant that two types of aggregate inventory calculations have been presented in some detail. This type of calculation can be made for any type of inventory by the practitioner who understands basic inventory concepts.

When materials planning component ordering methods are used rather than order points, the methods for calculating service *vs.* investment levels for the component inventories involve the following logic:

1. In a materials planning system, reserve stock takes the form of *time* (i.e., when uncertainty exists as to the exact requirement date for the component, it is ordered to be delivered somewhat earlier than the planned requirement date). The result in the aggregate inventory is that many components will be in inventory before they are required—this inventory is, in fact, provided to insure a high level of service or component availability.

2. The amount of inventory carried will determine the ultimate level of service, since the farther ahead of a planned requirement date material is put in the component storeroom, the better the protection against demands occurring earlier than planned.

3. The uncertainty of planned requirement dates is a function of the MAD (of the assembly being ordered in a make-to-stock company, for example).

Other inventories (such as work-in-process) can also be measured to determine the level required and the alternatives presented so that the inventory can be measured in aggregate. Work-in-process exists basically to even out the ups and downs in the flow between operations in a manufacturing company where these operations can not be balanced effectively by the engineer. In most companies, work-in-process usually results from poor planning and scheduling, but this does not mean that work-in-process does not serve a legitimate function. The minimum level of work-in-process required to keep operations in a plant from running out of work can be estimated by one of two general methods:

1. *Analysis*: This is done by sampling the backlogs and the downtime experienced behind machine centers and extrapolating this experience statistically to predict the levels of work-in-process required to give various degrees of certainty that there will be no downtime, etc.

2. *Simulation*: Using a computer program that simulates the flow of work through a plant, typical groups of factory orders can be run through the plant with varying work-in-process levels to evaluate the relationship between downtime and aggregate work-in-process inventory investment.

Work-in-process is one of the most significant inventories to reduce since it has a direct effect upon manufacturing lead time, and the analyst should remember that he should not just measure what the ups and downs in product flow are and prepare to cope with them when there is a good possibility that better planning and scheduling methods could reduce these fluctuations considerably.

If, in a manufacturing company, it is expensive or undesirable to change production levels, it may be necessary to work at a fairly stable rate all year, even though sales may be seasonal. This will require some inventory-building ahead of the peak season. On the other hand, a reduction in this anticipation inventory will require more production capacity changes throughout the year—requiring layoffs, hiring, training, overtime and other undesirable side-effects that these changes have in a plant. It is imperative that this type of inventory be managed with a clear-cut policy, since it affects not only costs, but also many workers' careers and the company's reputation for stable employment. The trade-off between seasonal inventory and changes in production level can best be seen in the form of a production plan discussed in Chapter 7.

Managing the total inventory investment

Most managers charged with this inventory responsibility are today in the unpleasant position of trying to execute inventory policies that have never really been formulated. Setting rational inventory policy requires a knowledge of existing alternatives, and this requires looking at inventory relationships in aggregate. The calculations required are rather tedious, but completely feasible using modern computers. The inventory manager who can present aggregate inventory information to higher levels of management and assist them in making reasonable policy decisions will be able to work with clearly established policies that recognize the basic trade-off in inventory management. The inventory manager who cannot present aggregate information will almost certainly have to work under a constant stream of criticism because policy has not been clearly established. In fact, it is questionable whether the man who does not prepare aggregate inventory information can truly be said to be *managing* inventories.

Bibliography

1. Brown, R. G., "Aggregate Inventory Management," *APICS Annual Conference Proceedings,* pp. 111–119, 1962.
2. ———, "Use of the Carrying Charge to Control Cycle Stocks," *APICS Quarterly Bulletin,* pp. 29–46, July 1961 Vol. 2, No. 3.
3. Eaton, John A., "New—The LIMIT Technique," *Modern Materials Handling,* Vol. 19, No. 2, February 1964.
4. Harty, J. D., Plossl, G. W., and Wight, O. W., *Management of Lot-Size Inventories,* A Special Education and Research Report of the American Production and Inventory Control Society, Chicago, Illinois, 1963.
5. Smith, Spencer B., "How to Make EOQ Fit Your Inventory Budget," *Purchasing Magazine,* Vol. 49, pp. 76–79, December 19, 1960.
6. Van DeMark, R. L., "Hidden Controls for Inventory," *APICS Annual Conference Proceedings,* American Production and Inventory Control Society, Chicago, Illinois, pp. 139–153, 1960.
7. ———, *Inventory Control Techniques,* Van DeMark, Inc., St. Clair, Mich. 1961.
8. Welch, W. E., *Tested Scientific Inventory Control,* Management Publishing Company, Greenwich, Connecticut, 1956.

# CHAPTER SEVEN

PLANNING
PRODUCTION CAPACITY

Lead time and inventories

In distribution industries, where inventories are purchased and resold, inventory control can be a fairly independent function as long as it balances the purchasing economies with the objectives of customer service and minimum inventory. In a manufacturing organization, the inventories exist either as a result of production or to support production. A manufacturing concern can change order points and order quantities but the resultant change in *total* inventory levels will not be significant until production rates are changed to increase or decrease factory output. Moreover, an inventory control function that ignores plant operating efficiency (specifically, the need to maintain a fairly stable rate of production for quality, morale, and cost considerations) is usually characterized by long lead times, poor service and high inventories. The reasons for this involve the basic relationship of lead time to inventories.

Lead time—the time it takes to replenish an inventory item—is composed of many elements, including the time it takes to generate the actual paperwork and the time it takes to update the records so that they reflect the fact that the item is back in stock. The manufacturing portion of this lead time is composed of the following basic elements:

1. *Setup time*
2. *Running time*

3. *Queue time*
4. *Move time*
5. *Wait time*

Running and *setup times* require no explanation; *queue time* is the time that a job spends behind a machine center without being worked on because there are other jobs ahead of it; *move time* is the actual time spent in transit between operations; and *wait time* is the term usually applied to the time a job spends waiting to be moved. In most functionally organized plants, checking a sample of manufacturing orders to see what percentage of the manufacturing lead time was running time and setup time typically shows them to be less than 10% of the total manufacturing lead time.

What, then, is the element that constitutes the bulk of this lead time? It is usually queue time—time spent waiting because there are other jobs in process. Since the bulk of the work in process inventory is typically not being worked on, it indicates that controls over work in process are poor. In fact, in many companies there is very little specific effort to control work in process, and the result is long queues and long lead times. In practice, the manufacturing inventory control function that assumes no responsibility to balance plant operating objectives usually makes high levels of work in process an operating necessity.

As an example, consider a company using order points to control its inventory without regard for plant capacity. Replenishment orders are generated at random by the inventory control system as inventories drop to the order points and are then sent to the plant, and inventory control personnel assume no responsibility for the efficiency of plant operation.

Plant operating people, recognizing that any increase in the number of orders that they receive may well represent just a random effect and having as one of their prime objectives the maintenance of a stable work force, will build up backlogs of work in order to stabilize the flow of work. This will increase the lead times, so that the "wanted" dates on the orders become less and less meaningful, and sequencing of manufacturing orders becomes extremely difficult. The only way to insure getting a specific order through the plant is to expedite it. Thus, the system typically degenerates into an "inventory control and expediting" system.

The usual reaction of the inventory control system to longer lead times is to reflect them in the order points or materials plan. The higher order points will then generate more orders (since more inventory items are below order point) and these orders will in turn generate a higher level of work in process which will generate *longer lead times*. The fact that most plants tend to operate this way is confirmed by looking at the work in process on the manufacturing floor. In most companies, work in process follows a variation of *Parkinson's Law*[1] and expands to fill available space on the factory floor.

The problem, of course, lies in the lack of production planning. It was stated earlier that the basic elements of a good production control system are:

> *Forecast*
>
> *Plan*
>> Inventory
>> Production rates (capacity)
>
> *Control*—through feedback and corrective action—of
>> Production rates
>> Input—scheduling and loading
>> Output—dispatching and follow-up

Control over work in process requires that production plans be made to give plant operating people enough advance notice to provide capacity when it is needed rather than after backlogs have been generated. It also requires that work be released to the plant to meet planned rates.

Recognizing that lack of production planning is self-defeating, some practitioners have tried to fix schedules far in advance to provide the basis for planning. The *quarterly ordering system* is an example of this type of production control.

The quarterly ordering system

Right after World war II, many industries had large backlogs of firm customer orders for their product stretching to 12 and sometimes 18 months. These provided the base upon which production plans could be made. It was logical and fairly easy to review these orders and make a periodic materials plan, starting with a required date for assembling one type of machine and then working backward to schedule subassemblies, component manufacturing and purchasing of needed materials, in order to meet this assembly requirement taking into account the intermediate levels of inventories and normal lead times. The requirements for parts, subassemblies and finished machines were then analyzed by machine center to arrive at the level of production required for each machine center. Component and subassembly orders were then written with release dates obtained by working back from the planned assembly date, using the normal materials planning techniques. In this way (since

---

[1] Parkinson, C. Northcote, *Parkinson's Law*, Houghton-Mifflin, Boston, 1962.

they far exceeded the lead times) the backlogs served as a known forecast of requirements, and planning could be done once each quarter, for example, with certainty.

During the late 1950's and early 1960's, these order backlogs dwindled to the point where they no longer supplied the necessary planning information. Consequently, a great interest developed in forecasting to supply the missing information. Because customers demanded shorter delivery times, many industries changed from *building to order* to *making to stock*. The typical approach was to make a detailed forecast by item of finished goods requirements for each month of the coming year, with a firm production schedule developed for the next quarter. This forecast would then be broken down into subassembly and component schedules, using it exactly as the order backlog had been employed. Once again, start dates would be assigned to orders and the orders put in the release file while awaiting their release date. The work on these orders would then be accumulated by machine center to determine the machine load for the quarter to insure that the actual capacity was adequate.

Unfortunately, as the period progressed, actual sales would vary from the forecast and the product scheduled to be produced would differ considerably from that required to meet the latest customer orders. The solution to this problem was to advance the schedule for the desired products and try to expedite them through the plant in addition to those orders already scheduled. As a result, demands on productive capacity usually became excessive (because the orders being expedited through the plant were really generating an additional work load) although the actual capacity was adequate to meet average requirements. Very few production control systems are sophisticated enough to identify those orders which can be rescheduled to make room for expedited orders, so that the total work load was typically above the planned level.

Another characteristic of this periodic scheduling system was a large overload at the beginning of each new quarter. As the inventory controller reviewed his requirements for the new period, he would find that many items had been sold in excess of what had been forecast at the beginning of the last quarter, and his schedules for the coming quarter therefore required a high concentration of production in the first month in order to take care of the urgent requirements. In theory, the quarterly ordering system attempted to level out production. In practice, when based upon a detailed item forecast instead of a firm backlog of customers' orders, it very seldom succeeded in attaining this goal.

The problem of planning production rates is not solved by this type of approach since the individual item forecasts are not at all likely to be accurate. In fact, production planning—which is so essential if work in process and lead times are to be controlled—creates something of a di-lemma: generating individual orders far enough in advance to give manu-facturing personnel a means to plan capacity is unrealistic when the basis for generating these orders is a forecast, yet if orders are only gener-ated *as required,* lead times tend to get extremely long. Both approaches usually degenerate into expediting systems in practice.

conflict

A rational approach to production planning

Since few companies have perfect forecasts, any successful system must be capable of coping with an imperfect forecast. This can usually be done if basic forecast characteristics disscussed in Chapter 2 are understood and applied. The two major characteristics involved are:

1. Forecast accuracy is a function of time. The farther out in the future the forecast is made, the less accurate it is likely to be.

2. Forecast accuracy is a function of the num-ber of items in the group being forecast. The larger the product group, the more likely the forecast is to be accurate.

Taking these characteristics into consideration, it would seem that production plans should be made *by the broadest possible product groups that go through similar manufacturing operations.*

Utilizing this principle, production plans can establish the produc-tion rates for these operations, while individual manufacturing orders are scheduled to the planned rate at the last possible moment and based on the latest requirements—whether these requirements are generated by an order point or materials planning system.

Choosing meaningful groups to plan by requires a thorough know-ledge of the plant's manufacturing processes. These groupings are seldom the same ones used by the marketing department or the inventory control system. The groups must be meaningful in terms of *demand on the manu-facturing facilities.* The important point is that the forecasts are inevitably going to be more accurate for the group than for individual items, and even a crude production plan is far better than no plan at all, since it provides:

1. A means of *planning* production rates

2. A means of *controlling* production rates to meet the plan

3. A means of *regulating* the rate of release of work to the plant in order to control the level of work in process

The balance of this chapter will be devoted to the development of production plans, emphasizing their use in the presentation of alternatives to higher levels of management and their use in planning production rates. Chapter 8 will cover the use of the production plan to control production rates and Chapter 9 will cover scheduling, with particular emphasis on controlling order input to meet the planned production rate.

Production planning—the link between inventory control and production control

The *Dictionary of Production and Inventory Control Terms*[1] defines production planning as "the function of setting the limits or levels of manufacturing operations in the future . . ." A good production plan is a projection of the level of production required for a specific production facility, but it is *not* a firm commitment to the individual items to be made within the plan. The production plan establishes the framework within which inventory control techniques will operate. It sets the rate at which orders must be generated to feed the plant.

Experience has shown that, of all the improvements that can be made in production control, the production plan is usually the most significant and rewarding systems revision for those companies without good production plans. Companies with seasonal production are especially vulnerable to high costs and inefficient operation when they lack effective production planning. The production plan lays out in advance the program for building inventory ahead of the peak selling season and charts a course against which actual performance can be measured. Without a production plan, it is typical in this type of operation to have management become alarmed by the inventory build-up ahead of the peak season but to lack specific information as to the level of inventory needed. Too frequently, the reaction is to get nervous over uncharted inventory increases and to cut back production rates just before the peak season, and then to react at considerable expense and increase the production rate again when sales rates pick up and the inventory disappears. With a production plan, the inventory buildup can be compared regularly to the planned levels, and the question of *too high* or *too low* can be decided

---

[1] Published by the American Production and Inventory Control Society, Chicago, Ill., 2nd Ed., 1966.

in time for corrective action to be effective without the problems of baseless discussions and panic decisions.

Making the production plan

Two basic principles must be observed in making a production plan. They are:

1. *The production plan should cover product families or groups that are processed by some common manufacturing facilities.* This, of course, means that the forecast used for production planning must be for these product groups and *not* for product groups that have meaning only to the sales department.

2. *The production plan should be expressed in the simplest terms meaningful to plant operating personnel;* that is, the measures of production should be *pieces, hours, etc.*

The steps involved in making a production plan are:

1. *Determine the period to be covered by the production plan.* Many companies make a general, overall monthly production plan one year in advance that is used to establish overall inventory/production policy and as a basis for checking equipment capacity requirements. They then make a detailed weekly production plan covering each quarter to plan and stabilize manpower requirements.

2. *Establish the base inventory level.* This is the sum of one-half the order quantities plus the reserve stocks for all of the items in the product group when an order point system is being used. This is the minimum inventory that should be on hand to meet the customer service level set by management policy. The logic for determining aggregate inventory levels using materials planning was discussed in Chapter 6.

3. *Spread the sales forecast over the planning period.* This should take into account regular cycles or peaks produced by promotions, which will have a significant effect on sales rates.

4. *Determine the total inventory for the product group at the beginning of the planning period.* This is usually net inventory available for new business, but may also include items manufactured but not yet packed or delivered to warehouses.

5. *Set the desired inventory level at the end of the period.* This will be the

base inventory level mentioned in paragraph 1, plus any inventory which has to be added to cover plant shutdowns, seasonal peaks or other requirements at the end of the period.

6. *Calculate the change in inventory level desired during the planning period.* This is simply the difference between beginning and ending inventories.

7. *Calculate the total production required for the planning period.* This is equal to the total sales forecast plus or minus any desired change in the inventory level from the beginning to the end of the period.

8. *Spread the total production over the period as desired.* This should be done considering holidays or other periods of lost production and the time required to increase or decrease production rates from present levels. 9. *Update plan at least quarterly - more if greater forcast error*

Starting with the actual inventory, if the desired inventory at the end of the planning period and the forecast of sales during the planning period are known, the weekly production rate can be calculated by using this simple formula:

$$R = \frac{D - S + \Sigma F}{N}$$

where: R = Weekly production rate to achieve level production over the planning period

D = Desired total inventory at the end of the planning period

S = Actual total starting inventory

ΣF = Total sales forecast for the planning period

N = Number of weeks in the planning period

As an example, assume that for a product line of stamped ashtrays:

1. Actual starting inventory is 130,000 units
2. Desired inventory at the end of the planning period is also 130,000 units
3. Total sales forecast equals 140,000 units
4. There are five weeks in the planning period

$$\text{Then: } R = \frac{D - S + \Sigma F}{N} = \frac{130_m - 130_m + 140_m}{5} = 28_m$$

Figure 7-1 shows the weekly production plan that would result. The starting inventory and the desired inventory at the end of the planning period are identical. Therefore, the total production is equal to the sales forecast. Note that the production plan has two lines for each week, *planned* and *actual*. During October, the actual sales, production and inventory will be posted against the plan in order to track and control the production rate. A production plan is used as a budget to compare

Figure 7-1

Weekly Production Plan for October

All stamped ashtrays (Figures in "pieces")			
Week date	Sales	Production	Inventory
Start			130,000
10 – 3 Planned Actual	20,000	28,000	138,000
10 – 10 Planned Actual	25,000	28,000	141,000
10 – 17 Planned Actual	30,000	28,000	139,000
10 – 24 Planned Actual	30,000	28,000	137,000
10 – 31 Planned Actual	35,000	28,000	130,000

actual performance against planned performance and to indicate when corrective action must be taken.

The production plan, in addition to planning and controlling the level of production, also regulates the flow of orders into the plant. Figure 7-2 shows a weekly *starting schedule* for the ashtrays covered by the production plan. Although there are approximately 50 different types of stamped ashtrays in the group only seven will be started through production during the week of 10-3. These have the lowest inventories and are at or near their order points. The total of all seven items to be scheduled is of course equal to the planned production rate for the week.

A production plan is a simple—yet essential—tool, and the information required is usually readily available in most companies. In fact, many companies that do not use production plans as such have all this information and are comparing performance against plans—but are doing this separately for sales, production and inventory. Most marketing and sales departments compare actual sales against forecasts. Financial people keep track of the actual inventory level against the data on which budgets of profit have been based. Like much financial data, however, these figures are usually from four to six weeks old and are of little use in controlling inventories. The production control manager or plant manager usually keeps records comparing actual production with the planned production rates.

Although this information is not often integrated, it has little meaning

when considered individually. Manufacturing control decisions can best
be made when all three factors—
sales, production and inventory—are
viewed together. It would be wrong to
insist that a plant meet a planned increase in production rate if sales were
not up to forecast and inventory was
higher than planned. On the other
hand, if production were up to the
planned rate, but sales were exceeding the forecast (causing inventory to
drop below the planned level), the
manufacturing rates would obviously
have to be increased. Looking at the
three factors together in a produc-
tion plan is the first and basic step to establishing a sound production
control system.

Figure 7-2

Weekly Starting Schedule

Stamped ashtrays Week of 10-3	
Item	Quantity
2" Round	14,000
2¼" Round	2000
3" Round	5000
4" Round	3000
6" Oval	1500
3" Hex.	1500
5" Hex.	1000
Total	28,000

Examples of simple production plans

Figure 7-3 shows a monthly production plan for all stamped ashtrays
for one year. This plan sets production at a level rate to satisfy the sales
forecast and to reduce the inventory from 150,000 units at the beginning
of the planned period to approximately 130,000 units one year later.
The calculations are as follows:

1. Cumulative sales forecast for the year = 1,456,000 pieces
2. Inventory change = −20,000 pieces (from 150,000 to 130,000)
3. Required production = 1,436,000 pieces
4. Weekly production rate (50 weeks) = 28,700 pieces/week

These figures have all been rounded off for simplicity of calculation.

An important point to note in this production plan is that after the
vacation shutdown period in July, the inventory will be below the base
inventory level until December. Consequently, service at that time will
probably be poorer than desired. The production planner should call
this to the attention of management and point out that it results from
holding a level production rate through the year. Two alternatives are
available: either run at a higher level during the early part of the year
(so that the inventory at the end of July is equal to 130,000 units) and
then reduce production during August to hit the year-end inventory
goal, or set a higher target inventory than the base level of 130,000 for

Figure 7-3
Yearly Production Plan

Month		Wk	Sales Month	Sales Cumul.	Production Month	Production Cumul.	Inventory* Dec. 31 150 M
			All stamped ashtrays (all figures in thousands)				
Jan.	Planned Actual	5	140	140	144	144	154
Feb.	Planned Actual	4	112 →252	252	115	259	157
Mar.	Planned Actual	4	112	364	115	374	160
Apr.	Planned Actual	4	112	476	115	489	163
May	Planned Actual	5	140	616	144	633	167
June	Planned Actual	4	112	728	115	748	170
July	Planned Actual	2**	112	840	57	805	115
Aug.	Planned Actual	5	140	980	144	949	119
Sept.	Planned Actual	4	112	1092	115	1064	122
Oct.	Planned Actual	5	140	1232	144	1208	126
Nov.	Planned Actual	4	112	1344	115	1323	129
Dec.	Planned Actual	4	112	1456	115	1438	132

* Base inventory level (1/2 order quantities plus reserve stock = 130 M)
** Vacation shutdown = 2 weeks

the end of December and maintain production at a level rate throughout the year.

For example, if it were decided to set the production level high enough so that the July-end inventory was equal to the base level of 130,000, approximately 500 more units per week would have to be manufactured. If the production level remained unchanged for the balance of the year and the sales forecast were accurate, the year-end inventory would be 157,000 units (500 per week times 50 weeks, plus 132,000) instead of 132,000 as previously planned.

At this point, it is well to keep in mind that production plans are only approximations. The chance that sales will be exactly as forecast is almost nil, as is the chance that the plant will manufacture exactly to the planned level of production. There is a point of diminishing return where added refinement of the production plan becomes meaningless.

The seasonal production plan

When making a seasonal production plan, three alternatives are available to the planner. They are:

1. To hold a level production rate at the expense of carrying high inventories

Figure 7-4

Yearly Production Plan #1

Month		Wk	Sales Month	Sales Cumul.	Production Month	Production Cumul.	Inventory* (Sept. 30 1 200)	Remarks
			All-steel cartridge automotive-type filters (all figures in thousands of hours of labor)					
Oct.	Planned	5	800	800	1120	1120	1520	Prod.= 224/wk
	Actual							
Nov.	Planned	4	600	1400	896	2016	1816	
	Actual							
Dec.	Planned	4	500	1900	896	2912	2212	
	Actual							
Jan.	Planned	5	1000	2900	1120	4032	2332	
	Actual							
Feb.	Planned	4	800	3700	896	4928	2428	
	Actual							
Mar.	Planned	4	800	4500	896	5824	2524	
	Actual							
Apr.	Planned	4	900	5400	896	6720	2520	
	Actual							
May	Planned	5	1200	6600	1120	7840	2440	
	Actual							
June	Planned	4	1000	7600	896	8736	2336	
	Actual							
July	Planned	2**	1000	8600	448	9184	1784	
	Actual							
Aug.	Planned	5	1500	10,100	1120	10,304	1404	
	Actual							
Sept.	Planned	4	900	11,000	896	11,200	1400	
	Actual							

*Base Inventory Level = 1400 M hours

**Vacation shutdown = 2 weeks

2. To hold inventories down by varying the production rate to meet the seasonal sales requirements

3. Some combination of these two extremes, with a few changes in the production rate made at strategic times to minimize excess inventory and meet the seasonal requirements

These three alternatives will be illustrated by the following example: Figure 7-4 shows a yearly production plan for making all-steel, cartridge, automotive-type filters. Two points in particular are worth noticing about this plan. The first is that it does not cover a calendar year, but covers instead a selling year. The production and inventory are planned to meet the seasonal demand pattern which starts from a low in December, increases to a peak in August and then drops back down. The plan should start near the end of the selling season since inventory will be lowest just before sales drop below the production rate. The second point worth noticing is that it measures inventory, sales, and production in terms of *labor hours*, which is the only meaningful measure for this large and mixed product group where some of the individual products in a group take far longer to manufacture than others. Nevertheless, all of these products go through the same basic manufacturing equipment.

Yearly Production Plan #1 (Fig. 7-4) attempts to set the production level and maintain it throughout the year. Inventory from January through June is quite high, but production is maintained at a steady rate. Yearly Production Plan #2 (Fig. 7-5) changes the production level four times during the year but succeeds in maintaining a much lower level of inventory. Yearly Production Plan #3 (Fig. 7-6) varies the production level twice during the year and arrives at a level of inventory that is a compromise between the first two plans. The summary below is based on value of inventory, costs of carrying inventory, and the cost of changing the production level as shown. With these assumed costs, Plan #3 gives the lowest total cost.

Summary Production Plans #1, #2, & #3

All-Steel Cartridge Automotive-Type Filters

	Avg. inv. level (M hrs)	Avg. inv. (M dollars) (1)	Avg. inv. carrying cost (2)	Changes in prod. level	Cost of changes (3)	Total cost (M dollars)
Plan #1	2060	$8240	$1648	1	$150	$1798
Plan #2	1313	5252	1050	4	600	1650
Plan #3	1622	6488	1298	2	300	1598

(1) at $4.00 per labor hour; (2) at 20%; (3) at $150M per change.

Figure 7-5

Yearly Production Plan #2

All-steel cartridge automotive-type filters (all figures in thousands of hours of labor)							
			Sales		Production		Inventory* (Sept.30 1200)
Month		Wk.	Month	Cumul.	Month	Cumul.	Remarks
Oct.	Planned	5	800	800	805	805	1205	Prod.= 161/wk
	Actual							
Nov.	Planned	4	600	1400	645	1450	1250	
	Actual							
Dec.	Planned	4	500	1900	645	2095	1395	
	Actual							
Jan.	Planned	5	1000	2900	1000	3095	1395	Prod.= 200/wk
	Actual							
Feb.	Planned	4	800	3700	800	3895	1395	
	Actual							
Mar.	Planned	4	800	4500	800	4695	1395	
	Actual							
Apr.	Planned	4	900	5400	950	5645	1445	Prod.= 238/wk
	Actual							
May	Planned	5	1200	6600	1190	6835	1435	
	Actual							
June	Planned	4	1000	7600	950	7785	1385	
	Actual							
July	Planned	2**	1000	8600	620	8405	1005	Prod.= 309/wk
	Actual							
Aug.	Planned	5	1500	10,100	1550	9955	1055	
	Actual							
Sept.	Planned	4	900	11,000	1240	11,195	1395	
	Actual							

*Base inventory level = 1400 M hours

**Vacation shutdown = 2 weeks

Basically, a seasonal production plan attempts to balance inventory investment against the costs of changing the production level. Just as with the economic ordering quantity problem, the costs needed to solve this planning problem are not readily available. Primary factors in these costs are overtime, hiring, training, and layoff (all of which can frequently be *estimated* with some confidence).

Other costs are more nebulous, though real just the same. Training new employees or low morale of workers facing layoff reduce quality, with higher scrap and rework losses. Frequent layoffs give a company a poor reputation in the labor market and make it difficult to hire and keep high-caliber workers.

Production rate changes, particularly increases, are very difficult to accomplish as scheduled. New employees are not able to produce at

Figure 7-6

Yearly Production Plan #3

Month		Wk.	Sales Month	Sales Cumul.	Production Month	Production Cumul.	Inventory* (Sept. 30 1 200)	Remarks
Oct.	Planned Actual	5	800	800	975	975	1375	Prod. = 195/wk.
Nov.	Planned Actual	4	600	1400	780	1755	1555	
Dec.	Planned Actual	4	500	1900	780	2535	1835	
Jan.	Planned Actual	5	1000	2900	975	3510	1810	
Feb.	Planned Actual	4	800	3700	780	4290	1790	
Mar.	Planned Actual	4	800	4500	780	5070	1770	
Apr.	Planned Actual	4	900	5400	780	5850	1650	
May	Planned Actual	5	1200	6600	975	6825	1425	
June	Planned Actual	4	1000	7600	1272	8097	1697	Prod. = 318/wk.
July	Planned Actual	2**	1000	8600	636	8733	1333	
Aug.	Planned Actual	5	1500	10,100	1590	10,323	1423	
Sept.	Planned Actual	4	900	11,000	1272	11,595	1795	

All-steel cartridge automotive-type filters (all figures in thousands of hours of labor)

*Base inventory level = 1400 M hours
**Vacation shutdown = 2 weeks

desired rates for varying periods and some, never able to attain minimum rates, must be replaced. Parts production increases must precede assembly rate increases, and manufacturing foremen are usually reluctant to add people until they "can see the parts there to work on."

It should be noted that Plans #2 and #3 require far more capacity to handle the peak production than Plan #1. This may be close to or even beyond the maximum capacity of plant and equipment available. Management should also recognize that with Plan #2 inventory will be well below the base level right after vacation.

It should also be noted that production is at a high rate going into the slow selling season in Plan #3. Unless sales are considerably higher next year, another change in production level may be required sooner in Plan #3 than in Plan #2. This may make Plan #2 potentially the lowest-cost plan. A few other considerations worth keeping in mind when making production plans are:

1. There is a definite period of time required for changing production levels. The change in production rate must be given to the plant soon enough for it to react.

2. The number of holidays during the year may be a substantial factor affecting the level of inventory. Setting a daily production rate and the working days per week in the production plan will handle this.

3. Under present union contracts, many people have 3-week or even 4-week vacations which result in production losses beyond the 2-week vacation shut-down. June through August is likely to be a period of slack production and it is important to pinpoint just where lost production will occur during this period.

4. Overtime work is expensive, but is in some circumstances more desirable than adding people (from a pure cost viewpoint). A good rule-of-thumb used by many practitioners is *never to plan to use overtime*. Their reasoning is that overtime provides flexibility in meeting unexpected surges in sales or overcoming losses in production caused by equipment breakdowns or similar failures. Moreover, planned overtime is much easier to start than it is to stop.

5. Seasonal production plans should attempt to store production *hours* in the cheapest form. Given the alternative between fabricating and storing a brass part that requires very little machining or processing a steel part with many operations, the steel part with lower material cost is definitely the better choice since the objective is to store the most labor and machine hours in inventory at the lowest possible cost.

As with most other problems in production and inventory control, when making a production plan it is important to obtain and use the most accurate data available and to present information to management to show them the alternatives that really exist.

Using the production plan

Production plans are frequently made out on a monthly basis for the year and on a weekly basis for each quarter, in order to give enough detail to permit following closely the planned production rate, sales and inventory levels. One of the most frequently-asked questions about production plans is: *How often should they be changed?* This question really misses an important point—the objective is to change production plans only when necessary. It is extremely important to determine ahead of time what set of circumstances will require a change in the production level. When these rules are not established ahead of time, there may be weekly discussions as to whether or not the present circumstances require a change in production level. In subsequent chapters, we shall discuss the decision rules that can be established for determining when to change production plans.

A plant should have a production plan for each major manufacturing area that it wishes to control. In fact, if there is a chance that it may be desirable to run two subareas within an overall manufacturing area at different production rates, two production plans—one for each of these submanufacturing areas—should be established. This might occur when one facility is feeding subassemblies into an intermediate inventory ahead of an assembly department. Separate production plans for the assembly and subassembly operations would make it possible to control (either raise or lower) the production rate of the subassembly area independently of the production rate for the assembly area.

Applications of production planning

The application of a production plan in a make-to-stock plant will be illustrated by taking as an example a company manufacturing a line of kitchen mixers. The mixers are marketed in 20 different models, each of which is made up of a motor, gears, bowls, beaters, and other miscellaneous castings and small parts. The general process flow is shown in Fig. 7-7.

Figure 7-7

General Process Flow
Kitchen Mixer Line

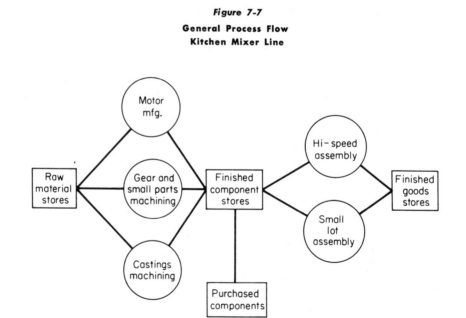

Production plans should be made for the following areas:

1. *Finished goods*: It will probably be necessary to have separate production plans for the high-speed assembly line for high-volume items and the small lot assembly line for the slow-movers.

2. *Finished component stores*: Separate production plans would be required for motor manufacturing, gear and small-parts machining and castings machining.

3. *Purchased components*: A less important—although very helpful—production plan could be developed for purchased components to regulate their flow into finished component stores. This same concept could also be extended to the flow of other groups of raw materials.

The production plan in each case would be for the *total* production expressed in meaningful terms for each particular facility. Picking the right measures of capacity to use in planning is particularly important—the production control man should use the simplest terms that are meaningful to manufacturing people. In motor manufacturing, for example, it would probably be sufficient to express the production rate in number of motors. In the case of gear and small parts machining, since the parts going through this department would have wide variations in labor content, *pieces* would not be so meaningful, and the total production plan would undoubtedly have to be made in terms of *hours*.

One of the best methods for determining "meaningful terms" is to go into the factory, talk to the foreman, and ask him about changing production levels—what personnel changes would he have to make if the number of *pieces* on the production schedule were increased? If these terms are meaningful to him, go no further. If he requires *hours*, which are much harder to get in the production control department, the added work is usually justified since it is important to generate information that is useful to those responsible for getting action in the plant.

Figure 7–8 shows a production plan for one quarter of a year for the final assembly area where all 20 models of mixers are put together. The sales forecast for the family is 2000 units per week, the starting actual inventory is 10,100 pieces of all models, and the desired total inventory at the end of the quarter is 14,000 pieces.

It is desired to increase the finished goods inventory from the base level of 10,100 pieces (which is required to insure giving 98% service for this product line) by 2-weeks' supply, (4000 pieces) in anticipation of the annual vacation shutdown. The plan, set up as explained earlier in this chapter, shows that a planned production rate of 2300 units is needed to meet the demand and build up the inventory to the desired level.

No provision has been built into this plan for holidays. It has been

Figure 7-8

Production Plan—20 Models Kitchen Mixers

(All data in thousands of pieces)

2nd Qtr. Week No.		Sales forecast		Production		
		Weekly	Cumulative	Weekly	Cumulative	Inventory
First Qtr.	Planned Actual		26.0 24.0		26.0 24.0	10.1 10.1
14	Planned Actual	2.0	26.0	2.3	26.3	10.4
15	Planned Actual	2.0	28.0	2.3	28.6	10.7
16	Planned Actual	2.0	30.0	2.3	30.9	11.0
17	Planned Actual	2.0	32.0	2.3	33.2	11.3
18	Planned Actual	2.0	34.0	2.3	35.5	11.6
19	Planned Actual	2.0	36.0	2.3	37.8	11.9
20	Planned Actual	2.0	38.0	2.3	40.1	12.2
21	Planned Actual	2.0	40.0	2.3	42.4	12.5
22	Planned Actual	2.0	42.0	2.3	44.7	12.8
23	Planned Actual	2.0	44.0	2.3	47.0	13.1
24	Planned Actual	2.0	46.0	2.3	49.3	13.4
25	Planned Actual	2.0	48.0	2.3	51.6	13.7
26	Planned Actual	2.0	50.0	2.3	53.9	14.0

assumed that an *average* weekly rate of 2300 mixers is required. If any weeks are short of working days, production in other weeks will have to exceed the average if the quarterly total of 29,900 is to be met. For this line, the refinement of planning around holidays was not believed to be warranted.

Cumulative sales and production figures are also shown in the plan.

These permit comparison of actual sales and production against planned values and against one another over the period. The plan in Fig. 7–8 shows that 26,000 mixers were to be produced and sold in the first quarter. Actual sales were below forecast but were equal to the 24,000 mixers actually produced, and the inventory goal was met.

The plan shows that the marketing department has not decided to change the weekly forecast of 2000 mixers because of the lower sales rate in the first quarter. They do not believe the first quarter deficit of 2000 mixers will be made up, and the second quarter plan therefore starts with a cumulative sales figure of 24,000. Had they anticipated overcoming this deficit *in addition* to selling 26,000 mixers in the second quarter, the weekly sales rate in the plan would have been 2150 pieces (26,000 plus 2,000, divided by 13 weeks).

Note that the cumulative totals of *actual* sales and production for the first quarter become the starting figures for the second quarter plan. The development of the weekly rates in making the new plan should be based on the desired inventory level at the end of the quarter and the expected total demand. Using these figures in making the plan takes care of production deficits in the preceding quarter.

In making a production plan for finished goods in a make-to-stock plant, the service *vs.* investment chart (cf. Chapter 6) is an extremely valuable tool. It establishes the *base inventory level* at which the production plans aim. It is important to remember, however, that the service *vs.* investment chart is based upon the average demand during the year. Where demand varies greatly during the year, the reserve stock required for a particular service level will also vary. In applications where there is a wide variation in demand during the year, the service *vs.* investment chart should be based upon the demand experienced at the time the inventory reaches its low point when there is no anticipation inventory on hand to assist the normal reserve stock in giving customer service protection.

The service *vs.* investment chart can also be used to evaluate the effect of dips below the base inventory level on customer service. Some production plan alternatives include a period during the year when inventory temporarily dips below an ideal level. This was illustrated by the seasonal plans for ashtrays in Fig. 7–3. The desirability of such an alternative can be evaluated better if a definite measure of the effect on customer service can be obtained. The service *vs.* investment chart gives this measure.

Production planning for functional departments

Functional departments performing basic starting operations, such as the motor manufacturing or general machining departments for the company manufacturing mixers, are usually more difficult to control. When they are controlled using only inventory control techniques and backlog measuring techniques such as machine loading, the erratic rate of order flow in these departments results in excessive and variable lead times and in very slow reaction to changes in the total demand caused by increasing or decreasing business. The same general principles of establishing a planned level of operation for these departments and then scheduling to meet this plan can reduce the lead time for components drastically, level out manufacturing operations very significantly and reduce reaction time when the business level changes.

A production plan for a functional department can be set up (using the same format as that in Fig. 7–8) for components by converting the sales forecast into *hours of machining* requirements. This would result in a production plan as shown in Fig. 7–9. As quantities of components are withdrawn from inventory they are converted into "hours of machining" in order to compare actual against planned demand. Production levels and component inventories are also expressed in the same terms.

Figure 7-9

**Quarterly Production Plan—Functional Department
In Terms of Machining Hours**

Week Ending		Orders		Production		Component Stockroom Inventory
		Weekly	Cumulative	Weekly	Cumulative	
4/7	Planned	2800	64,190	4300	55,390	12,820
	Actual	2750	64,200	5100	55,390	13,670
4/14	Planned	2800	66,990	4300	59,690	14,320
	Actual	3400	67,600	7580	62,970	17,850
4/21	Planned	2800	69,790	4300	63,990	15,820
	Actual	3260	70,860	4490	67,460	19,080
6/30	Planned	2800	97,790	4300	106,990	30,820
	Actual					

The inventory targets of such plans for parts-producing facilities are usually the base inventory levels of the group of parts. These are the average inventories (for purchased items) equal to one-half the order quantity plus the reserve stock, or (for manufactured items) derived from totals obtained by simulation or calculation based on the materials plan. Occasionally, it is desirable to increase these levels of parts inventory temporarily in preparation for periods of reduced production, such as would occur if factory equipment layouts are being rearranged or if a key piece of equipment were to be shut down for overhaul. Having a production plan for each major facility enables production control to plan for different production rates for these facilities when it is necessary to change parts inventory levels.

The timing of changes in production levels is very important. Assembly rates cannot be increased and sustained until production rates of components are picked up. Any change in production levels which requires hiring and training people will require a considerable period of time to accomplish. It is meaningless to increase the required production rate from a department before the raw material input rate has been increased. In a complex factory, production rates have to be increased successively through a sequence of departments, depending upon the starting inventory and lead time through the series of operations. The production plan makes it possible to accomplish such changes on an orderly basis with a minimum of lost time.

For service departments within a plant such as painting or plating departments, the production rates for significant equipment groups can also be planned—recognizing that it is not always possible to precisely control the flow of material into these departments since work does not originate there, but comes from many other departments. The scheduled input of orders into source departments should be balanced as closely as possible to meet the planned production rates in service departments.

While this can be a complex problem, even in companies with computing equipment available to make the calculations, there are ways to simplify the application of these techniques while retaining much of their effectiveness. The ABC concept applies here as well as in many other areas of production and inventory control. If the products going through the department are classed according to the work hours they generate, even though the total product mix is extremely varied, the "80-20" relationship is almost always apparent. A very few of the products going through the service department will generate the bulk of the man-hours required within the department. Controlling the input of only these items can effectively level the production rate, reduce the work in process, and consequently reduce lead time.

Production planning for purchased materials

Establishing a production rate and scheduling orders to meet this planned rate can also apply to purchased parts. It is of particular advantage when the vendor is a captive supplier with a large portion of his business coming from principal customers. Changes in the rate of orders flowing to him will generate severe ups and downs in his business level and result in widely varying procurement lead times for his customers. The fact that this is "his problem" does not lessen its effect on his customer's inventories.

The vendor's natural reaction is to generate a substantial backlog of orders in order to keep his business operating efficiently. By giving him a production plan by which to work and scheduling the mix of individual items to him regularly to meet this production plan, lead times can be reduced very substantially. As each mix schedule is issued, a review of the status of both new orders and previous orders should be made with the vendor. Such close communication is of great benefit to both vendor and customer.

The production plan can further be used by the customer as a control of the total dollar inventory. This can be done by determining the dollar value of material planned to be purchased from vendors weekly or monthly, and then generating orders to meet this planned rate. Actual receipts can then be compared with the budget to see that approximately this amount of inventory was purchased.

Planning the production level in a make-to-order plant

While the technique of production planning in make-to-stock plants is relatively easy to understand, it is more difficult to apply in a make-to-order plant. In a make-to-order plant, a customer order must be on hand before the finished product is produced. Most such plants therefore assume that they can only plan from customer order backlogs. In fact, this assumption ignores a basic forecast characteristic referred to earlier—large groups of items *can* be forecast with some accuracy, even where individual items cannot. Planning from forecasts rather than backlogs reduces lead time—and this can be a *real* competitive advantage.

The first step in production planning in a make-to-order plant is to decide upon the definition of manufacturing groups. These are not as readily apparent as they are in a make-to-stock plant. Nevertheless, there are usually groups of like products that go through similar manufacturing facilities which can be identified if the ultimate purpose of *planning the rate of production* is kept in mind. Even if the groups so identified do not account for the full load on the facilities, preparing a production plan for even a portion of capacity is far better than doing no planning, and almost invariably justifies the cost.

The next step is to look at the past history of *total demand* for the product groups selected. Figure 7-10 shows this type of analysis. This example covers a paper manufacturing company making a variety of grades of paper. Incoming orders for coarse paper have been reviewed for a 10-week period. This analysis does not break the incoming orders down into individual items, but instead totals them in terms meaningful to production (in this case, production hours). The forecast based on previous history was approximately 200 hours per week.

Figure 7-10

Incoming Orders for All Coarse Papers
(Expressed in production hours)

Week	Orders	Cumulative Orders	Cumulative Forecast	Deviation
Forecast = 200 hrs / week				
1	210	210	200	+ 10
2	220	430	400	+ 30
3	150	580	600	− 20
4	230	810	800	+ 10
5	300	1110	1000	+110
6	270	1380	1200	+180
7	215	1595	1400	+195
8	180	1775	1600	+175
9	140	1915	1800	+ 115
10	210	2125	2000	+ 125

Analyzing this 10-week period, it can be seen that cumulative sales deviated between plus 1 week (195 hours) and minus $\frac{1}{10}$ of a week (20 hours) of production. One of the great values of this type of approach is that it determines how much unreleased order backlog is necessary *if* a backlog is necessary at all in this plant. Rather than just assuming, for example, that "three to four weeks is normal" for this particular business, Fig. 7-10 indicates that one week of backlog is all that is normally required in order to keep production going at a fairly level rate. This information could then be used to set up a decision rule for changing the production rate. Based on these data, whenever the total backlog is greater than one week of work at the planned rate, the production level will have to be increased.

One of the distinct advantages of this type of analysis is that it focuses attention on the total demand rather than on individual orders, so that significant trends and factors are no longer buried in a maze of detail. Statistical approaches, further detailed in Chapter 8, can be used to refine this type of production planning in a make-to-order plant.

Once a reasonable weekly production rate has been determined, a schedule can be made out on a weekly basis, specifying the individual orders that make up the total. In fact, it is frequently possible to reduce the scheduling cycle to less than one week. For example, the plant could be told that it will be expected to turn out 200 hours' worth of coarse paper the following week, yet the detailed orders for individual sizes would be issued only for the first 2 or 3 days of the week. Orders coming in during the early part of the week would then be used to fill in the schedule for the balance of the week.

Most make-to-order plants have customers who place repeat orders for some regularly-scheduled items which can be used as buffers to absorb the ups and downs in incoming business for a product group. When total orders fall below the anticipated rate, these regularly-scheduled items can be run at something higher than the normal rate in order to make up the deficit in production level. This approach requires ingenuity and work, but it reduces the amount of backlog required and can pay off very handsomely in reduced lead times and better customer service.

The important point to remember in using scheduled items as inventory buffers or using a reduced backlog is to set up some controls. It is not unusual to find that this type of approach has been tried at some time previously in a make-to-order plant, but that the inventories of scheduled items used as "buffers" went completely out of control or the backlogs were not controlled properly. When decision rules are set up ahead of time, and when action is taken promptly on the basis of these rules to either reduce or increase the production level, these techniques can be used with a great deal of success. Like all forecasting, planning future production in a make-to-order plant must recognize explicity that no incoming order rate is likely to be fixed for a very long period of time.

Some considerations in production planning

Many shops are both make-to-order and make-to-stock plants, having the bulk of their business in make-to-stock products but receiving many orders for specials. The production plan for these shops can allow a portion of the total man-hours each week for specials, but the ups and downs inevitable in incoming order rate for special products can be handled by scheduling more or less of the make-to-stock items.

Production plans in any business must allow for rework and scrap. This can be done by adding enough capacity to the planned rate to cover scrap and rework or to provide additional manload above that required to meet the planned rate.

The production rate of feeder or secondary operations should also be planned in meaningful groups. Where there are particularly important operations supporting the main assembly level, these operations should be planned and their production rates monitored in addition to the total production of assembly operations.

Using this total hourly plan, the components that go into these facilities should be reviewed on a regular basis and scheduled into the machine groups to meet the planned production rate. This review will be facilitated if the parts are listed together according to the machine groups which process them and if the order quantities are expressed in machine hours. If the components in the groups are ordered by different individuals, each person can be assigned a quota of machine hours against which he must release orders in each period. The total of these quotas will, of course, equal the planned total for the machine group.

Production planning techniques

In the previous sections, production plans were prepared in hours and pieces. However, some practitioners prefer graphical techniques. Figure 7-11 is a graphical representation of the monthly production plan for filters shown in Fig. 7-4. The production plan shows generally that, during the early part of the year, production exceeds sales and, consequently, inventory builds up. It is reduced during the peak selling season (September through October) when sales exceed production. Upon close inspection of this production plan, though, some problems are apparent. Because the plan is based on a shop calendar that has two 4-week months and one 5-week month in every quarter, the graph of this production plan indicates that the production rate is quite erratic when, in fact, it is level at 228,000 hours per week.

To make this graphical production plan representative of the true situation, the time scale could be made *weeks* or *days* or *4-week periods* to eliminate the distortion. Another approach, however, would be to plot sales and production cumulatively (as shown in Fig. 7-12). In this case, the spacings for the months have been adjusted to be proportional to the number of production weeks available in each month. Consequently, the cumulative production total shows as a straight line, which is of more value in planning and following production than the monthly production line graphed in Fig. 7-11. Figure 7-12 also shows that inventory will be built-up during the early part of the year, but that as the sales and production cumulative lines "close the gap," inventory will be reduced.

Figures 7-11 and 7-12 illustrate standard approaches to graphical pro-

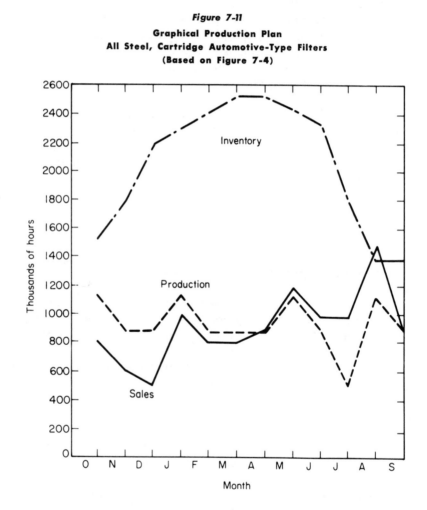

Figure 7-11

Graphical Production Plan
All Steel, Cartridge Automotive-Type Filters
(Based on Figure 7-4)

duction plans. It is evident that they require more work and that some study is required to understand them. Some people prefer graphs and can understand them more readily than columns of numbers. Graphical production plans can become extremely complex, particularly when actual

Figure 7-12

Graphical Cumulative Production Plan

All Steel, Cartridge Automotive-Type Filters

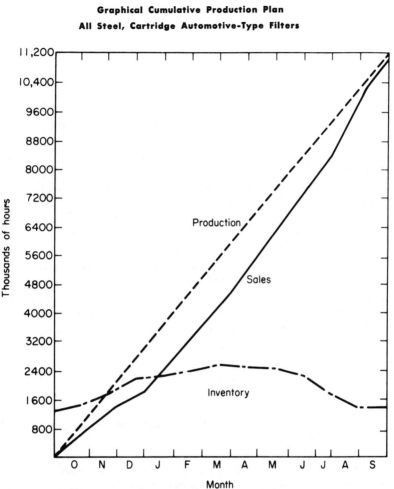

figures are plotted against the planned data and this, of course, is one of the most important uses of the production plan.

Many practitioners feel that graphical techniques have been somewhat over-emphasized in business literature. Most graphical production plans fail exactly where they should succeed: *conveying the picture rapidly*. The people who are to take action to correct deviations from plan want information in terms of hours, men, pieces, tons, etc. If given a graphical production plan, they must translate the graph into numbers in order to determine the degree of action that is required.

The practitioner who is considering using a graphical technique for production planning should try it together with the straight numerical technique. By running both techniques concurrently and presenting the information in both forms to management, he can determine which form is most readily understood.

In most multiproduct plants having many operations through which the products travel, the product lines can be classed in groupings that have a similar process flow. This condition exists far more often than is usually recognized. Capacity at the critical operations in the sequence can be established by a production plan and individual products can then be scheduled at the planned rate using the technique of *load balancing.*

Load balancing, discussed in detail in Chapter 9 under "Scheduling," is a technique to avoid overloading one operation in a sequence through which many products are passing. The product mix is fed in so as to achieve a balance among product groups which place widely variable demand on operations, so that the work load at any single operation will not be excessive during any one period. If, for example, there were two major product groups going through a sequence of operations, but one of the groups required twice the amount of milling, it would be foolish to schedule an extraordinarily large quantity of this product group in any one particular week. If this were done this group would take so long to process that other products would be delayed. Balanced loading is an extremely basic technique for avoiding bottlenecks in the plant and for allowing the scheduler to release work to the plant under a production plan, so that it flows through the operations rather than getting bottlenecked at a particular operation.

Tying the production plan and the budget together

Production control personnel, like accounting personnel, present information to management so that it can make decisions. Since both use cost data, it is therefore extremely important that they coordinate their activities so that they present information on similar bases. The accounting department should be familiar with the production plans used in the production control department and know how to convert these plans into dollars so that the accounting budget figures are based on the same anticipated sales, production and inventory figures as the production control budgets. This sounds like a very basic point, but it is one that is most often overlooked—probably because, in most companies, the similarities in the information requirements of the financial control and the production control systems have been obscured because they have developed independently. As the ability to design and implement integrated control systems develops with better applications of the computer, production planning and control systems will undoubtedly tend more and more to merge with financial planning and control systems. Until then, it is important for the production control executive to work closely with the financial executive to be sure that both systems present consistent information to higher levels of management.

Conclusion

Inventory control techniques cannot really control manufactured inventories by themselves since the inventory control techniques are designed to *cope* with lead time changes—but not to *control* them. Control of lead times, in practice, is dependent on control of backlogs which in turn requires some means of planning and controlling production rates.

The control of production rates was at one time handled by *machine loading*—basically a measurement of the actual backlogs of work at machine centers. With increasing pressures to ship "from the shelf" and provide shorter lead times, as well as increasing pressure to provide more stable levels of employment, it has been necessary to plan production rates according to *forecasts* rather than *backlogs*. While some machine loading techniques (which will be discussed in Chapter 9) are still useful in planning production rates in some companies, the principal value of machine loading is in showing where temporary overloads, underloads and bottlenecks exist. For most companies, some form of production plan by broad product groups that are meaningful in terms of manufacturing capacity can be developed to provide for capacity changes based on the forecast rather than backlogs. Since lead times are largely dependent on backlogs, a production plan is necessary to plan and control production rates and to provide a "regulator" to control order input so that work in process levels can be controlled. Orders are then put into production on regular weekly or even daily schedules to replenish those items required by the customers.

An outstanding example of an industry which has put this concept to work effectively is automobile manufacturing. Under the pressure of unions for a guaranteed annual wage, these companies have established an enviable record for keeping their plants operating at a level rate. This has been done in spite of consumer demand for a constantly increasing number of models. In the automobile industry today, a customer can order practically any car he wants with an immense choice of accessories and options. While the assembly plants know in general how many automobiles they will be producing, they only know the actual color, transmission option, upholstery, engine, etc., when they receive the customer's order. While the automobile industry is a highly mechanized mass-production industry, they have learned how to apply production planning techniques to keep their operations flexible and responsive to changing consumer demand.

The same principles can be applied in far smaller companies. A plant manufacturing an assembled product made up of many manufactured and purchased components was having chronic backlog problems in its screw machine department and lead times were excessively long. The inventory control system was generating orders based on needs and on lead times which historically averaged 12 to 14 weeks. The reason for the long lead times was the fact that the operating personnel had no basis for coping with the variations in work flow generated by the inventory control system, other than to maintain large backlogs by consistently running behind schedule. They did this in order to avoid temporary cutbacks in skilled labor, recognizing the high expenses generated by frequent changes in production level, the likelihood of not being able to rehire these skilled people when more manufacturing orders came to them, and the potential quality and cost problems involved with breaking in new machine operators.

In this instance, production planning principles were applied as follows:

1. Periodically, screw machine component demand was projected into the future based on an explosion of the projected assembly requirements.

2. These projected requirements were then added by machine group to establish anticipated capacity requirements, but the actual manufacturing orders were *not* generated (recognizing the forecast principle that the group forecast would be reasonably accurate while individual component requirements might change drastically).

3. The inventory requirements were then reviewed weekly so that the most-needed components were ordered *based on the planned capacity* and planned lead times of 4 to 6 weeks.

Note that in this example lead times were 12 to 14 weeks because of the paper backlog that was being used to level production. With a production plan and controlled order input, lead times were reduced drastically by simply eliminating the backlog. When an inventory system is generating requirements on production facilities, it is common to observe long lead times which exist only because the production control function has not developed effective production planning techniques.

The idea of assuming more responsibility for projecting capacity requirements and then controlling input to meet planned rates is relatively new. For many practitioners who have gained their experience through expediting, the idea of assuming more responsibility for plant efficiency is foreign, and since capacity planning methods must be tailored to the individual plant, there has not as yet been wide adoption of these techniques. As more pressures for lower inventories, stabler plant production rates and improved customer service continue to make themselves felt, there will be increasing development and application of techniques to plan and control production rates based on forecasts rather than backlogs.

Bibliography

The concept of planning and controlling the level of production in order to establish capacity requirements far enough in advance to react to them economically is fairly new and the references are therefore limited. Some information on this subject is available in the following:

1. Biegel, John E., *Production Control: A Quantitative Approach,* Prentice-Hall, Englewood Cliffs, New Jersey, 1963.

2. Holt, Charles C., Modigliani, Franco, Muth, John F., and Simon, Herbert A., *Planning Production, Inventories and Work Force,* Prentice-Hall, Englewood Cliffs, New Jersey, 1960.

3. Magee, John F., *Production Planning and Inventory Control,* McGraw, New York, 1958.

4. Scheele, Evan D., Westerman, William L., and Wimmert, Robert J., *Principles and Design of Production Control Systems,* Prentice-Hall, Englewood Cliffs, New Jersey, 1960.

# CHAPTER EIGHT

CONTROLLING
PRODUCTION CAPACITY

The need for control over capacity

If the fluctuations in production level for the average company were compared with the fluctuations in demand, it would quickly be apparent that most manufacturing executives tend to wait too long before deciding to change production levels, and that they overreact when they do change. The root of this problem is usually the information—or lack of it—on which they base their decisions. The manufacturing executive is basing this type of decision on uncertain information (i.e., forecasts) and when this uncertainty is not measured for him so that he can at least "play the averages," he tends to let changes in overall demand accumulate into large inventory overstocks or deficits before making a change in production rate. Since, in his company, no one has established what size inventory deficit or overstock justifies a change in production rate, the decision is postponed while the changes in demand accumulate week after week—building up to a genuine crisis which then forces a decision. In the meantime, in a make-to-stock company (for example) the inventory may decline far below the level required to give good customer service, while in a make-to-order company the delivery lead times quoted to customers may lengthen until business is lost because these lead times are uncompetitive. If, on the other hand, capacity ought to be cut, inventories will build up higher and higher while the decision is postponed. A good production control system should focus attention on the unpleasant decisions that must be made, the alternatives that exist (often unpleasant) and the consequences of not making the decision.

Control over any function requires at least these four elements:

1. A *norm* or plan against which to measure to know when the function is "on target."

2. Some *tolerance limits,* so that the system does not react to minute variations that will eventually be cancelled out by offsetting variations, but which will allow the system to recognize trends, and thus call for corrective action.

3. *Feedback,* so that actual performance can be compared against plan.

4. Some specific *corrective action* that can be taken to get back on plan when the function is out of control.

In production planning, the *norm* is the production plan discussed in Chapter 7 and the *tolerance limits* are based on measurement of the probable error in the forecast the plan was based on. The *feedback* consists of reporting actual production rates for the same production facilities included in the plan, and the specific *corrective actions* include hiring, layoff, overtime, subcontracting work, etc.

Some of the effects of poor production control and its impact on the national economy were discussed in Chapter 3. The need for control over production rates in order to control backlogs and lead time and the techniques of planning were discussed in Chapter 7. This chapter will be concerned primarily with using the production plan to control production rates, with particular emphasis on the techniques for establishing effective tolerance limits in the control system.

Using a production plan to control production rates

The production plan helps to avoid the pitfalls of overcompensation for business changes by requiring that production change *only enough during the planned period* to get the inventory back to the planned level. Figure 8-1 shows a production plan (taken from Fig. 7-4) with actual activity for the month of July posted against the plan. This was a make-to-stock production plan, and the base inventory level (that inventory required to give the desired level of customer service) was equal to 1400 units.

Figure 8-1

Make-To-Stock Production Plan

(From Figure 7-4)

Sales				Production			
Month	Week	Month	Cumulative	Month	Cumulative	Inv.	Remarks
July Planned Actual	2	1000 1120	8600 9400	448 470	9184 9600	1784 1400	
August Planned Actual	5	1500	10,100	1120	10,304	1404	
Sept. Planned Actual	4	900	11,000	896	11,200	1400	

It can be seen that in July, in spite of the fact that cumulative production totals were ahead of plan, sales were even further ahead, so that the inventory is now at the base level of 1400 units. If this base inventory level is to be maintained during the month of August, production will have to be 1500 units instead of the 1120 units previously planned.

Here is the type of basic decision-making that production control must assist management in handling. Two alternatives are:

1. To go below the base inventory level and have customer service go below the planned level.

2. To make a fairly substantial change in the production rate (although this change may only last a short period of time).

It is possible to make a production plan that includes tolerance in the form of *stabilization stock* in order to reduce the probability of having to change the plan too frequently. It is important, however, to determine how much stabilization stock must be included in order to accomplish the purpose without excessive amounts of inventory. This problem is analogous to that of determining the amount of reserve stock to carry for an item in order to reduce the possibility of a stockout.

This same type of problem occurs in a make-to-order business. Figure 8-2 shows incoming business stated in machine hours for a group of turret lathes. The forecast called for 1000 hours per week, and sales have varied quite widely around this forecast for the period shown.

One way to handle this incoming business would be to produce the following week the 1400 hours received during the week of 5-1, reduce production to 700 hours the next week to handle orders received during the week of 5-8, increase it once again to 920 hours for orders received in the week of 5-15, and continue to change production weekly to meet incoming sales rates. When production levels can be changed cheaply and easily, this is certainly feasible and will give the best customer service. Unfortunately, changing production levels in most plants incurs extra costs due to overtime, hiring, training, lost production, higher scrap rates from inexperienced operators, and many other factors.

Figure 8-2

Incoming Business—Turret Lathes

(Figures in hours)

Forecast	1000 hr/week
Week	Incoming business
5 – 1	1400 hours
5 – 8	700
5 – 15	920
5 – 22	700
5 – 29	850
6 – 5	1060
6 – 12	425
6 – 19	950
6 – 26	1300
7 – 3	1060
7 – 24	856
7 – 31	502

Looking once again at Fig. 8-2, it can be seen that the original forecast of 1000 hours per week seems somewhat high when compared to the actual incoming business average. If the weighted average forecasting technique discussed in Chapter 3 were applied to this particular set of data, a regular weekly updated forecast could be maintained. Figure 8-3 is based on the same incoming business for this group of turret lathes, but a simple weighted average is now used to make a weekly forecast for the following week. This forecast could actually be the production rate for the following week, if fairly small changes in production were easy and inexpensive to make.

Comparing Fig. 8-2 with Fig. 8-3, using the weighted average forecast as a means of controlling the production rate would reduce the weekly high rate from 1400 hours to 1080 hours and increase the low from 425 hours to 840 hours. By passing the full fluctuations in business level back to the plant, the production rate would have to vary almost 1000 hours (from a high of 1400 to a low of 425 hours), while use of the weighted average technique reduces this variation to just over 200 hours. It is apparent, however, that this second approach will require some order backlogs (not shown in Fig. 8-3), because full fluctuations are *not* passed back to production.

Figure 8-3

Weighted Average Forecast

Incoming Business—Turret Lathes (Figures in hours)

New forecast = W x incoming business + $(1-W)$ x old forecast					
Using weighting factors W = 0.2					
$1-W$ = 0.8					
Week	Incoming business	0.2 x Incoming business	Old forecast	0.8x Old forecast	New forecast
5−1	1400	280	1000	800	1080
5−8	700	140	1080	865	1005
5−15	920	185	1005	805	990
5−22	700	140	990	791	931
5−29	850	170	931	745	915
6−5	1060	212	915	731	943
6−12	425	85	943	755	840
6−19	950	190	840	672	862
6−26	1300	260	862	690	950
7−3	1060	212	950	760	972
7−24	856	170	972	778	948
7−31	502	---	948	---	----

Figure 8-4

Mean Absolute Deviation of

Incoming Business—Turret Lathes (Figures in hours)

Week	Incoming	Forecast	Deviation
5 − 1	1400	1000	400
5 − 8	700	1080	380
5 − 15	920	1005	85
5 − 22	700	990	290
5 − 29	850	931	81
		Total	1236
MAD = 1236/5 = 247			

In a make-to-order business, backlogs of orders are frequently used to absorb the fluctuations in incoming business. Our previous examples assumed that there were no backlogs of orders and that all production was handled the week after the orders were received. In actual practice, most companies find that it is not practical for them to change production rates frequently because such changes are expensive and take considerable time to accomplish.

The question which must be answered if backlogs are to be used to stabilize production is "How much backlog must be maintained?" In the previous chapter, this decision was made very roughly by observing deviations from the forecast of incoming business hours (Fig. 7-10). A more accurate method is to use the normal distribution, explained in conjunction with reorder systems in Chapter 5, to analyze the variations in incoming business and to determine the amount of backlog normally required to keep production fairly level.

Figure 8-4 shows this type of analysis of the first five weeks of incoming business. The individual weekly deviations are calculated and the mean absolute deviation is found to be 247 hours.

In the table of safety factors for the normal distribution, Fig. 5-7, the values are given for variations *above* the average only. Reserve stocks must protect only against *excessive* demand during the lead time. Since demand during the lead time will be *less* than the forecast approximately half of the time, no reserve stock will be needed to give 50% customer service. Therefore, the values given in Table 5-7 are those for service levels above 50%.

In determining how much backlog is needed to stabilize manufacturing operations, a different table must be used since backlogs will go down when incoming business is less than anticipated and will go up when incoming business is higher than anticipated. In other words, while only plus variations must be accounted for in setting reserve stock levels, both plus and minus variations must be accounted for in determining backlog requirements for a production plan. Figure 8-5 is the table to use for both plus and minus variations.

Figure 8-6 shows the results of level production, with backlogs starting at 617 hours ($2\frac{1}{2}$ mean absolute deviations) in the week of 6-5. Figure 8-5 shows that $2\frac{1}{2}$ mean absolute deviations should protect against running out of orders for more than $47\frac{1}{2}\%$ of the minus fluctuations in incoming business (if these fluctuations follow the normal distribution). Starting with a backlog of 617 hours and a production rate of 900 hours equal to the forecast average incoming business, the backlog would go below 617 hours whenever incoming business was less than the forecast production rate. Since incoming business should be lower than forecast only 50% of the time, over $47\frac{1}{2}\%$ protection should provide for fairly stable production without running out of orders too frequently.

Incoming business will be above forecast 50% of the time and backlogs will increase at such times. An additional 617 hours will include more

Figure 8-5

Table of Safety Factors for Normal Distribution
(Plus and Minus Variations)

Probable % of occurrences	Standard deviation	Mean absolute deviation
0.00 %	0.00	0.00
25.00 %	0.67	0.84
30.00 %	0.84	1.05
34.13 %	1.00	1.25
35.00 %	1.04	1.30
39.44 %	1.25	1.56
40.00 %	1.28	1.60
43.32 %	1.50	1.88
44.00 %	1.56	1.95
44.52 %	1.60	2.00
45.00 %	1.65	2.06
46.00 %	1.75	2.19
47.00 %	1.88	2.35
47.72 %	2.00	2.50
48.00 %	2.05	2.56
48.61 %	2.20	2.75
49.00 %	2.33	2.91
49.18 %	2.40	3.00
49.38 %	2.50	3.13
49.50 %	2.57	3.20
49.60 %	2.65	3.31
49.70 %	2.75	3.44
49.80 %	2.88	3.60
49.86 %	3.00	3.75
49.90 %	3.09	3.85
49.93 %	3.20	4.00
49.99 %	4.00	5.00

than $47\frac{1}{2}\%$ of the times when business is higher than forecast. The backlog could then go as low as zero (at which point production would have to be decreased) or as high as 1234 hours (at which point production should be increased). Figure 8-7 shows the turret lathe backlog graphically and shows the upper and lower control limits in a control chart to indicate when to change production rates.

The values in Fig. 8-5 show that $2\frac{1}{2}$ MAD will include 47.72% of the plus variations and 47.72% of the minus variations. In other words, the backlog should stay within the range of 0-1234 hours 95% of the time.

Figure 8-6

Backlog Hours with Level Production—Turret Lathes

Week	Incoming business	Production	Backlog hours
6–5	1060	900	617*
6–12	425	900	142
6–19	950	900	192
6–26	1300	900	592
7–3	1060	900	752
7–24	856	900	708
7–31	502	900	310

*2.5 x 247 (MAD) = 617

Figure 8-7

Turret Lathe Backlog Control Chart

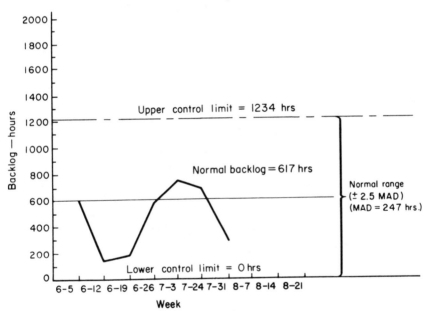

Expressed in terms of weeks, this means that one week in twenty the production level may have to be changed either upward or downward.

This backlog of hours behind the turret lathes is called *stabilization stock*. The greater the stabilization stock, the less frequently production level changes will have to be made. Fig. 8-8 shows the amount of stabilization stock required for various numbers of production level changes

Figure 8-8

Stabilization Stock vs. Production Level Changes

Production changes per year	Fraction of weeks without a change	% of weeks without a change	No. MAD* ± required (MAD = 247 hrs.)	Stabilization stock
1	49/50 =	98 %	2.91	1440 hrs.
2	48/50 =	96 %	2.56	1265 hrs.
4	46/50 =	92 %	2.19	1080 hrs.
6	44/50 =	88 %	1.95	964 hrs.
8	42/50 =	84 %	1.74	860 hrs.
10	40/50 =	80 %	1.60	790 hrs.
12	38/50 =	76 %	1.48	730 hrs.
14	36/50 =	72 %	1.36	670 hrs.
16	34/50 =	68 %	1.25	617 hrs.
18	32/50 =	64 %	1.15	568 hrs.
20	30/50 =	60 %	1.05	519 hrs.

*From Figure 8-5

during the year. If it is desired to change production only once during the year, the fraction of weeks without a change should be 49/50 or 98%. This 98% ($\pm 49\%$) stabilization should require ± 2.91 MAD according to Fig. 8-5, or 1440 hours of stabilization stock. If more frequent changes can be tolerated, less stabilization stock will be required, as shown in Fig. 8-8. The choice of particular numbers of changes depends on the economics of carrying the extra stabilization inventory *vs.* the costs of changing the production rate. This information can then be used to develop firm decision rules, without guessing at the amount of backlog required. Using the statistical concept of a normal distribution, a small sample can be used as a basis to determine what is *most likely* to happen over a fairly long period of time.

Value of decision rules

Decision rules have great practical value in industry. Determining when to change production levels is always difficult—there is a great deal of nuisance and money involved.

Established decision rules help manufacturing management avoid postponing decisions until a crisis has occurred. In making a decision rule, the production control manager is in effect setting the rules of the game *once* instead of each time it is played. Rather than having management teams spend a great deal of time each week deciding whether the present situation really justifies a change in the production rate, the decision as to *what justifies a change* should be made once. From then on, the weekly discussions can be concerned with the action to be taken to accomplish the change.

Whenever decision rules have been applied, the results have almost always been good. The actual form of the decision rules is probably secondary in importance to having a rational approach to the control of the production level. Application of this technique will not eliminate the ups and downs in the business cycle (although widespread use of more rational control methods would certainly dampen the usual amplifying effects in industry, since businesses are so dependent on one another), but decision rules can be of great value in measuring and coping with these changes in activity in the most effective and economical manner. They are part of the basic theme of good production control—*keeping out of trouble rather than getting out of trouble.*

Linear decision rules

More complex decision rules to assist in planning and controlling production rates and the work force needed to attain these rates have been developed as mathematical formulas.[1] These are intended to make possible (with or without a computer) routine calculations of the volume of production to be scheduled in the next month or week and the number of productive employees needed, based on a number of cost factors included in the derivation of the formulas.

The alternative ways to schedule production to meet fluctuating demand are:

1. *Vary production to match the demand.* This implies that demand must be known (at least for the period required to adjust the production rate). This is seldom the case, and planned production levels must be based on forecasts of demand. It also implies that plans will be carried out effectively and that planned rates will be achieved on schedule. Practitioners will recognize that this seldom happens. The variation can be obtained by:

   a. Adding people to the productive force or laying them off

   b. Working short shifts or overtime to vary the work hours of a constant labor force

---

[1] Holt, Modigliani, Muth, and Simon, *Planning Production, Inventories and Work Force,* Prentice-Hall, Englewood Cliffs, New Jersey, 1960.

c. Sub-contracting work to outside companies

d. Some combination of a, b, and/or c

2. *Hold production constant and let inventories of product take care of demand fluctuations.* This implies that production over the long-range is planned to provide enough inventory at the end of the peak season to satisfy the demand and that the business has the capital to invest in the required inventories and the space to store them.

3. *Hold production constant and let backlogs (inventories) of customers' orders take care of the fluctuations.* This implies that customers will wait varying lengths of time for delivery of their goods.

4. Some combination of 1, 2, and/or 3.

Each of these major and subalternatives has some costs associated with it. The problem of selecting that combination of alternatives which results in the lowest total cost of operations with relatively unknown future demand and performance is a formidable task.

Through the mathematical techniques of operations research, *linear decision rules* have been developed which give *optimal* solutions to this problem for certain well-defined assumptions about the related costs.

Figure 8-9

Costs of Hiring and Laying Off
Company "A" Linear Decision Rule

No. Men* Per Month	Total Cost
1	$ 150
2	400
3	700
4	1000
5	1500
6	2000
8	2800
10	4000
12	5000
15	7000
20	10,000
25	13,500

*Net additions to (hired) or reductions from (laid off) the workforce during the month

Figure 8-10

Inventory Carrying Costs
Company "A" Linear Decision Rule

Net Inventory Thousands of gallons	Monthly Cost
−200	$ 7000
− 150	5000
− 100	3500
− 50	2250
0	1600
50	1000
100	600
150	400
200	450
250	800
300	1250
350	1900
400	2800
450	4000
500	6000

An example will illustrate the form and use of a simple linear decision rule.

Company A manufactures glue using a semi-continuous process. Regular payroll costs are known, as are overtime premium payments. The costs associated with hiring and laying off employees are studied, and it is concluded that these as shown in Fig. 8-9. It is found that these costs increase *per man* with the number of men involved in a given period, hence it is more costly to make large work force changes in any one period. It is assumed that the costs of hiring are equal to those of laying off.

Inventory carrying costs are also studied and are determined to be as shown in Fig. 8-10. Negative inventory (backorders) is believed to be very undesirable, and high costs are associated with being out of stock. The minimum carrying costs occur at about 150,000 gallons—below this figure, backorder costs more than offset the savings resulting from lower inventories.

An operations research team studies these cost relationships and the pattern of sales demand, and develops two equations[1] which are intended to yield minimum cost decisions on manpower and production rates. These are:

$$M_{\text{Jan}} = 2.09 + 0.743\, M_{\text{Dec}} - 0.010\, I_{\text{Dec}} + \begin{cases} .0101\ D_{\text{Jan}} \\ +\ .0088\ D_{\text{Feb}} \\ +\ .0071\ D_{\text{Mar}} \\ +\ .0054\ D_{\text{Apr}} \\ +\ .0042\ D_{\text{May}} \\ +\ .0031\ D_{\text{June}} \\ +\ .0023\ D_{\text{July}} \\ +\ .0016\ D_{\text{Aug}} \\ +\ .0012\ D_{\text{Sept}} \\ +\ .0009\ D_{\text{Oct}} \\ +\ .0006\ D_{\text{Nov}} \\ +\ .0005\ D_{\text{Dec}} \end{cases} \quad (8\text{-}1)$$

[1] Holt, Modigliani, and Simon, "Linear Decision Rule for Production and Employment Scheduling," *Management Science*, 2:1 (Oct. 1955).

$$P_{\text{Jan}} = 153 + 0.993\ M_{\text{Dec}} - 0.464\ I_{\text{Dec}} + \left\{ \begin{array}{ll} & .463\ D_{\text{Jan}} \\ + & .234\ D_{\text{Feb}} \\ + & .111\ D_{\text{Mar}} \\ + & .046\ D_{\text{Apr}} \\ + & .013\ D_{\text{May}} \\ - & .002\ D_{\text{June}} \\ - & .008\ D_{\text{July}} \\ - & .010\ D_{\text{Aug}} \\ - & .009\ D_{\text{Sept}} \\ - & .008\ D_{\text{Oct}} \\ - & .007\ D_{\text{Nov}} \\ - & .005\ D_{\text{Dec}} \end{array} \right. \qquad (8\text{-}2)$$

The symbols used in these equations are:

M = Manload, number of men employed
I = Inventory, gallons of glue in thousands
D = Forecasted demand, gallons ordered in thousands
P = Production, gallons of glue in thousands

Although they appear to be formidable mathematical relationships, these equations may be expressed simply as:

Next month's manload (equation 8-1) equals:

a constant (2.09)
plus: a fraction (0.743) of this month's manload
minus: a fraction (0.010) of this month's inventory
plus: a fraction of the forecasted demand for each of the next 12 months (decreasing as the month is further in the future).

Next month's production rate is determined the same way, using a different constant and different fractions of the same factors: manload, inventory and forecasted demand (equation 8-2).

Using these two equations, simple calculations each month will determine the most economical manload and production rate for the following month, based on forecasts of demand for the next 12 months. For example, suppose that the data at the end of December were:

$$\text{Manload} = M_{\text{Dec}} = 80 \text{ men}$$
$$\text{Inventory} = I_{\text{Dec}} = 300,000 \text{ gallons}$$

Demand for the next year is forecast as:

$$D_{Jan} = 380,000 \text{ gallons} \qquad D_{July} = 565,000 \text{ gallons}$$
$$D_{Feb} = 370,000 \quad // \qquad D_{Aug} = 430,000 \quad //$$
$$D_{Mar} = 528,000 \quad // \qquad D_{Sept} = 360,000 \quad //$$
$$D_{Apr} = 720,000 \quad // \qquad D_{Oct} = 750,000 \quad //$$
$$D_{May} = 420,000 \quad // \qquad D_{Nov} = 683,000 \quad //$$
$$D_{June} = 800,000 \quad // \qquad D_{Dec} = 546,000 \quad //$$

In order to facilitate calculations, equations 8-1 and 8-2 use inventory and demand data expressed in thousands, dropping the last 3 zeros (for example, $D_{Jan} = 380$ and $I_{Dec} = 300$). Solving the two equations for January operating data gives:

Manload $= M_{Jan} = 82$ men (2 more than December)

Production $= P_{Jan} = 426,000$ gallons

The inventory will increase by the difference between production and demand (426,000 − 380,000 = 46,000 gallons). The planned inventory at the end of January will then be 300,000 + 46,000 = 346,000 gallons. This can be calculated in one step using the equation:

$$I_{Jan} = I_{Dec} + P_{Jan} - D_{Jan} \tag{8-3}$$

Some interesting observations can be made about the application of such equations to the real business world:

1. A practical management would want to test their effectiveness by simulating what would have happened if the equations had been used in the past and comparing against actual results.

2. Because of the complexity of the mathematical derivations, it is not possible to determine the effect on the decisions of changes in costs without deriving new equations. Negotiating a new union contract which increased wage rates would change the constants in equations 8-1 and 8-2, as would a revision of hiring and layoff costs, but just how these are changed could only be shown by working out new equations. This would require the services of the operations research team each time it had to be done.

3. Factors which were not included in the original derivation might become important, and it may be impossible to include them in new equations. As an example, suppose the company wanted to raise capital for expansion by liquidating part of the inventory, and management were willing to accept the lower level of service which would result. The inventory carrying cost is the only factor in the equations relating to this decision, and it is not easy to see how the effect of this decision can be expressed as a specific cost of carrying inventory.

4. The equations assume a specific amount of production per worker

on the payroll. The actual number of people employed and the hours worked would have to be increased if this productivity were not met or inventory levels would fall, causing customer service to suffer.

Linear decision rules have real potential for assisting management to control production level changes on a rational basis. Prudent management will test such rules thoroughly by simulation before using them in order to understand their use. They will also become familiar with the basic assumptions underlying the derivation so as to know which changes in operating costs and conditions will require new derivations or overriding decisions. The great danger is in assuming that management can be relinquished to formulas and that rules like these can reflect all significant considerations in any decision—they cannot!

Applied properly, linear decision rules result in improved control over production levels when compared to intuitive or other irrational approaches. Results would certainly be more stable and consistent as long as no major variations occurred in the factors which affect the basic assumptions used in the derivation of the equations.

As an interesting side-note, linear decision rules have found extensive use as the bases for production and manpower computer games used in production control and business management courses in colleges, industry and technical society seminars. They can be programmed for a computer which can make the calculations and print out results based on optimum decisions, while teams of men make decisions on rational or intuitive bases and match their results against the computer's.

Decision rules and reaction time

The application of decision rules assumes that production rates can be changed fairly rapidly once the decision to change has been made. In many real-life situations, this is not the case. It may take a considerable period of time to hire and train new people.

The construction of the decision rules determines how often a change in production level will have to be made. These rules are presumed to produce the most economical changes, but they do not take *reaction time* into account.

Reaction time is that time elapsed from the moment it is decided to change production levels until the production rates have either increased or decreased. This time usually includes placing a requisition through the personnel department to hire a man, actually finding and hiring the man, training him and, finally, getting his production output up to the normal amount. During this period, deviations from the forecast can continue to occur, and a rigorous calculation of stabilization stock levels would include some inventory to cover this period.

The calculation of this quantity of *reaction reserves* is fairly straight-forward. It involves estimating anticipated forecast error and the conversion of this estimate into an estimate of forecast error *over the reaction time*. This is the same type of relationship that exists in developing reserve stock, when the forecast error is calculated over a weekly time period and must be converted to forecast error over the lead time period, using tables such as Table 5-9. This calculation specifically recognizes the fact that the forecast error provided for in the stabilization stock calculation is for a one-week period, and that forecast errors may accumulate during the reaction time.

While this is an interesting relationship, it is rather academic since few of today's companies have developed decision rules or calculated stabilization stock. The student should be aware of this general relationship, while understanding that normal practice—even when stabilization stock requirements have been developed—is to use extraordinary production measures such as overtime to handle any significant increase in demand during the reaction period.

Practical considerations

In applying decision rules, some practical considerations can be of help to the production control manager:

1. Seasonal production: Controlling the level of production to meet a seasonal production plan provides some interesting problems. During the off-season, when production is being maintained at levels which will build-up inventories, there is little need for fast reaction to deviations from the production plan. The required reaction becomes increasingly crucial as the end of the peak selling season approaches and inventories are down to their lowest level (in fact, this level is at the base inventory level—the minimum inventory required to give the desired level of customer service). During the inventory-building season, the actual inventory can vary from the planned level by as much as a month's supply without causing any immediate problems as long as corrective action can be taken in time to meet the target set for the end of the peak selling season. It is often practical, for example, to maintain a monthly production plan during the inventory-building period, and then to switch over to a weekly production plan during the peak selling season.

The mean absolute deviation of forecast error calculated during the off-season is necessarily too small to be of much value during the peak selling season. A useful approach to handling this problem is to increase this mean absolute deviation in direct proportion to the anticipated increase in sales. A simple example will illustrate the application:

Weekly sales rate, January–March = 1000 hrs/week
Mean absolute deviation = 280 hrs
Weekly sales rate, April–June = 1500 hrs
Mean absolute deviation = 280 × 1500/1000 = 420 hrs

While this approach has much practical value, it should be tested on real data from the company concerned before assuming that it will work, since in some companies forecast error during the peak season seems to bear little relationship to error during the slow season.

2. Inertia in changing production: There is a tendency in most plants for production levels to have tremendous inertia. As previously mentioned, it is frequently difficult to get line managers to change production levels since they are far more conscious of the costs and difficulties involved in changing rates than they are of the dangers involved in not changing. This, of course, is the very reason for having decision rules—delays in changing the production rate can make the amount of change required so large as to be almost impossible to attain.

If, for example, in a seasonal business it is found that the actual inventory level is the equivalent of 1500 hours below target 20 weeks before the planned inventory low point, this situation can be corrected by raising the production rate over the planned level by 75 hours per week (1500 divided by 20). If this decision is postponed and the production rate is not changed until 5 weeks before the inventory will be at its low point, the production rate will have to be changed by 300 hours per week (1500 divided by 5). Such a change may be beyond the ability of the organization, and customer service will suffer over the longer period needed to restore the proper inventory levels.

This inertia exists when the production rate is cut back as well as when it is increased. Companies with incentive systems often find that they can produce as much after a reduction in hours (for example, from a 5- to a 4-day week) as they could on regular time because the workers increase their pace in order to earn their normal wage even though hours have been shortened.

3. Average production rates: Line manufacturing people often tend to look at planned production rates as ceilings rather than as averages. Production losses caused by holidays, unexpected equipment breakdowns, absenteeism, etc., tend to be overlooked if the planned rates are being attained during periods of full output. Only close attention to the cumulative production totals on the production plan will avoid serious effects resulting from the sum of many small losses.

4. Sequence of changes: In manufacturing assemblies such as the kitchen mixers discussed in Chapter 7, any change in the assembly production rate can only be made in the proper time sequence, following changes in plans to purchase raw materials, manufacture components and put together subassemblies. There is no practical value to increasing the assembly production rate if components will not be available to meet the planned increase in the rate.

Decreases in the production rate, on the other hand, can be instituted simultaneously at all stages of production. If they are expected to be long-term decreases, the purchasing and production rates should be set low enough to reduce the intermediate inventories of work in process, components, and semi-finished inventory.

5. Overtime vs. increased workforce: One debate that frequently goes on in a manufacturing concern is the relative value of overtime. Some companies try to enforce a rule that no overtime will be allowed while others feel that overtime is an extremely economical way to manufacture, and therefore include overtime in their production planning.

The real question is "Will the production increase be of a long enough duration to justify hiring people-" (assuming sufficient equipment is available, etc.) "-or should it be handled with overtime?" The answer to this question can be obtained by developing some approximate costs. The costs involved are those of overtime (including any additional overhead, which goes up proportionately with overtime) *vs.* the costs of increasing production to the new level and bringing it back down again. For example, if overtime costs for a change in the production level of a given magnitude were expected to total $200 in overtime premium per week, and the cost of hiring and training manpower, and the consequent layoffs to make this same change, equaled $1000 as a one-time cost, then the following rule could be used: Whenever the anticipated increase in the production level will last for more than 5 weeks—the breakeven point, or the point at which the total weekly overtime premium would equal the hiring and training costs—then people should be hired.

Like any attempt to assign costs to decision alternatives, this one must be handled with the practical recognition that the costs involved do not usually make the decision by merely being inserted into the formula. There might be other considerations—such as the company's reputation for employment stability—that should be considered. As with any decision alternatives, the proper approach is to gather the best available cost information, show the probable cost of the alternatives, point out the intangibles involved in the alternatives and, finally, to assist management in making a decision.

When using decision rules, it is recommended that production level changes made when the backlog first goes above or below the control limits for one week be of a temporary nature—that is, either overtime or a temporary cutback in hours. If the backlog continues above or below the control limits for two or more consecutive weeks (due to sales outside the control limits for two weeks running), then the changes should be more permanent, such as adding to or reducing the labor force. Two consecutive weeks of incoming business above or below the forecasted rate by more than $2\frac{1}{2}$ mean absolute deviations probably indicate that the original forecast is no longer valid and that a trend is occurring.

6. Simulation: When developing decision rules for changing the production level, the same approach should be taken as is used in developing forecasting techniques. Statistics and mathematics have real application in industry, but should not be adopted with blind faith. The production control manager should simulate—use past history, experiment with these techniques, and see what really would have happened if they had been in practice in the past. He can then evaluate these results and advise management as to what to expect before applying any type of decision rule.

Controlling the level of purchased inventories

One of the most significant aspects of any production plan is that it handles items in meaningful groups. A manufacturing production plan should include all items that go through common manufacturing facilities. A purchasing production plan, likewise, should include meaningful groups of purchased items. All of the components that go into a particular assembly can be grouped together and then broken down into subgroups that come from particular vendors. Looking at the total purchased inventory in relation to the total rate of use can give a quick overall control that cannot be attained by reviewing the great number of individual orders for items in the group.

This means, of course, that meaningful totals must be used in these purchasing plans (and to the purchaser, the most meaningful total is often dollars). The usual method for making a purchasing plan is to determine the number of components that will be needed to meet a planned production rate, and then to extend each of the individual component inventories and purchase commitments by the unit cost so that a meaningful total in dollars will result. In other respects, the purchasing plan is identical to the production plan, and its use as a control instrument is exactly the same.

The purchasing plan is a striking example of the similarity between the planning and controlling of production and using financial budgets. In fact, if the accounting system were able to give cost information within 24 to 48 hours after activities occurred, the production control system could be tied right into it. This similarity in the information required by all elements of the organization is what makes an integrated management information system so attractive. The idea of this approach is to develop and present the basic information necessary for running the plant in a standardized form (usually employing a computer) that can be used by all departments on a timely basis, so that it is of real value as control information.

Interrelated elements

One of the characteristics of production and inventory control that has caused practitioners great problems is the interrelationship of the elements involved. Capacity planning cannot be effective until there is an inventory control system that generates realistic requirements. On the other hand, the inventory control system that merely generates orders and releases them to the plant without regard for capacity usually generates its own excessive lead times and resultant higher reserve stocks. If the planning system has not been provided with controls, it is inevitable that production will eventually go out of control and that changes in the production level will occur too late to avoid crises.

It is essential that the production control system include some decision boundaries, and it is important that these be spelled out so that anyone might recognize when a change in production level is required. Such tools as the *service vs. investment curve*[1] can then be used to show the potential impact on customer service if production levels are not changed. In a make-to-order company, the impact on future delivery lead times can be projected to help other managers recognize the real alternatives involved.

The need for some decision rules or "boundaries" is so essential to control that it is recommended that they be implemented in any production control system, even if they must first be developed according to boundaries established by judgment (then later refined, using some of the techniques discussed in this chapter). Even if these control limits are less than scientific to start with, they should be better than the bases currently used to make production level changes. Establishing the boundaries only once provides far more rational control than having to debate where the boundary is and postpone corrective action until a crisis makes it obvious that action was indeed required.

---

[1]Figure 6-13.

Control over the level of production is necessary in order to insure that the right items come through production. If sufficient capacity does not exist, techniques such as expediting will only get some of the items through. It is folly to increase expediting efforts when the real problem is lack of capacity, since expediting only "robs Peter to pay Paul." If the requirements generated by the inventory control system are realistic, yet a great deal of expediting is required in a particular plant, the chances are that this is merely a symptom of the real problem: *lack of control over production capacity.*

The next two chapters will deal with the problems of controlling the flow of individual orders through the plant within the planned capacity. This requires controlling input to select the best jobs that balance inventory and customer requirements against plant capabilities, and insuring that these jobs flow in the proper sequence through succeeding manufacturing operations.

Bibliography

1. Biegel, John E., *Production Control: A Quantitative Approach,* Prentice-Hall, Englewood Cliffs, New Jersey, 1963.

2. Holt, Charles C., Modigliani, Franco, Muth, John F., and Simon, Herbert A., *Planning Production, Inventories and Work Force,* Prentice-Hall, Englewood Cliffs, New Jersey, 1960.

3. MacNiece, E. H., *Production Forecasting, Planning, and Control,* 3rd Edition, Wiley, New York, 1961.

4. Magee, John F., *Production Planning and Inventory Control,* McGraw, New York, 1958.

5. Scheele, Evan D., Westerman, William L., and Wimmert, Robert J., *Principles and Design of Production Control Systems,* Prentice-Hall, Englewood Cliffs, New Jersey, 1960.

CONTROLLING INPUT :
SCHEDULING

The role of scheduling in effective
production control

Up to this point we have developed the methods of planning inventory levels and production rates and controlling production rates. The control of input to the manufacturing facilities must be a function of both the inventory controls and the available capacity if work-in-process, backlogs, and lead time are to be controlled. The broad categories of input control can be broken down into:

1. *Selecting* the right orders to feed into the plant, based either on the materials control system or customer orders and the planned production rates.

2. *Scheduling*—assigning desired completion dates to the operations that must be performed on each manufacturing order.

3. *Loading*—comparing the hours required for each operation with the hours available in each work center in the time period specified by the schedule.

The techniques of capacity-planning establish and control the overall flow rate through the production facilities, often in fairly crude form, with the objective of providing required capacity and providing a means for controlling total work-in-process levels and resultant lead times. The input selection system deals with the individual manufacturing orders and tries to choose those orders that best balance the requirements of the inventory system and the capabilities of the plant. Scheduling provides a basis for following job progress through the succeeding manufacturing operations, and the machine loading system is a short-term detail capacity-control technique that highlights day-to-day bottlenecks and underloads.

The control of input naturally precedes the control needed to meet schedule dates in the factory. In practice today, input control receives far too little consideration and, as a consequence, excessive expediting, dispatching, and effort in locating jobs—including, sometimes, searching for lost jobs—frequently reduces the production control function to a group of "hurry clerks" working extremely long hours and trying desperately to answer a constant barrage of questions relating to late jobs and interrupted schedules raised by both sales and manufacturing personnel. When this production control effort is channeled into better planning and control of input, conditions usually improve substantially. When a better input control is achieved, less time and effort are required for job location, expediting and dispatching, but, far more important positive benefits will be obtained through getting more jobs completed on schedule.

Selecting the input

Once a production level is established, it is important that schedulers be disciplined to feed in the right items at the rate needed to meet the planned production level. Even when production rates are established, overzealous schedulers will usually overload the factory—principally, it seems, from a desire to insure meeting required dates by "getting jobs started as early as possible."

An inventory control system in a manufacturing company will generate random peaks and troughs of shop orders, and the flow of these orders must be regulated in order to control work-in-process levels. Some examples follow, showing how this control over input can be accomplished.

Chapter 6 showed how base inventory levels are determined so that a production plan can be prepared. The base inventory level depends on the desired level of customer service and the specific order points and EOQ's or the materials plan used for generating replenishment orders. Once the level has been planned, these inventory control techniques must be used properly to control the mix input.

Figure 9-1
Production Plan—All Models of Lamps
(All figures in pieces)

		Sales	Production	Inventory
Week 8 (Actual starting inventory)				22,000 pieces
Week 9	Planned Actual	5200	6000	22,800
Week 10	Planned Actual	6200	6000	22,600
Week 11	Planned Actual	6200	6000	22,400
Week 12	Planned Actual	7200	6000	2 1,200
Week 13	Planned Actual	7200	6000	20,000*

*Base inventory level

Figure 9-1 shows a simple production plan for a company making several models of lamps. This production plan is used to control the assembly operation, while other production plans would be needed to control the component manufacturing sequences. Note that this plan calls for level production over a five-week period and a reduction of inventory to the base level.

Figure 9-2 shows the weekly production scheduling report for the lamps included in the production plan in Fig. 9-1. This production

Figure 9-2
Weekly Production Scheduling Report
(All figures in pieces and weeks)

Lamps	Weekly incoming business	Year to date incoming business	Net stock available	Factory order	Order point	Weekly weighted average incoming business	Total weeks of stock	Order point expressed as weeks of stock	Economic ordering quantity
#7W	341	17,933	1739	3078	2730	485	10	5.6	2250
#7D	288	9837	1224	832	1436	274	7	5.2	1500
#9W	894	35,329	4007	1956	4242	924	6	4.5	2000
#9D	251	10,120	2189	662	1386	259	11	5.3	1500
#9P	1187	46,690	8371	- - - -	6250	1290	6	4.8	2500
#11D	1332	47,078	2844	7050	6768	1345	7	5.0	2500
#11P	598	21,896	778	3302	3346	639	6	5.2	2000

scheduling report has many of the elements found in a standard *stock status* report. It shows data on incoming business for each item, net stock available, the amount currently on order with the factory and the order point and economic ordering quantities. However, other features of this report are specifically designed to make it useful in generating orders to meet a planned production rate. In this report, the exponential smoothing technique explained in Chapter 2 has been used to update a weekly weighted average of incoming business to serve as a forecast of demand for each item, so that the latest sales trends can be identified. The order point itself has been recalculated each week for the new demand forecast, using an updated calculation of the mean absolute deviation (explained in Chapter 5) to revise the reserve stock portion. The total inventory (the sum of available stock and quantities on order with the factory) and the order point are both expressed as weeks of stock by dividing them by the latest forecast of incoming business for each item. The scheduler can use this report in selecting lamps to fill his starting schedule to meet the planned production level.

The total inventories of lamps shown on the production scheduling report in Fig. 9-2 are above their order points. This is a fairly normal situation when inventories are being built-up in anticipation of seasonal sales or a vacation shutdown. Nevertheless, this production scheduling report can be used to choose the proper items to be scheduled in order to meet the planned production rate of 6000 lamps per week shown in the production plan. To do this, the scheduler may select those lamps closest to their order points—those with the lowest total weeks of stock—and schedule them so that inventories are kept in balance. There are three items that have a six-week inventory level: the first is the #11P (pin-up lamp) which is closer to its ordering point than any other, the next is the #9P (pin-up lamp) and the third the #9W (wall lamp). Scheduling these would release a total of 6500 lamps for assembly production. While this is slightly in excess of the 6000 planned production rate, the scheduler would release these this week and compensate for the small excess in succeeding starting schedules.

This production scheduling report thus provides the technique for generating a starting schedule to meet a planned production rate, rather than having order points generate orders at random with widely varying demands on the plant's production capacity. Another extremely valuable feature is that it also eliminates the need to recalculate order points when it is desired to build up inventory levels in anticipation of periods of high sales or low production. The production plan indicates the rates needed to raise the inventory and the scheduling report shows which items to start in order to meet the planned production rate. Tinkering with order points is unnecessary.

Figure 9-3

Ranked Weekly Production Scheduling Report

(All figures in pieces and weeks)

Lamps	Weekly incoming business	Year to date incoming business	Net stock available	Factory order	Order point	Weekly weighted average incoming business	Total weeks of stock	Order point expressed as weeks of stock	Economic ordering quantity
# 11 P	598	2 1,896	778	3302	3346	639	6	5.2	2000
# 9P	1187	46,690	8371	- - - -	6250	1290	6	4.8	2500
# 9W	894	35,329	4007	1956	4242	924	6	4.5	2000
# 7D	288	9837	1224	832	1436	274	7	5.2	1500
# 11 D	1332	47,078	2844	7050	6768	1345	7	5.0	2500
# 7W	341	1 7,933	1739	3078	2730	485	10	5.6	2250
# 9D	251	10,120	2189	662	1386	259	11	5.3	1500

The production scheduling report would be easier to use if all the items were ranked, so that the scheduler might readily see which were close to their order point level. Figure 9-3 shows a ranked weekly production scheduling report with the items arranged in order of increasing total weeks of stock and decreasing order point weeks. If there is a large number of items involved and a computer is available to do the sorting, this type of ranking can speed-up and eliminate errors from the work of preparing a schedule.

The production scheduling report provides the link between inventory control and production control. It provides the tool the scheduler needs to do an effective job of selecting the items that must be included on the starting schedule to feed work to the plant so as to meet planned production rates. This eliminates the need for large starting backlogs that inevitably result when orders are generated without regard to the plant's production capabilities.

Other factors must often be considered in addition to the overall capacity of the manufacturing facility when preparing schedules. When scheduling a press department, a screw machine department or a line of extrusion presses, for example, the ability of the department to perform the required number of setups is as important as its total of available machine hours. For this situation, a periodic review of all the parts made in the department (using a scheduling report such as Fig. 9-4, Weekly Schedule Review—Turret Lathes) will make it possible to schedule to both a total of machine hours and a limiting maximum number of setups.

First, a target of hours must be set, based on the forecast rate of usage

Figure 9-4

Weekly Schedule Review—Turret Lathes

Week ending _____12-10_____

Week no. _____48_____   70 planned weekly schedule hrs.

Dept._____84_____   10 maximum setup hours

Machine center #1700   110 total hrs. in machine center

Part no.	A B C	Description	Used on	Annual use	Next planned order release	Order qty	Order qty cost	Order qty hours	Setup hours
21	A	2 nd–spindle	"A" motor	3000	Week #47	200	1222	22	5
30	A	Upr. spg. carr.	"A" motor	6000	Week #48	700	281	31	3
59	A	Piston	"A" motor	6000	Week #3	400	298	31	2
64	B	Lwr. spg. carr.	"A"motor	6000	Week #50	1000	235	40	3
18	C	Pack washer	Gear box	1000	Week #51	500	41	12.5	2
27	B	Roller	Gear box	2400	Week #51	400	138	20	2
29	C	Spg. guide	Coupling	200	Week #50	500	25	50	3
34	C	Adj. screw	Coupling	2400	Week #50	2300	85	77	3
54	C	Ball seat	Emerg. relse.	275	Week #50	150	37	30	2
55	C	Spg. plug	Coupling	275	Week #51	250	29	25	3
56	C	Floor plate	"B"motor	92	Week #2	100	82	9	3
46	C	#3–1st,#5–2nd — lens holder	Control box	850	Week #49	450	131	15	5

of all the parts, adding or deducting the effects of any desired changes in inventory levels of these parts. This is identical to preparing a production plan as discussed in Chapter 7, except that hours of machining time are used instead of pieces or dollars.

Next, a maximum limit is established for setups, based on the number of setup men available or the number of machine-hours which can be devoted to setting up without cutting into needed capacity for making parts.

Using these two factors, total hours and setup hours, the planner or scheduler can review the inventory position of all items, as shown in the *Next planned order release* column of Fig. 9-4. As an example, suppose a review of the report indicates that Components 21, 30, and 46 should be started in the next week. If he were to schedule these for the next week, the scheduler would release:

Component	Order quant. hrs.	Setup hours
21	22	5
30	31	3
46	15	5
Totals:	68	13

He would be close to the planned weekly schedule of 70 total hours, but he would exceed the maximum of 10 setup hours. Consequently, the shop could not run on this schedule.

By reviewing other items in the group near their release dates, he would find Component 27 would soon have to be reordered. Substituting this for Component 46, which is in better condition than either 21 or 30, his schedule would be:

Component	Order quant. hrs.	Setup hours
21	22	5
30	31	3
27	20	2
Totals:	73	10

This would be practical for the shop. He would then have to be sure to schedule Component 46 the following week, and might even have to expedite subsequent operations on this part to cut the normal lead time and get it in stock on time. While greatly oversimplified, this example illustrates a very useful technique for scheduling to meet two limitations on production capacity.

Scheduling sequenced operations

Many intermittent, semi-process and even so-called "job shops" have a definable flow of work through the plant. While even the crudest attempt to control work-in-process will result in some improvement, anytime that flow lines of reasonably-sequenced operations can be identified, some specific scheduling techniques can be adopted that will enable the scheduler to reduce work-in-process without risking excessive downtime. In this type of plant, control can be greatly improved by having the scheduler look beyond the first operation to any subsequent operations which are critical because of limited capacity or because the operation is inflexible. Releasing work into a starting operation that will be backlogged later is self-defeating.

In many plants, it is quite practical to generate a weekly schedule to meet the planned production rates and then have the planner release the work to the plant on a daily basis. Each day, he can release a day's work for the first operation which he also knows to be a day's work for later critical operations. Consider, for example, the Pattern Panel Company, making control panel housings. The general sequence of operations is:

1. Shear—*Press department*
2. Blank—*Press department*
3. Pierce—*Press department*
4. De-burr—*Subassembly department*
5. Insert bushings—*Subassembly department*
6. Subassemble fasteners—*Subassembly department*
7. Plate or paint—*Finishing department*
8. Inspect—*Quality control department*
9. Pack—*Shipping department*

Figure 9-5

Pattern Panel Co.

Production Scheduling System

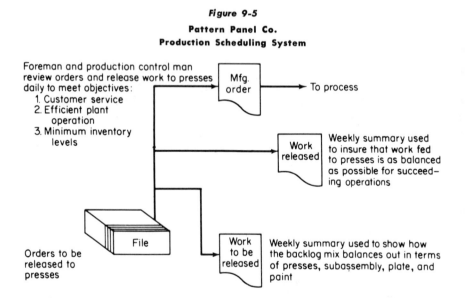

The Pattern Panel Company, following the simple production scheduling system shown in Fig. 9-5, releases a balanced load into this sequence of operations each week. Their emphasis is on rapid flow. They receive many individual orders, most of them requiring fairly short processing times. Figure 9-6 shows the weekly release summary used by the production planner for scheduling all operations.

For each major load center, the production planner has a target number

Figure 9-6

Pattern Panel Company

Weekly Release Summary

		Week #14
Load center	Hours released	Weekly capacity
Press department	2̶0̶ 4̶8̶ 1̶0̶8̶ 1̶6̶8̶ 180	240 hours
Subassembly	4̶0̶ 6̶0̶ 1̶0̶5̶ 115	120 hours
Plate	5̶ 1̶4̶ 2̶4̶ 28	80 hours
Paint	1̶0̶ 1̶8̶ 36	40 hours

of cumulative hours to be released per week. He and the foreman review daily the orders ahead of the press department. As he releases orders to the press department, he tries to select orders which provide the proper load within the capacity of subsequent departments. For example, based upon the information shown in Fig. 9-6, the planner would try to release orders totaling as near 240 hours as possible to the press department, without exceeding 120 hours in the subassembly department, 80 hours in plating or 40 hours in the painting department. This approach encourages rapid flow through the sequence of operations.

An adjunct to the weekly release summary is a weekly analysis of orders to be released showing how much work is about to be generated for the press, subassembly, plating and painting departments. Thus, any drastic change in the mix of hours to be sent out into the plant can be seen ahead of time, and plans can be made for additional or reduced capacity. Particularly where there are some make-to-stock products manufactured along with make-to-order items, it is sometimes possible to see a temporary drop-off in plating coming because of the mix of make-to-order business. This can be offset by generating more make-to-stock orders that will help level the load on the plating facility. This *input load balancing* is a most effective technique for controlling semiprocess flow operations characteristic of many of the plants that call themselves "job shops."

Figure 9-7 shows this type of load balancing for a series of three of the most critical operations in a metal-fabricating plant: the second, eighth, and tenth operations, respectively. Prior to the actual order scheduling, the machine load has been projected monthly to estimate the required capacity. This was a capacity-planning function and actual orders were generated separately using a materials plan. It is reasonable to expect that adequate average capacity should be available at each

Figure 9-7

Balancing Input for Sequenced Operations

	Running time in hours		
	Operation 2	Operation 8	Operation 10
Job A	– – – – –	2.22	3.99
Job B	2.76	4.96	6.00
Job C	– – – – –	– – – – –	6.75
Job D	0.63	0.50	1.30
Job E	8.75	7.80	8.75
Job F	13.52	11.84	12.64
Job G	7.64	6.56	7.24
Job H	1.46	– – – – –	3.26
Job J	2.52	2.00	5.20
Job K	4.38	4.44	8.04
Job L	7.30	8.00	14.00
Job M	16.90	13.80	13.40

Schedule #1 = Jobs A, B, C, D, E, F

Schedule #2 = Jobs A, B, C, D, E, H, J, K

	Operation 2 20 hr/wk	Operation 8 20 hr/wk	Operation 10 40 hr/wk
Planned Cap.			
Schedule #1	25.66	27.32	39.43
Schedule #2	20.50	21.92	43.29

operation, but it is known that just releasing orders into production at random would cause temporary overloads and underloads on the factory floor. Orders are rechecked weekly to put them in the latest proper priority (designated alphabetically—order "A" being highest, etc.). These manufacturing orders are put in a "Hold for release" file and reviewed weekly by a planner whose objective is to get the needed orders into process while generating the best balanced load on the facilities.

Schedule #1 containing orders A, B, C, D, E and F would generate overloads at operations 2 and 8 over the 10% excess allowed in this company. Removing job F from the proposed schedule—since it has the lowest priority and a high percentage of its hours in operations 2 and 8—gives an underload at all operations. From the next lower priority jobs in the unreleased file, choosing jobs H, J and K results in a better-balanced schedule that does not exceed the 10% allowance for overloads or underloads. Job G (there is no I) is left out because it will generate the same unbalanced conditions that job F did.

Obviously, jobs F and G will have a very high priority on next week's schedule. This approach really just keeps backlogs on the scheduler's desk rather than out on the factory floor, but the result is to avoid releasing work to a starting operation that will simply get bogged down at a succeeding operation.

Scheduling a balanced load means that plant backlogs will be kept to a minimum and that the lowest level of work-in-process will be maintained while keeping all operations working. This type of approach is often difficult to "sell" to a scheduler who has been in the habit of releasing work into the factory as it arrives on his desk, but he will soon see the advantage of having small backlogs on his desk, where he can react to changing priorities, engineering changes, etc., rather than out in the plant where an expediter has to try to arrange the "reacting."

Load balancing is an organized approach to controlling shop input which can be used in conjunction with conventional scheduling and loading techniques. If work does not usually follow the same path, it may be necessary to take time periods into account when balancing the load. A painting operation, for example, might be the fifth operation on one job or the twelfth operation on another job. Under these circumstances, it would be important to take arrival times into account when loading these jobs. This approach becomes practically identical to the *finite capacity loading* technique described later in this chapter.

Load-balancing techniques have been shown in their simplest form in order to explain the concept, but where more than two operations have to be balanced, the calculations can become very tedious. When a computer is available, this logic can be programmed and the computer can actually select the optimum starting schedule.

Some principles of shop input control

The techniques for selecting input and load balancing do not keep customer requirements from creating uneven demands on the shop, they merely try to smooth out the random ups and downs in the demand in a controlled manner rather than by having large inventories on the plant floor. This approach assumes that backlogs can be controlled better in the production control office than on the factory floor and this is indeed one of the most important principles of shop input control. The following paragraphs explain this and some related principles that are important to use if work-in-process is to be controlled.

1. Select the input using techniques like the production scheduling report (Fig. 9-2) or the weekly schedule review (Fig. 9-4) to meet the planned production rate. If the plant is not actually producing to meet this plan, the amount of work released into starting operations should not exceed actual output. This is a difficult point to make to the scheduler who knows that he needs the output. Learning to use the production plan rather than backlogs of work-in-process to control capacity may require a considerable education program for schedulers, foremen and even many managers.

2. Keep backlogs off the shop floor wherever possible. When backlogs get out on the shop floor they:

a. Are more difficult to control
b. Make engineering changes more expensive to implement
c. Generate more expediting
d. Create physical problems (newer jobs pile up in front of old work that gets pushed back into corners)

One of the most difficult things for any scheduler to resist is the temptation to "get it started." It is comforting for the scheduler to get everything "on order" with the factory and to emphasize this point when the factory is not meeting schedules. Unfortunately, the more work there is in the factory, the more expensive it becomes to control the actual job selection. Excessive backlogs on the factory floor can seriously compound the problems of getting the right items through production, and it is precisely when the plant is behind schedule that job selection becomes most critical.

3. Sequence orders based on latest requirements rather than "release" dates established when the order was first generated. When some backlog of orders must be kept in the production control office and there is a demand forecast involved in establishing the release dates, the production control system should be designed so that planners or schedulers release orders based upon dates established at the last possible moment. Even when other requirements make files of "To be released" orders useful, the advent of the computer (which can compare changing inventory requirements for many items with production requirements), and the introduction of such techniques as *Critical Ratio*—described in Chapter 10—make it possible to review desired schedule dates periodically, to be sure that orders are released to the factory based only upon the latest possible information on requirements.

4. Schedule only items the factory can make. In generating orders to meet a planned production rate, it is meaningless to release orders if they cannot be run during the scheduled period. One of the first steps that should be taken to improve the operation of any production control system is to force planners or schedulers to keep on their desks all orders for which raw material, components, tools or other necessary materials are not available. This practice will clearly define where the basic problems lie in getting work completed. It will be immediately evident if the inability to meet production rates results from production control's failure to provide purchased materials or to allow necessary lead times on manufactured parts or from the factory having insufficient manpower or equipment to produce at the desired level. Another benefit which should not be underrated is that releasing firm orders representing real work for the factory increases plant operating personnel's respect for the abilities of production control people and also develops confidence in the latter's decisions, leading to better cooperation and resulting in greatly improved operation of the plant. There are some exceptions to the rule that orders should not be released until all necessary materials are available. Where a finished product will take three weeks to assemble and the only component missing is one which is added at the last operations, assembly orders can be issued to the plant to start work immediately if the scheduler is confident that the missing component will be available by the time it is needed. There are other exceptions based on unique situations in the drug, electronic and similar industries where it is impossible to determine before a schedule is released whether the product *can* actually be produced.

5. Schedule to a short cycle (weekly or even daily). This not only helps to get the latest and most accurate requirement dates on the orders scheduled, but it also assists in controlling the orders flowing through the factory. The point was made very well by John F. Magee[1] who said, "the more frequently scheduling is done, i.e., the shorter the scheduling period, the lower the in-process inventory can be, and the faster can material be processed through the departments. For example, in the case described, a change in the scheduling period from one day to one week would mean increasing the total processing time from roughly 13 days to roughly 6 weeks."

In the typical manufacturing operation, having a semiprocess flow and with many intermittent operations, generating a monthly schedule for the department performing most of the starting operations gives that department a broad choice of items to run on any particular day. They will normally run those items that suit their convenience and the load flowing into subsequent departments will probably not match their capacities. The result will be to have large backlogs of work ahead of these departments in order to maintain their production at the level rate.

---

[1] J. F. Magee, *Production Planning and Inventory Control,* McGraw, New York, 1958, p. 235.

Moreover, if a department can be considered on schedule if a job is manufactured on the first day of the month or on the thirtieth day of the month, quoted lead times will have to be exceedingly long in order to give customers realistic delivery dates.

An interesting fallacy that has gained wide recognition among production control and manufacturing personnel is that the schedule period must equal the lead time. The question "How can we possibly have a weekly schedule when it takes us one month to produce the product?" is frequently heard. Although it sounds perfectly rational, there is no reason why schedule periods must be equal to the total lead time.

Even in the extreme example of a company with a 9-month lead time required for a sequence of 50 different operations, someone must make a decision practically on a daily basis as to which items will be started in the first operation. A firm 9-month starting schedule is *not* required. It is certainly more sensible to issue a weekly starting schedule which is based on the latest available information on customer requirements, the inventory status and the plant workload. Only in this way can a factory be kept flexible enough to meet changing demands in an economical manner. These principles will help to control the flow of work into the plant at the first operation. Scheduling techniques then provide a basis for keeping jobs flowing into succeeding operations.

Standard scheduling techniques

One of the first steps that can be taken by any company to improve its delivery performance is to establish schedule dates by operations. Frequently, in companies where production control is basically a stock-chasing function, even the stock-chasing doesn't begin until jobs have failed to meet their shipping date. The next step beyond this approach is to review jobs that are due to ship this week and next week as well as those that are past due, to determine what problems are causing delays. Figure 9-8 shows this type of *production schedule review*. This can be a very effective type of report if used in conjunction with an operations-scheduling system to make sure that no slip-ups have occurred, and also as a means of keeping the sales department informed. The production schedule review can be sent to personnel in the sales department so that they know which jobs will be shipped on time and which won't, thus providing them with the means of telling the customer ahead of time if his job will not be shipped out as promised—a very important element in customer service.

Figure 9-9 lists the steps in operations scheduling. The first step is, of course, to provide the data for the scheduling system (which must include the operations sequence of factory routing). Figure 9-10 is a typical manufacturing order, including the operations sequence and showing

Figure 9-8

Production Schedule Review

Customer	S.O.	Past due	This week	Next week	Nearest lot		Next lot		Remarks
					Loc.	Qty.	Loc.	Qty.	
Stalco	17624	577			D-32	1150	---	---	Will ship next week
Chambers	11318			40	D-40	94	---	---	On salvage (?)
Trild Inc.	10628		1100		D-29	1000	---	N.A.	Call complete
Morton	10959		1780	2500	D-32	5200	---	---	Balance 6040 stock
Padsing	11003		7000		D-22	7500	---	---	O. K.
Pennbush	11004			20,000	D-22	10,750	D-2	10,750	Will ship 10 M, balance 3/26
Stalco	11008			7000	D-40	8240	---	---	O. K.

Figure 9-9

Scheduling Steps

1. Provide data
   A. Operation sequences
   B. Standards, engineered or estimated

2. Develop system
   A. Shop calendar
   B. Scheduling rules

3. Choose scheduling method
   A. Back-scheduling
   B. Forward-scheduling

4. Schedule
   A. Multiply order quantity by time per operation
   B. Add transit time
   C. Add allowance for delays

the setup hours and running time required. On this factory order, the running hours for this lot have been calculated by multiplying the quantity on the order (expressed in thousands) by the time figure shown in the column headed *Running hours*/1000. This manufacturing order is designed to travel with the work through the factory, so that the operator

Figure 9-10
Typical Manufacturing Order

Part name	Drawing no.	Used on	Date	Order	Qty.
Pinion spindle	E-17352	Frame assembly E-0014	wk. 21	2950	5000

Material
Steel bar stock – 0.500" Spec. #A-407

Remarks
Note thread is left–hand

Dept.	Mach. group	Op. no.	Operation description	Set-up hr.	Run hr./1000	Run hr. this lot	Man no.	Qty. comp.	Qty. scrap	Qty. salv.	Insp.
#040	Truck	01	Draw bar stock from stores	—	—	—					
#517	#14	02	Make pinion spindle on screw machine	14.5	3.1	15.5					
#319	#18	03	Mill slot to B/P	1.3	9.5	47.5					
#771	#42	04	Tumble for burrs	—	—	2.0					
#624	#06	05	Drill hole for pin	0.2	4.0	20.0					
#771	#40	06	Degrease	—	—	0.5					
#771	#43	07	Plate – dull zinc	—	—	4.7					
#009	#04	08	Inspect	—	—	AQC 403					
#040	Truck	09	Deliver to stock	—	—	—					

can note his time and quantities directly on it. In some companies, this operation sequence is maintained on a master form which can be reproduced when repetitive orders for the same product are run through the factory. In others, this type of routing is maintained in a deck of punched cards or in a computer's tape or disc file. When an order needs to be generated, the manufacturing order is printed out, along with a punched card for each operation which can be used by the machine operator to report his time. Note that the traveling order by itself does not usually provide the means to report an operator's time and quantity to the timekeeping department.

Time standards, either engineered or estimated, are essential to any scheduling system. Since there will always be orders for new items that have to be scheduled into production before engineering standards have been developed, some means of estimating these standards will have to be provided in either the industrial engineering or the production control department. Accuracy is not vital, but consistency in estimating these standards is important. Quite often, there will be an experienced man in production control who can estimate such work well enough so that there is no delay in getting the information and using it to schedule the job into production.

Figure 9-11 shows a shop

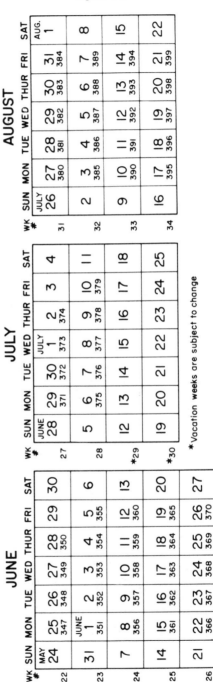

Figure 9-11

calendar of the type used by many companies to facilitate scheduling on which each *working day* is numbered consecutively—in the case of a "thousand-day" calendar, the consecutive numbering covers a period of four years. This enables the scheduler to establish dates easily and directly without correcting for weekends, plant shutdown periods or holidays, since these have been omitted from the shop calendar.

Some simple scheduling rules are shown in Fig. 9-12. These are over-simplified when compared to the rules needed in most companies, but they illustrate the type of rule which must be developed before scheduling can begin.

Figure 9-12

Typical Simple Scheduling Rules

1.	Multiply hours per thousand pieces by number of thousands on order
2.	Round up to nearest 16-hour day (2 shifts) and express time in days, round down to nearest day when excess hours are less than 10% of total, minimum 1 day for operation
3.	Allow five days to withdraw stock from stockroom
4.	Allow one day between successive operations within the same department
5.	Allow three days between successive operations in different departments
6.	Allow one day for inspection
7.	Allow one day to get material into stockroom
8.	Allow two extra weeks for screw machine parts

The next step is to choose one of the two principal scheduling methods available:

> 1. *Backward-scheduling* is done by starting with the date on which the order is required in the stockroom, on the assembly floor or to be shipped and calculating the schedule backwards to determine the proper release date for the order. Backward-scheduling assumes that the finished date is known and that the start dates must be computed for each step in the manufacturing sequence.

2. *Forward-scheduling* starts with either today's date or the first open time at the first operation and computes the schedule date for each operation to determine a completion date for the order.

Forward scheduling is most frequently used in companies such as steel mills, where jobs are manufactured to customer order and delivery is usually requested as soon as possible. One characteristic of plants where forward-scheduling is used is that the product is usually *not* an assembly requiring a great many components. Even when forward-scheduling is used, the scheduler will probably check the customer's requested date before doing his scheduling. If the required date is far enough away, he will not schedule the order immediately so that, in effect, he is really combining backward-scheduling with forward-scheduling.

Backward-scheduling is typically used where components are being manufactured to go into an assembled product. Components usually have different lead times, some considerably shorter than others. After determining the required schedule dates for major subassemblies, the scheduler uses these as the required dates for each component and works backward to determine the proper release date for each component manufacturing order. If he were to schedule forward, he would be releasing all orders at the same time, and a good many of the components would be on hand long before they were required. More important than this, parts would be competing in the factory for the same produc-

Figure 9-13

"Block" Scheduling Rules

1. Allow one week for releasing order and drawing material from storeroom
2. Allow six weeks for screw machine operations
3. Allow one day for each 400 pieces in the Milling Department; round upward to next full week
4. Allow one week for drilling and tapping, burring and similar operations using minor equipment
5. When operations are especially short, combine within the same week
6. Allow one week for inspection and delivery of completed material

tion facilities that were required for orders that were actually needed earlier.

Many companies do not spell-out detailed scheduling rules such as those shown in Fig. 9-12, but use instead general rules such as the *block-scheduling* rules shown in Fig. 9-13, where large increments of time are used to roughly estimate the amount of time required for each operation. Block-scheduling saves computation time, but usually results in extremely long lead times.

Figure 9-14 shows two ways of scheduling the manufacturing order shown in Fig. 9-10. In both cases, the order has been backward-scheduled from the required date (week #51 or day #445). Block-scheduling is done according to the rules listed in Fig. 9-13 with scheduled completion dates expressed by week numbers. This method results in a total of fourteen weeks' lead time.

The operation time scheduling starts with the required date expressed

Figure 9-14

Scheduling

Operation no.	Block scheduling		Operation time scheduling	
	Time allowed	Week	Time allowed	Day
Release date		#37		402
01	1 week	#38	5 days	407
02	6 weeks	#44	12 days	419
			T = 3 days	
03	3 weeks	#47	3 days	425
			T = 3 days	
04	1 week	#48	1 day	429
			T = 3 days	
05	1 week	#49	2 days	434
			T = 3 days	
06			1 day	438
	} 1 week	#50	T = 1 day	
07			1 day	440
			T = 3 days	
08			1 day	444
	} 1 week	#51		
09			1 day	445
Date required		Week #51		Day #445

* T = transit time

as a day number and works backward using the shop calendar day numbers to compute the required completion date at each operation. This schedule requires 43 working days, or about 9 weeks to complete. Notice in the computation that the transit time is always added to the next operation. For example, operation #7 must be completed on day 440 in order to allow 3 days' transit time and one day of running time at operation #8. *Transit time* is really a very loose term that is used to cover the following elements:

1. The time the job spends waiting to be picked up for movement out of the department—*wait* time.
2. The time the job spends actually in transit—*move* time.
3. The time the job spends in waiting to be started at the next machine center—*queue* time.

Note in Fig. 9-14 that the setup time has also been taken into account. For example, in operation 02 one extra operating day is included because of the setup time required on the screw machine.

Operation time-scheduling is more complex than block-scheduling and requires considerably more computation. The allowed lead time for block-scheduling is, however, considerably longer than that required by operation-scheduling (five weeks less in the example in Fig. 9-14). One of the further advantages of operation time-scheduling is that it provides input data for the machine-load report. If, for example, a weekly machine-load report were kept for the drilling department, the next step would be to add the 20 hours required for operation 05 (see Fig. 9-10) for drilling to be performed during the week which includes day 434.

Machine loading

Figure 9-15 shows the steps in machine loading. The first of these is to choose the load centers. Some companies load by department only. If all the machines in a department are interchangeable, this simplified approach can be justified, but when different machine centers within the department have different capabilities (as in a general machining department), loading the total department does not really accomplish much. The next refinement is to break the machines down into similar machine groups. All 24″ boring mills, for example, might be included in the same group if jobs are interchangeable among the machines. In some instances, as in the case of a screw machine with a milling cutter attachment, but otherwise identical with other machines in the group, individual machine coding should be set up so that such a machine can be singled out if a job can only be done on that machine. For example, a machine group might

Figure 9-15

Loading Steps

1. Choose Load Centers

    A. Department

    B. Group

    C. Machine or work station

2. Develop Efficiency Factors by Load Center

3. Choose Loading Method

    A. To "infinite" capacity

    B. To "finite" capacity

    C. Combination

4. Load Scheduled Orders into Load Centers

5. Unload "Completed" Hours

be designated as group 2400 containing a specialized machine designated as 2407. All jobs that could go on any machine would be loaded into machine group 2400, while a job that could only be done on that particular machine would be designated as being loaded for machine 2407. It is important to group as many machines together as possible, however, since this will reduce the size of the report and tend to stabilize the load. Trying to load individual machines when there is considerable interchangeability is poor practice and will result in very erratic loads.

One of the most important factors in machine loading is to develop *efficiency factors* by load center. For example, a load center with two men working in it would theoretically be turning out 80 hours of production per week, but a history of actual output might show that their real output is considerably less than 80 hours if part of their time is spent on setup work and indirect activity. If they are working on an incentive system, on the other hand, it's possible that they could be turning out work that is equivalent to more than 80 "standard hours" of production. Without efficiency factors, a machine loading system can be very unrealistic.

The next step is to choose the actual loading method. In the previous section, for example, it was explained how 20 hours of drilling time would be added to the machine load in the week in which this drilling time should be done to meet the finished product schedule. This type of loading is called *loading to infinite capacity* if the load is shown in the week in which it should ideally fall, without regard to the current load already existing in that week. If the department were loaded only according to its present capacity (*loading to finite capacity*), scheduling could not be done in one continuous calculation. Each scheduling step would involve checking the machine load for the time period required to see if there were sufficient capacity available for the order being scheduled in the week in which the work was required. The order in the previous example would have been scheduled out of the plating department on day 440 only if there were available capacity to handle 4.7 hours of plating in the week required.

Loading to finite capacity by operation is more complex than infinite capacity-loading since any plant activity that does not go according to schedule will require that the load be recalculated, since loads will now fall in different time periods. Finite capacity-loading also requires that the scheduler establish the priority for loading the jobs, since the first jobs loaded will tend to go through quickly because capacity is available while the last jobs loaded will tend to have long lead times because they must fit into remaining capacity at each operation.

There's a great deal of misunderstanding about the terms *infinite capacity-loading* and *finite capacity-loading* and there is some misuse of these techniques. A production control department is certainly not doing its job properly if it merely generates a machine load to infinite capacity and publishes the load report. It is also necessary to investigate how additional capacity can be made available—whether or not work can be subcontracted or if overtime can be worked when there are overloads—and whether or not orders can be rescheduled to take care of underloads or overloads. Infinite capacity-loading shows only how the orders would fall on an ideal basis. At that point, load-leveling will either take place as a planned function in the production control department or it will take place on the factory floor as a nonplanned function. The means for leveling the factory load are only:

1. *Start orders earlier than required*
2. *Start orders later than required*

When the production control department does not do some form of load-leveling, the plant will always be behind schedule because the leveling will occur on the factory floor in the form of backlogs.

In practice, finite capacity-scheduling is by itself unsatisfactory since it assumes that present capacity is all that is available and does not show the time periods in which overloads will occur if an attempt is made to meet desirable schedules. Without the latter information, action cannot be taken to improve the plant's performance in meeting customer requirements.

In practice, a good machine-loading system involves a combination of both techniques. Orders are first scheduled and loaded to infinite capacity to see where overloads will occur, then orders are rescheduled in order to level the load based on available capacity after corrective actions have been taken wherever possible.

One of the most important elements of a machine load system is the *unloading* technique. In a manual system, it is frequently necessary to take shortcuts such as considering a job to be completed when the first time card is turned in. This saves posting many production lots and recalculating load balances, but results in a machine load which is always understated by the number of hours remaining on each job that has been unloaded from the system. Another shortcut approach uses the last time card on a lot to relieve the load. This results in a load constantly overstated by the hours completed on each job but not removed from the machine load. A good machine load should deduct hours as they are completed and show the true number of hours remaining in the load. One point sometimes overlooked is that the number of hours to be unloaded for any job must be equal to the number of hours loaded for that job. For example, if an estimated time standard of 12 hours has been set on a job, but the job is actually completed in 9 hours, 12 hours must be relieved from the load in order to correctly state the work remaining in the machine load. This is done by multiplying the number of pieces reported by the standard rather than deducting actual elapsed time from the load.

Figure 9-16 shows a typical machine-load report covering a department with six load centers and with three men working on the eleven

Figure 9-16

Weekly Machine Load Report
(In standard hours)

Department No. 47								
Load center	Total Men Mach.	Adjusted* capacity	Behind schedule total	Produced last week	Week 41 load	Week 42 load	Week 48 load
2401	2 4	64	140	96.4	55	56	26
2402	1 2	32	10	0.6	2	3	1
2403	– 1	--	4	----	--	--	--
2404	– 1	--	13	3.6	4	3	1
2405	– 2	--	108	8.5	23	14	4
2406	– 1	--	11	0.5	2	1	--
Totals	3 11	96	286	109.6	86	77	32

*At 80% Efficiency

available machines. This machine-load report shows that the department is almost four weeks behind schedule since there are 86 hours scheduled in the current week #41 and there are 286 hours behind-schedule to be handled at a capacity of 96 hours per week. A frequent problem encountered in setting-up machine-load reports is that the system is designed so that any job which has not been shipped out of a department by its schedule date shows as being behind-schedule for that department. While this is certainly a true picture it is not complete. If, for example, the foreman of this department knew that material for many of these orders had not yet arrived in his department, he would not put much credence in the machine-load report shown in Fig. 9-16. A good report should show not only the work on which the department is charged with being behind-schedule, but also the amount of that work that is *actually in the department.*

When companies operate from large backlogs of orders, switch men around among machine centers freely or hire and lay off as they see fit, machine-loading is a satisfactory means of controlling capacity. Without this flexibility, machine-loading is only a good short-term technique for showing where overloads or underloads are occurring, but it is not a satisfactory means for long-term capacity planning. Some form of production plan or simulation of anticipated requirements is necessary in almost every company today, since few have enough firm orders upon which to base an effective machine load, and the pressures for stabilizing manpower have become very strong. In some companies, the machine-loading system itself is used to estimate future capacity requirements by introducing forecasts into the system. A simple test of whether or not the machine load of actual orders can be used by itself to plan and control capacity is to find out how much time a foreman will require to add a man to his work force and then how long he should keep that man to justify having hired him in the first place. If the machine load does not cover this total period, it will not give enough advance notice to add people when they are required and the plant will run behind schedule.

Scheduling and loading are effective techniques only when applied with a full understanding of the problems of controlling the flow of individual production orders and the objectives and principles to be observed. Frequently, orders are generated at random by an inventory control system, schedules are sent down to the plant and backlogs are measured in a machine-load report without any attempt to control the rate of flow of these orders into the plant and without any recognition of the fact that the required dates may change before the orders are completed. This problem of reacting to changes in requirements that occur after the jobs have been released will be discussed in the following chapter.

Controlling input to vendors

Distributors who do not manufacture anything generate an input of orders to their vendors. Most manufacturing companies purchase a large percentage of their components from outside vendors. Relations between the production control and purchasing functions within many companies are perpetually strained because of the problems involved in getting the right items in from these vendors. Some of the most significant of these problems are:

1. Quantity discounts: If the materials control system does not recognize that quantity discounts must be considered in ordering purchased materials, the purchasing department will probably want to increase the quantities on the requisitions sent to them and this will, of course, increase inventories. These quantity discounts should be recognized in the materials control system and the overall policies on what constitutes an acceptable discount should be established, considering the aggregate effect on inventory. These ordering rules should then be built into the materials control system.

2. Buyer delays in placing orders: A good purchasing department concentrates much of its efforts on buying—the actual negotiation of prices. This is an extremely important function since, in most companies, the cost of purchased material often far exceeds the actual labor cost by so that much industrial engineering effort is directed at controlling. To the scheduler, however, the objective of reducing costs seems rather shortsighted when a missing component holds up delivery of a customer order and he learns that the requisition he sent to purchasing was held up by the buyer while he negotiated prices. This problem cannot be eliminated, but it can be handled better if the production control department will:

a. Tell purchasing its anticipated yearly requirements of standard components and insist that price negotiations be handled on a planned basis, and *not* as requisitions are received.

b. Show purchasing what requisitions are *most likely* to be generated for some period—perhaps two months—in the future. A computerized materials planning system can do this quite readily and can thus give the buyer advance notice so that the buyer can negotiate.

c. Try to allow time for negotiation of price in the planned lead time of some infrequently ordered items and request a follow-up report from purchasing to tell when any requisition for this type of item has not been placed within the planned time period.

3. Purchased component lead times: It is not unusual to hear purchasing personnel tell a vendor "We aren't too concerned about your lead time, as long as you meet your delivery promises." Unfortunately, longer lead times on the vendor's part will probably increase his work-in-process level and *impair* his ability to meet delivery promises. Beyond this consideration, however, the longer lead times will require higher reserve stocks in the materials control system—or else poorer service will result. A program to educate purchasing people to understand some of the fundamental relationships in production and inventory control can generate many tangible benefits in this area.

4. Lack of follow-up: Nothing generates more friction between production control and purchasing than late deliveries of purchased items. Techniques for improving control over the vendor's output are discussed in Chapter 10. Frequently, however, poor vendor deliveries—like plants that are always behind schedule—can be overcome more by improving control over input rather than by concentrating solely on better control over output.

Probably the most significant step that can be taken to improve a vendor's output, especially if most of his business is with a few companies, is to assist him in planning production levels and then to provide him with a regulated amount of work on a weekly basis. Many companies are repelled by this idea, since they feel that they have enough to worry about at home without trying to help their suppliers, just as many production control personnel feel that if they generate orders and show where the overloads are, it is then "the factory's responsibility" to get work out on time. Recognizing that a vendor is running a manufacturing facility too, and using some of the techniques described to help plan his production level and control input to meet this plan, will usually improve vendor performance substantially. Far from being an altruistic gesture, this approach will usually result in shorter, more dependable deliveries of purchased parts.

Scheduling assembly operations

In many plants assembly times are short, manpower is very flexible, and assembly scheduling is straightforward. The assembly department can often be broken down into a few major flow lines that can be loaded to finite capacity. In other companies that have complex assembly operations, such as those manufacturing sophisticated electronic equipment, detailed scheduling of assembly operations can become very important indeed. Where this is true, the scheduling and loading job often becomes as detailed as scheduling component manufacturing operations, and schedules for assembly can best be planned operation-by-operation, using the techniques described earlier in this chapter.

In automotive or appliance manufacturing, where a distinct assembly-line flow exists, it is necessary to balance the workload on the line so that each worker has a reasonable amount of work to perform as the product moves through his station. While *line-balancing*,[1] in terms of defining what work will be done at each station, is usually done by the industrial engineer, the scheduler must then feed work into the balanced line.

The basic steps in line balancing are:

1. Establish time standards for all operations on all products to be assembled in as small elements as possible.

2. Determine by assembly line zone which operations *must* be done in each and which operations *can* be done there if desired.

3. Work backwards from the finished-product end of the line to get the optimum balance among jobs, considering all products to be run. This is usually done using a trial and error approach, and is most effective when a computer can be used for simulating all of the possibilities that exist.

4. Make up the production schedule that will give the most flexibility in production mix with the best utilization of available manpower.

No scheduling technique can generate production from an assembly line that is short of components and, in many plants (especially where the assembly department is being fed by many functional departments), chronic parts shortages always seem to exist. This is an excellent example of the interactions in the production control system and also an example of the need for a disciplined system that *really* controls. Too often, lack of good basic systems discipline generates problems, and attempts at "quick-and-dirty" solutions merely compound the problems.

---

[1]"This is Line Balancing," *Factory*, April 1963.

Many companies have been through this cycle:

1. Because inventory records are inaccurate, parts shortages occur at assembly (since parts that were shown by the system to be available are not).

2. This causes serious disruptions in the assembly line and someone suggests that kits of parts for assembly be *laid out* or *"staged"* farther in advance. If the procedure has been to make up these kits one week in advance of the assembly schedule, the suggestion is often to increase it to four or six weeks. The reasoning is that the additional time will then be available to expedite parts through manufacturing to fill unexpected shortages at assembly.

3. Staging components farther in advance then generates these problems:

a. Generating an extra four or five weeks of components laid out against future assembly schedules requires substantial increases in component inventory, which usually are not readily available. This is the equivalent of writing this inventory off the records, since this 4- or 5-week supply of components will no longer be available to be used on new assembly requirements, yet it will not be available in the form of an assembled product either.

b. Increasing the advance layouts to determine parts shortages earlier places a peak load of real magnitude on stockroom personnel to pull the required components faster than they are being assembled.

c. More advance layout requires more space.

d. A layout shortage record file must be developed and maintained, indicating which components are short in each of the layouts. This file, by itself, can become extremely cumbersome and time-consuming.

e. Typically, where there is multiple use of a given component, the advance-layout technique will result in components being improperly allocated. A component laid out for an assembly that can't be made for lack of other components will be found to be the only part missing from another layout kit.

f. Shifting components from one layout to another is inevitable and increases with the layout period. As a result, record accuracy is more difficult to maintain and usually decreases.

g. The work of putting away excess components is increased tremendously. The original quantity of each component pulled from stock to make a given assembly is based upon the desired finished assembly lot size. When the component which is in shortest supply finally comes in—typically, in less than the desired quantity—it must be distributed among several assembly layouts, none of which can be assembled in the desired lot-size. Consequently, the leftover components must be put back into the stock bins.

h. When the advance layout technique is used, control over the sequence of assemblies run in the assembly department is usually lost by the production control department. In times of extensive parts shortages, any product for which components are available is seized upon and run by the assembly department foreman. This adds to the shortages by using up scarce interchangeable components.

The "quick-and-dirty" solution of staging components usually generates far more problems than it solves, and the result is poorer utilization of the limited supply of available components and a complete degeneration of the inventory records because so many extra transfers of components are taking place.

Too frequently, inaccurate inventory records are only one of many deficiencies in the system that cause problems at assembly. Component shortages may also be due to poor reordering practices, where simple order points may be used to replenish items whose demand is not uniform, but depends on assembly schedules. Shortages may also result from too-low a level of component production resulting from poor production planning.

Good control over the flow of components to support assembly operations requires:

1. Accurate inventory records that are checked by regular "cycle" inventories rather than by an annual physical inventory, and which are supported by the education of all personnel entering the system so that they understand the proper techniques for handling each transaction and realize the importance of following the proper procedure.

2. A reorder system that bases component requirements on anticipated assembly schedules —rather than average past usage—and reacts to changes in these assembly requirements by changing the requirements shown in the materials plan.

3. Means to plan the level of component production in advance of desired changes in the assembly department production rate.

Scheduling component manufacture, component purchasing and the assembly department are the necessary elements in controlling input to most plants. The techniques described in this chapter can be implemented manually, graphically or on a computer. There are also specialized manufacturing situations for which specific techniques have been developed. The following sections cover one particularly important graphic method and some specialized scheduling approaches.

Loading and scheduling devices

The Gantt chart, developed by Henry L. Gantt at Frankford Arsenal in 1917, is one of the oldest planning tools known to production control. Figure 9-17 shows a Gantt chart used to plan a project in which a large purchased motor, a housing fabricated on a frame and a machined casting are to be assembled, inspected, packed and shipped. The scheduled dates for each activity, starting and finishing, are shown by the short vertical lines at the ends of the light horizontal lines. Each project activity has its own set of lines, and the chart shows the full period from start to finish of the project. The carat mark above the date headings shows the present time (end of Week 9).

At the end of the 9th week, the heavy horizontal lines (representing actual progress) show that the motor has been ordered on time, that the frame steel has been ordered, received, and fabricated, and that the housing is now being fabricated around the frame. The chart also shows that the base casting has been ordered but has not been received and, in fact, is behind schedule, thus threatening the desired delivery date in the 17th week if corrective action is not taken at once.

In this example, the Gantt chart is used to show a project schedule only. It can also be used in a slightly different form to show machine loads by labeling the rows to represent machine centers and drawing lines within the columns to represent the amount of capacity that is loaded.

There are many commercial devices available today that are really mechanical Gantt charts. Some of these use strips of paper to represent the amount of work that has been loaded into a particular department and then combine these strips of paper with colored signals to show where critical overloads have occurred. Other mechanical devices are perforated boards with pegs attached to strings that can be manipulated

Figure 9-17

Gantt Chart—Order #008160

Project Plan

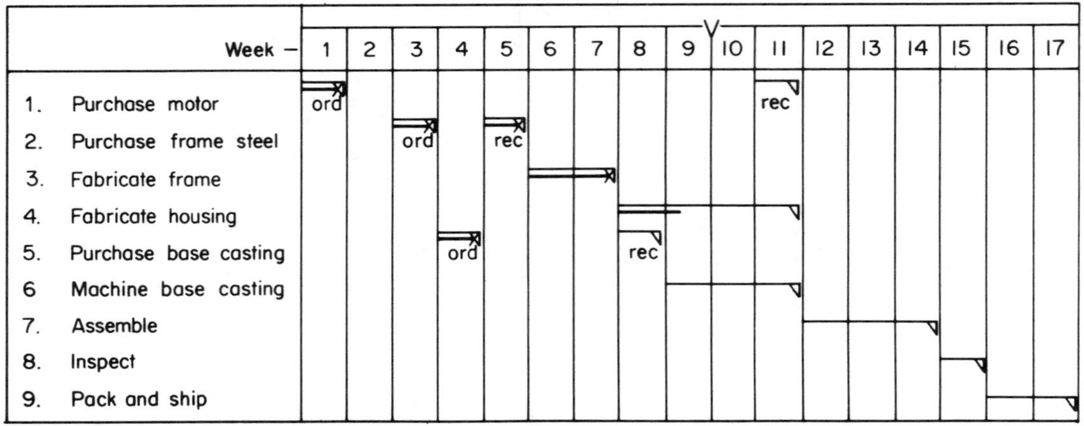

to make a Gantt chart, showing either project plans, machine loads or work center backlogs.

These mechanical Gantt charts can be of assistance in presenting information in visual form. By themselves, they are not a production control system. Basically, they have application where a Gantt chart is required to display scheduling and loading information—they are successful only if the system used to generate the information presented is sound. These techniques present some problems in recording, duplicating and transmitting their message. A Gantt chart made on paper can be duplicated readily and sent to all personnel who require information. A mechanical Gantt chart can only be duplicated by taking photographs of it (some companies do this), by summarizing the information manually on paper or by bringing the people to the information display.

These mechanical Gantt charts have a real place in production control. They are useful in presenting information visually but, like any other tool, they should be used with discretion by a professional who understands the principles behind the techniques and knows how to apply them properly.

Project planning and control

Since the introduction of the Gantt chart, there have been some dramatic innovations in project planning, brought about by the need to plan and control complex projects involving many suppliers. The critical path method (CPM) or critical path scheduling (CPS) is a form of project planning called "network planning." Network planning involves setting up a chart of the elements and activities making up a complex project showing the necessary sequence and interrelationships and determining the *critical path* or longest sequence of events that really determines when the project can be completed. Figure 9-18 shows the same project covered by the Gantt chart in Fig. 9-17 as it would be handled by CPM. It is presented as a series of *events* shown by the circles, and *activities* shown by the lines that connect these circles. Event #1, for example, is to place requisitions, and the activity is to then "Purchase" (which requires four weeks, as shown on the chart by the notation "4W"). Once the critical path chart has been made up, the total time required to complete the activities which follow any path can be determined. In Fig. 9-18, for example, the critical path is 1-5-8-9, and it determines the ultimate completion date for the project. If the base casting happens to be received one week late, for example, this would not affect the final project completion date because there are three weeks' "slack" time available—path 1-4-7-8 requires 10 weeks, as compared to 13 weeks for 1-5-8. The critical

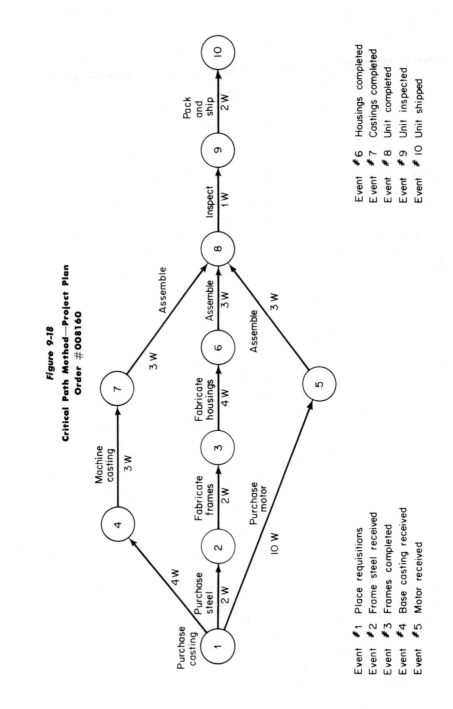

Figure 9-18
Critical Path Method—Project Plan
Order #008160

Event #1 Place requisitions
Event #2 Frame steel received
Event #3 Frames completed
Event #4 Base casting received
Event #5 Motor received

Event #6 Housings completed
Event #7 Castings completed
Event #8 Unit completed
Event #9 Unit inspected
Event #10 Unit shipped

274

path method has been applied to many complex projects, and an entire science of network planning has been developed.

Perhaps the most publicized network planning technique is PERT (*Project Evaluation and Review Technique*). This is a refinement of the critical path method in which estimates of "most optimistic," "most likely," and "most pessimistic" times are made for the completion of each element in the project. These data are introduced into a computer where the statistical probabilities of completing the various paths are calculated and the critical path is determined. The computer also prints information on those activities that have "slack" time and can tolerate delays, so that effort, manpower, machines and money can be diverted from slack to more critical activities, reducing the total project time at no extra cost.

These project planning techniques can also be used in project control, but just making the original plan can do a great deal to get the project started properly. Once a PERT chart is established, progress of the project can then be reviewed periodically and the chart can be updated. Frequently, substantial changes will be noted in the critical path as some events are completed ahead of schedule and some fall behind. Maintenance of the updated information necessary to use project planning as a control technique requires a considerable effort as time passes and changes occur in the project. Nevertheless, the effort is considered worthwhile by many companies involved in highly complex project type manufacturing. The United States Government specifically requires that PERT or similar techniques be used to supply status information on a regular basis for many of their contracts.

The production control practitioner should be familiar with network planning techniques and should know where to apply them to his advantage. He should be very much aware that they do *not* replace the normal production control functions of planning, scheduling, dispatching, etc.

Most project planning techniques treat the project elements as if they were entities without recognizing that each element is itself a series of activities. A project to deliver 100 completed units, for example, might require fabricating or purchasing components at a rate of 10 per week to meet the specified delivery. There are projects that require this type of monitoring, and the *line-of-balance* technique is designed to handle them. It uses graphical techniques to extend a project plan into a series of stepped lines representing component or subassembly quantity requirements at any point in time. This line of balance is then the objective against which bar charts showing actual completions are plotted. When the bars do not come up to the line, the component involved is shown as being behind schedule. Where the bar extends above the line of balance, it indicates that deliveries of this component are ahead of schedule. LOB is a project planning technique that is especially applicable when the project contains many units to be completed over a period of time—it is more valuable as a monitoring technique than as a planning technique. It might, for example, be used to monitor a multi-unit project that was planned using the critical path method.

Another technique that applies particularly to complex project-type industry is the *learning curve*. The learning curve is a tool for planning manload on projects where experience improves ability and speed in performing a given task. The aircraft industry, electronic equipment manufacturers and shipbuilding companies find, for example, that the first airplane, radar unit, or submarine in a new model line will take a given amount of manhours to complete; the second takes considerably less time, and subsequent units take less and less because the design problems are solved, tooling is debugged, inspection procedures are perfected and the workers are learning to manufacture it properly.

The general relationship shown in a learning curve is that the amount of time required to make one unit of the product will be smaller by a standard percentage (which varies among industries and products) as the number of manufactured units doubles. Figure 9-19 shows an 80% learning curve for a missile. The total project calls for 128 missiles to be manufactured. The first one is expected to take 1800 hours, and since experience has shown that an 80% learning curve applies in this particular company, the second missile will take only 1440 hours (0.8 × 1800). The fourth, 1150 hours (0.8 × 1440), and so on, according to the relationship shown on the right-hand side of Fig. 9-19.

The learning curve is used for establishing capacity requirements and estimating costs and delivery dates in industries making large or

Figure 9-19

Learning Curve—"Blackbird" Missile

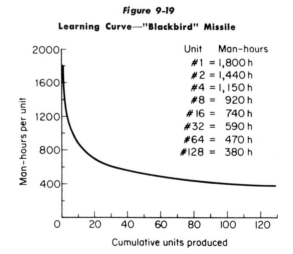

complex products. The production control manager does not have to participate in preparation of the curve in all its sophistications, but he should be aware of the general relationship and should know how to use the principle behind it in scheduling and loading.

Linear programming

Linear programming is a name given to a family of techniques which solve simultaneous linear equations through a systematic routine that typically involves many repetitions of the basic routine (*iterations*). Having received much publicity a few years ago, linear programming is probably the best known and most characteristic of the "operations research" type techniques used in production control areas.

Linear programming can be applied to problems having the following general characteristics:

1. There are definable objectives (such as profit, cost, maximum possible production within a time period, etc.)

2. There are alternative solutions available. For example, a job could be run on one machine or on another at different costs, or warehouse replenishment orders could be filled from separate manufacturing plants at different manufacturing costs and freight costs.

3. Resources are limited. For example, the capacity of the lowest-cost machine is not sufficient to make all the product required, and less profitable machines must be used to turn out some of the jobs.

4. The relationships among variables can be expressed in linear (first-order) algebraic equations.

Linear programming methods have been applied to several production control problems, principally in machine scheduling and production planning, although such techniques are in limited use in practice at the present time. Several different methods are available, varying in difficulty and complexity. Arranged in order from simplest to most complex, these are:

1. Index method
2. Modified distribution (MODI) or transportation method
3. Simplex method

These methods have several features in common. While they are based on mathematical solutions of systems of linear equations, only simple arithmetic is required in the application of all but the Simplex method. Mathematics has been applied to develop a set of organized procedures to be followed using tabular arrangements of data and simple arithmetical calculations. Similarly, although calculus is required in deriving the equation for economic order quantities (Appendix III), only arithmetic is required to use the equation.

The *Index* method will be illustrated by an example showing ten jobs to be assigned to one of four similar machines capable of running it in the number of hours shown in Fig. 9-20. A dash indicates that the job cannot be run on that machine. The problem is to assign each job to one machine following a schedule which will result in the *minimum number of machine hours* (hence, minimum cost) required to get the work completed in the shortest elapsed hours. Such a schedule will not necessarily get these jobs done in the minimum total elapsed time and, obviously, any individual job may not be completed as soon as if it were given highest priority.

As shown by the data in Fig. 9-20, the ten jobs cannot all be run on the most economical machine (shown by the underline), since this would put 102 hours (Jobs 01, 02, 04, 05, 06, 07, 10) on machine 100 and only one job on each of the other three machines, requiring over $2\frac{1}{2}$ weeks

Figure 9-20	Figure 9-21
Hours Required for Jobs on Machines	Dispatcher's Assignment of Jobs by Inspection. First-come, first-served

Job no.	Machine number				Job no.	Machine number			
	100	200	300	400		100	200	300	400
01	1̲0̲	20	25	25	01	10			
02	1̲8̲	21	24	--	02	18			
03	17	1̲7̲	17	28	03		17		
04	1̲6̲	20	19	22	04	16			
05	1̲2̲	22	18	20	05		22		
06	1̲6̲	--	26	35	06			26	
07	1̲2̲	18	27	32	07				32
08	15	30	29	1̲2̲	08				12
09	25	25	1̲4̲	27	09			14	
10	1̲8̲	25	22	28	10	18			
Totals	159	198	221	229	Totals	62	39	40	44

of one shift operation to complete the last job. Machine utilization for machines 200, 300 and 400 would be very low unless more jobs came along which were better run on these than on machine 100.

By inspection, attempting an "economical" assignment after putting the most economical jobs on machines 200, 300 and 400, a dispatcher might assign the jobs as shown in Fig. 9-21.[1] He has made a good balance of the first nine jobs among the four machines—only the tenth will be completed much more than a week later and it was the last received.

Figure 9-22
Calculations of Indices and
Index Method of Assignment of Jobs

Job no.	Machine number			
	100	200	300	400
01	10	20 (2.00)	25 (2.50)	25 (2.50)
02	18	21 (1.17)	24 (1.33)	--
03	17	17	17	28 (1.65)
04	16	20 (1.25)	19 (1.19)	22 (1.38)
05	12	22 (1.83)	18 (1.50)	20 (1.67)
06	16	--	26 (1.63)	35 (2.19)
07	12	18 (1.50)	27 (2.25)	32 (2.67)
08	15 (1.25)	30 (2.50)	29 (2.42)	12
09	25 (1.79)	25 (1.79)	14	27 (1.93)
10	18	25 (1.39)	22 (1.22)	28 (1.56)
Total most econom. jobs	119	0	14	12 145
Move 1 Job 03	$\frac{-17}{102}$	$\frac{+17}{17}$	$\frac{--}{14}$	$\frac{--}{12}$ ---
Move 2 Job 02	$\frac{-18}{84}$	$\frac{+21}{38}$	$\frac{--}{14}$	$\frac{--}{12}$ $\frac{+3}{}$
Move 3 Job 04	$\frac{-16}{68}$	$\frac{--}{38}$	$\frac{+19}{33}$	$\frac{--}{12}$ $\frac{+3}{}$
Move 4 Job 10	$\frac{-18}{50}$	$\frac{--}{38}$	$\frac{+22}{55}$	$\frac{--}{12}$ $\frac{+4}{155}$

---

[1]The student will notice improvements possible for *individual* jobs and is urged to attempt to improve this assignment intuitively to get a better understanding of the problem.

A much more economical distribution is possible using an organized approach provided by the Index method. The basis of this approach is to calculate an index number for each alternative job assignment, comparing it to the most economical machine. For example, job 01 is done most economically on machine 100 in 10 hours. It would require 20 hours on machine 200, so the index for this machine is $20/10 = 2.00$. It would take 25 hours on the other two machines, so their indices are $25/10 = 2.50$. Figure 9-22 shows all the indices for the less economical machines. Obviously, if job 01 were to be rescheduled from machine 100, the most economical, less penalty wuld be incurred by putting it on machine 200 than on either of the other two machines.

The lower the index, the lower the penalty—therefore, the basic principle of the index method is to move work from the most economical machine to another, starting with the job/machine combination with the lowest index number, and making the fewest possible moves to attain a reasonable balance. Subsequent moves are always made to the machine with the lowest remaining index number.

The tabulation at the bottom of Fig. 9-22 shows a simple technique for recording the effect of making each move. The totals for each machine are the sums of the hours for running the jobs for which that machine is the most economical (actually, those jobs for which no index number is shown). Machine 100 must be relieved of several jobs to achieve better balance.

The most obvious move is to put job 03 on machine 200, since this carries no penalty of extra hours. Move #2 is made by finding the lowest index number in the table, indicating that job 02 should be run on machine 200. The next lowest index number sets up move #3 by indicating that job 04 should be assigned to machine 300. Move #4 transfers job 10 to machine 300, and a reasonable balance has been obtained. Figure 9-23 shows the final assignments of the index method. Note that any attempt to bring machine 400 up to a more equal share of the load carries rather severe penalties in added hours.

Figure 9-23

Final Index Method of Assignment of Jobs

Job	Machine number			
no.	100	200	300	400
01	10			
02		21		
03		17		
04			19	
05	12			
06	16			
07	12			
08				12
09			14	
10			22	
Totals	50	38	55	12	155

The total machine hours required to complete all ten jobs on the most economical machine is 145 hours. Figure 9-21 shows that the schedule laid out by the dispatcher would require a total of 185 hours, while the index method total is only 155 hours. The total elapsed time to complete all jobs has also been reduced from 62 to 55 hours.

The final assignment of jobs by the index method may not be the best possible arrangement, particularly if there is a larger number of jobs and machines than was used in this example, but it will be a substantial improvement over assignments made by intuitive means or visual inspection. The solution can also be improved for some situations by recalculating the index numbers after each move is made, moving some jobs twice but keeping the penalty incurred by each move to a minimum.

The index method considers only machine hours for running each job. It does not handle the economics of sequencing jobs to take advantage of setup savings, neither does it weight the cost factors involved in delaying running a job in order to get it on the most economical machine. It is a very workable technique which can be used without calculating equipment and which can be learned quickly by schedulers and dispatchers.

The *Modified Distribution* or *Transportation Method* of linear programming was originally developed to solve problems involving transportation of materials from a number of sources to a variety of destinations. For example, it was desired to minimize the costs of distributing a product (such as a specific size of automobile tire) which could be manufactured in several factories and had to be delivered to and stored in a number of different warehouses. This technique was later applied to other problems involving allocation of limited facilities, such as multiple machine scheduling.

One direct method of solving such a problem would be to calculate the total cost for each different solution among the many possible alternatives and select the lowest cost solution. Even with high-speed computers, this quickly becomes impractical if the number of sources and destinations exceeds four or five. Four of each would have 24 possible solutions; with five, the number would climb to 120. Linear programming was used to develop a step-by-step method of arriving at an optimal solution.

There is a substantial portion of operations research literature devoted to explanation and discussion of the details of the method, and these will not be repeated here. One easily-understood explanation is contained in the book *Production Control—Text and Cases*, by William Voris (Richard D. Irwin, Inc., Homewood, Illinois, 1956). Other references are listed in the bibliography at the end of this chapter.

The Simplex method is, ironically, the most complex of the linear programming techniques. It requires the greatest knowledge of mathematics and can handle the widest variety of problems.

Whereas the mathematical theory behind the Index and MODI methods is based on the solution of linear equations, the theory behind the Simplex method is based on *inequalities,* such as that stated by: "The load on Machine 100 cannot exceed 80 hours in two weeks." It is obvious that this statement has many solutions *in addition* to: "A load equal to 80 hours." Therefore, the Simplex method permits arriving at one of the other solutions while minimizing the total scheduling costs or maximizing profits, and will be much more powerful than a method which can only handle the case where machine 100 works 80 hours.

This method not only solves general problems in linear programming, but it can also be used to develop solutions which take into account the effect of added restrictions or changes in the data used. This has two benefits:

1. The solution can be modified as changes in the real-life situation develop, rather than requiring a completely new solution.
2. Expected changes can be simulated to show how they would affect the solution if they did occur, permitting the study of many more variables such as overtime, the addition of machines or shifts, cost increases and other common variables with which management must deal regularly.

The Simplex method requires a knowledge of matrix algebra and other mathematical techniques which are beyond the scope of this book. The interested reader should consult *An Introduction to Operations Research,* by Churchman, Ackoff and Arnoff (Wiley, New York, 1957).

Three of the classical applications of linear programming in business problems are:

1. The machine scheduling problem described above.
2. The transportation-distribution problem, where several warehouses are to be supplied by a number of manufacturing facilities, some of which produce overlapping product lines, thus providing a choice as to the best source of supply for each warehouse for at least some products.
3. The mixing problem of determining the best mix of products for a particular refinery run or the optimum mixture of ingredients for a steel furnace charge utilizing scrap steel and raw materials so as to get a particular grade of processed steel.

As with other techniques, linear programming techniques should be used where they apply, and not just for the sake of using "advanced" techniques. They are not ideal techniques any more than any other scheduling and loading technique, and they have to be combined with other methods of production planning and control in order to establish a sound system for a particular application.

Practical considerations

For the practitioner, here are some practical considerations in controlling input:

1. When a finished product is being assembled, it is important to explode product assembly requirements into component requirements as frequently as possible and reschedule the purchased or manufactured components. Techniques for handling the rescheduling are discussed in Chapter 10.

2. Component manufacturing facilities can be scheduled as effectively as assembly facilities. In most plants, someone is deciding—practically on a daily basis—which items should be started. Firm commitments to long-range schedules should be avoided in both cases.

3. Control over input to the factory is essential. This can be as elaborate as holding components in a central storeroom between operations and releasing them only as directed by production control, so as to have complete control of all items. Frequently, however, functional departments (such as plating or painting) work on practically all of the diverse products of a plant. Detailed control of all items of input to these departments is impossible. It is quite feasible, however, to use the "ABC" principle to determine the parts that generate the bulk of the man hours in these secondary departments. Most companies will find that these will be a small percentage of the total parts going through such departments. If this small percentage of items is scheduled carefully, a balanced load can be maintained on these secondary operations.

4. The same general "ABC" principle applies to the components that make-up a particular assembly. It is normal to find that a few components have extremely long lead times, while the majority have considerably shorter lead times. If demand for these long lead time components is difficult to predict, it is worthwhile to maintain a substantial inventory of these parts in order to obtain flexibility with a minimum investment. The short lead time components can be controlled more tightly.

5. Manufacturing costs associated with setting up machines can be substantially reduced if items are scheduled in "family groups." In a

screw machine plant, for example, only minor setup changes are required between items in a family which uses the same-diameter stock. Substantial economies can be realized by having the scheduler review all products within a family group and order all of them when he orders any one of them, using a review sheet similar to Fig. 9-4. The economic lot-sizes should be calculated for each item using the technique discussed in the "Major and minor setups" section of Chapter 4.

6. Determining the proper shop input in a seasonal business is extremely difficult. It will usually be found that the forecast of requirements during the inventory building period is rather inaccurate. A reasonable approach to this problem is to prepare work input schedules based on the forecast until the season has progressed far enough for the actual demand to be used to indicate what the real product mix should be. Typically, a greater amount of setup time and flexibility will be required during the peak season than during the off-season. Many companies handle this by having skilled personnel perform both setup and manufacturing operations during the off-season, bringing in relatively unskilled personnel for manufacturing operations during the peak season and letting the skilled personnel handle only changeovers.

Applications of scheduling and loading techniques

There are many planning, scheduling and loading techniques, and the mark of the novice is to learn only a few and try to apply them everywhere. Part of this problem has been generated by articles which discuss specific techniques without relating them to others and without presenting application criteria. In earlier chapters, the materials control techniques were presented along with some application criteria—this section will suggest criteria for choosing the most effective planning, scheduling and loading techniques.

The criteria for selecting proper materials control techniques revolve around product configuration, while criteria for the selection of planning, scheduling and loading techniques revolve around the amount of lead time (and consequent backlog) available and the plant manufacturing configuration. Companies are often classified as:

1. **Distributors** who purchase materials, maintain inventories and resell, but do not manufacture.

2. **Make-to-order companies** that manufacture a product but maintain very little finished product inventory.

3. Make-to-stock companies that manufacture
their product and also maintain inventories.

Distributors are concerned only with inventory management, make-to-order companies are concerned primarily with planning and controlling production, while in a make-to-stock company these two basic functions must be meshed together very carefully to get optimum results. The student should recognize that, in practice, most manufacturing companies usually have some make-to-stock and some make-to-order products, but this classification of their activities is still helpful in determining the proper techniques to use. In considering criteria for choosing the proper planning techniques, it is helpful to think of one other type of make-to-order company: the project-oriented company manufacturing aerospace products, computers and other complex products, where long engineering lead times have made long delivery lead times traditional and acceptable to the customer.

Recognizing the fact that control over capacity is the prime purpose of a planning function, the following conclusions can be drawn about the techniques that are most appropriate for each general manufacturing classification:

1. *Project type make-to-order:* In this situation, the amount of lead time available usually provides the planner with a reasonably firm backlog of orders which he can use in conjunction with standard machine-loading techniques to project capacity requirements. For broad scheduling of projects, techniques like CPM, PERT, learning curve, etc., can supplement the regular detail scheduling and loading.

2. *Short lead time make-to-order:* If the amount of backlog normally available is less than the time required to make a capacity change (i.e., minimum manufacturing lead time is 4 weeks and customers require 4- to 8-week delivery times, thus backlog can go as high as 4 weeks, but it takes 10 weeks to hire and train a machine operator), the machine-loading technique will be useful for showing temporary overloads and bottlenecks, but supplementary techniques will be required to plan production rates.

3. *Make-to-stock:* Unless extremely long lead times are acceptable, machine-loading alone will not provide for capacity to be available when it is required and, with this type of company, there is no excuse for not projecting capacity requirements based on the projected inventory requirements (as explained in Chapter 7). Input should be controlled (using techniques described in this chapter) to regulate the level of work-in-process.

The choice of specific planning, scheduling and loading techniques should be made recognizing that the better the input control can level out the flow of work through the plant, the less in-plant backlogs will be required. The plant manufacturing configuration (within any of the service classifications above) could be further broken down into:

1. *Intermittent production,* where products are largely one-of-a-kind. Examples of this type of plant would be die-making and ship-building.

2. *Semi-process flow,* where departments may be broken down functionally (with similar equipment segregated by department rather than lined-up in the sequence in which it will be used)—but many jobs follow the same general series of operations, and there is much repetitive manufacture.

3. *Process flow,* such as automotive assembly or a textile finishing plant specializing in dyeing and finishing cloth.

For a process-flow type of plant, control over input determines control over output since every job will go through all operations in the same sequence in which it was started. Capacity can usually be planned in terms of total output (cars per day, yards of cloth, etc.) Line balancing techniques can help to define the constraints on the scheduler to get optimum use of manpower. There is no need for operations scheduling, since each job flows through the same series of operations and there is no real need to follow job progress. *Load reports* are only of value in showing the amount of unreleased backlog since, once in-process, jobs don't stop long enough for a load report to be meaningful.

In most plants, there is a great deal of semi-process flow (even if it exists only within certain product lines). Wherever this type of flow exists, any forecasting that can be done in terms of broad product groups that go through similar manufacturing sequences can be very useful in planning production rates. Control over input can be refined to the point of load-balancing for series of operations, as explained earlier in this chapter. Operations scheduling will provide a basis for following job progress, and machine-loading will show where short-term bottlenecks and overloads are occurring.

In a genuinely intermittent production-type factory (most plant people *think* of their factories as "job shops"), planning can usually be done only in the crudest terms, but it has value in controlling work in process. Forecasts can often be simulated through the machine-loading system to predict capacity requirements. Control over input can usually be done only very roughly—and even then only in starting operations. The machine-load report will be the prime document in controlling capacity.

These, then, are broad guidelines for selecting from among the available techniques. The more input can be controlled, the less output will have to be controlled. Most plants tend to concentrate on output control instead of planning input. *Some* control over plant output is necessary in any plant that is not pure process flow—the principles and techniques for controlling output are the subject of the following chapter.

Bibliography

1. Magee, J. F., *Production Planning and Inventory Control*, McGraw, New York, 1958.

2. Plossl, G. W. and Wight, O. W, "You Can't Eliminate Expediting, But . . .," *APICS Quarterly Bulletin*, Vol. 5, No. 1, April 1964.

3. ———, "Achieving Operating Efficiency through Production Planning and Scheduling," *The Manufacturing Man and His Job*, American Management Association, New York, 1966.

4. Putnam, Arnold O., Barlow, E. Robert, and Stilian, Gabriel N., *Unified Operations Management*, McGraw, New York, 1963.

5. Scheele, Evan D., Westerman, William L., and Wimmert, Robert J., *Principles and Design of Production Control Systems*, Prentice-Hall, Englewood Cliffs, New Jersey, 1960.

6. Van DeMark, R. L., *Production Control Techniques*, Van DeMark Inc., St. Clair, Michigan, 1964.

7. *PERT Guide for Management Use*, 1963, Supt. of Documents, U. S. Government Printing Office, Washington, D. C. 20402, Catalog No. D1.6/2: P94/2.

# CHAPTER TEN

CONTROLLING OUTPUT

The objectives of shop control

There are many techniques for controlling factory output, and most of them try to handle the following functions in one manner or another:

1. *Job selection and assignment* on the factory floor—the actual choice of which job behind a work center should be done next.

2. *Shop planning* to be sure that tooling is available, materials are on hand, setups will be completed in time, etc.

3. *Rescheduling* the jobs in process to meet changing requirements.

4. *Lot-control* to provide the basis for job location, means of auditing the counts reported by machine operators and accumulation of costs against the manufactured lot.

5. *Feedback* from the shop so that performance can be measured against plan and corrective action can be generated when required.

Job selection on the shop floor increases in importance as the number of jobs behind a machine center increases. The more shop input can be controlled, the less problem job selection becomes. Nevertheless, in a plant with intermittent operations and functional manufacturing departments, some provision must be made for job selection on the factory floor. In many companies, job selection is handled by the line foreman according to information given to him by the production control department. Other companies feel that choosing the job that best balances shop and customer requirements is the responsibility of a representative of the production control department—the *dispatcher* or *shop planner,* usually located out in the manufacturing department. This choice might involve deciding whether a job that can follow in the setup currently in a machine should run next, or whether a job urgently needed to meet service requirements should be run. The dispatcher who makes this decision is not only responsible for the customer service that will result, but for the setup costs as well. Assignment of a particular machine operator to the job is sometimes left to the foreman or one of his representatives, because it involves considerations of the operator's skills and a fair distribution of the more difficult or less desirable jobs (when an incentive pay system is used).

Shop planning can be a very worthwhile function when it is designed to take the responsibility for coordinating arrival of materials, availability and preparation of tooling, and issuing of proper shop paper (such as payroll cards) away from the foreman, so that he can spend more time supervising. The shop planning function frequently handles the assignment of jobs to actual machines within a machine center, while the machine-loading function usually assigns jobs only to a machine center. When machines within a machine center have special capabilities, such as a screw machine with a milling cutter attachment, the shop planner assigns jobs based on this ability (often conferring with the foreman or setup man on a daily basis) and reports any overloads on a particular machine that would not appear in the broader machine load reporting system. Shop planning can also generate savings by seeing that jobs that go through similar setups are run together, or by overlapping lots. This involves starting work on one manufacturing lot at a machine center before the entire lot has been completed at the previous operation—it can very significantly shorten lead times in some plants.

In many companies, the required date on an order issued to the plant is subject to change once the job is in-process. In a make-to-stock company for example, some items may sell faster than others and the inventory position may change drastically in a few weeks' time. Ability to react to these changing requirements can be a real asset in improving customer service. The section on *Priority rules* discusses techniques for *rescheduling* jobs once they are in the plant, so that when there is a choice of jobs to be run, this choice can be based on the latest requirements.

Lot control usually involves assigning an identification number to a particular manufacturing quantity for an item. By accumulating the counts that machine operators report against the quantity started on this lot number, the accuracy of labor claims—the basis for the operator's pay—can be verified. In some companies, costs are accumulated against each manufacturing lot and, in most companies, the movement of this lot is the basis for updating job location records so that job progress can be followed.

The shop control system should provide additional *feedback* besides job location—such as delay reports indicating which jobs are not moving, and why. Feedback is essential to good control and is the subject of Chapter 11.

There are many techniques for shop control. Some of the most important of these are discussed in the following sections.

Expediting

Expediting is probably the best known technique for shop control and the one in widest use today in industry. Expediting consists principally of finding and rushing "hot" jobs through the production facilities by pushing them ahead of other jobs competing for the same facilities. The simplest type of expediting consists of locating (among the work-in-process) items which are out-of-stock or those past-due and getting immediate attention to move these items through production. It begins to function after trouble has occurred. A more advanced form of expediting attempts to prevent trouble by setting-up check points along the way to start expediting if the job does not get through the check-point operation on the scheduled date.

Expediting has fallen into disrepute because it is expensive, frequently overdone and often does little for the factory besides generating confusion and undermining confidence in production control. Nevertheless, some follow-up and trouble shooting is usually required, since all activities cannot be predicted and there is always a gap between planned and actual results. Some companies claim that they don't have expediters, but there is someone in every company who is conscious of the customers' requirements and has the responsibility for troubleshooting and solving problems so that schedules are met. A valid comment frequently made is that the expediter only urges other people to do what they should have known enough to do by themselves.

The qualifications of an expediter are important factors of his success. Expediters should be highly energetic and resourceful people. They must get along well with plant personnel, and yet be forceful and effective in getting foremen, inspectors, engineers and others to face their problems and solve them quickly.

In practice, an expediter's activities are usually poorly organized, and much of his time is wasted. This condition can be improved by having a supervisor plan the expediters' daily activities so that their time is spent effectively and so that some measures of accomplishment may be used to evaluate each expediter's results.

Most expediting, however, is generated by poor planning – scheduling that is too rigid and that assumes that customer orders will come in exactly as predicted. Since orders seldom come as forecasted, the expediter must change schedules frequently and rush jobs through in his attempts to give good customer service. Poor scheduling will result in large backlogs of work-in-process, requiring the services of more expediters trying to sort out the backlogs and insuring that needed jobs move through.

The addition of a dispatching function to reduce the need for expediting is usually unsuccessful when the real problem is poor scheduling. The expediter is still required to tell the dispatcher about changing job priorities. A need for excessive expediting is also a symptom of under-capacity. Whenever enough product is not being manufactured, shortages arise. Too frequently, the attempted cure is to increase the expediting effort. If the real disease (too little capacity) is not cured, customer service will continue to deteriorate. Requests for special service and high priority will come first from the sales correspondents, next from sales managers and, finally, from the general manager. The problem seems to compound itself—if a small amount of expediting has been successful, there will be much pressure to increase the effort.

One expediter can usually do an effective job of rushing individual orders through production. Lines of communication are simple and there are no priority conflicts. The common assumption is therefore that two expediters would be twice as effective. Unfortunately, this is *never* the case.

Expediting consists of picking one job out of the backlog and running it through ahead of all others. As expediting efforts are increased, the number of selected rush jobs increases. If the real cause of the backlogs is not eliminated, all jobs soon become rush jobs, and a special designation must be developed for those with top priority. These become "special rush" jobs. It isn't long before only the special rush jobs seem to come through on schedule. All jobs then become "special rush," and the vicious cycle continues. This is the history of all priority systems operating under continuing shortages—including gasoline and metal rationing during national emergencies.

Expediting can be effective only as an exception technique. It works only when a small percentage of jobs are given priority over others, regardless of the number and caliber of the expediters. The basic principle is: *The less expediting there is, the more effective it will be.*

Dispatching

The dispatcher is a production control man who usually has an office in a manufacturing department where his function is to choose the sequence of jobs to be run. He has a file of orders representing jobs released to his department. He usually also has a copy of all manufacturing orders generated in the production control department, whether released or not, on which his department has operations. He holds the latter orders in a *dead load file,* waiting for notification that the job has been released to his department. When he receives this, and *before* the material has arrived in the department, he initiates action to get the tools, fixtures, gages, etc., needed to run the job. Immediately after the material arrives, he moves the order into a *live load file* behind other jobs already waiting to be run. This file has a section for each machine center or machine to which he is dispatching work. When he wants a job to be run, he issues the authorization to the production floor, frequently sending with it specifications, blueprints, time cards and related paperwork.

While the dispatcher can have positive control over job selection, he is an expensive means of attaining it. To accomplish his job of sorting out the backlog, he must find out which jobs are the "correct" ones. This is frequently difficult since the original wanted dates and priorities no longer hold and delays in other areas often prevent his receiving needed material in time to meet original schedules.

On the other hand, he may find that work moves a great deal faster than its accompanying paperwork. Many dispatching functions are not control functions at all, but simply serve to confirm with paperwork what has already been done in the plant. Paperwork originally designed to control the sequence of jobs going through production is thus only used to record history—the actual work that has been done by machine operators. It is not uncommon for a dispatcher to spend most of his time in his office while machine operators tell him which job they have started so that he can issue the proper "authorization."

Commercial equipment is available to assist the dispatcher. The simplest are *load boards,* mechanical devices to represent jobs in the backlog. Cumbersome manual dispatching techniques have often been replaced by communication hardware, such as the *teletype, data-collection terminal* and other data-transmission equipment.

Centralized dispatching

This equipment makes practicable a centralized dispatching function without individual department dispatchers. Centralized dispatching can be more practical than having dispatchers in each department because it helps solve two of the major problems of dispatching:

1. It requires less manpower than having a dispatcher in each department.

2. It provides for ready communication among dispatchers so that they can all be aware of the latest job requirements and shop status.

Centralized dispatching requires, however, that some form of communication equipment be used to report job completions to the central location (such as data-collection terminals, where the operator reports his time through the terminal and a punched card is generated in the central dispatching location). The actual job assignment is usually handled by a telephone call to the assistant foreman or setup man, who places job-assignment cards in the proper sequence in a rack at the input station on the shop floor where the operator must report to "clock off" the job he is completing.

A typical centralized dispatching control center is shown in Fig. 10-1; an input station is shown in Fig. 10-2. Each dispatcher in the picture controls several departments, and each department is represented by a card rack. Each machine center is represented by a slot in the rack, jobs being worked on are represented by punched cards in the proper slot at the front of the rack and jobs in backlog or queue are placed in corresponding slots on the back of the hinged racks. Immediate notification of job activity is received via the card punch shown at the right of Fig. 10-1 when the operator inserts the proper job card and his badge into the input terminal shown in Fig. 10-2.

This type of control center is often better than having a dispatcher in each department. It provides job selection information to the plant floor, maintains job location information for each job and immediate auditing of labor claims. The next step is to have a computer actually maintain status information and print a dispatching list on the shop floor, based on preprogrammed dispatching logic.

Flow Control

A simple system for controlling plant production in a semi-process flow type of operation has been applied very successfully in several companies.

Figure 10-1

Control Center

Called "Flow Control"[1,2], it is based on the principle that jobs started through a semiprocess flow will progress with a minimum of paperwork and formality if work in-process levels are kept low. There are six basic elements of flow control:

1. *Planned production levels of major activities:* Planned production rates for every operation or every product line are not necessary, the ABC principle applies here as it does in so many other areas of production control. There are a few products that require the bulk of available man-hours in a given manufacturing process. By controlling the rate of input in these few areas closely, production rates can be maintained at a fairly even level.

2. *Well-defined "In" and "Out" stations for material:* Clearly marked

---

[1]Robert E. McInturff and John B. Robinson, "Flow Control," Arthur Andersen & Company, New York, *Factory,* January 1963.

[2]Philip A. Link, "Successful Control over Parts Manufacturing," Automatic Electric Company, Northlake, Illinois, *APICS Quarterly Bulletin,* October 1961.

Figure 10-2

Production Floor Input Station

In and *Out* locations should be available in each department, so that all work coming to a machine center is easily recognized as new and all work completed at that machine center is immediately brought to the attention of the material handlers who will move it to the next "In" station.

3. *Clearly visible dating and identification of work-in-process:* The Flow Control approach emphasizes *visual* control of work-in-process. As each operation is completed, the work identity and completion date are marked on a tag on each move-lot of material, so that anyone concerned can tell how long each job has been at each operation.

4. *Delay reports on slow-moving work:* At regular intervals (usually twice each week), lists are made of those jobs that have been in any machine center more than a stated period of time (usually one or two days) without actually being processed. This delay report is used to bring delayed jobs to the foreman's attention so that he can take action to get them moving.

5. *A priority system:* A simple priority system is sometimes needed, but the short lead times and rapid flow of work through machine centers resulting from flow control techniques usually reduces the importance of priorities outside the production control office.

6. *Good housekeeping and shop floor discipline:* Since Flow Control is a visual way to control material on the factory floor, it depends heavily on good housekeeping and discipline in handling, arranging and locating shop containers so that material is in its proper location and is readily identifiable.

Flow Control is a thoroughly practical method for applying the principles of work-in-process control discussed in this chapter. It applies when there is a semi-process flow of work—the practitioner should be sure this is true of his plant before attempting to use Flow Control. This technique places on production control the responsibility for sending out to the factory only those jobs actually required and for gearing input very closely to actual plant capacity. It leaves the burden of shop planning to the department foreman and does not, by itself, provide for lot control. Job location and auditing of counts must therefore be handled by a separate system.

Rescheduling and priority rules

Since the problems introduced by forecast error have been discussed so frequently and since their effects are so important in designing a shop control system, a characteristic example of the type of forecast errors encountered is worth consideration. Figure 10-3 shows the results of a study of a sample of 17 items ordered to arrive in week #21. The order system indicated that these items would be required during week #21, based on estimates of demand made 13 weeks in advance. Subsequent experience showed that 5 of these items were actually required before week #19 and an equal number were required later than week #23. One item was actually needed in week #14 and another item, for which sales slowed down, was not needed until week #26. This may seem like an extreme example, but those in industry who work with long forecasts will agree that it is quite typical of their actual experience.

A good production control system should provide the means for reviewing required dates periodically, so that the proper items are started based on the latest possible information. It should also provide the means for reviewing required dates for any items already started so that these can be rescheduled if changes in forecast demand make revisions to required dates necessary or desirable. A technique that handles rescheduling

Figure 10-3

Effect of Forecast Error on "Required" Dates

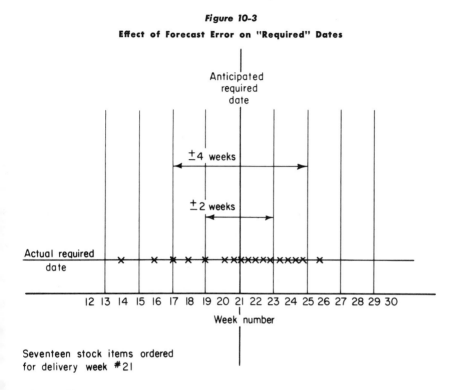

Seventeen stock items ordered
for delivery week #21

and relates it to the current status of the job in process as well as its latest requirements is called the "Critical Ratio" technique.

The Critical Ratio technique was developed by Arnold O. Putnam, of Rath & Strong, Inc.[1] This technique compares the rate at which inventory of an item is being depleted to the rate at which manufacturing lead time is being used up. The stock depletion rate is the numerator and the manufacturing lead time rate is the denominator of the Critical Ratio, which is then used to set up priority for jobs in the plant or in the *hold for release* file. It represents the latest information on actual requirements— jobs with high ratios are not urgently required, while those with low ratios should be expedited.

To calculate a Critical Ratio, accurate data are needed on:

1. Reorder points for each item in inventory
2. Inventory of every particular item on hand and available at any given time

---

[1] Putnam, Barlow, and Stilian, *Unified Operations Management,* McGraw, New York City, 1963.

3. The total manufacturing lead time required by each item

4. The remaining manufacturing lead time required by each item (in-process in the factory, or in the *hold for release* file in the production control office) at the given time

Using these data, two factors are then determined:

$$\text{Stock depletion factor } A = \frac{\text{Available stock}}{\text{Reorder point qty.}}$$

This factor will usually be less than 1.00 since another lot would not be ordered if the available stock were above the reorder point. Customer returns or order cancellations may increase the available stock and sometime cause this factor to be more than 1.00.

$$\text{Lead time factor } B = \frac{\text{Std. lead time remaining}}{\text{Total mfg. lead time}}$$

This factor will also usually be less than 1.00, since some part of the total lead time will have been used up if the part is in process.

The Critical Ratio is determined from the following relationship:

$$\text{Critical Ratio} = \frac{\text{Stock depletion factor } A}{\text{Lead time factor } B}$$

For example, suppose the order point of an item is 2000 pieces. Three weeks after a new lot is ordered, only 1000 pieces are available in the storeroom. The stock depletion factor A will be:

$$A = 1000/2000 = 0.5$$

The total time required to complete one lot of this item is six weeks, of which three weeks remain. The lead time factor B is:

$$B = 3/6 = 0.5$$

and $$\text{Critical Ratio} = A/B = 0.5/0.5 = 1.00$$

By its magnitude, the Critical Ratio indicates to production control personnel that the order is in one of three general conditions:

1. Good ratio: A/B is between 0.80 and 1.20

Available stock is being used up about as fast as lead time, and the replenishment lot should be completed about on time. No action is needed on such jobs. The example above is in this condition.

2. Expedite ratio: A/B is less than 0.80

For example, $A = 0.2$ and $B = 0.5$ (giving a critical ratio of $0.2/0.5 = 0.4$), indicating that the remaining stock has been reduced to 20% of the order point—yet 50% of the total lead time remains to complete the order now in process to replenish the inventory. With this condition, the job will have to be expedited or a stockout will occur.

3. Slack ratio: A/B is more than 1.20

Such ratios indicate that the rate of consumption of the available stock is less than was anticipated when the order point was established and/or the manufacturing order has moved through the plant faster than normal. Regardless of the cause, replenishment of this item can be delayed without risking a stockout. If it is not delayed, the new lot will come into inventory while there is still a substantial quantity on hand and inventory carrying costs will increase. Such jobs should be delayed unless the work is needed to avoid idle men or machines.

This technique, although requiring a computer when handling the large volume of data and calculations involved in most companies, is an extremely effective one for reviewing and revising schedule dates for work-in-process, orders held in the release file or for directing effective action to control work-in-process.

This type of ratio can also be used to improve the job sequencing in a plant where order due dates are generated from a materials plan or from customer's requirements. Consider two jobs in a machine center on day 105; both originally scheduled to be run on day 104. Both of them seemingly should have the same priority but Job A is due to be shipped on day 106 while Job B has more operations remaining and is due to be shipped on day 110. Job A should be assigned a more urgent priority because there is so little time left to get back on schedule. A priority ratio can be developed as follows:

$$\text{Ratio} = \frac{\text{Required date} - \text{today's date}}{\text{Required date} - \text{operation schedule date}}$$

$$\text{For Job } A: \frac{106 - 105}{106 - 104} = \frac{1}{2} = 0.50$$

$$\text{For Job } B: \frac{110 - 105}{110 - 104} = \frac{5}{6} = 0.83$$

A dynamic system of this type can be used to generate a daily dispatch list such as that shown in Fig. 10–4. Here jobs are ranked in priority sequence starting with the lowest (most urgent) number for the ratio.

One of the greatest aids to shop planning is to show not only the jobs that are in a department but also those that are expected to arrive during the next few days. This approach provides advance notice, so that tool preparation, sequenced setups, and overlapped operations can be planned more effectively.

Figure 10-4

			Daily dispatch list		
			(In priority sequence)		
	Work center #4010			Date 3/21	
				Shift 1	
Job #	Part #	Op. #	Operation description	Ratio	Remarks
71823	7123X	030	Blanchard grind	.55	Hopper feed
30756	1937A	070	Grind	.68	To B.P. 23789
63117	6424B	040	Rough grind	.82	
92318	7702X	060	Finish grind	.94	Commercial tolerance
94413	6866M	050	Rough grind	1.60	Remove case harden only

The importance of accurate, up-to-date information to the success of this type of reporting cannot be overemphasized. Dispatch lists are best when issued daily because of constant changes in shop status—their value to the shop will be very low if the status represented on the report is more than a few hours old.

The use of data collection terminals in the plant was mentioned in connection with dispatching, and it is important to note that most companies using dynamic priority rules for shop rescheduling do use some mechanized system for shop feedback. The terminals solve one technical problem related to a mechanized system: when prepunched time cards are sent to the plant along with the shop order, only one card need be sent out for each operation, no matter how many times work is reported on that operation, since the card can be inserted in the terminal over and over again. Without terminals, the prepunched reporting cards—usually called a *shop packet*—must be supplied in sufficient quantity so that there will be a card available to be returned to the production control office at the end of each shift (or other period for reporting labor).

Nevertheless, the principal advantage of using this type of equipment is neither to make technical improvements possible nor to reduce the number of timekeepers, as has often been supposed. When considering this type of mechanization, justification should not be based on clerical savings, but on its contributions through improved control.

Purchasing follow-up

Many hours of discussion concerning follow-up of purchased material have taken place in most companies. Production control people usually maintain that if purchasing would only follow-up each order to make sure it came in on schedule, most of the problems would be solved—while purchasing people argue that there aren't enough hours in the day to follow-up on all items, particularly since there are so many "RUSH" orders, and that if *all* the material came in on schedule, there would be no room to store it. The problems of controlling output from vendors revolves largely around the rescheduling problem discussed above: the real objective of purchasing follow-up is to make sure that material arrives in time to meet latest requirements. As expected, many purchasing requirements will change after the requisitions have been made, and it is more important to relay these changes to the purchasing department and have them try to effect these changes than it is to insist on adherence to original scheduled dates. If material for which requirements have dropped off is received late, no harm will result.

One technique used by many purchasing departments is the *blanket order,* calling for delivery of a portion of the order at a particular weekly rate. By contracting in advance for a large supply (usually either six months' or a year's supply), they are able to take advantage of quantity discounts. Because of the long range of the forecast, accuracy is a serious problem and it is important for the production control department to review actual required dates constantly.

Figure 10-5 shows a weekly report issued by the production control department reviewing blanket orders (in this case, for the components required to manufacture the lamps discussed in other examples in this book). This type of review is necessary in order to be sure that schedules based upon the original estimates are still realistic. A significant point concerning this blanket order review form should be remembered. The forecasted average weekly usage for each component is based upon a weekly weighted average of incoming business. However, this has to be adjusted to meet the anticipated total requirements indicated by the production plan.

The weighted averages of past actual demand for 11D and 11P lamps might indicate, for example, that requirements for X27 switches would equal approximately 2000 units, while the production plan indicates that the production rate will be substantially higher than this, requiring 2300 units per week to support the planned production rate rather than the 2000 units forecast.

The inventory range in weeks on the blanket order review form is

Figure 10-5
Blanket Order Review
Purchased Lamp Components

Week ending 2/25

Week number 8

Part no.	Part name descr.	Used on	Est. avg. wkly. use	Req. this week	Inv. range in wks.	On* hand	Past due	Scheduled delivery						Remarks
								Due Wk.8	Due Wk.9	Due Wk.10	Due Wk.11	Due Wk.12	Due later	
X18	Switch	7W,7D 9W,9D,9P	3,700	4,500	2-3	7,105	—	5,700	4,000	4,000	3,000	4,000	42M	—
X27	Switch	11D,11P	2,000	2,300	3-4	15,423	—	3,400	—	—	—	—	34M	Bought against fm. invr.
4107	Cord set	All	6,000	6,500	1-2	6,400	8,000	7,200	6,000	6,000	6,000	6,000	40M	P.D. prom. for Fri.

*Note — If out of range more than one week's use, action must be taken based upon the variability in demand anticipated for these components. The 4107 cord set, for example, is used on all lamps, and its total weekly demand will be equal to the planned production level. Thus, an inventory range of one to two weeks should be sufficient. The X27 switch is used on only two lamps, and its demand might be expected to fluctuate rather substantially from week to week; consequently, an inventory range of three to four weeks is considered desirable. At the present time, the inventory is considerably above this level because material has been purchased in anticipation of a price increase.

The X18 switch inventory range is two to three weeks since it is used on the majority of the lamps, and demand for it—while not as stable as that for the 4107 cord set—should still be considerably steadier than the demand for the X27 switch.

The basic purpose of the blanket order review is to provide control over a blanket order schedule originally set v ɹ with the vendor according to long-range estimates of future demand, and to allow a tolerance for adjusting it when actual requirements turn out to be considerably different from the original estimates. The principle involved is fundamental to all purchasing follow-up systems: the production control department is responsible for supplying information regarding any changes in requirements—advances or deferments—and a tolerance must exist in the system so that it will not overreact to small changes in requirements.

Lead time control

Before attempting a program aimed at reducing lead time, practitioners should analyze a sample of actual orders completed recently to determine the elements of lead time, such as setup time, running time, delays, and (particularly) paper-processing time. A customer considers lead time to start when he sends in his order. Delays of ten days may occur in some companies before the production control department first sees the order.

Actual processing time, including setup, cannot be reduced by the production control department—only the manufacturing and industrial engineering groups can change this element of lead time. The percentage of manufacturing time to waiting time for each department will show in which departments the greatest delays occur. Through proper scheduling and attention to delays, by pointing out where better balancing of shifts would cut down elapsed lead time and by making sure that paperwork processing time has been reduced to a bare minimum, production control can reduce both the length and variability of lead times.

There are three major areas of improvement in seeking a reduction in lead time:

1. Order processing time: This is the time which elapses from the moment an order leaves the customer's hands until the material is actually pulled from storage in a make-to-stock plant, or until it is being scheduled into production in a make-to-order plant.

Actual delivery time of orders from customer to vendor rarely comprises an important fraction of this element of lead time. If it does, the use of teletype equipment, telephone or modern data-transmission equipment can cut this very substantially. Most long order processing times result from two basic causes: every order is handled as an exception, or all paperwork operations—order entry, updating sales records, inventory adjustments, invoicing, etc.—is completed *before* the order is released for processing. In many companies, the credit manager must look at each order that comes in, rather than merely checking credit risks, and the sales department wants someone to look at each order as it comes in to pick out unusual ones. If these people handle orders in sequence, even if they do their review promptly, this order handling time can require two or three days.

While order processing is a complex system beyond the scope of this book, it is important to recognize its contribution to lead time and to control it as well as factory lead times. Ingenuity in reducing paperwork lead time can improve a company's performance as much as new processing equipment or improved production control systems. For example, copying machines make it possible to get a customer's order to schedulers promptly in order to start factory work before beginning the required formal paperwork (type the order, edit it, and check it through engineering, credit, and sales). In most plants, the order will not have progressed far if there is reason to stop it because of poor credit or engineering questions.

2. Scheduling: Backlogs constitute a considerable part of total lead time in many companies. As discussed in Chapter 7, some means of leveling production are required and, if these are not provided by planning, it will be achieved by maintaining backlogs ahead of the starting operations. In a make-to-order plant, incoming business fluctuations make starting backlogs inevitable. If there is no attempt at production planning, these backlogs may add weeks of unnecessary lead time.

Controlling input as described in Chapter 9 can assist in reducing scheduling lead time by keeping total production geared closely to total demand and feeding individual orders into production according to the latest customer requirements. Lead time can also be reduced by scheduling to the shortest possible cycle.

3. Reduced work-in-process backlogs: In most intermittent operations, analysis of the lead time will indicate that the greatest gains are to be made in reducing waiting time at individual operations.

Figure 10-6 is a simple chart that can be used to analyze lead time. This is a frequency distribution which can be maintained by a clerk in the production control department who reviews all of the receiving documents, or by a computerized system. As receipts are posted against the purchase order or factory order records, a tally is made of the actual lead times. The production control manager can then use this analysis to see how lead times are changing. When he sees lead times increasing, he should attempt to correct the problems causing this rather than increasing his planned lead times.

Figure 10-6

Monthly Lead Time Analysis

Forgings Purchased from Ace Foundry

Forgings purchased from Ace Foundry			
Lead time	Occurrences	Cumulative	Percent
0-1 week	‖	2	3.9
1-2 weeks	‖‖	6	11.5
2-3 weeks	ℳ ℳ ‖‖	19	36.4
3-4 weeks	ℳ ℳ ℳ ℳ ‖‖	42	80.8
4-5 weeks	ℳ	47	90.4
5-6 weeks	‖	49	94.2
6-7 weeks	‖	51	98.1
Over 7			52	100.0

Control of lead time is not well understood in most manufacturing companies. Many believe that their actual lead times are appropriate. Unfortunately, if lead times are *expected* to be long, they most likely *will* be long. The vicious cycle of rising business activity, stepped-up ordering, lengthened lead times, increased order points, additional ordering and further increases in lead time will generate severe shortages and unnecessary increases in inventory.

A major sales job will be needed to convince scheduling personnel that by planning and reducing its backlog, a department that couldn't meet its requirements with 15 weeks average lead time will now be able to give them deliveries with five weeks average lead time!

Figure 10-7 represents a memorandum sent by a purchasing agent to his company's production control manager. This illustrates a not-uncommon reaction by a purchasing agent to increased pressure from production control when suppliers get so busy they cannot give deliveries. In this case, Mr. Jones' company is the only supplier of bearing inserts to the Fairville

Figure 10-7

Fairville Division
of Johnson – Fairville

Interoffice correspondence

To: **Mr. J. R. Moss, Production Control**   Date: 1/14

Subject : **Lead Times**

I called Mr. R. Jones in reference to Bearing

inserts which we wanted at once.

Mr. Jones said their bearing insert department

is now operating on a six-week delivery time.

He suggested we increase our inventory to take

care of future delays.

J. Seagar,

Purchasing Agent

Division and the question of what Mr. Moss (Production Control Manager) should do is an interesting one. The only way to increase his inventory is to place more orders on Mr. Jones' company which, in all probability, will result in longer quoted delivery lead times.

Mr. Moss' estimates as to which bearing inserts he needs and when he needs them will become less and less accurate as he tries to predict further in advance. Even if the supplier's service did not deteriorate as his in-plant backlogs increased (which is most likely), the ability of the Fairville Division to give its customers good service would certainly deteriorate since they would be less able to predict their actual requirements over the extended lead time.

Earlier ordering is requested of their customers by suppliers who imply that they will then reserve enough capacity to meet the customers' needs. Poorer forecasts of customer requirements over the longer lead times, however, actually result in wasted vendor capacity. Reserving vendor capacity in terms of machine hours, tons of castings or some other meaningful total units and committing this capacity to specific customer items at the latest possible time avoids this waste. Generating larger backlogs will never solve the problem of inadequate capacity.

The essence of lead time control is control over work-in-process through planned production rates and controlled input. Much of the need in many companies today to control output is caused by their inattention to control over work-in-process. In most intermittent production plants, it is necessary to have *some* work ahead of each machine center to smooth out the flow of production and to insure that there is a minimum of machine down-time caused by lack of work. Nevertheless, most production control operations do not recognize the great effect that the level of work-in-process has upon lead time, output control and, consequently, customer service. Missing this, they fail to exert sufficient efforts toward keeping work-in-process to a minimum.

The fact that the basic relationship between the level of work-in-process and the control of mix output is not generally recognized is not surprising. It has received far too little emphasis in the literature of production and inventory control. One of the few published items on this subject is a most interesting article titled "The Case of Management Versus Excessive Inventories" which tells of a company that made a very drastic reduction in work-in-process inventory and thereby reduced average lead time from five months to two weeks. Their approach was simple: they tagged all work on the floor and removed all material that was not actually being worked on. This insured that the right jobs would go through production. This article appeared in the September **1930** issue of *Factory and Industrial Management* magazine. Unfortunately, its message seems to have gone almost unheeded in the four decades which have followed its publication.

The benefits of a reduction in work-in-process in most plants are much easier to recognize than to attain. The real problem is teaching the value of getting along with less floor-work to people such as:

1. *The foreman,* who wants more work on the floor before he adds manpower to meet rising demand.

2. *The inventory control man,* who believes his job is to generate orders to replenish stocks without concern for planned production and proper scheduling.

3. *The expediter,* who feels that if he had "just two more weeks of lead time," he could get every job completed on schedule.

4. *The scheduler,* who wants to "get the jump" on important jobs by getting them on order with the factory as soon as possible, believing that extra lead time will insure getting them through on schedule. This puts him in the very comfortable position of being able to say "It's on order with the factory!" when asked the status of a particular job.

5. *The production control man,* who recognizes that work-in-process is too high but is too busy trying to get the right job shipped out on schedule to do anything about it.

6. *The setup man,* who waits to start one job so that he can combine its run with that of another he knows will come through sometime soon.

This education job is a major stumbling block in reducing work-in-process, but the necessity for this effort is obvious in most plants. Most plants with intermittent production seem to have very little control over their level of work-in-process. There are very few where all available space on the factory floor is not taken up with work-in-process. Almost any foreman in these plants will quickly attest that he could do his job much more effectively if he had "just a little more space." It is common to find recurring shortages of skids, pallets, shop boxes and other work containers.

When this is true, it is important that the effects of excess work-in-process inventory throughout the system be emphasized to all concerned and that they recognize the results that can be attained by reducing it. These benefits include:

1. *Lead time*—decreases as backlogs decrease

2. *Forecasts*—more likely to be accurate as lead time decreases

3. *Dispatching and communication*—easier as backlogs are decreased

4. *Production control manpower*—decreases as the need for expediting and dispatching decreases

Reducing work-in-process requires major adjustments by both production control and manufacturing people. Taking the responsibility for keeping work flowing in the factory at a smooth rate requires a new perspective of production control departments who have historically depended upon large factory backlogs to do this. Factory operating people will be deeply concerned when they see in-process inventory levels decreasing—a reasonable time period should be allowed for building the foreman's confidence in production control's ability to keep work flowing to him and for learning to use the control system to detect backlogs when they occur.

During this transition period, foremen and production control personnel will have to work together very closely to iron out the problems that may arise. A machine operator may occasionally run out of work when work-in-process levels are first reduced. If they investigate this objectively, production control personnel can usually see how better scheduling might have avoided this situation. To make a work-in-process reduction permanently effective, production control personnel will have to check every reported case of machine down-time or operator idle-time, determine what caused it and try to insure that it does not happen again.

One legitimate reason for having inventory is to provide insurance against breakdowns of equipment, and plant people often cite this as a primary reason for having high levels of work-in-process. Unfortunately, a little checking will show that normal work-in-process inventories provide very little protection against breakdown because they have not been planned properly. If a critical machine is subject to breakdown, spare parts should be available, preventive maintenance should be used and repair actions should be taken to get this machine back into operation quickly when it breaks down. If, in spite of the best planning, it is still necessary to have inventory ahead of this machine, that inventory should be chosen so that it represents a balanced load on subsequent operations and should be physically removed from process, so that it will not interfere with normal operations but will only be available when a breakdown occurs.

For most companies, work-in-process can be reduced drastically with no ill-effects, but it is worth determining *proper* levels of work-in-process. Work-in-process is justified when the rates of flow between operations cannot be controlled precisely. Estimating the proper levels of work-in-process involves measuring the variation in these flow rates—which can be done by simulation or by observation. When chronic backlogs exist, they can be sampled from time to time and, for example, if these backlogs range between 50 and 75 skids of work, the variation in flow would justify maximum actual backlog of 25 skids. Of course, it follows that any scheduling techniques that can reduce this variation will get at the heart of the problem.

Any work-in-process reduction program should begin by determining the amount of man and machine down-time that exists with current factory backlogs, so that direct comparisons can be made with down-time that occurs with lower levels of in-process inventory. Unless this comparison is available, excessive down-time will be cited as the principal result of reducing work-in-process. Such a reaction is understandable. It is a major change for plant operating personnel who have been used to large banks of work ahead of each operation to watch these banks dwindle and to have to learn to work today without having tomorrow's material on hand. In spite of such difficulties, more and more practitioners are recognizing that reducing material in the shop is the most effective means of lowering lead times and is fundamental to real control over output.

Job shop simulation

Simulation is a useful tool when there are so many variables that a direct mathematical solution is impractical. The answers to many problems involved in intermittent or job-shop scheduling obviously fit this description and, since the advent of the computer, considerable time has therefore been spent on *job shop simulation*.

In the typical job-shop simulators, numerical data—the language of the computer—are used to describe how many machines of each type are available, how many shifts each one is manned, and how many productive hours can be expected from each work center. Each of the jobs to be studied is described in one of a deck of punch cards, including each work center in the manufacturing sequence, setup time and running time for every job. With this information, the computer is programmed to simulate actual factory operations and print out the results, showing starting and finishing dates, etc. The equivalent of months of experience can be developed in a few hours of computer time.

Several firms and universities have used computer simulation to test dispatching rules that could be used when deciding which job to run next. Many dispatching rules have been applied, but four fairly typical and frequently used ones are:

1. *First-come, first-served:* The oldest job at each machine center should be run first.

2. *Value priority:* Preference is given to the "A" items (those having the highest dollar value for the lot) so that work-in-process dollar inventory investment is kept low.

3. *Critical machine:* Those jobs are run first which must later go through critical machines of limited capacity. The rule was designed to get jobs to bottleneck machines sooner, permit-

ting the highest utilization of critical equipment and reducing the likelihood of delays.

4. *Least processing time:* The next job to be run is
   the one requiring the least time to complete
   the lot at the machine center (the easiest job
   to get done.)

Published results would appear to show that the best all-around dispatching rule is the *least processing time* rule. This rule typically results in:

1. The most jobs completed—this makes sense, since by picking the
   easiest jobs first, the dispatcher will be able to help the shop complete more jobs within a given period.

2. The lowest in-process inventory.

3. The shortest average lead time.

4. The best machine utilization.

5. The fewest late jobs—this is particularly interesting, since this
   dispatching rule pays no attention to job schedule dates at all.

Using this rule over a long period of time, however, might mean that
jobs with long processing time *never* get done. They will be worked on
only when there is no other work at the machine center requiring less
time, and this might never happen! Simulation study of dispatching
rules in a job shop has not yet come up with the answer to finding the
best dispatching rule, but it has demonstrated one point that has been
emphasized throughout this book: Any technique that keeps work-in-
process low—this is the principal effect of the least processing time rule—
will improve plant performance by almost every measure.

One of the requirements for a good dispatching rule, in practice, is
that it be capable of reacting to changing required dates (as the forecast
changes and according to the relative progress of the job in process).
The Critical Ratio rules meet this criterion and, in current business
applications, seem to be more practical than any fixed dispatching rules.
Nevertheless, other dispatching criteria could be combined with techniques such as the Critical Ratio if more sophistication were desired.

One of the most effective future applications of the computer in simulating the flow of work through factories will undoubtedly be for studying
shop flow (especially delays and interruptions), and for developing the
optimum schedules needed for complex operations. Schedules based on
computer simulations can take cognizance of critical operations and
balance the input to provide uniform loads for these operations as well as
for the starting operation. Computer simulation can also be used to determine the optimum level of work-in-process. While the majority of plants

Figure 10-8

Simulated Work Input and Flow Times (SWIFT)*

Simulation Printout

Time			Work ctr.	Status	Ident.	Hrs. Remain	Queue		Hours to date			
Clk	Day	Shift					Jobs	Hrs.	Run	S/U	Idle	Avail.
7.0	1	1	1	R	8	0.7	1	2.7	6.3	0.7		7.0
			2	R	13	9.2			2.4	0.6	4.0	7.0
			3	R	1	17.8	2	12.1	13.0	2.0		14.0
				S	6	16.1						
			4	R	15	1.9	1	6.0	0.8	8.2		14.0
8.0	1	1	1	S	16	2.4			7.0	1.0		8.0
			2	R	13	8.2	1	6.1	3.4	0.6	4.0	8.0
			3	R	1	16.8	2	12.1	14.9	2.1		16.0
				R	6	15.1						

*SWIFT was developed at The Stanley Works, New Britain, Connecticut
by J. D. Horty, G. W. Plossl, and O. W. Wight.

have high levels, there is a practical minimum and simulation offers a convenient tool for attacking this problem.

Figure 10-8 shows a printout from a computer simulation of production flow in a factory. In making this simulation, the computer has been programmed to employ a model of a typical intermittent manufacturing facility in which time is represented in increments that can be chosen at the discretion of the user. In the example shown, time is being recorded in one-hour increments, beginning with the seventh hour and showing the work status in the various work centers—whether the work center is running or being set up, the identification of the particular job currently being run, the time remaining for that job, and the other jobs in queue at that work center. This computer printout also shows a machine activity summary through the current simulation clock interval. A simulation of this type can be used to test different scheduling methods, to determine how best to balance the load of work through sequences of operations and to determine the optimum level of work-in-process.

Simulation has been used in some companies to prepare daily shop schedules showing not only jobs in each machine center, but also those coming in during the next few shifts, so as to provide better information for shop planning. Simulation will undoubtedly become one of the most important tools for controlling shop operations efficiently.

Applications of output control techniques

One of the most challenging tasks for student and practitioner alike is to sort out the various production control techniques in his own mind and to recognize where they apply properly. Since so many articles are devoted to one particular technique or another, it is easy to rely entirely on individual techniques for their own sake instead of seeing them in their proper perspective. Guidelines for selecting the proper output control techniques should be considered with a particular company application in mind.

One of the first points to determine is whether output control (essentially job selection) is a real problem or whether problems that appear to revolve around output control are just a result of lack of planning or input control. This question can be answered by checking actual elapsed lead time for a sample of manufactured items. If average lead times are reasonable but some items take very long times to be completed while others are manufactured considerably ahead of schedule, then job selection is the problem. If, on the other hand, average lead times are extremely long, it should be recognized that no amount of expediting or dispatching is likely to improve this average.

If job selection is the real problem, the next problem is choosing the proper technique to apply. When many jobs follow similar patterns of flow in production, techniques such as Flow Control should be considered. Here again, it is important to keep techniques in perspective. The general elements of Flow Control (such as planned rates, well identified *in* and *out* stations and delay reports) make sense in any system and do not necessarily have to be used in conjunction with a visual follow-up if the visual approach is not appropriate. The general concepts of Flow Control could be applied using electronic data-collection terminals if other objectives (job location, count control, etc.) were required by the production control system. Any system used in a plant that has some degree of flow should focus the greatest attention on control of input to the plant and keeping jobs moving.

If work flow is truly intermittent, dispatching can best handle job selection and might be introduced only in bottleneck departments. When dispatching is to be used in many departments, a centralized approach should be considered. It is sometimes worth having a production control man assigned to a manufacturing department when job selection is not particularly critical just to handle shop planning. This type of department is characterized by the need for considerable detail planning to handle tool preparation, job sequencing, and the most effective use of available setup time.

In a make-to-stock plant where the actual requirements may change considerably *after* jobs have been sent into the plant, dynamic priority rules will be very effective in reflecting these changing requirements to the plant. Critical Ratio can be applied if order points are used for materials control and adapted to a materials plan updated regularly. The application of techniques of this type should improve customer service by helping to move the right items through production.

When purchased components are particularly important, consideration should be given to the use of better follow-up techniques. This follow-up should be based on latest requirements rather than required dates set some time ago. Insisting that the purchasing department bring all material in on time and bring the rush jobs in ahead of time does not recognize the fact that for every rush job, there should also be one that can be rescheduled to a later date. Knowing this will help purchasing to reschedule their vendors more effectively. Close attention to vendors' delivery lead times (using summaries such as that shown in Fig. 10-6) can help to spot trouble before it is highlighted by excessive shortages or inventory increases.

If average lead times seem too long, some items can be sampled to see what percentages of the overall lead time are represented by order entry, scheduling time in production control, setup time, running time, move time and wait time. If order entry represents a large part of total lead time, it's a likely candidate for systems improvement. In most companies, queue time is the largest lead time element by far. Long queue times are symptomatic of lack of control over work-in-process, and if work-in-process seems to have filled all available space, the first step is to develop better planning and input control techniques, and then to gradually reduce work-in-process levels while conducting a continuing education program to help personnel learn to live with lower levels of work-in-process. Each major backlog area should be analyzed to determine what purpose the inventory serves and approximately how much is really needed.

The job of selecting the proper technique for controlling output requires a knowledge of the range of techniques available and where each best applies. Beyond this, however, production control systems design requires an understanding of the way the elements of a good system must interrelate. Shop control can be very expensive and sophisticated, yet achieve very little if lack of attention to planning and controlling capacity has let work-in-process levels build up too high. Even the most dynamic priority system will decrease in effectiveness as shop backlogs get out of control. On the other hand, if the materials control system does not truly reflect requirements or changes in these requirements, efforts to get items through production according to unrealistic schedules will be largely wasted effort. Output control is a vital part of any production control system, but it should be remembered that *it can only function as part of a well-designed overall production control system.*

Bibliography

1. Conway, R. W., "Priority Dispatching and Job Lateness in a Job Shop" *Journal of Industrial Engineering,* Vol. XVI, No. 4, July–August 1965.

2. Gomersall, Earl R., "The Backlog Syndrome," *Harvard Business Review,* Vol. 42, No. 5, September–October 1964.

3. Link, P. A., "Successful Control over Parts Manufacturing," *APICS Quarterly Bulletin,* Vol. 2, No. 4, October 1961.

4. McInturff, Robert E. and Robinson, John B., "Flow Control," *Factory,* Vol. 121, No. 1, January 1963.

5. Myer, H. C., "Shop Scheduling," *APICS Annual Conference Proceedings,* 1964.

6. Putnam, Arnold O., Barlow, Robert E., and Stilian, Gabriel N., *Unified Operations Management,* McGraw, New York, 1963.

7. "Small Backlogs = Big Control," *Executives Bulletin,* No. 228, April 30, 1965.

# CHAPTER ELEVEN

FEEDBACK AND
CORRECTIVE ACTION

Feedback—the basis for control

In essence, control consists of feedback and corrective action. Use of the production plan to control production levels (as discussed in Chapter 8) is an example of effective feedback to compare progress against plan. A forecast of demand and the desired change in inventory level was used to determine the production rates. Actual incoming business, production and inventory status are then compared periodically with the plan. If the inventory is outside acceptable range, some corrective action must be taken. Control of input also requires feedback of sales and inventory information to indicate exactly which items should be started into production. Output control, involving shop planning, expediting and dispatching, requires regular feedback of information about what has been produced, the location of jobs in process and the problem areas that require attention.

Production control is primarily an information system. This does not mean that it should be a passive function merely turning out reports, but it does mean that the basis for control is information and that the production control department has the responsibility for generating the proper information so that the plant can be managed to meet established goals. This is not a simple task—the job of establishing the goals for operating the plant, tracking progress against these goals and recommending proper corrective action is an extremely challenging one.

Production control managers frequently find themselves in difficulty because customer service, inventory levels or plant operating expenses are out of control. Since they have no authority over the manufacturing operations that can correct the conditions, they sometimes feel that it is unfair to place the blame on them. Unfortunately, in many instances, this is exactly where the blame should be placed since the basic cause of the problems is that not enough information was presented to management to show them the real alternatives available in solving these problems. It is the production control manager's job to be constantly distilling the information that comes to him and to provide guidance to plant management in making operating decisions.

There are three links in the chain of production control. All must be present and tied together effectively in order to have good control. They are:

1. *A production control system—a discipline for handling information*

2. *Use of the system by production control personnel to generate timely information*

3. *Use of this information by plant operating personnel to manage manufacturing operations effectively*

The production control system should be designed to be an effective *control panel* for the plant manager, so that his activities are directed to solving the most important problems in order to correct a situation that is out of control. The system should be designed to present information *to those responsible for taking action.*

For example, a quality control problem which is hindering delivery should be reported immediately to quality control personnel who can generate corrective action. The information should be reported objectively, briefly, and with the best recommendations that the production control man can make for resolving the problem. This relationship also exists with other organizational groups, such as industrial engineering, product engineering, etc. Any problems which are not solved promptly and effectively should then be reported to the next higher level of management.

Developing timeliness in a control system is one of the most difficult problems. In some plants, for example, it often appears economical to use tabulated payroll cards to report job location in the plant. This employs common source data already in machine language for two important jobs. In most companies, payroll customarily comes first, and adjustments required before processing it delay work on job location reports, so that this report will be two to three days old before it is delivered to those who need it. They then find that many jobs have moved, and soon come to look upon the report as useless. The use of electronic data collection terminals on the factory floor to collect this information at the point of origin so that it will be more accurate and timely is increasing in industry today, primarily because of its impact on improving feedback.

Inventory reports which show the stock status as it existed two or three days ago are another common violation of the principle of timeliness. Control cannot be exercised over things that have already happened, only over things that are going to happen. Control information which is outdated is not control information at all.

Once an effective production control information system has been set up, getting personnel to use it properly requires an effective education program. Production control personnel who have not had a good information generating system consider that their principal jobs are expediting and troubleshooting, and they often resent the discipline that a production control system imposes. They are too busy drowning to save themselves. They find it difficult to comprehend that the routine of reviewing items that require reordering and generating replenishment orders promptly, for example, is really far more important than expediting an individual job that has fallen behind schedule. Many of the action-oriented production control troubleshooters of the "old school" never do learn to come to terms with the routine paperwork, detailed planning and difficult thinking-ahead that is required in a good production control system. Consequently, they always have plenty of troubleshooting problems to occupy their time.

Education of management is needed to avoid emasculating the system by "cost reduction" programs which save the pay of one or two clerks at the expense of poor customer service, excess inventories and upsets in the factory. The system itself must be based on information provided by up-to-date routings and bills-of-material. Penny-pinching in the maintenance of this basic information can be very costly in the long-run.

The existence of a production control information system and its effective use by production control personnel accomplishes nothing, however, until line personnel take action. Top management is frequently looking for changes in their production control system to cure an out-of-stock problem, for example, when the present system has already pointed out quite effectively that finished goods inventory levels are not high enough to give the desired level of customer service—yet no real action is being taken by plant management to restore these inventory levels. The most effective system and the most competent production control personnel cannot succeed where the third link in the chain of production control is not provided. The business of production control is *information,* information which must be presented promptly, briefly, and frequently in such a fashion that the required action will result.

Feedback and corrective action in a make-to-order plant

While more planning is possible in a make-to-order plant than is usually done, it is usually not possible to preplan activities as well as in a make-to-stock plant. It therefore becomes extremely important to report problems more promptly in a make-to-order shop. The orders being run (even though there may be repeat orders from customers) require more engineering, tooling and supervision because they are run less frequently than those in a make-to-stock plant. For this reason, the personnel are not as familiar with the individual jobs and there tend to be more manufacturing problems. In a make-to-order plant, the emphasis must be on prompt reporting and quick reaction to solve the problems in tooling, materials, schedule changes and the like.

Many make-to-order plants have a large percentage of business in new orders, which must start with individual engineering and special tooling for each job. In such situations, it is almost mandatory for production control to schedule the engineering and the tooling required. If these elements proceed on schedule, it will not be necessary to make up for the time lost in engineering and tooling by reducing manufacturing lead time. Since fewer people are involved, it is much more economical to use extra help or overtime in the engineering department to meet the original schedule or to work some overtime in the tool room rather than to disrupt other schedules and work many overtime hours while trying to make up time lost in earlier phases of the project. Project planning techniques outlined in Chapter 9 can be used to monitor activities against check points set up for each major element in the project.

Establishing check points by operations scheduling is one of the first improvements usually made in a make-to-order production control operation. Most companies progress from having expediters chase only those jobs that have appeared on the *past-due* list (jobs still in the plant beyond the shipping date promised to the customer) to a system that establishes a date when critical operations should be completed and takes action to get operations completed on time in order to meet a promised completion date. Up-to-date job location records are, of course, essential.

The next step is to report unavoidable schedule changes to the customer promptly so that he can adjust for them. While this requires an amount of courage that is often hard to muster, it generally results (over the long-run) in far better customer relations than telling him nothing unless he asks. Having the customer initiate the call to find out why a job is late and hearing "We'll check and call you back" gives him the impression that his order has been forgotten and that there is little control over production in this plant.

Most make-to-order companies can gain a considerable competitive advantage by having shorter lead times and by meeting promised dates. For this reason, it is important to develop a management team within this type of company that is fast on its feet and quick to react to changes. This requires a good feedback system, so that management attention can quickly be focused on delays and the alternatives available to correct them. For example, as the backlog ahead of starting operations increases, the alternatives open to management are relatively few and are all unpleasant:

1. Either:
   a. Quote longer lead times—and therefore turn away some business (many companies don't change their quoted lead times as their starting backlog increases, and lose their reputation for service because they do not meet the delivery promises they make)
   or:
   b. Increase the production level

2. If it is decided to increase the production level, this means either:
   a. Working overtime
   or:
   b. Adding personnel

3. The decision to work overtime or add personnel hinges principally on predicting the duration of the increase in business, which must come from the sales or marketing personnel, and which would indicate either:
   a. The increase is short-term and should be handled with overtime
   or:
   b. The increase is long-term and should be handled with added personnel

Unfortunately, few production control departments are effective in pointing out these alternatives quickly enough. Management personnel are themselves frequently guilty of not facing the real alternatives available and not insisting upon assistance from production control personnel in pointing out these alternatives. The final result is customers who are disappointed in the service they are receiving and a general manager who is thoroughly disappointed in his management team because he sees service deteriorating and costs going up.

Providing the information to permit management to weld the sales and marketing personnel, plant operating personnel, engineering, quality control and other major elements of the business into an effective operating team is one of the challenges that faces the production control man in any plant. An effective production control manager must be able to show management its real decision alternatives in specific terms, such as which orders will suffer when rush orders are forced through the plant. In fact, a good production control manager may sometime have to advise management to turn down a specific order to avoid jeopardizing service on a great many others. Organizing information effectively enough to point out the rational basis for making this type of decision is an extremely challenging job requiring a great deal more skill than the expediting that usually occupies so much of the production control manager's time in a make-to-order operation.

Feedback and corrective action in a make-to-stock plant

In a make-to-stock plant, there must be much more emphasis on planning production levels, controlling input and output and planning the total production of individual parts requiring substantial investments in tooling or equipment. While it is a mistake to release orders any further in advance than necessary, it is possible to plan tooling, machine capacities and the like by estimating total requirements for a stock part well ahead of the time individual orders are generated.

In a make-to-stock business, such standard techniques as machine loads, job location reports and job progress comparisons are used much as they are in a make-to-order business. Job location records show the location of each individual job based upon feedback from the plant, usually in the form of a payroll card turned in by the machine operator or entered through an electronic data-collection system.

The most difficult problem to overcome in controlling any make-to-stock operation arises when all planning is based on a forecast. No matter how much effort is devoted to improving the forecasts, many operating changes are bound to be needed to meet changing demand. Most operating and production control personnel have a natural aversion to the uncertainty involved in working with a forecast—they try to develop fairly rigid production control systems with firm plans made far in advance to overcome this uncertainty. As the systems usually fail, these people then blame the failure on lack of a reliable forecast. Since the reduction of lead time helps make the forecast more accurate, short lead times are every bit as important in a make-to-stock business as they are in a make-to-order business.

A considerable improvement in customer service can be made if flexibility is introduced into the planned schedule and it is recognized that the original scheduled dates are subject to change as customer demand changes. This requires some form of priority system and the means for revising these priorities. The Critical Ratio presented in Chapter 10 is one very practical technique for revising priorities. It should be kept in mind, however, that the necessity for revising plant priorities is reduced as the level of work-in-process and (consequently) the plant lead time are reduced.

In most make-to-stock companies, customer demand is quite effective in calling the attention of the production control department to those items which are selling at a higher rate than forecast, since they will go low in inventory or out of stock, and therefore require special attention. Very few companies today have an equally good system for pointing out the items which are *not* selling up to forecast rates, and which can therefore be rescheduled in order to get more urgently needed parts through.

In a make-to-order business, the original schedule date should be a fairly firm target (excepting occasional rescheduling required by breakdowns). In a make-to-stock business, however, the original schedule dates should always be subject to revision based upon changing conditions of inventory of the individual items. It is at least as important to have timely feedback information on the stock status of individual items as it is to know where they stand in production.

The requirement for schedule flexibility can be especially trying in a plant that has partly make-to-stock and partly make-to-order business, and where stock items and make-to-order items are competing for the same facilities. It is very tempting and, in fact, usually the practice in such companies to give make-to-order items priority over make-to-stock items. Under these conditions, the service rendered to those customers who buy stocked items from inventory deteriorates to such a low level that considerable sales department pressure is exerted to improve it.

The usual reaction is to have a management dictum that schedule dates on make-to-stock orders are just as important as those on make-to-order items, and that both must be observed religiously. This policy usually stays in effect until an individual case comes up where a stock item is run in accordance with its originally scheduled date and pushes aside a make-to-order item which is competing for the same manufacturing facility. Someone then finds out that the stock item wasn't really needed on that date because actual sales were below the rate forecast at the time the manufacturing order was scheduled. This customarily results in make-to-order items being assigned higher priority than stocked items, and the cycle begins anew.

What is actually required in a make-to-stock business is some means of reporting both the status of jobs in-process and the condition of the inventory of those items. The Critical Ratio method discussed in Chapter 10 is a thoroughly practical technique for comparing feedback information from both inventory and manufacturing to determine up-to-date plant priorities. It can also provide a rational means for deciding whether a make-to-stock or make-to-order item deserves preference.

The problems of uncertainty are compounded in a plant that makes an assembled product. An inventory must be maintained for multiple-end-use components that are needed in a number of different finished assemblies. The usual approach to maintaining this component inventory is to determine an order point for each component; when the inventory goes below the order point, a new replenishment order is generated. The order point is made up of two elements—the expected average demand during lead time and the reserve stock needed to cover upward variations in demand and lead time. Since many finished assemblies are produced intermittently, it will frequently be found that some parts are being manufactured to bring a component inventory up to a desired level although this inventory will not be drawn upon for some time to come. On the other hand, order points based on estimated *average* usage will not handle extraordinary requirements for components, such as might result from peak demands caused by sales promotions or heavy buying preceding a price increase. For this reason, it is extremely important to have feedback between the expected demand for finished goods and the scheduled production of components. The materials planning approach is an effective technique for accomplishing this feedback.

Feedback in a make-to-order operation is concerned principally with job progress and the effects of problems in the plant. Since there is not likely to be a high percentage of repetitive operations and new problems will be arising constantly in a make-to-order plant, emphasis must be placed on good feedback to find out what the problems are and to report them to someone who can take corrective action. In a make-to-stock plant, on the other hand, manufacturng tends to be routine, with the same items processed over and over again. In order to have an efficient operation and to get the best customer service for the inventory investment, feedback is needed both from the plant (to report job progress) and from the inventory, so that significant changes in finished goods stock status can be reflected in manufacturing priorities.

Feedback from purchasing

The more a company depends upon purchased components in the manufacture of its product, the more important it is to have good feedback from purchasing. In a make-to-order business, the purchasing department should have the responsibility of following-up vendors to be sure that all material is received as close to the required date as possible. They should rate each vendor according to his delivery performance and take this into consideration in the selection of vendors. They should also prepare their own delivery performance report showing (for example) the percentage of jobs delivered from vendors on time as compared with the total number of jobs required in any given week. This type of performance report should emphasize the number of jobs that the production control department requests within shorter-than-usual lead times. However, production control should accept the responsibility for showing purchasing personnel the real advantages of exerting as much pressure as possible to reduce vendors' lead times. These benefits come from the improved accuracy of forecasts of demand over shorter lead times.

Most important, though, is the need for the purchasing department to set up feedback systems whereby vendors can tell them *in advance* of anticipated late deliveries, so that production control can also be advised and can take whatever action is possible to counteract this situation. When the item that is going to be late is a component used on many assemblies, it is very useful to have bills of material in *where used* format, so that the affected assemblies can readily be identified.

The relationship between production control and purchasing and the amount and type of feedback information required between them is also a function of the type of operation. In a make-to-order operation, delivery dates may be relatively firm once established; in a make-to-stock operation, they are less firm and more emphasis must be placed on purchasing's ability to react to changes in schedule, since many items in a make-to-stock operation may not actually be needed on the original schedule date.

Likewise, in a make-to-order business, shopping around for bids on individual items typically starts when a requisition is received for that item, since it may only be purchased for one order for a particular customer. This will delay processing the purchasing requisition, and an acceptable period for this delay should be agreed upon ahead of time. In a make-to-stock business, on the other hand, where items are purchased repeatedly, there is no reason for waiting until the purchase requisition is received to negotiate new prices with the vendor or to seek new vendors to compete for the business. The production control department should regularly provide the purchasing department with information on the anticipated usage of various purchased components. This information should serve as the basis for asking vendors to compete on price, quality, etc. There is then no reason why requisitions should be held up in a make-to-stock business.

Like many other difficulties in running a company effectively, problems between purchasing and production control often exist because these sections do not recognize common goals. To solve this problem, it is frequently recommended that all of these activities be grouped under the same executive, and this is one reason why the *materials management* concept has generated considerable interest. Developing a good method of measuring the performance of the purchasing department in meeting production control requirements and the performance of the production control department in communicating those requirements to purchasing can mean a long stride forward in reducing the friction that so frequently exists between these two functions.

Some feedback techniques

In some companies, the out-of-stock list or the past-due lists are used to analyze the causes of these delays. An interesting relationship usually exists between the problems that cause delays in meeting schedules and the number of falldowns they generate. This is the same relationship that is the basis for the "ABC" classification of inventory. Generally, in analyzing schedule upsets by cause, it is found that approximately 20% of the causes generate 80% of the problems. With this information, corrective action can be directed where it will do the most good.

When individual departments or machine centers are set up as checkpoints at which the status of each job is compared to its scheduled completion date at the particular checkpoint, it is practical to maintain a performance report for each department showing how well it is able to meet schedules. This report is of value principally as a means of comparing present performance against past performance, since departments farther along the manufacturing sequence are likely to receive more jobs *already* behind schedule and thus have a more difficult time completing jobs on schedule. Whether or not the report can be adjusted for this handicap is of secondary concern. The important point is to measure improved departmental performance in giving customer service and to consider this measure of performance to be as important as the foreman's ability to meet his budget. Many line managers profess concern over the difficulties in getting foremen to be customer-service-oriented, but they persist in measuring a foreman's performance against other goals, and really consider customer service to be primarily the responsibility of the production control or sales departments.

A very effective feedback device from the plant is a regular *delay report*. The daily delay report shown in Fig. 11-1 is made out by the department dispatcher, indicating jobs delayed on the shop floor and the reasons for their delay as well as the action being taken. Since it is extremely important that this information be up-to-date, and since only those jobs delayed are listed, it can often best be handled by the dispatcher

Figure 11-1

Daily Delay Report

| | | | | | | Dept. *Sub-Assembly* |
| | | | | | | Date *10/20* |

		To:				From:
To:		Supv. of dispatchers:				Dept. dispatcher:
Dept. foreman:						
C. Brown		*S. Tobias*				*J.C.T.*
Name		Name				Name

Part no.	Part name	Order no.	Qty. delay	Days delay	Problem and action
10-1762	X-Type Panel	4321	1200	4	Jig being repaired – promised 10/21
17-1105	Switch Assy.	4004	2500	2	Q.C. 100% Insp.

as a visual review of all work on the floor ahead of each machine center, listing all jobs delayed beyond some acceptable interval.

An essential element of feedback that is often neglected is a regular report that capsulizes plant activity and problems so as to direct management attention to the important problems to be solved. Figure 11-2 shows a weekly summary of activity and problems summarized by the production control manager and addressed to the plant manager and other individuals concerned with operating the plant. It contains a general summary of activity for the week, a listing of the major problems, and the production control manager's recommendations. Space is provided to indicate the action being taken by the manager responsible. In Fig. 11-2, for example, major problem #2 concerns delivery of some switches from a vendor, and the purchasing agent has written the action he is taking in the right-hand column. This type of summary serves many functions:

1. Preparing it forces the production control manager to think through the plant's problems each week, put them in perspective,

Figure 11-2

Weekly Summary of Activity and Problems

From: Prod. Cont. Mgr.   To: Plant Manager   Week no. 13

cc: Chief Industrial Engr.
General Foremen (4)
Quality Control Mgr.
Purchasing Agent
Production Planners (2)

Summary of activity:

1. Current finished goods inventory = 56,000 pcs. – one week below 72,000 pcs. goal.

2. Service level last week = 96% vs. 98% goal.

3. Incoming business 22% ahead of forecast for 1st quarter. Marketing revising forecast; due Monday.

Summary of major problems	Recommendation	Action
1. New people in Elect. Subassembly not producing acceptable product.	Continue overtime to meet prod. reqt's. Q.C. aid foreman in finding specific operators responsible and retraining.	Replacing one girl. Adding temporary supervision. J.P.V.
2. Popco switches still one month behind scheduled deliveries.	Second source.	Buyer to visit Popco weekly. 3 potential suppliers bidding this week. F.W.W.

organize his knowledge of plant activity and problems and condense this for the plant manager.

2. It serves as the agenda for a weekly production meeting of the people most concerned. When managers tend to postpone making decisions, its use will quickly point out the effects of such inaction. The report gives the chief manufacturing executive a means to follow up decisions and insure that needed actions are taken.

The principal requirement of a weekly summary of activity and problems is that it be brief. Some companies set an arbitrary rule, limiting the number of problems that can be listed in any one week to ten or twelve. A long catalogue of problems, however genuine, will serve little useful purpose. The normal management team of six or seven can take effective action on only a few problems each week—listing any more will only cause confusion, discouragement and dilution of effort.

The proper presentation of this type of information to plant management is an essential function of the production control manager. Developing this information properly is far more important than troubleshooting out on the factory floor, although one way of obtaining feedback from the factory is a regular tour of the factory to see how operations are progressing. Nevertheless, there must be a balance between close contact with factory operations and the desk work required to operate a satisfactory management information system.

The production control manager starting a formal report of this type may find initial reaction to it negative, since it points out problem areas for which other managers are responsible. Its preparation requires a great deal of objectivity on the part of the production control manager—he should be very careful to be diplomatic (though factual) and to be honest in pointing out failures within his own department. Other managers must know *in advance of the weekly meeting* the problems to be listed. This avoids generating resentment at being "put on the spot" and gives managers time to decide on corrective action. In practice, this type of report brings real problems to the attention of the managers (when it is developed effectively by the production control manager) and almost always results in getting solutions to these problems.

Performance yardsticks

There are many performance indicators for a production control department. One of the most important measures of performance is customer service. Statistical measures of customer service were discussed in Chapter 5. Other measures in a make-to-stock business can be based on the number of items stocked, the total number of line items backordered as a percentage of the total number of line items received as incoming business, or the percentage of the total number of orders on which a backordered item occurs.

Figure 11-3 shows one type of report of service from finished goods inventory in a make-to-stock business. For this company, the goal is 95% service (in this case, the measure used is demand filled as a percentage of total demand). An upper limit of 97% has been set, based on the understanding that service at a higher level will require more inventory than can be justified by the improved customer relations. It has also been decided that 92% is a low limit of customer service, and that service below this level will jeopardize their position as a vendor to many of their customers. The comments made by the production control manager indicate that inventories have been reduced in this particular product line and, as a result, service has come back down to about 95% from a range that was considered too high to be economical.

In a make-to-order business, service is usually measured by how well orders are shipped to customers in relation to scheduled dates. Figure 11-4 shows a product delivery performance report for a make-to-order company. There were 20 jobs due to be shipped in the first week of the fourth quarter and all were shipped on schedule; delivery performance was therefore 100%. Note that this report also shows delivery performance on orders with revised promises.

The problem in developing a suitable measure of customer service is that a great many factors are involved. In a make-to-stock company, the *number* of items out of stock affects customer service, but frequently more important are *which* items and *how long* they remain out of stock. A very popular item will generate a great many backorders, while a less popular item may not even be missed by most customers. In companies where a tabulated card is used to represent each individual backorder, counting the total number of cards in the backorder file at any particular moment may give a fair measure of performance.

Nevertheless, critics can point out that this still does not measure the *duration* of the backorder. Some items may stay out of stock for extremely long periods, causing customer dissatisfaction that cannot be measured by merely counting the number of backorder cards. Even if this factor were included in a more complex system for measuring customer service, it could still be pointed out that it is often desirable to give some customers preference—because they are new and have a high potential business, or because they are old and loyal customers.

This approach can lead to the development of a highly complex method for measuring customer service which requires more effort than it is worth. Measures of customer service should be as simple as

Figure 11-3

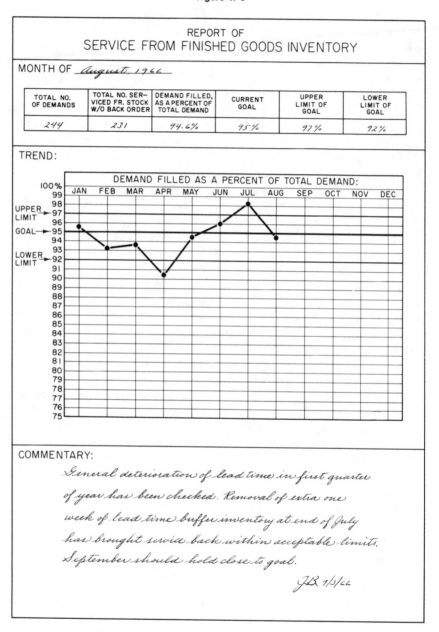

REPORT OF
SERVICE FROM FINISHED GOODS INVENTORY

MONTH OF _August, 1966_

TOTAL NO. OF DEMANDS	TOTAL NO. SERVICED FR. STOCK W/O BACK ORDER	DEMAND FILLED, AS A PERCENT OF TOTAL DEMAND	CURRENT GOAL	UPPER LIMIT OF GOAL	LOWER LIMIT OF GOAL
244	231	94.6%	95%	97%	92%

TREND:

DEMAND FILLED AS A PERCENT OF TOTAL DEMAND:

COMMENTARY:

General deterioration of lead time in first quarter of year has been checked. Removal of extra one week of lead time buffer inventory at end of July has brought service back within acceptable limits. September should hold close to goal.

JB 9/5/66

Figure 11-4

PQR Company

Products delivery performance

	Last 13 wks	Week #1	Week #2	Week #3	Week #4	Week #5	Week #6	Week #7	Week #8	Week #9	Week #10	Week #11
		10/16	10/23	10/30	11/6	11/13						
Jobs due to ship		20	23	23	22	17						
Jobs shipped		20	22	23	22	15						
Delivery perform. %	91%	100%	96%	100%	100%	88%						
Repromised jobs due to ship		0	0	1	0	0						
Repromised jobs shipped		0	0	1	0	0						
Repromised delivery performance %	97%	0	0	100%	0	0						
Number of jobs past due		0	1	0	0	2						

possible—their prime value consists in showing that customer service either has been improved or has not. Discussion about whether or not any particular measure of service is "fair" or "unfair" is wasted effort which might better be devoted to improving the company's performance under simpler measures.

The second major area for measuring performance of a production control department is inventory control. This is most effectively measured using a customer service *vs.* investment relationship developed by means of the techniques (explained in Chapter 6) for determining a reasonable level of inventory for a desired service level. Once a production plan has been introduced, level production may result in building some inventory with seasonal demand. Consequently, inventory control performance should be measured against this production plan rather than against some fixed target that does not recognize desirable inventory fluctuations.

Inventory turnover is a performance measure that has some real meaning, but is abused more often than not. There are today many practitioners who refuse to use an inventory turnover measure because they are too aware of these abuses. In some companies, where inventory turnover has been used as a performance measure without balancing it against related costs, some managers have forced inventories down by holding back deliveries until the first of the following month, bringing in small quantities toward the end of the month and using other approaches that generate excessive costs in other areas that must handle the flood of material that arrives in the first few days of the new month. These tactics do not reflect on the validity of inventory turnover as a performance measure, but they do underscore the fact that it cannot be used effectively unless related costs and customer service are considered at the same time.

Like many other performance measures, inventory turnover has little meaning when used to compare the activities of one company with those of another. It can be used for comparison of one company with *averages* for an industry if used with restraint. Two companies in the same business may have extremely different rates of turnover, depending upon the degree of manufactured *vs.* purchased material contained in the end product, whether the business is make-to-stock or make-to-order or both, consignment stocking policies, distance from suppliers, the number of warehouses maintained and many other considerations that very substantially affect the companies' ability to turn inventory.

Far more important than attaining a certain turnover is establishing reasonable inventory levels to give desired customer service, and then measuring a company's performance over the short-term in meeting these inventory levels, and over the long-term in improving the service attained with a given amount of inventory. Inventory turnover has most meaning as a measure of improvement in inventory control performance.

The proper formula for determining inventory turnover is:

$$\text{Turnover} = \frac{\text{Cost of sales in period}}{\text{Cost of average inventory on hand}}$$

Since turnover figures are so often obtained from published data in profit and loss statements and balance sheets, the most common figures are obtained by dividing the inventory at year-end (at cost) into the annual sales (at net selling price). The use of cost figures in calculating inventory value and sales figures in calculating annual sales activity gives an unrealistic basis of comparison. Although industry-wide comparisons will have to continue to use available data, each company should measure improvement of its own performance using cost data which gives the most meaningful results and is unclouded by pricing policies.

Inventory turnover is a good performance measure when used judicially. Like any other measure, it should be thoroughly understood by those applying it, and comparisons between companies, between divisions and even between departments should be made with extreme caution and with full knowledge of all the elements that affect their ability to perform.

Most production control departments have been slow in recognizing their responsibility for keeping the plant operating efficiently and, consequently, very few companies measure such performance. This requires measures that relate overtime, machine down time and the number of hires and layoffs during the year to production control performance. Since production control is concerned with balancing customer service, minimum inventory investment and efficient plant operation, any effective set of performance measures must include measures of plant operating efficiency against goals, just as any measure of a foreman's activities should include performance in meeting *both* scheduled delivery dates and budget goals.

Finally, one objective implicit in running any staff department is to have the lowest level of manpower consistent with good performance. Devising a means of measuring the amount of work turned out by production control personnel and the number of personnel required is extremely challenging, yet has been handled effectively by some companies. A comparison of the number of people in the production control department and the production control budget with plant activity measures should be made on a regular basis. This can be as infrequent as once a year, and should be used as an incentive for better performance on the part of the production control manager.

Most production control departments have increased their functions and have required more and more personnel over the years. Whether or not this is justified, it is more often than not true that inefficient use is being made of the personnel now available. Each additional person requires a greater percentage of the group's time in communicating among personnel—nowhere is this more evident than in a production control department. In a small plant, it is relatively easy for a few people to know what other personnel are doing, but in a large plant, communication among production control personnel and with purchasing or manufacturing people becomes a formidable task. Before adding manpower to his staff, the production control manager should ask himself whether or not he really solved the problem the last time he added manpower to his department, and whether or not he is going to increase his communications problem disproportionately to the amount of improvement he gets by adding another staff member.

Measures of performance are extremely important in any company. Before any improvement program is started, measures of performance should be established to show how future performance will compare with the present situation. It is always easy to see today's problems while forgetting how big yesterday's problems were. If measures of performance are not started before the improvement program begins, few people will remember how bad the "good old days" really were. Measures of performance are by themselves one of the best ways of improving performance, and thus should be one of the fundamental elements of any production control system. It is a recognized fact that performance measures in any field of activity tend to generate a healthy spirit of competition, and that people will work hard to meet or better a realistic goal.

The neophyte production control manager (particularly if he is under the pressure of criticism within his company) is usually anxious to get performance information from other companies. He asks other production control managers how many people they have in their department, how good their customer service is, how much inventory they carry and similar questions, hoping that he can use some of these figures to convince his boss that his performance isn't really so bad after all.

The more experienced production control manager recognizes that performance comparisons between companies are not meaningful. He, much as a good golfer, plays against par rather than against his opponent, and devotes his attention to improving his own performance rather than justifying his poor showing by trying to find someone who is a little bit poorer.

The production control checklist

The true function of the production control department is to generate the information that is required in managing the plant so as to *keep* out of trouble rather than just handling the day-to-day activities required to *get* out of trouble. The production control system is a discipline for handling information and requires that specific activities take place at specific times. Production control managers, like managers of other functions, find that they can best organize their activities by making up a daily list of things that require their attention and following this list in doing the most important jobs first.

Since no production control manager can give attention to all of the problems he faces, it is extremely important for him to sort out these problems and handle first the more important ones. A checklist such as is shown in Fig. 11-5 will help him to be sure to include in this daily list those routine activities that require regular attention in order to keep the production control system running effectively. This particular checklist shows that schedules must be made out weekly, that production plans must have actual activity posted against planned activity weekly and that they must be reviewed and revised (if necessary) on a monthly basis.

Figure 11-5

Production Control Manager's Checklist

	11/23	11/30	12/7	12/14	12/21	12/28	1/4	1/11	1/18
Schedules prepared									
Production plans posted									
Production plans revised	X		X		X			X	X
Stock status reviewed									
Out-of-stock report prepared									
Percent out-of-stock graph updated									
Turret lathe machine load updated									
Raw materials inventory report issued									
"C" stock review made	X			X		X			X
Finished goods card inventory audit	X								
Summary of activity and problems prepared									
Mfg. areas delay report compiled	X		X	X	X	X		X	X
Purch. comp. delay report compiled							X		
Explosion of requirements made	X	X				X			

In companies with a highly seasonal business, for example, it is difficult for the production control manager to remember that he should be planning to increase certain inventory levels well in advance of the peak season. Some production control managers use a production control calendar which lists the major activities that must take place during the year, including such regular chores as reviewing order points and order quantities, preparing for physical inventory, reviewing personnel performance, making up lists of obsolete material for disposition and the many other activities that take place very infrequently but must be handled in order to perform the job properly.

Generating corrective action

The three links in the chain of production control discussed earlier in this chapter were:

1. A system for generating information
2. Use of the system to generate the information
3. Action on the part of plant operating personnel to react to the information generated

The weekly summary of activity and problems shown in Fig. 11-2 is a good example of the type of information that the production control manager must provide to the plant manager. This information must be generated on a timely basis—control can only be exerted over events that have not yet occurred. A good index of the production control manager's ability is the number of times the plant manager has to ask him about a problem rather than having first been informed of it by the production control manager. An effective production control manager will be telling the plant manager about upcoming problems *ahead of time* and recommending actions to keep them from becoming serious interferences to good customer service or efficient plant operation. The difference between excuses and control information is simply a matter of timing.

Bibliography

1. Cunningham, M. A., "Systems of Feedback of Production Data," *APICS Quarterly Bulletin,* Vol. 5, No. 1, January 1964.
2. Link, Philip A., "How to Evaluate Production Control Standards of Performance," *APICS Quarterly Bulletin,* Vol. 1, No. 1, January 1960.

CHAPTER
TWELVE

DESIGNING AND
MANAGING THE PRODUCTION
CONTROL SYSTEM

Systems design

Designing an effective production control system requires a knowledge of the techniques of production control and a sound understanding of principles so that these techniques are understood in their proper perspective. It is relatively easy to learn a few techniques and to try to use these as solutions to all production control problems. This is particularly tempting since so many symptoms of production control problems can be misleading.

The challenge for the systems analyst is to look beyond the symptoms and find the real underlying problems. For example, he may see that incoming business is highly erratic and that production control personnel feel that a better forecast would enable them to cope with this in a more effective manner. Looking deeper into the problem, he may find that customer orders are not really erratic but that fluctuations are due to warehouse replenishment orders. The real problem is that each warehouse manager is using an ordering system that looks good from his isolated point of view but makes little sense from the overall company point of view.

The systems analyst may find that so-called "production control problems" go far beyond the production control department. He may learn, for example, that the marketing department constantly adds new items to the product line without ever eliminating obsolete products, and that no one in the organization recognizes the effect this has in increasing the number of setup hours required in the plant and thus reducing the level of customer service that can be provided with a given level of inventory investment.

A few common symptoms and their most probable underlying causes are:

1. *The forecasts are inaccurate*—this usually indicates an inflexible production control system and a lack of communication between production control and marketing or sales (along with a great deal of buck-passing). There is often room for considerable improvement in the marketing forecast, however, and this should start with a real understanding of the use that will be made of the forecast and of the consequences of poor forecasting.

2. *Nothing gets through our plant unless it is expedited*—this generally indicates that the plant is not operating at the proper capacity and that production control is forcing more and more work into the plant. Instead of recognizing and curing the real problem—*capacity*—they are attempting to cure the symptom (poor control over individual orders) by expediting.

3. *We never have enough lead time*—this indicates too much work-in-process. Ironically, allowing longer lead time will probably generate a higher level of work-in-process and compound the problem.

4. *We never seem to have the right items in production*—this is common in a company making complex assemblies, where the component inventory is replenished via order points rather than a materials plan using the latest forecast of assembly requirements, or where requirements are not generated frequently enough to relate component schedules to changing assembly requirements.

5. *We don't have time to follow production control system routines—there are too many crises*—production control people seem to enjoy firefighting more than fire-prevention. The longer planning is postponed, the more firefighting becomes a way of life. As systems deteriorate, patchwork subsystems develop which compound the problems further and expand production control's job to the point where it can't possibly be handled properly by the available personnel.

The systems designer must probe these apparent problems to diagnose the real ills and, in order to cure the problems, it is essential that he tie all the elements of the production control system together if he is to get lasting and effective results. A better forecasting system or inventory control system, for example, may improve performance temporarily—but if business increases and a large workload develops, the lead times can get out of control and undermine the system. On the other hand, a system that includes good capacity planning and control will be sadly lacking if the generation of shop orders is based on an ineffective inventory system. By the same token, the installation of a dispatching system without a capacity planning and control system will not solve production control problems. The message cannot be repeated too often: *No single technique is a panacea. Techniques must be selected with a proper understanding of principles and applied as parts of an integrated production control system.* Two examples are used below to show how the system can be tailored to an individual application.

A company with a 12-week component lead time manufacturing an assembled product to maintain a finished goods inventory might use the following approach:

1. Finished product groups are forecast every quarter to cover the next 12 months by the marketing department. Production control uses exponential smoothing to prorate these forecasts over the individual products in each group and then updates these item forecasts weekly, extending them for the next 12 weeks.

2. From these forecasts, a master schedule is made up for each of the finished products and revised whenever the forecast changes significantly.

3. From the master schedule, a materials plan is made up for all components showing those to be ordered and weekly start dates.

4. The level of production for each of the major component manufacturing facilities is estimated each month from the materials plan by simulating it and making an estimated machine load.

5. Orders are released into these major manufacturing facilities at the planned rate on a weekly basis. These are selected to give the best balanced load on these facilities, taking into account not only the starting operations but subsequent critical operations as well.

6. Individual shop orders are scheduled through each operation and a machine load report is generated weekly to show where short-term bottlenecks are occurring.

7. Using the Critical Ratio technique, a dispatching list is prepared daily for each of the manufactured components.

8. The central dispatching function uses the daily dispatch list to control the flow of components through production.

9. Branch warehouse inventories are centrally controlled and replenished using the techniques explained in Appendix VIII.

A make-to-order company manufacturing a single-component item

—gasket material made in sheets on large rubber-rolling machines— might use a somewhat different approach:

1. The gasket materials are forecast by overall product group designated by the machine group through which they must be run.
2. A production plan is made for each machine group. While no finished inventory is stocked, the production plan is designed so as to keep the backlog of customer orders to a minimum.
3. Statistical backlog controls based on past experience are set up so that plant operating people know when the production level must be changed.
4. Raw materials and production capacity are planned from the forecasts of anticipated orders for the various production groups. The schedules are firmed up only as orders come in. A machine group may often be working against a production commitment from production control for a popular size and type sheet, but the specific orders for which the material is being produced will not be given to them until near the end of the schedule week.
5. There are secondary operations such as curing, branding, slitting and packaging. As individual orders are fed into the starting operation, they are balanced so that overloads are not created when they reach subsequent critical operations. From work-in-process files, a weekly machine load report is generated, and orders which would aggravate the situation should backlogs develop ahead of an operation are not released. They are issued only after action has been taken to clear the backlog.
6. Since most jobs follow the same general operation sequence and work-in-process can be kept low, the lead times tend to be short and job selection is left to the foreman, who uses a semi-weekly dispatch list. There is little requirement for shop planning since tooling is relatively simple and there is no need to audit laboi claims very rigorously because all employees work on a salaried basis.
7. The general techniques of flow control over work-in-process are used rather than having a dispatcher in each department.

Here are two plants with extremely different types of production applying the same basic principles. A production control system is very much like a man's suit—from a distance, all may look the same, but differences become apparent once the observer stands close enough. With a production control system, the same general elements are found in most companies, even though those who are closest to the operation may think their company entirely unique. While systems cannot be transferred successfully from one company to another, specific techniques can be tailored carefully to fit the individual requirements of every company.

One of the pertinent questions the systems designer must answer is the degree to which he plans to use a computer in his system. Most medium-and large-size companies now have computers and while their use is often concentrated on accounting reports, their most profitable areas of application, according to a survey of companies using the computer, are *"the crucial decisions of the business: in sales forecasting, in manpower and production scheduling, in inventory management."*[1]

The following list should be considered typical, though not at all comprehensive of the almost unlimited number of applications of the computer in this field:

1. Forecasting—the computer is particularly well-adapted to performing the complex mathematical computations involved in regression analysis, correlation analysis, calculation of exponential smoothing forecasts, mean absolute deviations and forecast tracking signals as described in Chapters 2 and 3.

2. Planning inventory levels—this can be done by calculating individual lot sizes, order points and reserve stocks, summing-up the resulting aggregate inventory by using such techniques as LIMIT, and statistical order point calculations for thousands of items. When a dependent type of demand is involved, the computer can be used to generate a materials plan and to use its basic materials planning program for simulating the levels of inventory required to maintain planned production levels in the future. The computer can also break component requirements down by short time cycles, so that these can be ordered to come in at a particular time rather than in a broad time block (such as is used in most manual systems).

3. Planning production levels—individual item needs (in hours) can be projected and then totaled by machine group to determine the required production capacity. This information must then be broken down further by labor grade in order to do an effective job of manpower planning.

4. Controlling levels of production—information output from the plant must be prompt, accurate, and in a form that is meaningful and compatible with the production plan. This requires exception reports and can be greatly enhanced through the use of a computer to process the data and perform the mathematical and statistical operations.

---

[1]Garrity, John T., *Getting the Most Out of Your Computer*, T OO1153, McKinsey & Company, Inc., New York.

5. Controlling input—stock status reports for independent inventory items and issuance of regularly-updated requirements for dependent type components can then be used to generate shop orders that dovetail with the planned capacity. Component requirements can be determined level-by-level, so that excess components are not ordered inadvertently (as they would be if sets of parts based on the bill of material were used for ordering). These shop orders can then be scheduled and loaded using logic built into computer programs. The computer can also be used to update the stock status and control reports for warehouse inventory control.

6. Other computer applications—control of output, job location, the use of techniques such as the Critical Ratio for dispatching, updated dispatching lists, expediting reports, job reporting and the like are all techniques that lend themselves to computer application. Modern electronic data-collection terminals facilitate prompt and accurate reporting from the factory floor and can provide the timely updated information to make techniques such as these—and the centralized dispatching discussed in Chapter 10—practical. Production flow can be simulated with a computer to determine the level of work-in-process that will give the shortest possible lead time with a minimum of machine down-time. Many other functions of production control (such as summarizing the physical inventory and correcting records for discrepancies, taking cycle counts in the factory and making analyses to determine the ABC distribution) are all fairly straightforward computer applications.

An important distinction to recognize is the difference between *analysis applications* and *control applications*. LIMIT, for example, is an analysis program used to study lot-sizes. A system that schedules and loads each order into available capacity reporting by exception when orders cannot be loaded and still meet required shipping dates is an example of control application. Because analysis programs, while extremely valuable aids in decision-making, may be run intermittently, their potential profit contribution is usually not as great as that of control applications. Control systems, on the other hand, are more difficult to design and install and are far more dependent on disciplined handling of input information and proper use of the system by the many people involved.

Computer applications offer unlimited potential, but rarely pay for themselves when the systems designer simply mechanizes his manual procedures. The computer makes possible the use of techniques beyond the reach of manual methods. One company, for example, enters customers' orders into its computerized inventory control system as they are received, checks material availability (since they custom-assemble

needed at NIKE

the product ordered by the customer), generates component orders for unavailable parts and prints out a schedule date for each order based on estimated component availability. It also loads the assembly department to capacity and balances the line so that manpower is used most effectively. The computer prints out the daily final assembly schedule by model number and quantity, including all options—such as color, accessories, etc. This is an ambitious computer application uncommon today, but only a taste of things to come as we develop the ability to capture commonly-used logic and identify the exceptions that require human intervention, reducing the drudgery of the production and inventory control job (and, consequently, its cost) and immeasurably increasing its scope.

Once the systems designer has decided on the application to which he feels the computer can make the greatest contribution, he must decide whether or not the company can afford the computer if it does not already have one available. Computer justification in manufacturing control should be approached not on the basis of clerical savings, but rather on the benefits from increased control: better customer service, lower inventory investment and more efficient plant operation. This type of justification requires a commitment from an executive who has foresight and courage enough to recognize how better information can give him better control. It is important that this justification be based on a sound system, however, because the computer cannot make the existing system better—it is not the panacea some executives imagine, but it is a sound tool that can (in today's business world, perhaps *must* is a better word) be applied.

A computer system requires good design and documentation, programming, training, good discipline and management support. Even a good manual system requires everything but the programming. Good documentation is required in the form of written procedures, and any new system requires as its most important element an effective training program. The need for discipline is only a little greater in computer systems than manual ones and, in fact, many manual systems today can be shown to be ineffective largely because the need for discipline has not been recognized. A company that cannot maintain accurate inventory records is certainly not going to be able to utilize materials planning very effectively. The computer system, like any system, will require management support and the company that has not been able to make its manual systems effective because of management aloofness and dislike of the disciplines imposed by a system will probably not be able to realize the full potential of the computer.

To many students of management, the computer appears to be the tool that will transform production control from an art to a science.

But the production control man who is sitting back and waiting for someone else to design a production control system for him will undoubtedly be disappointed, as will also the man who feels that the computer is an optional device which he can choose or reject as he wishes. The challenge is for the production control man to teach himself how to use the computer with discretion and wisdom to give him the solutions he needs to his problems. Basically, the production control man has always been working with an information system; nothing will undoubtedly have a more profound effect upon this system than the computer.

Whether the system will be manual or computerized, the involvement of production control personnel in the systems design is essential and can best be handled by assigning experienced, yet imaginative, personnel to the systems job on a full-time basis. All but the very smallest production control departments should be able to detach at least one man from day-to-day duties to plan for the future. If the system is computerized and crosses departmental lines, he will probably be a member of a team responsible for systems design. Under any circumstances, it will be the job of this man to insure that production control personnel understand and contribute to the systems design as it evolves. Nothing invites failure as much as a system that was designed by outside "experts."

In designing a production control system, some of the objectives of good systems design that go beyond pure production control considerations should be kept in mind. Some of the most important of these objectives are:

1. Management information in the form that will assist management most in making timely and profitable decisions.

2. A system that dovetails with other systems within the company to minimize duplication, contradiction and suboptimization, and builds logically toward an "ideal" system.

3. Best use of the abilities of computer and man, recognizing that the computer can process data faster and more accurately— but with less recognition of changing conditions. An overly automatic system can encourage a "hands-off" attitude and lead to trouble when the preprogrammed computer logic is no longer appropriate for the current conditions.

4. A profit-oriented system designed not just

to reduce cost but primarily to improve profits and growth through improved customer service, better management control of operations and greater flexibility to detect and respond to significant change.

5. A minimum of paperwork within a system that provides for "management by exception."

Each of these objectives could be the subject of a complete chapter, but two require further clarification: the techniques for building the system logically toward an "ideal" system and the hackneyed expression, "management by exception."

It is difficult to resist the temptation to design a system that will cure a particular problem, and this may be necessary, but it is extremely important to have some kind of master plan indicating how this will fit into the overall system and how it will build logically toward an overall control system. Failure to consider these questions and develop an overall plan before taking the first step inevitably results in duplication of effort and redoing major parts of the system from time to time.

The system design objective that is discussed most—and implemented least—is the last: management by exception. Especially when a computer is being used, management by exception can be implemented today in ways that were impractical a few years ago. Conditions can be preprogrammed into the system so that exceptions, such as an item below order point, can be flagged by the system. The inquiry capability of modern computers can be used to generate information on such topics as job location on only those jobs that are of interest, rather than generating voluminous reports giving the location of all jobs. Beyond this, modern data storage and retrieval techniques make it practical to generate customized reports in infinite variety that give management timely data on specifically requested topics, making the term "management by exception" a reality in a well-designed system.

Even this sophisticated type of system, however, will only succeed if it has management support. Introducing any system—manual or computerized—will require unpleasant changes and imposition of new disciplines. If top management does not recognize the need for the system and does not give it enthusiastic support, it will probably become a political football and degenerate rapidly. There is a real job to be done in getting some managers to recognize that results are dependent on such fundamental disciplines as accurately reporting counts from the shop floor.

Once the overall systems design concepts have been determined, a proposal should be made to management in order to obtain necessary funds and manpower to continue the design and start the implementation of the system. In making this proposal, there are four important points for the systems designer to remember:

1. He will gather a great deal of detailed information and get deeply involved in making his analysis, but his report will be just one of many things competing for management attention. His proposal must be brief, preferably in outline form, with supporting documentation in an appendix where those specifically interested may read it. The body of the report should be written so that the average manager can determine the important elements in 15 or 20 minutes.

2. He must be as objective as possible. His very presence implies criticism of someone. If he is not effective in gaining the cooperation of the people who must use the system, their apathy may doom the system before it starts. No production control system can function effectively if it is simply used mechanically, without understanding or intelligent adaptation to actual situations. Active and interested people are essential to the success of any new systems installation.

3. The systems analyst must constantly remind himself to avoid overselling. He should not imply that the system will be a panacea for all of the problems in production control—negative reaction arising from continuing problems may hamstring an otherwise effective system that was oversold.

4. The systems analyst is usually a specialist with detailed knowledge of techniques and equipment capabilities, but he must always keep in mind that a system cannot work unless people use it. He should spell out as clearly as possible everyone's responsibility in making the system successful. Only people can generate real results.

Systems implementation

A step-by-step implementation program should be developed within the master plan. The individual steps should be planned to generate results, and the choice of initial installation may have to be made according to its potential for generating some results that will encourage management support. Results can silence critics and generate enthusiasm for the systems effort better than any selling efforts.

Since all production control operations are interrelated, it is usually necessary to have installation steps overlap because the inventory system may well flounder if a production planning system is not available to support it. When installing a system, such as an electronic data-collection system that is intended to provide the basis for a dynamic control system such as Critical Ratio, the systems designer should be careful to point out the fact that no significant results are expected from the data-collection system itself, and that it provides the unglamorous—but essential— foundation for the control system.

It is important that performance measures be established *before* any production control systems revisions are started. Even though great improvements may be made and a reasonable semblance of order may be attained, operating people will tend to feel that today's problems are bigger than yesterday's and that progress really isn't being made. The systems designer should determine the current level of customer service, today's ratio of inventory to sales, and the present setup, down-time and other costs before he tries to improve the system.

He should also get clear statements of policy from management in areas that are more difficult to measure, such as changing levels of production. The plant that makes frequent, drastic changes in its pro-duction level incurs high expenses, often difficult to evaluate. One of the surest results from an effective production control system is the reduc-tion of wide fluctuations in the production level. Unfortunately, measur-ing this improvement is quite difficult and the systems designer will be challenged to find an effective way to indicate to operating people how many more crises they had in the past. It is extremely difficult to demonstrate how many times crises *have not occurred* because of an im-proved production and inventory control system.

Another problem facing the systems analyst in maintaining morale and a cooperative spirit among the people involved in operating the new production control system is that other factors are also changing. While the production control system is being changed, the sales pattern is varying, personnel are joining and leaving, business is getting better or worse and facilities are being added or torn down. Any man who attributes all improvements or deteriorations in performance to the production control system alone is not being realistic about the dynamic business environment that normally exists.

One of the questions most systems designers must answer is whether or not they will run operations in parallel. This involves running the old system while getting the new system going—and while it may sound like a good approach, it seldom works because there simply aren't enough "hands" to get a new system started while keeping the old system running. The objective of parallel operation is usually to insure that the plant will operate while the bugs are worked out of the new system, but there are other approaches that are usually more practical in achieving this end:

1. Audit record accuracy scrupulously on a sample basis, determine where and why errors are occurring and correct them.

2. Provide alternate routines to handle situations if hardware breaks down, so that a failure in the system can be handled routinely without stopping production.

3. Wherever practical, set up the new system on a pilot basis on part of the product line or for part of the plant, so that it can be debugged before installing it on a large scale that would complicate the debugging process and increase the harmful effects of problems.

In short, there will be problems with any new system, and they should be anticipated and solved as quickly as possible. Running in parallel usually tends to perpetuate the old system rather than solving the problems associated with the new one.

The actual systems installation can be planned using one of the project planning techniques, such as the Gantt chart, and the responsible manager should receive periodic reports on progress, noting where problems are occurring and what is being done to solve them. This project plan should also tie in with the project budget so that the manager can keep posted on the use of the funds he has allocated for the systems installation.

One of the critical areas of systems implementation—and one that is often left out of the budget—is training. Experienced systems personnel will attest that training of personnel in the use of the system is extremely important. Some pointers on internal training programs in general are discussed later in this chapter.

The comments concerning involvement of operating personnel made in the previous section apply equally well to systems implementation. The more directly the people who will use the system can become involved in implementing it, the more successful it is likely to be. For very good psychological reasons, the other man's system never seems to work as well as one's own.

Finally, throughout the design and installation phases, it will be necessary to get management policy decisions. If policy concerning inventory turnover has not related rationally to customer service in the past, it will now have to if the system is to operate satisfactorily. Most companies find themselves thinking through basic policies that they once took for granted or established by default as they install new production control systems, and this is often among the most significant contributions the new system makes to better plant operation.

Managing the production control function

It has frequently been mentioned in this book that production control's primary function is managing an information system. It is important to emphasize that this management cannot be done passively. The production control manager *must take the initiative* in the presentation of alternatives to management with his best estimate of the costs and results of these alternatives. In a company with seasonal sales, the production control manager should develop alternative production plans to show how much extra inventory would be carried if production were leveled completely, what added capacity would be needed if production were geared directly to sales, how many times manpower levels would have to be changed during the year, etc. The production control manager should estimate the costs of these various plans to the best of his ability, recommend one plan to management and assist in making the basic decision. Once this decision has been made, the production control manager's job is generating control information to keep the plant on course. Since there will be many deviations from plan along the route, this will require constant corrective action.

Ironically, a production control system is rarely considered successful when the line people have not taken the proper corrective action. A production control system is necessary, but not sufficient. Merely generating the proper information—even going to great effort to show the line managers what needs to be done—does not guarantee that the proper action will be taken. The timid production control manager will be most vulnerable if he permits his performance to be judged by the actions of others. Even if his system indicates that additional capacity is required and he has given them this estimate of capacity sufficiently in advance, but plant operating people postpone adding this capacity, the production control department is usually blamed when customer service deteriorates as a result. Almost everyone recognizes poor customer service, but few can identify the true causes. By the way he manages information, the production control manager should be able to generate action. If he does his job of handling information expertly, it will be obvious to all concerned that actions are needed and who is responsible for taking them.

The information generated by the production control system often puts a great deal of pressure on line managers, even on the plant manager who is often the production control manager's superviser. If the production control manager does not have confidence in his system, if he does not take the initiative in his company and identify problems vigorously and courageously, he may become the "nice guy" who is blamed for someone else's failure to take the proper action. The production control system must be able to stand up to considerable back pressure and nit-picking from line managers who try to postpone taking action by questioning the information generated by the system and requesting exhaustive reviews or further analysis. There is a limit to the amount of skepticism that can be justified or tolerated. At this point, the production control manager deserves the solid support of his superiors in overcoming passive resistance and getting effective action without further demands that the system justify itself.

Keeping the initiative requires a courageous manager with a good system and competent people to operate it. It also requires that the production control manager remember that his job always looks easy to other people. Every day, the production control manager and his staff must make hundreds, even thousands of decisions about the future. Inevitably, hindsight will show some of these decisions to be wrong and critics will be able to point out mistakes that were made in the production control department. Beyond this, many of the other managers with whom the production control manager must work may be suboptimizing —working toward objectives different from those of the overall business. They may feel that the production control manager does not understand his job properly when he disagrees with these objectives. This situation is aggravated in companies which practice to extremes the *unique accountability* theory of organization, which sets up the sales manager as solely responsible for sales, the chief engineer as solely responsible for product function, etc.

Effective production control requires an objective approach which recognizes that firefighting is necessary, but that fire prevention is preferable. One of the most serious temptations in production control is to become a firefighter—to come in each morning prepared to charge out at every phone call and handle most of the expediting personally. It is undoubtedly satisfying to action-oriented people, it creates the impression of great activity in production control and of a production control manager who has his finger on the pulse of the factory and knows what's going on all the time. Unfortunately, it is usually such firefighting activity which indicates clearly that the unromantic task of fire prevention is being neglected. The work of finding out the anticipated life of major dies and whether or not they are being replaced on time to meet the needed volume, or analyzing the facilities of the proposed new product line to see where bottlenecks might occur and what can be done to avoid them can appear prosaic and dull indeed. The production control manager who neglects his fire prevention activities can be sure that tomorrow will bring bigger and better firefighting opportunities.

The production control manager must expect trouble. "Murphy's Law"—*what can go wrong will go wrong*—is always in operation. He should be a "happy pessimist" who recognizes that problems are a way of life and that tomorrow's troubles are undoubtedly brewing today. Crises in plants very seldom develop overnight—they usually grow over a long period of time and are frequently the result of continued inaction. The production control manager has the responsibility for pointing out ahead of time where troubles are likely to occur, showing what the alternatives are, and doing all he can to see that operations continue as planned or are quickly corrected to prevent crises.

One of the most important characteristics of effective production control operation is timeliness. Very simply, this is the difference between giving excuses and presenting information soon enough so that someone can take action to prevent problems. If the production control manager is asked by his boss why a particular product went out of stock and, after some investigation, replies that it was caused by a bottleneck in the plating department last week, he has only given an excuse. If, on the other hand, the production control manager pointed out the bottlenecks ahead of time, made positive recommendations to overcome it and predicted that if it were not overcome the product would be out of stock, he did generate control information. The simple difference is timeliness— information supplied in time for plant operating people to take the necessary corrective action *in advance* of trouble.

If the production control manager is to continue to be effective, he must use his power of information and knowledge in an objective, constructive way. He should be realistic and avoid the wishful thinking of optimists who hope that troubles may not occur or will go away if ignored. Since he is constantly calling attention to existing and potential troubles, however, he must do this in a positive way, avoiding accusations and implications of incompetence in others and resisting the temptation to prove he is always right.

Since the production control manager's success will be largely dependent on the accuracy and promptness of his information system, the use of simple techniques to insure that things are being done on time can do much to insure that the requirements of the system for attention and activity are met. Frequently, some of the most important but routine activities (revising the materials plan or updating order points) are postponed because of the pressure of urgent interruptions. It is sometimes difficult to associate the poor results that show up later with the actual cause. A check list to insure that important routines are being followed regularly and on time can be of great assistance in the proper organization of activities in the production control department.

A vital mental exercise for the production control manager should be to sit down regularly (at least once a month) and do an "ABC Analysis" of known and anticipated problems in the next six months, sorting out the biggest ones, and insuring that he has activities projected to handle or prevent these problems. A good habit to form is the preparation of a daily "To Do" list of the activities to be performed in priority sequence. Half an hour spent before each working day getting this list prepared will result in much better direction of activities and higher productivity.

The production control manager should also set aside some time each day to visit major or critical production areas in the plant. Often, a quick tour through the plant will detect potential problems a great deal faster than even the most up-to-date information system. The production control manager must also set aside some time—and this will probably have to be after regular plant hours, when the telephones have stopped ringing—to do the thinking and planning that is essential to his department's future performance. This is the time when fire prevention projects are conceived and when long-range programs required to improve his department's performance are developed. A good production control manager has to strike a balance between action to solve today's problems and planning to prevent tomorrow's. While the weight of his office is needed in solving many daily crises, he must avoid getting directly involved in too much expediting. He must counterbalance this with a disciplined program of preparing for the future.

One of the most important steps in preparing for the future is education. This includes education in new techniques, new data-processing equipment, and a broadening of scope through participation in professional societies and the attending of special courses to gain exposure to areas of business management outside of his own field.

This education should take place within the company as well. In the past, most people got into production control work without study or preparation in the field. Not only did they not know much about production control, they frequently did not realize that there was very much to know. Such people frequently became expediters and firefighters, and developed little ability to control production effectively.

Correcting this requires training and, since it involves adults, this training must be as practical as possible. Adults must see the practical applications of the training material if it is to be effective. Studying economic lot sizes will be a waste of time to men in a make-to-order plant, where most of the lot sizes are dictated by the size of the orders. If an individual can specifically see how each technique applies to his company and how the failure to use these techniques properly has caused problems in the past, he will respond enthusiastically. Almost everyone has some desire to become more proficient in his work.

Training related to production control systems, however, goes well beyond production control department personnel. In many companies, other department supervisors have been able to use the production control department as a whipping boy, challenging any information that came out of the department, and thus reducing their need to take action because of this information. Training them to understand what a production control system really is, how they must work with it and use it and how they affect its performance through the information they supply and the action they take is vital to the success of any production control system. Top management people often have little understanding of the true role of production control. They do not recognize the limited alternatives available to them in managing inventories and production and are not always aware of the need to balance the conflicting objectives in day-to-day operation. Production control must accept the responsibility for pointing these out. An extensive communication program may be needed to develop full awareness of the function of production control.

Since the production control department is often the purveyor of bad news and frequently presents management with some rather unpleasant alternatives, it is worth putting some effort into explaining (really *selling*) the production control function to management. A good production control manager will take every opportunity to clarify his department's function to management. One of the best techniques is to volunteer to present to top management a brief program explaining the latest systems revision project in the production control department, how an important new product is to be introduced or to summarize the results of projects.

A very effective program of self-development can be undertaken by any production control department conducted by the senior members of the department—both for training the junior members and in order to provide orientation programs for marketing personnel, foremen, inspectors and others who must work effectively with production control. In this way, the latter group learns what to expect and what not to expect from production control.

In the final analysis, though, success in the job of selling production and inventory control to management and others in the company will rest upon results. The production control manager who is willing to risk setting ambitious goals, who works hard to improve the operation of his department and succeeds in developing and administering programs that improve the performance of the plant as a whole in the areas of inventory control, customer service and profitable plant operation will have little difficulty convincing management of the importance and value of his work.

Production control—the future

Production control originally developed as a paperwork function: maintaining records, issuing shop orders and handling other necessary shop recordkeeping functions. From there, it developed to include stock-chasing and some departmental machine-loading—but most techniques were crude and functions were highly decentralized, to the point of separating inventory control from production control in many companies.

Decentralization was the solution that most companies tried to use as problems of increasing size and complexity faced them. While it often offered some improvements, it also introduced its own problems (such as duplication of effort and considerable suboptimization), with each manager tending to concern himself with limited goals rather than overall company objectives. Some companies went so far as to have separate production control functions for each major manufacturing area within a plant. While this trend toward decentralization was evident in production control, it was also compounding the production control job since it aggravated the problem of getting financial, manufacturing and sales managers to work toward common goals.

There have since been three major developments: operations research —generating a more scientific approach to management; the computer—providing a means for overcoming the communications problems that made it necessary to decentralize in the first place; and the founding of the American Production and Inventory Control Society—providing a means for practitioners to exchange knowledge. The result has been a revolution in production control, as techniques and the means for implementing them have become known. More and more companies have recognized that business can no longer be managed by the "seat-of-the-pants," with a few trusted employees carrying most of the knowledge in their heads. As companies tried to develop control systems—or simply tried to solve problems of customer service, inventory investment control, or plant operation—they recognized that their basic problem was lack of a production control system worthy of the name. This new attention to production control has created a demand for an organized body of knowledge that could be passed on from those practitioners who have learned the practical application of modern techniques. It has brought into sharp relief the fact that much of our progress to date has been in developing techniques, while these techniques have seldom been satisfactorily related to one another or to specific applications. The development of a practical body of knowledge that can be readily taught offers the best encouragement to the further use and development of scientific techniques of production control.

The demand for improved production and inventory control has also created an immediate demand for trained people. An article in *Fortune* magazine made the following observation: "Up until recently, there was a critical shortage of engineers; now there is a shortage of people who can set up inventory problems and the like on a computer."[1] The problem of getting and keeping competent personnel has been compounded by the fact that management has recognized that production control is a field that develops a manager's perspective and understanding of the major segments of the business, and many of the most successful practitioners have been promoted into higher levels of management.

Undoubtedly, the same influences that focused management attention on production control in the last decade will make it increasingly important in the future. Product complexity and variety are increasing dramatically while there are ever-stronger pressures to level production. Most companies must maintain inventories under control in order to keep capital available for other profitable investment opportunities. Above all, there will be pressures for better customer service—frequently the most fertile area for profit improvement as well as the basis for increased market penetration against competition if the improvement is to be sustained and not an isolated spurt.

While there will continue to be many contributions from operations research, probably the most important in the next ten years will come from the improved application of many known techniques whose uses have so far been limited by lack of understanding or lack of ability to handle the vast amount of computation involved. Unquestionably, the greatest influences on the field of production control will come from a growing professionalism, better education and the wider application of the electronic computer.

There will undoubtedly be a return toward centralization in many companies where decentralization was originally adopted as a solution to the difficult communications problems that existed. Once such systems are centralized, departmental boundary lines will begin to break down and new organizational forms will be seen. There will probably be a strong trend to combine the efforts of the financial and production control managers, since they basically deal with the same information and are

---

[1]Robert Sheehan, "New Report Card on the Business Schools," *Fortune*, December 1964, p. 148.

the staff functions most concerned with management controls. The problems and the resulting benefits of such an approach are illustrated in companies that have tried to set up standard cost systems. Typically, the standard cost system was initiated by the financial department and suffered recurring problems. Every two or three years major inventory adjustments were necessary because of errors that crept into the system. If the standard cost data are also used by the production control manager in planning and controlling production, the system is always more successful since discrepancies become quickly apparent when data that do not make sense are used daily. Detecting errors at the source eliminates decisions based on incorrect data and prevents wasted time incurred by chasing down the reasons for such errors long after they have taken place.

The new organizational forms that will develop as a result of the current revolution in information management are difficult to predict today, but there is no question that traditional organizational forms are going to change drastically and that the "production control" department, as we know it, may disappear. The title of the function is really of secondary importance—no matter what it is called, the basic information required to manage a manufacturing operation in the face of intensive competition will become more and more vital to every company. This planning and control function will not only become more important in the operation of the company, but will become a vital training area as well. A background in systems, particularly manufacturing control systems, will undoubtedly be one of the requisites for top managers of the future.

Bibliography

1. Garrity, John T., *Getting the Most Out of Your Computer,* T OO1153, Mc-Kinsey & Company, Inc., New York.
2. Orlicky, Joseph A., "Production Control Yesterday, Today and Tomorrow," *APICS Quarterly Bulletin,* Vol. 4, No. 3, July 1963.

PROBLEMS

Chapter 1:

1-1 a) What are the principal reasons why effective inventory and production control are vital to the successful operation of a manufacturing firm?

b) What effects can one company's inventory and production control activities have on another company? On the national economy?

1-2 Why are the functions of inventory and production control receiving increasing recognition and attention from business management and educators?

1-3 Explain why the activities of sales, financial and manufacturing people are not likely to meet the objectives of customer service, inventory investment and plant operation if each group concerns itself only with its own function.

1-4 a) What are the major policies management should establish for balancing customer service, inventory control and plant operation objectives?

b) Give specific examples of some unrealistic management policies and point out the problems these cause.

1-5 a) Does the electronic computer contribute to achieving better balance among conflicting objectives?

b) Is the introduction of a computer to the inventory and production control system likely to achieve this balance?

1-6 Sketch a flow chart including the major departments and the basic elements of an inventory and production control system as you would imagine it, showing the flows of information for:

a) An auto parts distributer

b) A machine tool builder of special-purpose automated equipment

c) A manufacturer of electric razors

1-7 a) Why are inventory control and production control separate functions in many companies?

b) What are the disadvantages of such separation in a manufacturing company?

1-8 Visit a local industrial firm. Outline how it provides the elements of the production control system and how it recognizes the balancing of the conflicting objectives.

Chapter 2 :

2-1 a) Under what general conditions would a forecast based only on statistical analysis of past history be reliable?

b) When would a prediction made without reference to history be preferred as a forecast?

2-2 Is the demand forecast (incoming business) or is the sales forecast (shipments) of more importance to inventory and production control?

2-3 What factors would determine whether or not a company should spend more money on improving its forecasts?

2-4 What do you think are the underlying causes of forecast characteristics leading to greater accuracy for larger groups of products and for shorter periods?

2-5 Actual incoming orders (in units) for a product for three years are:

	1st year	2nd year	3rd year
Jan.	200	220	250
Feb.	290	310	350
Mar.	350	370	430
Apr.	410	430	500
May	450	470	520
June	500	530	580
July	850	860	900
Aug.	920	940	990
Sept.	730	760	810
Oct.	520	550	600
Nov.	310	340	380
Dec.	230	260	300

Using exponential smoothing, calculate and plot forecast *vs.* actual orders for Year 3, assuming a starting forecast of 230, using:

a) First order smoothing with $\alpha = 0.1, 0.2, 0.3$

b) Second order smoothing with $\alpha = 0.1$, and $B_{old} = 200$

c) First order smoothing (as in a) plus seasonal index based on Years 1 and 2

d) Second order smoothing (as in b) plus seasonal index (as in c)

e) Comment on the quality of each forecast

2-6 Using an available computer and software program* for exponential smoothing, test the various combinations of simple, trend and seasonal forecasting techniques for assumed data showing random, increasing, decreasing, seasonal, rising seasonal and falling seasonal characteristics. How could mathematical tests for accuracy of fit be applied?

2-7 Visit a nearby manufacturing company and determine the source, number and type of forecasts prepared. What units are used for forecasts needed by the following departments:

Sales
Marketing
Treasurer (controller)
Engineering
Manufacturing (production)
Purchasing

Chapter 3 :

3-1 How does capital invested in inventory earn a return? Answer separately for raw materials, work-in-process, finished goods, supplies, lot-size material, safety stocks, transportation goods and anticipation material.

3-2 Make up a company, indicating its major product and manufacturing departments. Classify its inventories by "condition" and then indicate how each inventory "function" exists for inventory in each condition.

3-3 a) Divide the various costs associated with ordering and carrying inventory into Fixed, Variable, and Mixed (Fixed or Variable) classes.

b) Why do accounting systems rarely develop such costs directly?

3-4 What kind of inventory control technique is best adapted to:

a) High usage rivets totaling $25,000 worth annually?

b) A $250 casting with 15 pieces used per year?

3-5 How does the application of a computer to inventory control affect the techniques used to control C items?

---

*Most computer manufacturers have these available.

3-6 What factors might account for recent indications that proper inventory management is reducing the effects of inventory fluctuations on the business cycle?

3-7 Would you expect the ABC curve to differ in shape for a discount department store, a specialty camera supply shop, a hand tools manufacturer and a steel casting foundry?

3-8 Make an ABC analysis for all the items in the inventory of a local business.

Chapter 4 :

4-1 Name at least three situations in which the EOQ concept does *not* apply.

4-2 a) What factors might account for the reluctance or failure of many companies to apply EOQ's, in spite of substantial potential benefits?

b) What should be done to correct or overcome each factor?

4-3 a) What specific savings can result from using EOQ's?

b) What intangible benefits?

4-4 a) If an item passes through several successive operations in different machines having short and long setups, how would you calculate setup costs to be used in the EOQ formula?

b) Standard unit costs usually include a prorated amount of setup in burden or overhead. Should such costs be used in calculating EOQ's?

4-5 Why might the cost of carrying inventory be different:

a) In two successive years?

b) For two different inventory items?

4-6 What approach would you use to calculate EOQ's for:

a) A blanket order for an annual requirement to be delivered in weekly lots?

b) 50 items shipped weekly to a branch warehouse?

c) A highly seasonal item?

d) A part purchased as a casting, put in a raw material inventory, machined in an automatic chucking machine, held in semi-finished component inventory, finished in milling, boring, drilling, tapping and grinding machines, kept in finished component inventory and used continuously on an assembly line?

4-7 a) Calculate EOQ's from the following data:
   1. Fixed ordering cost = $7.00
   2. Inventory carrying cost = 15%
   3. Annual demand = $1500, $3000, $6000, $12,000, $18,000

b) Repeat for inventory carrying costs of 10% and 20%.

c) Repeat for fixed ordering costs of $5.00 and $10.00.

1) For a $3000 annual demand, would you buy twice the EOQ if a discount of 2% were offered? (Use costs in a.)

4-8 Contact the production control or controller's department in three local companies and determine:

a) What inventory carrying cost is used, and

b) How it was determined.

Chapter 5 :

5-1 a) Distinguish between *order point* and *order quantity*.

b) What factors are common to both?

5-2 What important factors are usually overlooked when reserve stocks are determined intuitively?

5-3 a) Using the first order smoothing forecast with seasonal index for year #3 in Problem 2-5 and a starting MAD of 100 pieces, calculate the MAD for each period.

b) What MAD would be used to calculate the order point as of Oct. 1 if the lead time were 2 months? 4 months? 2 weeks?

5-4 The number of pieces of an item sold in the last 26 two-week periods (replenishment lead time = 2 weeks) were:

18	21	5	14
12	13	11	6
9	12	17	13
7	13	10	15
14	15	12	19
13	8	11	13
	7	4	

a) Assuming a fixed forecast of 12 pieces per period, sum up the deviations to determine MAD.

b) With an EOQ of 40 units, how many orders will be placed per year?

c) What order points are required to give the following service:
1. 2 stockouts per year?
2. 1 stockout per year?
3. 1 stockout every 2 years?
4. 1 stockout every 5 years?
5. No stockouts?

d) What is the average total inventory required for each service level in "c"?

5-5 a) What are the similarities and differences between the fixed quantity-variable cycle (*order point*) and the fixed cycle-variable quantity (*periodic review*) systems?

b) What types of businesses would use each?

5-6 What service level would be obtained for Item X on pages 108–109 if reserve stock were set at one week's supply? Two week's supply? One month's supply? What are the corresponding average inventory totals?

5-7 What are the advantages of time series materials planning?

5-8 In addition to production control, what other departments require bills of material data?

5-9 Assuming an average finished product demand for one year of 200 units per month and fixed order points and order quantities as shown, which approach gives the best results?

a) The finished product and components are controlled by order points.

b) The finished product is controlled by order point as above and components are ordered by time series planning. These parts are used in this assembly only. The following data apply:

	Fin. prod.	Part A	Part B	Part C	Part D
Unit cost	$20.00	$1.00	$ 5.00	$ 1.50	$ 0.50
Lead time	4 wks.*	4 wks.	4 wks.	8 wks.	8 wks.
OQ	1200	1400	800	1000	6000
Inv. cost	12%	12%	12%	12%	12%
Setup cost	$250.00	$75.00	$25.00	$11.25	$135.00
OP	1000	1000	1000	2000	2000

*Assembly, testing and packaging time included.

Assume that manufacturing rates can be varied each month to meet the demand (leveling not necessary) and that starting inventory of finished product is 2000 units and of each part is zero.

5-10 Calculate the EOQ's for the four parts making up the finished product in Problem 5-9 if they are manufactured to a time series plan.

5-11 How do statistical concepts of forecast error pertain to a time series materials plan?

Chapter 6 :

6-1 When order quantities are set intuitively, why are they usually far from the economical lot-size calculated by formula?

6-2 Trace the actual sequence of events which might occur if orders for EOQ's were released to a department which lacked the capacity to handle the required number of setups.

6-3 If EOQ's are introduced where they have not been used formerly and lot sizes change substantially, what are the specific sources of savings:

a) If inventories increase

b) If inventories decrease

6-4 Could the application of LIMIT result in a need to recalculate reserve stocks for the items included?

6-5 How would you use LIMIT to assist in deciding whether or not to add capital equipment?

6-6 Four items are made on one machine. Pertinent data on these items are:

	1	2	3	4
Annual use	1,000	40,000	1,500	1,000
Unit cost	$1.00	$0.25	$2.00	$3.00
Setup cost	$2.00	$2.00	$12.00	$25.00
Invent. cost	20%	20%	20%	20%
Pres. ord. quant.	250	10,000	375	250

a) By means of LIMIT, calculate individual lot sizes which will keep the same annual setup cost as the present order quantities.

b) Show the average cycle stock inventory for present, LIMIT and theoretical EOQ, and the corresponding total setup cost.

6-7 A department has three men engaged in setting up machines. These setters also perform in-process quality control inspections. The superintendent wants to double the amount of time these setters spend on this inspection to improve quality. What data are needed and how would you proceed to solve this problem?

6-8 Will reducing finished product inventory always result in poorer customer service?

6-9 Why is it usually impossible to guarantee 100% customer service?

6-10 What classes of inventory do not lend themselves to service vs. investment calculations?

6-11 In making service vs. investment calculations:

a) What items should be grouped together?

b) How frequently should the calculations be updated?

6-12 Many companies use industry averages of inventory turnover as their goals.

a) Why?

b) What are the limitations of this approach?

c) What better definitions of *optimum turnover* are there?

6-13 What actions should management investigate if it wishes to improve customer service without increasing inventory investment?

6-14 There can be only one *real* cost to carry inventory. Why calculate various LIMIT order quantities?

Chapter 7 :

7-1 In making a production plan, how is forecast error taken into account?

7-2 How does production planning provide for reducing the backlog of unshipped orders?

7-3 a) Prepare a production plan for a 13-week period for Widgets based on this year's calendar and working days as in 7-6a.
Forecast incoming business = 105 pieces per wk.
Starting inventory = 855 pieces.
Closing inventory = 920 pieces to meet sales promotion.

b) Revise the plan to meet a closing inventory goal of 600 pieces.

7-4 Compare and contrast the three basic types of production planning:

a) The quarterly ordering system

b) The "order point-order quantity only" approach

c) The production plan as described in this chapter.

7-5 a) What cost elements must be considered when making a production plan?

b) Which costs would be highest using level production?

c) Which costs would be lowest using level production?

7-6 Monthly forecasts of incoming orders for a product group are:

Jan.—220	Apr.—430	July—860	Oct.—550
Feb.—310	May—470	Aug.—940	Nov.—340
Mar.—370	June—530	Sept.—760	Dec.—260

a) Make an annual production plan for level production: Starting inventory = 900; ending inventory = 500; plant vacation shutdown last 2 weeks in July, no other official holidays throughout the year.

b) Make an annual production plan, changing production rate only twice and minimizing inventory buildup.

7-7 Why is introducing production level planning frequently the most rewarding systems improvement in a company experiencing difficulty in maintaining customer service?

7-8 If lead times average 15 weeks and it requires 10-12 weeks to accomplish a change in production capacity, could the quarterly ordering system be used effectively?

7-9 What difficulties may result if an order point/order quantity inventory control system is allowed to generate orders for manufactured components without any planning of production level?

7-10 Visit a company in the area and determine:

a) Who sets capacity levels? How? How are they changed?

b) What unit of measure best expresses capacity in each major department?

c) Do they use machine loading? If so, how is it related to capacity planning?

Chapter 8:

8-1 It has been said that a 5% variation in retail sales can be amplified to 10% at the assembly plant, 20% at the parts manufacturing level, and 40% for raw material demand.
How can better production planning help reduce this type of amplification?

8-2 What control benefits are obtained by having sales, production and inventory data shown together on a production plan?

8-3 A "30-day sales rule" is being used to control an inventory of manufactured items. The factory management complains about the large fluctuation in ordered quantities. What alternative method could be used and what are its advantages and limitations?

8-4 a) How large a backlog of incoming orders would have to be permissible to permit level production during the year if no inventory was maintained for the product in Problem 7-6?

b) What backlog level would you recommend for the following year to limit random changes in production level to one change? (Note that these sales data are the same as Year 2 in Problem 2-5)

8-5 Calculate and plot monthly production, manload and inventory for the glue demand data given in this chapter, using linear decision rules, equations 8-1, 8-2 and 8-3. Assume second-year monthly forecasts 10% above first year.

8-6 Prepare a production plan for the glue factory (base inventory = 420 Mgal.) and compare the inventory with the data obtained in Problem 8-5.

8-7 Assume you are the leader of the operations research team working with the operating managers to fit linear decision rules to the glue factory:

  a) What questions would you expect from them?

  b) How would you answer them?

Chapter 9:

9-1 In addition to improved customer service, what benefits can be expected from effective scheduling?

9-2 a) How do the time elements (setup, running, move, inspection, etc.) used in scheduling relate to the *lead times* used in calculating order points?

  b) What is the effect of using "comfortable" move and delay times in scheduling on:

  1. Work-in-process inventory levels
  2. Finished component inventory levels
  3. Finished product inventory levels

9-3 List the advantages and disadvantages of using detailed operations scheduling rules *vs.* block scheduling.

9-4 Compare and contrast loading *to infinite capacity* and loading *to finite capacity*.

9-5 What are the limitations of machine loading as a means of controlling production capacity?

9-6 Discuss the effects of effective scheduling on an inventory control system using floating order points and economic order quantities.

9-7 Justify the statement that "There is no reason why schedule periods must be equal to the total lead time."

9-8 Visit a local continuous production plant and an intermittent production plant and report on:

  a) Scheduling techniques used

  b) Sources of scheduling data

  c) Reliability of lead times

Chapter 10:

10-1 What are the basic problems of shop floor control, and how do techniques of dispatching, expediting and Flow Control contribute to their solution?

10-2 Discuss the statement "There will always be a need for expediting." Do you agree? Does it apply to all businesses?

10-3 a) Why is there no single "best" dispatching rule?

b) What additional action would you recommend for a company which wanted to use the " least processing time " rule?

10-4 What system elements are needed before you can use the Critical Ratio technique?

10-5 Why is it true that the amount of work-in-process on a factory floor usually expands to fill the space available?

10-6 Taking the basic elements of Flow Control, discuss the effect of omitting each on the control of work-in-process.

10-7 a) Analyze the lead time in a local company, from receipt of a customer's order to shipment of the material or rendering the service.

b) What should be done to improve service to customers by reducing lead times?

Chapter 11:

11-1 What problems would you expect with an inventory control system which lacked any of the four control elements? (Take each element in turn.)

11-2 How can the organizational level at which production control is located affect the performance of the feedback and corrective action elements of the system?

11-3 What differences would you expect to find in the application of computer programs to inventory and production control activities in a make-to-stock plant, as compared to a make-to-order factory.

11-4 What differences in inventory and production control activities in make-to-order *vs.* make-to-stock plants affect the level of organization to which the production control manager should report?

11-5 What actions would you recommend if the first issue of a daily delay report for a milling machine department contained over one hundred items?

11-6 In addition to delays to specific parts of finished products, what classes of problems might appear on a production manager's weekly summary?

11-7 What are the advantages and disadvantages of using more than one measure of customer service at one time?

11-8 Study the production control system of a local manufacturing company and identify specifically each of the four control system elements for control of:

a) The level of production
b) The level of customer service
c) Make detailed recommendations for any missing or deficient elements.

CASE STUDIES

Case study #1: Inventory control

The companies described in this case are all having serious problems with their inventories. Customer service is poor and factory operations are frequently upset by shortages, even though inventories are very large. Inventory losses due to obsolescence, loss and deterioration are high.

> *Company A* manufactures drill bushings. The product begins as rod or tubing and moves through screw machines, milling, grinding, heat treating, plating and packaging. A total of 3500 different, single-piece, finished products is maintained in stock made from 150 different items of raw material. The company tries to maintain a 45-day supply of raw material and a 60-day finished stock level.

> *Company B* manufactures small electrical appliances, including accessories. Demand for their products seems to fluctuate rather widely, and the company therefore maintains a very high level of component inventories. Finished goods inventories of the 100 products and the component stocks of several thousand parts and subassemblies are all controlled using statistical order points. Their most serious problem is that components never all seem to be

available when an assembly is to be started on the line.

Company C makes composition friction material for clutches, brakes and similar applications. Finished goods inventories of several hundred items are maintained by statistical order points. These consist of cut shapes of material, some riveted and some bonded to metal backing plates.

The total lead time from raw material to finished stores is 6 to 8 weeks, with only 1 to 2 weeks required for the final operations that convert a basic piece of material into a specific item. For this reason, a semi-finished inventory larger than the finished stores is maintained from which a given piece of material can be processed quicly to make any one of several different items.

The total of semi-finished and work-in-process inventory for each item is maintained at 3 months' supply by ordering 1 month's replenishment lot when the semi-finished total drops to a 2 months' supply. These inventories are very high, but it often seems that needed items are in short supply, particularly when business is picking up. There are also many very slow moving items in the semi-finished stores.

Company D produces a limited line of specialized machine tools comprised of 11 basic machines with many optional features. They normally have a backlog of 12 to 18 months of customer orders on hand. Each month, a Manufacturing Planning Group consisting of the President and the Vice Presidents in charge of Sales, Manufacturing, and Finance review the order backlog and develop a firm production schedule for the 9th month in the future.

Production Control uses this authorization (usually for 20-25 finished machines) to order purchased materials and release orders to the plant. The eight months' lead time is adequate to cover all except a very few critical materials.

The most critical problem is that customers request many changes in the optional features from those on the original order, and often several months after placing the order. Production Control finds difficulty in working these changes into the firm schedules already issued. The shop spends much time working on components for items no longer needed.

Questions

Answer for each company individually. State any assumptions you believe necessary.

1. What is your opinion of the strengths and weaknesses of the present inventory control system?

2. What changes would you recommend to improve the system's performance? Justify each recommendation.

3. What problems would you anticipate in making the changes? What timetable would you follow and what actions would you take to resolve these problems?

4. What specific improvements would you expect? Give reasons and some means to measure the amount of improvement.

Case study #2: Production control

The length and variability of lead times measure the effectiveness of any production control system. Long lead times lengthen the forecast period over which the inventory control system must predict the requirements, and accuracy decreases as this period grows longer. Variability of lead times prevents setting dependable delivery dates. Both necessitate carrying higher reserve stocks or giving poorer customer service.

An important factor in the control of lead times is the size of backlogs of work-in-process. This can be verified by a simple manual simulation using small cardboard boxes to represent shop boxes, each containing a different job. In this simulation, there are two work stations—both drill presses—the first one doing a drilling operation and the second a tapping operation. Each job goes into the drilling operation first, requiring one day to complete. It then goes into the tapping operation, which also requires one day to complete. These operations are perfectly balanced—a day's work at the drilling operation also represents a day's work at the tapping operation. Once a job has been tapped, it is completed.

The shop boxes consist of two groups, those without any markings and those numbered 1 through 10. The objective of the simulation is to start with a given shop workload, represented by a number of unmarked boxes, and try to run jobs 1 through 10 through in the proper sequence with *no scheduling, dispatching, or expediting*. Running the simulation requires four people:

1. A production control manager who sends the jobs down from his office in the proper sequence. (That is, Job #1 goes out on the factory floor to the drilling operation on Day #1, Job #2 on Day #2, etc.)

2. An operator at the first drill press who looks only at the back of each shop box in the queue at his machine, cannot see the number on the front so that he makes a random choice, works on the job chosen and then passes it to Machine Center #2.

3. An operator at the second drill press who takes each job that has been drilled and taps it. He cannot see the numbers on the front of the boxes either and makes a random choice from the total workload ahead of his machine.

4. A record clerk who watches the jobs coming out of the second operation and posts the order in which they are completed.

As the jobs are completed, they are recorded on the form shown in Fig. 1. The spaces in Fig. 1 numbered 1 through 30 represent completion days. The X's in these squares represent unnumbered jobs that were completed on that day. A number in the square indicates that one of the numbered jobs was completed on that day. Total lead time is easy to calculate. In the example shown in Fig. 1, an unnumbered job came through on each of the first three days and Job #2 came through on the fourth day. Since Job #2 started on the second day, its total lead time was 2 days.

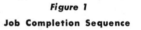

Figure 1

Job Completion Sequence

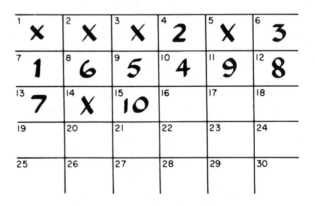

Figure 1 data are typical of the lead times obtained when this simulation is run with two jobs ahead of each machine center. Jobs #1 through #10 are released by the production control manager in their proper sequence. In order to insure that the operator always has two jobs ahead of his machine center to choose from, the production control manager also released blank jobs into production once the ten numbered jobs had all been started. Because the operators choose jobs at random out on the factory floor, the jobs are not completed in the same sequence in which they are started.

Figure 2 shows the lead time summary for the simulation, with 2 jobs in backlog or queue at each machine center. The shortest lead time for any job was 2 days, the minimum possible. The longest lead time was 6 days (and three jobs required this long to complete). The average lead time for the ten numbered jobs was 4 days—as might be expected when there are two days of work already in process ahead of each machine center.

After this first simulation has been completed, a second can be run with just one change—this time there are 5 unnumbered jobs ahead of each machine center at the start. As before, the production control manager releases in sequence the 10 numbered jobs to be worked at random. Again, the production control manager releases unnumbered boxes after Job #10 to keep the queues full.

Figure 3 shows a typical job completion sequence with five jobs in queue at each machine, and Fig. 4 gives the lead time summary for this simulation together with the previous one.

Figure 2

Lead Time Summary

Job no.	2 Jobs in queue	5 Jobs in queue
1	6	
2	2	
3	3	
4	6	
5	4	
6	2	
7	6	
8	4	
9	2	
10	5	
Total	40	
Avg.	4.0	

Figure 3

Job Completion Sequence

1	2	3	4	5	6
X	X	X	X	X	3
7	8	9	10	11	12
X	1	X	X	X	X
13	14	15	16	17	18
8	5	4	7	X	X
19	20	21	22	23	24
X	6	2	9	10	
25	26	27	28	29	30

Figure 4

Lead Time Summary

Job no.	**2** Jobs in queue	**5** Jobs in queue
1	6	7
2	2	19
3	3	3
4	6	11
5	4	9
6	2	14
7	6	9
8	4	5
9	2	13
10	5	13
Total	40	103
Avg.	4.0	10.3

Questions

1. What two conclusions regarding the effects of backlogs on lead time can be drawn from this demonstration?
2. How could this demonstration be modified to illustrate the effect of expediting on lead times?
3. What effects do backlogs have on dispatching? Machine loading?
4. a) What actions would be necessary to reduce the backlogs from 5 jobs to 2 in controlling this oversimplified manufacturing operation?
   b) How would you accomplish this reduction if the backlogs were still "on paper" instead of in physical parts?
5. What reaction toward small backlogs would you expect from:
   a) An expediter
   b) An inventory control supervisor
   c) A shop foreman
   d) A machine operator
   e) The company controller (treasurer).

Case study #3

The Black Pot Company manufactures small electrical home appliances such as toasters and coffee pots. The basic components of these appliances are stampings manufactured in their press department, purchased electrical subassemblies, plastic bases to which the heating units, switches, etc. are assembled at the plant and cord sets which are purchased from a single vendor.

Sheet metal components start in the stamping department, move into the forming department where secondary operations are performed, then through the plating department and into finished component stores. Electrical parts are subassembled in a separate department and sent to finished component stores. These electrical subassemblies, the sheet metal subassembly and the cord set are withdrawn from finished component stores, assembled into finished products, inspected, packed and shipped.

The principal participants in this case study are:

> General Manager, J. F. Black
> Sales Manager, R. B. Forsythe
> Plant Manager, Fred Atkins
> Controller, R. C. Braken
> Production Control Manager, **You**

History

Before World War II, the Black Pot Company was a small appliance firm concentrating principally on one model of six-cup coffee pot and a standard toaster. The coffee pot was very well accepted as a low-priced yet dependable appliance and was purchased by many retailers as well as private brand outlets who marketed it under their own name.

During World War II, the company made minor electrical subassemblies, particularly those employing stampings, for military use. When World War II was over, they had a large number of orders in backlog for the standard coffee pot and toaster which carried them into 1953. In the meantime, some new model appliances were introduced.

The production control system was a very simple one. Since the order backlog was never under six months, it was standard procedure to make out a quarterly production schedule which was firm for the assembly department. It was also broken down into required electrical subassemblies, stampings and purchased parts ordered by the Production Control Department from the supplying department and vendors to meet the assembly schedule dates. This ordering system worked very well as long as the order backlog existed.

Late in 1953, the order backlog had diminished to approximately four weeks of production and the quarterly ordering system became increasingly difficult to work, since there were not enough firm orders to make up a schedule for the next quarter. Recognizing the seriousness of the situation, the company hired a Marketing Manager who set up forecasting procedures in order to develop a quarterly forecast to be used by the Production Control Department for planning production. He was also instrumental in urging new ventures in small appliances. Consequently, many new products have been added since 1953, including drip-type coffee makers, large coffee urns in 20-to 100-cup capacities, many different models of toasters, toaster-broilers, waffle irons and, most recently, an electric plug-in bean pot in three different sizes and a dozen different canister sets.

While the Marketing Manager was highly capable in new product development and introduction, his forecasting ability was somewhat less enviable. The Production Control Department's records showed that 50% of his forecasts for individual items were off by plus or minus 25% over a thirteen-week period. With such inaccuracy the quarterly ordering system could not work very well and, in fact, a great deal of expediting was required to get the proper items through the plant. The plant people complained that the Production Control Department always wanted something extra in addition to the quarterly schedule given to them. The Production Control Department in turn complained that the forecasts were inaccurate and they had to spend the necessary time and effort in expediting, not only to get the proper assemblies made, but to get the needed components through manufacturing and purchasing.

One of the most serious problems was the fact that the requirements for components were reviewed only quarterly, when the quarterly assembly schedule was drawn-up. At this time, the assemblies were exploded into component requirements and component orders were scheduled throughout the plant. While this system was intended to generate a fairly level amount of work for the plant, the degree of forecast inaccuracy caused some very serious lumps in the production schedule. Each time Production Control reviewed their quarterly assembly requirements, they found that these had changed drastically from the last review and that many components were required immediately. This meant that demands on supplying departments (in particular, the stamping department) tended to crowd into the first month of the quarter, and there was a decided bulge in the workload at the beginning of the quarter.

Management was very concerned about these problems, particularly since inventories had increased substantially since 1953 and customer service was still very poor by industry standards. The Sales Department believed that the service given by the Black Pot Company factory was among the very worst in the appliance industry.

Two years ago, Mr. Black, under heavy pressure from his Sales Manager, called in a management consultant to recommend improvements in the production control system that would solve the customer service problem. This consultant recommended applying economic order quantities and order points to control manufacturing and inventory and these recommendations were adopted. The economic order quantities resulted in larger lot-sizes, but these were accepted because of the managements' understanding that this

Solution

larger investment in inventory would be economical. Order points were established for all assemblies, manufactured and purchased components, and many raw materials.

Present situation

After running this system for more than eighteen months, many problems still exist. The inventory has been increasing steadily, the level of work in the plant is very unstable and has been more erratic in the last two years than it had ever been in the past. Customer service—far from improving—has grown poorer and the pressures have been so great that the Production Control Manager recently left the company.

Mr. Black called together his executive group and discussed the problem. They talked about calling in another consultant, but felt that their past experience did not justify the expense. They have decided to hire another Production Control Manager (You) and to act as a task force to assist you in analyzing the problem. Each member of the task force is to write a memorandum outlining his analysis of the problem and making specific recommendations for solutions.

As the new Production Control Manager, you are to review the memos submitted by the other members of the task force and develop a program embodying their recommendations and your own improvements. Your presentation should contain specific comments on the task force recommendations. Your program should include *specific techniques* to be used in:

1. Utilizing forecasts, together with recommendations for improving them
2. Planning and controlling inventory levels
3. Leveling the load on the factory, including the plating department
4. Reducing and controlling work-in-process
5. Measuring and improving customer service
6. Preparing for and implementing a computer installation in Production Control
7. Improving procurement of purchased items.

Include a timetable and comments on required manload to install any recommended system changes.

As a separate project, discuss this company's approach to the use of a management consultant.

Interoffice Memorandum

THE BLACK POT COMPANY

To: *J. F. Black,* Gen'l Mgr.
From: *R. B. Forsythe,* Sales Mgr.
    SUBJECT: *The production control problem*

If we are going to resume the rate of growth in the future that we had in the past (you'll note that sales have leveled out during the past few years), we have to provide competitive customer service. We're supposed to be a make-to-stock company and we're supposed to have our appliances on the shelf when our customers ask for them. Unfortunately, we don't seem to be able to do this consistently.

We in the Sales Department are constantly in the position of trying to push our new products to our customers who tell us that they're not interested in the new products until we can deliver our old ones. We have more ideas for new products, but see no sense in suggesting these when our factory seems to be completely incapable of handling our present business properly.

Reviewing the situation from a common-sense point of view, I can make two observations:

1. When we recently got in trouble with our major private brand account, we added an expediter who concentrated his efforts on this account. Since that time, we have had very few complaints about service to this customer. I believe that it would be well worth the expense to add more expediters to the payroll so that we could improve our service to our valued customers. *[handwritten: too expensive]*

2. We constantly emphasize the need to improve inventory turnover at Black Pot. It would be a good idea to invest the needed funds in inventory before it's too late. *[handwritten: high investment]*

I'm not qualified to tell you how to run a factory, but I can tell you about sales: *You can't sell from an empty wagon!*

R. B. Forsythe

Interoffice Memorandum

THE BLACK POT COMPANY

To: *J. F. Black,* Gen'l Mgr.

From: *F. Atkins,* Plant Mgr.

SUBJECT: *The production control problem*

In my opinion, our switch from a quarterly ordering program to an order point-order quantity system has aggravated our problems at Black Pot and cured almost none of the basic ills. As I see it, we have the following problems:

1. The order point system tends to generate many orders for parts and products that are not really needed and exaggerates the ups and downs in our business cycle. When business picks up, a lot of orders are generated and sent out to the plant. Unfortunately, we don't know how to recognize this flood of orders as a true pick-up in business because the order point system seems to cause a high degree of variability, even under normal circumstances. Typically, there will be one week of heavy orders, followed by two weeks of very light orders and then another week of very heavy orders generated and sent down into the plant. It is impossible for plant operating people to determine from the size of the order backlog when to add men or when to lay men off. It's easy for the Production Control Department to say that we should be reacting by increasing or decreasing production rates, but this is a long slow process. We can't get press operators hired and trained overnight, and once we lay them off, we never seem to see them again. Until we see a ten to twelve week build-up of work ahead of our manufacturing departments, we do not feel justified in adding manpower or increasing production other than by occasional overtime. *coordinate*

    For example, at the present time, we know that sales are down (judging by the dollar incoming business reports), yet there is a very substantial backlog out in the plant. Would you feel that we would be justified in adding manpower to work off the backlogs of work in the plant?

2. The system for generating orders in Production Control doesn't seem to be connected to actual requirements. We have many orders now in the plant that were released four and even six months ago, yet no one has asked us to run them. Specifically, our colonial coffee pot that is made for the Ace Premium Company only twice a year was assembled for the Christmas order, and the components were immediately reordered from the stamping department and the electrical subassembly department in January. These components aren't used on any other product and could not possibly be needed before the next Ace vacation promotion order in August. This work just lies around on the floor until some expediter comes down to push it.

3. Expediting concentrates on putting pressure upon our factory people, but

it doesn't seem to exert as much pressure on people outside our company. We are doing rush jobs every day of the week and getting blamed for missing the schedule on our regular work, yet we find many orders in the plant for which there is no material. The expediters don't seem to know when the vendors are going to ship the material. In fact, a recent survey of the orders in the stamping department indicated that while we had a twelve week backlog, only six weeks of this could be worked on since material was not available for about half the orders ahead of the department.

4. There have been very heavy surges of work in the plating department. All plating work seems to come at one time with everything wanted at once. We simply cannot hire and train new plating people to do the quality work that Black Pot expects quickly enough to keep up with these surges. This department is a constant bottleneck because Production Control does not feed a level rate of work into the department.

In my own opinion, the following actions are needed to solve our immediate problems:

1. Lengthen the lead time allowed on components. The lead time for press parts was lengthened from six weeks to eight weeks recently, but right after that we received a flood of orders from Production Control which bogged the department down so badly we haven't recovered yet. We need to increase the lead time on these parts to a minimum of twelve weeks. If the Production Control Department could plan further ahead, it would certainly be of assistance in keeping this department operating smoothly and on schedule.

2. We are in constant trouble in the assembly department because we have sets of parts laid out for assembly with one or two parts missing. I feel that we should be laying out at least four weeks in advance of our scheduled assembly date instead of just two. If we did this, we would find out earlier which components were short and the Production Control Department could use this shortage list for effective and timely expediting of critical parts rather than expediting everything through the plant.

3. I don't see why the Purchasing Department can't institute a regular follow-up procedure to get purchased materials—particularly special steels for the stamping department, plastic bases for the subassembly department and cord sets—in on time.

4. We used to have a firm quarterly schedule that worked out very well. When we lost our order backlog, our biggest problem was that we could no longer get a good quarterly forecast. An improvement in forecasting by the Marketing Department and some discipline and restraint on the part of the Sales Department (so that we could have a firm quarterly forecast to work with) would make substantial improvements in plant economy and in service to customers.

5. Our Sales Department is constantly asking for new and different products. From a small company making two or three products when I first joined it

as a press operator, we have expanded to where we are now making sixty different assemblies averaging ten components each, and the Sales Department is still clamoring for more. It must be recognized that we are basically a job shop, and that we cannot turn out the volume of production in the variety required by the Sales Department.

A return to our quarterly ordering system with reliable forecasts is probably the best solution available to the current problems at the Black Pot Company. I will certainly do everything I can to cooperate with those parties who will participate in this or any other program.

Fred Atkins

Interoffice Memorandum

THE BLACK POT COMPANY

To: *J. F. Black,* Gen'l Mgr.

From: *R. C. Braken,* Controller

SUBJECT: *The production control problem*

Recognizing the very serious problems in our company in the areas of inventory control and customer service, I have had an audit group working in the plant during the last few months. Listed below are their findings and recommendations:

1. Economic order quantities were installed approximately two years ago and have resulted in larger lot-sizes. So far, there have been no offsetting economies in setup or ordering cost. *Recommendation:* these economic ordering quantities should be reviewed, using an inventory carrying cost approved by the controller. ✓

2. The amount of work in the plant is excessive; there is far too much work-in-process. One of the serious problems that results is a "last in, first out" effect in front of machine centers. The work is piled so deeply ahead of these machine centers that the oldest jobs are ignored because they get pushed so far in back and the more recent jobs get done first. *Recommendation:* reduce the amount of work-in-process. ✓

3. Our audit group has found that many orders are lost in the plant. Production Control expects these orders to come through when, in fact, they can't even find them. Occasionally, they assume that these orders have been completed and adjust inventory records accordingly. This results in large inventory write-offs at year-end. *Recommendation:* A reduction in work-in-process would help solve this problem also.

4. The inventory records were checked and found to be inaccurate in over 10% of the cases. These records are now prededucted when orders are sent out to the assembly floor and, consequently, they cannot be reconciled with the physical inventory. *Recommendation:* a permanent roving audit team should be checking inventories of components against stock records, and these component inventory records should be kept on an actual rather than a prededucted basis.

5. There is a lot of inventory all over the assembly floor, practically every lot lacking in some required components. Productive time is often spent borrowing components from Order A to use on Order B, even though Order A was laid out first. *Recommendation:* more accurate records would help in avoiding this type of waste of time and money.   ✓

6. There are indications of loose control in the Production Control Depart-

382

ment. Production Control personnel accept as complete an order with 90-95% of the material delivered against it rather than checking to see where the balance of the order is. Other basic disciplines seem to be lacking in Production Control. *Recommendation*: such well-recognized devices as commercial Schedule Control Boards should be installed wherever applicable.

7. Too much time is spent expediting various orders in the plant. Since job location records are frequently two to three days late, most of the expediters' time is spent in actually looking for the job. Black Pot has grown enough to require and be able to afford a data collection system and the latest electronic computer equipment to keep our job location records up-to-date. *Recommendation*; a computer could be used to print out job location records on a day-to-day basis for Production Control. Such a computer could also handle inventory control and machine loading—a function sadly lacking in our present Production Control system.

R. C. Braken

APPENDICES

Appendix I

Table of square roots

No.	√	No.	√	No.	√	No.	√	No.	√	No.	√
1	1.0	30	5.5	300	17.3	3,000	54.8	30,000	173.2	2,000,000	1,414
2	1.4	35	5.9	350	18.7	3,500	59.2	40,000	200.0	3,000,000	1,732
3	1.7	40	6.3	400	20.0	4,000	63.2	50,000	223.6	4,000,000	2,000
4	2.0	45	6.7	450	21.2	4,500	67.1	60,000	244.9	5,000,000	2,236
5	2.2	50	7.1	500	22.4	5,000	70.7	70,000	264.6	6,000,000	2,450
6	2.4	55	7.4	550	23.5	5,500	74.2	80,000	282.8	7,000,000	2,646
7	2.6	60	7.7	600	24.5	6,000	77.5	90,000	300.0	8,000,000	2,828
8	2.8	65	8.1	650	25.5	6,500	80.6	100,000	316.2	9,000,000	3,000
9	3.0	70	8.4	700	26.5	7,000	83.7	150,000	387.3	10,000,000	3,162
10	3.2	75	8.7	750	27.4	7,500	86.6	200,000	447.2	12,000,000	3,464
11	3.3	80	8.9	800	28.3	8,000	89.4	250,000	500.0	14,000,000	3,742
12	3.5	85	9.2	850	29.2	8,500	92.2	300,000	547.7	16,000,000	4,000
13	3.6	90	9.5	900	30.0	9,000	94.9	350,000	591.6	18,000,000	4,243
14	3.7	95	9.7	950	30.8	9,500	97.5	400,000	632.5	20,000,000	4,472
15	3.9	100	10.0	1,000	31.6	10,000	100.0	450,000	670.8	25,000,000	5,000
16	4.0	110	10.5	1,100	33.2	11,000	104.9	500,000	707.1	30,000,000	5,477
17	4.1	120	11.0	1,200	34.6	12,000	109.5	550,000	741.6	35,000,000	5,916
18	4.2	130	11.4	1,300	36.1	13,000	114.0	600,000	774.6	40,000,000	6,325
19	4.4	140	11.8	1,400	37.4	14,000	118.3	650,000	806.2	45,000,000	6,708
20	4.5	150	12.2	1,500	38.7	15,000	122.5	700,000	836.7	50,000,000	7,071
21	4.6	175	13.2	1,750	41.9	17,500	132.3	750,000	866.0	60,000,000	7,746
22	4.7	200	14.1	2,000	44.7	20,000	141.4	800,000	894.4	70,000,000	8,367
23	4.8	225	15.0	2,250	47.5	22,500	150.0	850,000	922.0	80,000,000	8,944
24	4.9	250	15.8	2,500	50.0	25,000	158.1	900,000	948.7	90,000,000	9,487
25	5.0	275	16.6	2,750	52.5	27,500	165.8	1,000,000	1,000	100,000,000	10,000

Appendix II

Square root curve

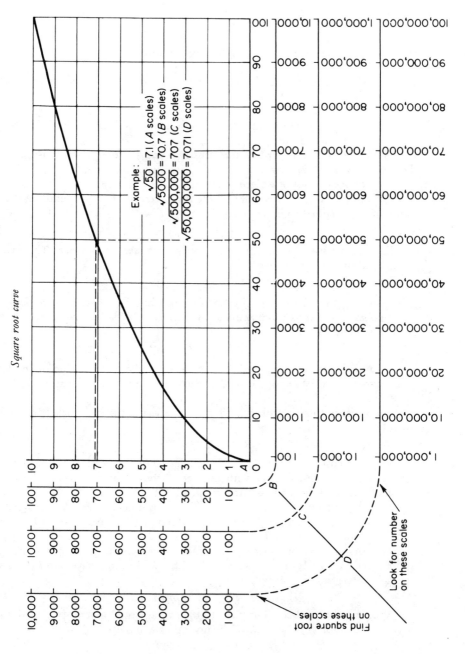

Example:
$\sqrt{50} = 7.1$ (*A* scales)
$\sqrt{5000} = 70.7$ (*B* scales)
$\sqrt{500,000} = 707$ (*C* scales)
$\sqrt{50,000,000} = 7071$ (*D* scales)

Find square root on these scales

Look for number on these scales

Appendix III

Formula derivation economic ordering quantity

This derivation covers the formula for determining the most economic ordering quantity (EOQ) for one item carried in inventory, whether the item is purchased or manufactured. The term *received* will be used to cover delivery into inventory; the word *issued* for usage out of inventory. All assumptions will be written in italics.

The daily rate of receipt of the item is p and the daily rate of issue is u. *Both are assumed to be uniform over the whole cycle of receipt and issue.*

To produce one lot of q pieces requires q/p days.

The rate at which pieces will be added to inventory is $p - u$, and the maximum quantity added to inventory will be:

$$(q/p)(p - u) \qquad (1)$$

The reserve stock inventory is R, *assumed constant over one year.* The maximum total inventory will be:

$$R + (q/p)(p - u)$$

Assuming that the *storage space and handling charges are directly proportional to the maximum inventory and are measured by w dollars per year per piece,* the annual cost of storage will be:

$$w[R + (q/p)(p - u)] \qquad (2)$$

Assuming uniform rates of receipt and issue, the *average* value of the lot-size inventory will be one-half the maximum given by equation (1), or $(q/2p)(p - u)$.

The average total inventory will also include the reserve stock R and will then be:

$$R + (q/2p)(p - u) \qquad (3)$$

The unit cost per piece is C and includes labor, material and that portion of the overhead which varies with the size of the lot produced, but does not include ordering charges associated with each lot procured.

The ordering cost is S and includes all preparation charges, such as writing orders, setting up machines, inspecting the setup, and other charges incurred each time one lot is procured.

The total cost of one piece is $C + (S/q)$, and the total cost of a year's requirement with daily issue rate u and with N working days *based on using lot-size q throughout the year* will be:

$$Nu[C + (S/q)] \qquad (4)$$

Applying the total cost per piece to the average total inventory quantity as given by equation (3), the value of the inventory will be:

$$[C + (S/q)] \times [R + (q/2p)(p - u)]$$

The cost of carrying this inventory (expressed as I dollars per dollar of inventory) will include elements for cost of money, obsolescence, deterioration,

taxes, insurance and *other factors not included in this derivation as separate costs.*
The total annual cost of carrying the average inventory will be:

$$I \times [C + (S/q)] \times [R + (q/2p)(p - u)] \tag{5}$$

The grand total T of the costs for one year's operation will be the sum of:

1. The storage cost, equation (2)
2. The direct cost, equation (4)
3. The carrying cost, equation (5)

$$T = w[R + (q/p)(p - u)] + Nu[C + (S/q)] \\ + I \times [C + (S/q)] \times [R + (q/2p)(p - u)]$$

This expands to:

$$T = wR + (wq/p)(p - u) + NuC + (NuS/q) + ICR \\ + (ICq/2p)(p - u) + (ISR/q) + (IS/2p)(p - u)$$

The minimum value of T will result when the lot-size q is set at the "most economic" size, the EOQ. This is determined by differentiating this equation with respect to q and setting this equal to zero:

$$dT/dq = (w/p)(p - u) - (NuS/q^2) + (IC/2p)(p - u) - (ISR/q^2) = 0$$

Combining terms:

$$\frac{NuS + ISR}{q^2} = \left[\frac{IC + 2w}{2}\right] \times \left[\frac{(p - u)}{p}\right]$$

from which:

$$q^2 = \frac{2(NuS + ISR)}{(IC + 2w)(1 - u/p)}$$

and the final step:

$$\text{EOQ} = \sqrt{\frac{2NuS + 2ISR}{(IC + 2w)(1 - u/p)}} \tag{6}$$

In practical use, the annual usage is expressed as a single factor A instead of the daily rate u times the number of days N. Also, the *storage charge w* is not handled as a separate factor but *is considered part of the inventory carrying cost I.* This reduces equation (6) to:

$$\text{EOQ} = \sqrt{\frac{2AS + 2ISR}{IC(1 - u/p)}} \tag{7}$$

If reserve stock is a relatively small factor whose influence does not justify the complication of including it in the calculations, the *reserve stock* factor $(2ISR)$ can be omitted, and equation (7) reduces to:

$$\text{EOQ} = \sqrt{\frac{2AS}{IC(1 - u/p)}} \tag{8}$$

This is the common form used where the rate p at which the item is received is not large when compared to the rate issued u, called the Noninstantaneous Receipt case.

Where the ratio of these rates "u/p" is small enough to be considered negligible (which is often true in practice) the most frequently used form of the EOQ equation results:

$$EOQ = \sqrt{\frac{2AS}{IC}} \qquad (9)$$

Summarizing, the symbols used are:

EOQ = most economic ordering quantity, pieces
A = annual total issues, pieces
S = total ordering cost for one lot, dollars
I = inventory carrying cost, dollars per dollar of inventory
C = unit cost, not including setup, dollars per piece.

Appendix IV

Effect of changes in order quantity on total inventory investment

When calculating economic lot sizes, it is frequently assumed that a reduction in the lot-size portion of the inventory will reduce the total inventory by the same amount. This is not exactly the case. Reductions in the order quantity result in more frequent exposure to stockout and require larger reserve stocks for the same level of customer service. Table IV-I shows a series of possible order quantities for an item with an annual forecast of 96,000 units. The service level desired is one stockout in two years and the mean absolute deviation is found to be 1680 units. The table shows how reserve stock will have to increase as order quantity decreases in order to maintain the same service level.

Figure IV-1 shows a graph of the average lot-size inventory and the average total inventory including reserve stocks, showing that reductions in lot-size inventory will not be reflected in their full amount in the total inventory because reserve stocks will have to be increased.

Table IV-1

Effect of changes in order quantity on total inventory investment

Annual forecast = 96,000 units
Desired service level is 1 stockout in 2 years
Lead time = 4 weeks
Mean absolute deviation = 1680 units

Order quantity	Exposures per year	Service factor	Service ratio	Required number of MAD[1]	Reserve stock	One-half order quantity	Total inventory
96,000	1	1/2	50.0	0	0	48,000	48,000
48,000	2	3/4	75.0	0.84	1,410	24,000	25,410
32,000	3	5/6	83.3	1.20	2,020	16,000	18,020
24,000	4	7/8	87.5	1.43	2,400	12,000	14,400
16,000	6	11/12	91.7	1.74	2,920	8,000	10,920
12,000	8	15/16	93.8	1.93	3,240	6,000	9,240
8,000	12	23/24	95.8	2.16	3,630	4,000	7,630
4,000	24	47/48	97.9	2.55	4,280	2,000	6,280
2,000	48	95/96	99.0	2.91	4,890	1,000	5,890
1,000	96	191/192	99.5	3.20	5,380	500	5,880
500	192	383/384	99.7	3.44	5,770	250	6,020

[1]From Fig. 5–7, Chapter 5, interpolated where necessary.

Looking at Table IV-I, it can be seen that an extremely small order quantity (in this case, one that represents considerably less than a one-week supply) would actually result in a slightly higher total inventory than that for the next larger order quantity. This is, of course, because the increase in reserve stock due to the additional exposures more than offsets the decrease in the average lot-size inventory for the smaller order quantity.

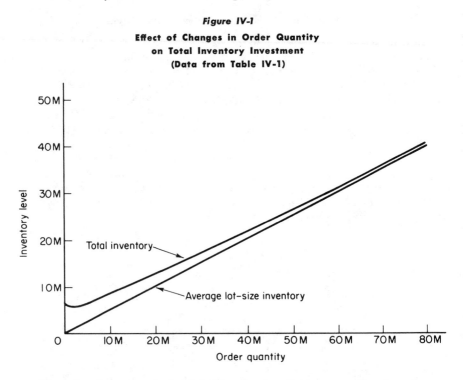

Figure IV-1

**Effect of Changes in Order Quantity
on Total Inventory Investment
(Data from Table IV-1)**

When lot-sizes are calculated independently of reserve stocks, there is no assurance that the total inventory that results will necessarily be the lowest inventory for the specified level of service. Frequently, a slightly larger lot-size will result in a lower total inventory because reserve stock requirements will be reduced. Without using fairly complex mathematical approaches, the best technique is an iterative trial and error approach.

In practice, so many other factors can affect inventory investment that this effect is of little importance. The student should be aware of it and the practitioner should consider iterative calculations only on the very high value items, where the inventory savings would justify the additional computations.

Appendix V

Derivation of LIMIT mathematical formulas

This Appendix contains the derivation of the LIMIT formulas to adjust economical ordering quantities to conform to restrictions on setup (which may be expressed in hours or dollars) for a family of items manufactured on a common group of facilities.

LIMIT Formulas:

The following symbols are used—with lower case letters applying to individual items and capital letters to totals—for all items in any group:

a, A = annual usage, dollars
q, Q = Economical ordering quantity, dollars
s, S = setup or procurement cost, dollars
I = inventory carrying cost fraction
h, H = setup or ordering time, hours
c = setup or ordering cost, per hour

Subscripts 1, 2, 3, ... n are used to designate symbols applied to individual items. The setup cost, c, and the inventory carrying cost fraction, I, are assumed constant for all items and hence carry no subscripts.

The economical ordering quantity is given by the basic equation:

$$q = \sqrt{2as/I} \qquad (1)$$

The number of orders needed per year for each item to produce the annual total demand is:

$$n = \frac{a}{q} \qquad (2)$$

Each item will require h setup hours at c dollars per hour, so that the total annual setup cost for each item is:

$$nhc = \frac{ahc}{q} \qquad (3)$$

For an inventory of n items, the total annual cost of setup will be:

$$S = \left(\frac{a_1 h_1 c}{q_1}\right) + \left(\frac{a_2 h_2 c}{q_2}\right) + \cdots + \left(\frac{a_n h_n c}{q_n}\right) \qquad (4)$$

Equation (1) can also be written:

$$q = \frac{\sqrt{2as}}{\sqrt{I}} \qquad (5)$$

Substituting equation (5) in equation (4) for each item:

$$S = \frac{c\sqrt{I}\,a_1 h_1}{\sqrt{2a_1 s_1}} + \frac{c\sqrt{I}\,a_2 h_2}{\sqrt{2a_2 s_2}} + \cdots + \frac{c\sqrt{I}\,a_n h_n}{\sqrt{2a_n s_n}} \qquad (6)$$

A basic assumption of this derivation is that I, the inventory carrying charge, is equal for all items in the group. Also, c, the cost of a setup hour, is assumed equal for the group of items. Equation (6) can then be rearranged:

$$S = c\sqrt{I}\left[\left(\frac{a_1 h_1}{\sqrt{2a_1 s_1}}\right) + \left(\frac{a_2 h_2}{\sqrt{2a_2 s_2}}\right) + \cdots + \left(\frac{a_n h_n}{\sqrt{2a_n s_n}}\right)\right] \tag{7}$$

Squaring both sides:

$$S^2 = c^2 I\left[\left(\frac{a_1 h_1}{\sqrt{2a_1 s_1}}\right) + \left(\frac{a_2 h_2}{\sqrt{2a_2 s_2}}\right) + \cdots + \left(\frac{a_n h_n}{\sqrt{2a_n s_n}}\right)\right]^2 \tag{8}$$

Solving for I:

$$I = \frac{S^2}{c^2}\left[\frac{1}{(a_1 h_1/\sqrt{2a_1 s_1}) + (a_2 h_2/\sqrt{2a_2 s_2}) + \cdots + (a_n h_n/\sqrt{2a_n s_n})}\right]^2 \tag{9}$$

The total annual setup hours, H, will be equal to the total annual setup cost, S, divided by the cost per hour, c, or:

$$H = \frac{S}{c} \tag{10}$$

Substituting equation (10) in equation (9):

$$I = H^2\left[\frac{1}{(a_1 h_1/\sqrt{2a_1 s_1}) + (a_2 h_2/\sqrt{2a_2 s_2}) + \cdots + (a_n h_n/\sqrt{2a_n s_n})}\right]^2 \tag{11}$$

For simplification, let the quantity in brackets equal T, so that:

$$T = \frac{1}{(a_1 h_1/\sqrt{2a_1 s_1}) + (a_2 h_2/\sqrt{2a_2 s_2}) + \cdots + (a_n h_n/\sqrt{2a_n s_n})} \tag{12}$$

Note that T is constant for a group of items and is independent of I. Equation (11) then becomes:

$$I = H^2 T^2 \tag{13}$$

If the individual item lot sizes, q, are calculated for a family of n items, using the best estimates available for the cost factors (S_n, c and I), a corresponding value of total setup hours, H, for the group can be obtained from Equations (4) and (10). This can be repeated for different values of I.

Each value of I will yield one value of H. Let subscripts a, b, c, ..., etc., designate corresponding values of I and H, and from equation (13):

$$I_a = H_a^2 T^2 \qquad I_b = H_b^2 T^2$$

The total setup hours, H_a, resulting from EOQ's calculated in the usual manner (using estimated costs) may be impractical to attain immediately, or beyond the capacity of the manufacturing facilities. This total of setup hours can be adjusted to any predetermined desired value by determining the proper value of I to use in the individual EOQ calculations. This is found by taking the ratio of the two equations:

$$\frac{I_a}{I_b} = \frac{H_a^2 T^2}{H_b^2 T^2} = \left(\frac{H_a}{H_b}\right)^2 \tag{14}$$

or, solving for I_b, the desired value of the carrying cost:

$$I_b = I_a\left(\frac{H_b}{H_a}\right)^2 \tag{15}$$

Equation (15) gives the "apparent" value of I to use in equation (1) when calculating each item's EOQ so that the resulting total setup hours will equal the desired value H_b.

To simplify the calculations for a family of items and avoid recalculating the square roots for each item, note from equation (5) that:

$$\text{For } I_a, \quad q_{na} = \sqrt{\frac{2a_n s_n}{I_a}} \tag{16}$$

$$\text{and for } I_b, \quad q_{nb} = \sqrt{\frac{2a_n s_n}{I_b}} \tag{17}$$

Dividing equation (17) by (16):

$$\frac{q_{nb}}{q_{na}} = \sqrt{2a_n s_n/I_b} \div \sqrt{2a_n s_n/I_a}$$

or:

$$\frac{q_{nb}}{q_{na}} = \sqrt{2a_n s_n/I_b} \times \sqrt{I_a/2a_n s_n}$$

and:

$$q_{nb} = q_{na}(\sqrt{I_a/I_b}) \tag{18}$$

Equation (14) can be restated as:

$$\frac{H_a}{H_b} = \sqrt{I_a/I_b} = M \tag{19}$$

Therefore, individual item order quantities can be adjusted by the multiplier M (a constant for all items) calculated from equation (19) by:

$$q_{nb} = M \times q_{na} \tag{20}$$

Equation (20) will adjust individual item order quantities to give the least total inventory and hold the setup total for the family to any predetermined level H_b.

Appendix VI

Storeroom techniques

In many companies, the responsibility for storeroom control is assigned to the production and inventory control department. Even where it is not, the department has a vital interest in these functions. It is sound policy to have one manager responsible for operation of the storeroom and the accuracy of the inventory records used to control the storeroom.

One of the problems present in every storeroom is lack of space. When space is inexpensive and the design life of parts fairly long, each item in inventory can have space permanently assigned to it and storeroom personnel will not need a location index to find it. The maximum number of parts to be stored using any type of storage usually approximates the economic lot size plus two times the reserve stock. Reserve stock is intended to cover above-average demand, but it is reasonable to expect that demand will be below-average just as often. If normal reserve stock for an item is equal to 100 units then, on the average, there should be 100 units on hand when the new supply arrives. When demand has been lower than normal, there might be as many as 200 units still in the storage bins when the new lot arrives.

With each storage space assigned to a part, no advantage can be taken of bins or shelves that are empty or partially filled because the items normally stored in them are nearing the replenishment time. Storage space must be provided for the maximum expected quantity.

Because it does require more space, very few companies use a pure *reserved space* storage system. Even those that are theoretically using it find that many items of stock are actually juggled from one location to another as part of the normal operating procedure.

Another alternative is to have *random space* storage, where parts are assigned to available empty space when they reach the storeroom. This requires a location index telling the storeroom personnel which spaces are empty and available and where each item is stored. Random storage is more economical, since the total space required need handle only the average inventory on hand (approximately one-half the economic lot sizes plus the reserve stock). The clerical work of maintaining the locator file can be time-consuming if done manually, but it does lend itself to mechanized information control.

A compromise system frequently used with either reserved or random space storage is called *zone storage*. Using this approach, all related components (for example, all those that go into a particular assembly) are located in the same general zone within the storeroom. This reduces the amount of back-and-forth traveling by the material handlers in collecting related components.

Space requirements and the material handling effort in a storeroom can be greatly reduced by keeping working stocks of low-value items on the assembly floor and maintaining in the storeroom only the *minimum* or *order point quantities* equivalent to the maximum anticipated demand during lead time. When more low-value items are needed on the assembly floor, the required quantity is sent out and a replenishment lot is ordered at the same time.

Locator records often consist of a simple 3″ × 5″ card file, with a card for each item listing its bin location. In some systems, material handlers report where they put the material to a clerk who handles the locator file. In others, the space is preassigned and the material handler is dispatched from a central location and told where the material should go.

Locator files duplicate inventory records to the extent, at least, of part number and description and, at most, of "where-used" information and issues, receipts, and balance-on-hand quantities. They must also be referred to each time a receipt or issue of parts is handled. A question that must be decided in each company is whether the inventory records should be kept in the stockroom or in the inventory control office. They are generally more accurate and up-to-date if kept in the stockroom, where people find it easier to understand their function, to relate stockroom activity to the information on the records, and where mailing delays affecting requisitions can be eliminated. Unfortunately, this makes it difficult to get the information required to plan production, makes it harder for the supervisor of inventory control to review the records and it uses space for an office function in an area needed for physical storage. The ideal system would make it possible for both stockroom personnel and production and inventory control office personnel to have simultaneous access to the records. This is approached by modern computer and data collection systems.

The number of storerooms and their location should be of primary interest to production control. Whenever new storerooms are being considered, production control should be deeply involved in the question of whether there should be one storeroom or many, and should simulate the amount of activity in the storeroom—the number of withdrawals and receipts—to help in deciding on manload, layout and equipment needs. They should recognize that the needs for accurate storeroom control must be balanced against the extra material handling cost that can be easily generated by too-rigid a system.

One of the basic problems faced by production control managers in maintaining records that control storeroom inventories is that of assigning responsibility in the storeroom for record accuracy. Almost all but purely clerical errors in the inventory records can best be eliminated in the storeroom. There are many sources for these errors:

1. Extra material withdrawn from the storeroom to replace material that is lost, scrapped or, for other reasons, is not available on the assembly floor without making the necessary corrections in the records.

2. Withdrawal of material from the storeroom by unauthorized personnel— night-shift operators, department foreman, sales or service people, etc.— without informing the records. Some companies handle the night-shift problem by giving a watchman or guard a storeroom key and the responsibility of filling out the proper paperwork.

3. Direct delivery of urgently needed parts from manufacturing departments to assembly departments without going through inspection or the storeroom and having the proper paperwork made out. Handling this problem requires discipline and an understanding on the part of everyone

concerned of his responsibilities and of the benefits to be realized from maintaining accurate records. Rigid enforcement of material movement into storerooms will avoid this problem, but will add extra material handling cost and will delay the movement of urgent parts, so that it is rarely justified or enforceable. The combination of data collection terminals in fabrication departments informing computer-stored inventory records when work is completed permits developing a system that can determine whether or not there are any emergency requirements, deducting these from the records properly, and delivering the components directly to the area that requires them.

4. Misidentification of parts, particularly if the same part is stored in various stages of manufacturing which are not easily recognized. One solution to this is to have the order number and part number transmitted to the inventory records clerk so that he can verify the identification by referring to the original manufacturing or purchase order.

5. Inaccurate piece counts, compared with requisitioned quantities—caused by human error or deliberate delivery of shop box quantities which are different from the ordered amounts. This causes additional work because some components must be returned and put away again. The use of counting scales and standardized shop boxes helps to ease this problem, but the only real solution is good storehouse discipline.

6. Delayed flow of paperwork between material handling personnel and the inventory records, plus loss of some copies of important receipts or requisitions. One technique that can be of some assistance in being sure that all paperwork is getting into the inventory records is to have serially numbered forms for all documents that affect the inventory control records, so that missing documents can be traced.

Undoubtedly, most problems in controlling storeroom inventories can be traced to poor education and lax discipline. Personnel whose activities have the most effect on record accuracy frequently have a poor understanding of their duties or of the results from their failure to follow the proper procedure. Manufacturing, material handling and other shop people seem to have a disdain for paperwork that can only be overcome by training and enforcing the rules. The introduction of sophisticated computer systems can hardly be expected to generate real improvement until control of information flows at all levels has been attained.

Appendix VII

Physical inventory techniques

Many companies take an annual physical inventory which is intended to satisfy the auditors that the inventory records represent the value of this major asset accurately. Of more direct interest to production control is the use of the physical inventory data to correct any inaccuracies that may have occurred in their records during the year. The responsibility for taking physical inventory usually falls upon the production control manager—he should be sure that sound techniques are used to get the greatest benefits from the substantial costs incurred in such inventory-taking.

Taking an inventory is very much like painting; the results depend principally upon the effort put into preparation. Preparation for physical inventory involves four phases:

1. *Housekeeping*—getting materials arranged and located properly so that they can easily be inventoried.

2. *Identification*—the quality of the inventory depends on the accuracy of parts identification, and there are only a limited number of people who can identify them. All identification work should be completed prior to taking the physical counts.

3. *Instruction*—letting everyone know what to do in taking the inventory: which things are to be inventoried and which are not, the control disciplines that must be observed.

4. *Training*—actual training in counting and checking must be given to those people who will do the counting. Since physical inventory is usually taken on a yearly basis, even experienced personnel need to have their memories refreshed.

In taking the inventory, four basic steps are usually involved:

1. Count the goods and record the count on a ticket left on the material

2. Verify this count either by recounting or by sampling

3. List the inventory items in each department from the tickets

4. Adjust the inventory records for differences between record and physical quantities and dollars. Auditing recounts may be made of large discrepancies.

Production control cannot take a passive approach to the annual physical inventory, even if it is not directly assigned to them. Production control personnel should be active in organizing the inventory and supervising its taking. They should also be available to answer questions on procedure or identification during the actual inventory. Production control should also have checking teams available so that, as inventories are reported and posted against the records, obvious discrepancies can be checked immediately before production is resumed and recounts made impossible.

Some general pointers that will help make a successful annual physical inventory are:

1. Auditors will usually agree to physically inventory low-value items less frequently than once a year. Inventory records, if available, may be used. Many companies are determining by review of past data the value of low-value items as a percentage of other inventory totals, and using this percentage to calculate the low-value item inventory each year.

2. In choosing inventory teams consisting of inventory counters, checkers and an inventory writer, one individual should be able to identify material so that he can catch and correct misidentified items in the plant.

3. Serially numbered inventory identification tags provide a method of ensuring that all items counted have been accounted for in the records.

4. Prepunched tabulating cards can assist greatly in processing inventory data since they can have the correct item identification number, description, price, etc. punched into them from master records, eliminating handwriting and other human errors. The problems with prepunched cards are in determining how many of each card to prepare in advance for each item and in finding the correct card quickly while identifying material. If the number of prepunched cards is based on high-volume items, there will be far too many cards for most items, creating a very bulky file of cards to be searched. Preventing physical damage to cards (which makes them unfit for machine processing) is another serious problem. Nevertheless, the tremendous gains in increased accuracy and speed of processing make the use of prepunched cards a necessity for inventories of a large number of items.

5. The most important concern in reconciling inventory records with the physical inventory data is the establishment of cutoff dates, so that paperwork in the system is accounted for properly. An inventory of all parts on paper records, receiving reports, scrap tickets, requisitions, shipping orders, etc., is just as important as the physical inventory of the parts. Input and output papers should be posted properly to inventory records so that a valid comparison of record balances and physical counts is possible.

6. Production control records should be posted and verified during the inventory if possible, and always before physical inventory information is passed on to accounting. This permits rechecking physical counts and clearing up other questions immediately, so that the inventory data is purified and so that production can be resumed based on accurate records. It can be extremely helpful to have duplicate inventory information available so that both production control records and accounting records can be posted simultaneously.

One of the most helpful techniques to improve physical inventory-taking is a post-inventory review. This is usually the time when people are least inclined to even think about physical inventory, but this is the time when problems that occurred during physical inventory-taking are freshest in mind. If the people most directly involved are assembled in a post-mortem briefing, problems can be reviewed and specific program revisions can be developed for improving physical inventory-taking procedures for the coming year. This is also the time to determine which items should be written off the inventory records.

All companies, particularly fast-moving industries where obsolescence is a real problem, should have a policy for writing off unsaleable items so that their financial statements accurately reflect the value of materials in inventory.

There are many disadvantages in taking a yearly physical inventory, and many companies are getting away from this timehonored procedure. Taking a physical inventory usually involves shutting the plant down and losing production. The manpower and paperwork can be very expensive. Since it is usually done under pressure, there is much hurrying to complete the inventory and it is frequently done poorly. Under any circumstances, using a large number of people who are not used to the job of taking inventory almost always results in waste and errors. Not the least of the disadvantages of an annual physical inventory is that it results in correcting record errors only once a year for the great majority of items. Because of these disadvantages, many companies are turning to periodic cycle inventories.

Cycle counting involves having inventories on specific items taken at regular intervals throughout the year, so that records can be verified regularly rather than on an annual basis. Cycle inventory avoids the costly shutdown of production facilities and the high labor costs and overtime premiums that almost always result from the pressure to complete the annual physical inventory in minimum time. In addition, it can usually be handled by stockroom personnel during the offpeak hours, and these employees can be trained to be far more accurate counters than the factory personnel who only take an inventory once a year.

A cycle inventory system should be designed so that fast-moving items are counted more frequently. Some cycle inventory systems count items only when they are reordered. Since more popular items are reordered more frequently, they will be counted and verified more frequently. Other cycle inventory systems specify how many times each item must be counted, often calling for A items to be counted twice during the year, B items once, and C items every two years (for example).

A cycle inventory system may be based on a check of the quantity in the bins when a replenishment lot is received in the storeroom. This system also results in a greater number of inventory counts and verifications for the faster moving items. This technique is particularly practical since the quantity to be counted is a minimum—the clerk putting stock away is already at the bin and the inventory record clerk has the item card out for posting. In simple paperwork systems, it is sufficient to have the stockroom man write the inventory quantity on the bottom of the receiving document. The inventory clerk can then check that quantity against his records while he is entering the quantity received.

There are disadvantages to cycle counting as well as advantages. The problem of establishing paperwork cutoff dates is difficult enough for annual physical inventory, but it becomes extremely challenging to handle effectively for cycle counts to be made while normal factory activity is going on. Picking up the paperwork in the system so that the inventory can be properly reconciled to the records requires considerable ingenuity and discipline. The most serious disadvantage of the cycle count system is that it is usually done by regular stockroom personnel who normally have sufficient time to handle it. When activity in the factory picks up, however, there is always great reluctance to add more personnel in the stockroom. In order to give stockroom personnel more time during heavy activity periods, cycle counting is too often discontinued. More cycle count systems have failed for this reason than have successfully been continued, in spite of the obvious advantages of cycle counting. The best solution is a team of cycle counters permanently assigned to this work.

Annual physical inventories or cycle checks are not a substitute for good records and discipline in handling paperwork. Many companies recognize their failure to maintain accurate records because of the resulting problems generated in the plant (shortages, overstocks, etc.), but they often depend solely on the physical inventory to straighten out their records. Unless the failures that caused the records to go wrong are corrected, the records will be in error again and again.

Appendix VIII

Controlling branch warehouse inventories

The basis for successful branch warehouse inventory control:

Increasing competition to provide better service to customers has resulted in a growth in warehousing in recent years. Many large cities such as Atlanta, Chicago, Dallas, Los Angeles, New York and San Francisco have branch warehouses representing practically every major manufacturer in the country, and most of these warehouses are fairly new. They provide the customer with an extension of the factory in his own city, reducing delivery time to a minimum.

Unfortunately, many companies have been extremely disappointed with the results of their warehouse programs. Part of this disappointment has resulted from a lack of understanding of the fundamentals of inventory management. Managers have frequently been surprised to discover that the freight savings from carload and truckload *vs.* LCL (*less than full* carload) and LTL shipments are largely offset and often exceeded by the costs of running the warehouse and the added inventory required. This added inventory might well be justified to achieve the increase in customer service, but it has too often come as a distinct surprise to the managers concerned.

Figure VIII-1

**Warehouse Replenishment Transportation Inventory
Transit time 4 weeks**

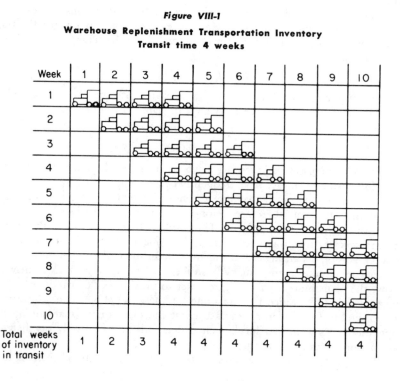

Week	1	2	3	4	5	6	7	8	9	10
1										
2										
3										
4										
5										
6										
7										
8										
9										
10										
Total weeks of inventory in transit	1	2	3	4	4	4	4	4	4	4

In Chapter 5, the problem of splitting inventory among several locations was discussed, and a general rule formulated that the total inventory level increases as inventories are divided. A manufacturer in the Chicago region who decided to set up branch warehouses in New York, Atlanta, Dallas and San Francisco would find that the total inventory required to maintain the same level of customer service would increase. With the total inventory now divided among a number of locations, the number of demands on individual locations of the inventory would be only a fraction of that on the original single location. Thus, there would be a higher degree of variability and, necessarily, more reserve stock required in total.

In addition to this higher reserve stock inventory, there is also a *transportation inventory* that must be maintained—material in transit to the warehouses. Before the warehouses existed, this inventory belonged to the customer—since the shipment was en route to him—but now the transportation inventory belongs to the company.

Figure VIII-1 shows the amount of transportation inventory that would result from weekly shipments with a transit time of four weeks. On the first week, a truckload of material is dispatched to the warehouse; on the second week, another truckload is dispatched—but the first truckload has not yet arrived. By the third week, there are three truckloads of material in transit and, by the fourth week, the system stabilizes with four truckloads of inventory in transit.

Thus, when warehouse inventories are maintained at constant levels with deliveries replacing shipments, the simple rule can be applied that the transit inventory will be equal to the transit interval times the selling rate. Written as an equation:

$$I_t = T \times R$$

For example, a warehouse with a 3-week transit time and average sales of $30,000 per week would have an average in-transit inventory of:

$$I_t = 3 \times 30,000$$
$$I_t = \$90,000$$

Even if increases in inventory have been expected, results in the accompanying customer service have frequently been disappointing. Many companies have taken the approach that the warehouse inventories are part of the distribution system and, therefore, belong either to a separate distribution department or to the sales department. The result is that the responsibility for balancing service, inventory and efficient plant operation is no longer assumed by one person or department, and much wasteful internal competition develops. Instead of having a great many customer orders coming in at a fairly even flow, the plant finds itself trying to react to very erratic demands from a few large warehouses. Since the personnel at these warehouses feel little or no responsibility for inventory levels back at the plant or for maintaining plant operations at an efficient level, their orders will be based only on their own evaluation of future demand.

The result will almost always be to amplify the effects of changes in the rate of actual customer demand on the production level. This adds very drastically to the costs of operating the manufacturing facilities, because of the frequent and substantial changes in production rates, and, for customer service, the results are frequently just the opposite of what the sales or distribution people intended. When each warehouse controls its own inventories, it is almost certain that production levels cannot be controlled to respond properly, and that the inventory will not be distributed efficiently.

These facts can be verified by using the following approach: warehouse demand on the factory can be compared with actual customer demand on the warehouses to see how much the warehouse demand amplifies customer demand. Then, all warehouse inventories can be checked for the items that are currently out of stock at the factory. It will almost always be found that some warehouses have a very good supply of these items. In addition, there will be some items on order with the factory that would not have to be manufactured at all if the inventory were properly distributed. This not only means that unnecessary inventory is being produced, it also means that *production capacity vitally needed to manufacture out-of-stock items is being used to produce items that are not needed.*

The warehouse problem is one of the best examples of what the language of operations research calls "suboptimization." Suboptimization simply means that different groups within the company pursue their own limited objectives rather than the overall company goals. When each warehouse is responsible only for its own inventory, the warehouse manager's chief concern is to fulfill his imagined needs without regard to the effects his demands will have on the other warehouses or the main plant. He also feels no responsibility for helping the plant maintain operating efficiency. The authors know of instances where branch warehouses had available space, but were reducing inventory in order to meet their own budget goals—while the main plant, keeping production rates up in order to retain its hard core of trained manufacturing personnel, was renting public warehouse space to hold the material the warehouses weren't ordering. This is certainly suboptimization at its worst.

This approach is usually defended by saying that the warehouse "buys" its inventory from the plant and that the warehouses are "the plant's best customers." Unfortunately, very few companies would be in business very long if their "best customers" scheduled their manufacturing operations. This approach makes as much sense as eliminating the production control department and just having the shipping room foreman (as the plant's "best customer") walk into the factory once a week and tell them what he needs.

The distribution of warehouse inventory is therefore part of the responsibility of managing all the inventory that results from manufacturing. The production control manager or materials manager should assume the responsibility for distributing inventories to the warehouses and maintaining service at these warehouses. This is just a further extension of his responsibility for balancing the three conflicting objectives. He must, for example, plan on any increase in warehouse inventory levels in order to plan for the manufacturing of this inventory. He must likewise plan for any decrease in inventory levels at the warehouses when he is making his plant production plan. Once these production levels have been set, it is necessary to have information on the inventory status of individual items fed back from the warehouses so that these items can be replenished as needed.

Establishing warehouse inventory control

The successful control of warehouse inventories involves the following steps:

1. Integrate the responsibility for warehouse inventories under the same executive who is responsible for the inventories at the main plant and make sure that the management of these inventories also includes maintaining customer service and plant operating efficiency to avoid suboptimization.
2. Establish an economical replenishment period for sending shipments to each warehouse.
3. Set the warehouse inventory level and allow for any increases or decreases required when planning the production level at the plant.
4. Develop inventory targets for each specific item in the inventory.
5. Replenish the warehouse inventory as it is sold, taking into consideration efficient shipping quantities and minimum package quantities. This technique involves replacing approximately the same quantity of each item that was sold during the replenishment period—it is called the *sales replacement* technique. It ensures that the level of warehouse inventories will not change, but that the mix will respond to sales requirements.

Integrating warehouse inventory control

The problems involved in setting up an integrated warehouse inventory control system are usually more political and educational than technical. If the branch warehouse inventories come under the jurisdiction of a sales, marketing or distribution function, they will usually argue vigorously against losing this control by stating:

> 1. *"Home office people are not close enough to the specialized needs of our region."* While usually grossly exaggerated, this problem is a real one and underscores the need for the branch warehouse personnel to be educated to assume their responsibility for notifying the central inventory control function of special local situations.
>
> 2. *"Red tape will keep us from servicing special requirements quickly."* This potential problem can be avoided by giving the local branch manager the authority to order any extra quantity of a standard item or any nonwarehouse stock item with the understanding that as long as such items are handled on an exception basis, the rule will be to "ship first and ask questions later."

3. *"The home office people will not give us a fair share of short supply items."* With most decentralized systems, the orders from branch warehouses are often very difficult to evaluate in trying to allocate scarce items, and the personnel at the main plant may have developed the attitude (usually partly justified) that the "warehouses are ordering beyond their needs and taking stock needed for main plant customers." The challenge then is to develop an effective information system that will make it possible to distribute scarce items equitably among all customers served by the main plant and the warehouses and to hold the central inventory control personnel responsible for customer service at the branch warehouses as well as the main shipping warehouse. Distributing copies of main plant stock status reports to the branch warehouses will also help by letting them see that scarce items are being distributed equitably.

The feedback of information from the branch warehouses can take many forms:

1. Branch warehouse sends in a copy of customer order (by mail, teletype, etc.,) and it is posted against an inventory record for this warehouse maintained manually or by data-processing equipment.

2. Branch warehouse uses punched card output order processing equipment, and data are transmitted by data-phone, wired, or mailed back to main office.

3. A summary of branch warehouse sales activity is sent in periodically to coincide with the shipping schedule. This summary can be manual, punched card form, paper tape, etc.

One of the most effective techniques (though not always the most economical) is to continue to maintain inventory records in the branch warehouses and have them report periodically on the stock status of all items that are active during the review period. This approach has the advantage of keeping the responsibility for the records within the branches. It eliminates discussion about whether or not the records are correct, and it gives the branch warehouse manager up-to-date stock status information with which to answer customer inquiries.

The rapid progress that has been made in reducing data transmission costs has made it practical to send information from the branches to the central control center daily or even more often. A fairly standard approach is to type the orders at the branches on a machine that generates a card output, and then load these cards into a terminal for transmission by telephone line (usually by having the control center call in, using a wide area telephone service—WATS—line). The unattended terminal starts transmitting cards as soon as it receives the call, and records are immediately updated at the central inventory. Whatever techniques are used, however, the key to success will always be in developing good working relationships between the main plant and the branch warehouses.

Establishing an economical replenishment period

One of the most important considerations in setting up a warehouse control system is the replenishment period. Trucking companies, railroads and even steamship lines have freight rate schedules based upon the amount of freight included in each shipment. Consequently, any warehouse replenishment system must plan to include in each shipment sufficient quantity to obtain the lowest possible freight rate that is consistent with maintaining reasonable inventory investment and good customer service.

Figure VIII-2 shows the type of basic calculation involved in determining an economic warehouse replenishment period, assuming some of each item is handled in each shipment. In this example, the annual forecast is $1,375,000 worth of material to be shipped to this particular warehouse. There is a cost associated with picking an item off the shelf in the storeroom at the main plant and putting it away on the shelf in the warehouse. This cost is fairly constant for a wide range of quantity involved since it requires a trip to the location where the item is stored, one shipping document, etc. It is similar to the setup cost that must be considered in calculating economic lot-sizes.

The average cycle inventory is also similar to the average cycle inventory that results from an economic lot-size. If a shipping quantity of $27,500 were chosen, the order cost would be $2,000 (50 shipments times $40 picking cost) and the average cycle inventory (that portion of the inventory that results from the lot-size—which can never be smaller than the usage during the replenishment period) would be one-half of the shipping quantity, or $13,750.

Consequently, the costs can be calculated for any proposed shipping frequency by considering:

1. The order cost (order frequency times fixed order picking and put-away cost).
2. The inventory carrying cost (one-half the shipping quantity plus the reserve stock, times the inventory carrying cost expressed as a percentage).
3. The annual freight cost (which will diminish as larger shipments are made).
4. The change in reserve stock required as total lead time changes due to the change in shipping interval.

In this particular example, the lowest total cost would result when a shipping schedule was set up so that the warehouse was replenished every third week.

Figure VIII-2
Economic Warehouse Replenishment Period

Inventory carrying cost = 10%
Annual shipments forecast = $1,375,000
Fixed order picking and put-away cost = $40

Shipping frequency	Order frequency	Order cost	Shipping quantity	Average cycle inv.	Average* reserve stock inv.	Total average inv.	Inv. carrying cost	Annual freight cost	Total cost
Every week	50/yr	$2000	$27,500	$13,750	$50,000	$63,750	$6375	$25,000	$33,375
Every 2nd week	25/yr	$1000	$55,000	$27,500	$58,500	$86,000	$8600	$22,000	$31,600
Every 3rd week	17/yr	$680	$81,000	$40,500	$66,500	$107,000	$10,700	$20,000	$31,380
Every 4th week	13/yr	$520	$106,000	$53,000	$74,000	$127,000	$12,700	$19,000	$32,220

*Assuming that a three-week replenishment lead time plus 1-week review period (4-week total lead time) requires $50,000 reserve stock inventory and using Table in Fig. 5-9, to estimate added reserve required as longer replenishment periods increase total lead time.

409

As stated earlier, this example assumes that each item on which there was sales activity is replenished in the following shipment and that there is a fairly uniform number of items in each shipment, so that a constant order cost is valid.

Economies can be realized by shipping low-value items less frequently in larger quantities. In such a system, "C" items could be replenished in every third or fourth shipment, requiring less handling at both ends and resulting in fewer items in each shipment.

The use of computer techniques makes it possible to accumulate warehouse requirements until a shipment totaling a truckload is required, and then to dispatch this to the warehouse. In practice, many companies prefer to make their shipments on a regular schedule, so that the storeroom, shipping room and warehouse can each schedule their work on an orderly basis, and so that the warehouse will know when to expect shipments and advise customers of deliveries. This requires adjusting each total shipping quantity to meet a predetermined minimum (carload, truckload, etc.) quantity. Techniques for meeting this requirement are discussed in the following sections.

Setting branch warehouse inventory levels

The same principle of setting the level of inventory and selecting the mix according to the latest customer demand applies to branch warehouse inventory levels as well as to main plant inventory levels. Control of individual items in inventory is usually based on target inventory levels. The construction of these targets is discussed in detail in Chapter 5 (*Periodic review systems*), and further specific applications to branch warehouse inventory control are discussed below. The base inventory level for a branch warehouse is the same as that for a main plant finished goods inventory—equal to approximately one-half the sum of the order quantities plus the reserve stocks for all items (not counting, of course, the material in transit to the warehouse).

Branch warehouse total inventory levels can then be planned using the same general format as the production plan.[1] *Production,* however, will now be the amount shipped from the main plant, while *sales* are, of course, the shipments to (or, preferably, orders received from) customers. The reason for making out a warehouse inventory plan is to make sure that the production plans at the factory include any increases or decreases in the total warehouse inventories so that the effects of these fluctuations can be reflected in the total production level.

In practice, for most fairly stable product lines, it is not necessary to make a detailed branch warehouse inventory plan, but it is imperative that main plant production planning include changes in the warehouse inventory levels. These changes can usually be kept to a minimum and, for most stable product lines, the only significant build-up in the branch warehouse inventory would be to anticipate the annual plant vacation shutdown or to prepare for a major sales promotion effort. Changes in the level of inventory for individual items

---

[1] See Chapters 7 and 8.

would normally be accounted for as target inventory levels for each item are recalculated.

Establishing target inventory levels

The target inventory level for each stock item is made up of three elements:

1. Anticipated demand during the **lead time**
2. Anticipated demand during the **review period**
3. **Reserve stock**

The construction of a simple target inventory level was discussed in detail in Chapter 5. Its use for warehouses is analyzed below.

Lead time

The lead time for a branch warehouse consists of the total elapsed time from the moment that it is decided to place a stock replenishment order on the main plant until the stock has been received at the branch warehouse and put away in the bins and is once again available to the customers. The total replenishment cycle usually includes:

1. Time for making up, transmitting and processing the stock replenishment order.
2. Time for picking and packing the replenishment order at the main plant.
3. Transit time from the main plant to the branch warehouse.
4. Put-away time at the branch warehouse.

Total replenishment lead time is worth investigating in some detail, to find out what it is (as opposed to what some people think it should be). Information should also be gathered on the dependability of replenishment lead time. This is an area that normally receives very little consideration. It is not unusual for shipping rooms to use branch warehouse replenishment orders as fill-in work around shipments to regular customers. The variability in replenishment lead time and the total replenishment lead time should be reduced to the lowest possible levels, because longer and more variable lead times require greater reserve stock (since forecast reliability decreases as the forecast period is extended).

If, for example, it is felt that the shipping room should handle branch warehouse replenishment orders on a fill-in basis, then the total extra warehouse inventory (over that required to maintain customer service) caused by the resulting increase in variability in lead time should be spelled out clearly by production and inventory control personnel so that management is aware of the effects of this decision.

Review period

For all practical purposes, the length of the review period is the same as that of the warehouse replenishment period and, as the former is increased, the total replenishment lead time is increased by the same amount. In determining an economical replenishment period (as described in an earlier section of this Appendix) it will be found that reserve stock requirements increase very substantially as the replenishment period is increased.

It might be argued (from a purely theoretical point of view) that as the review cycle increases, the order quantities become larger—thus giving fewer exposures to stockout and requiring less reserve stock (refer to Chapter 5 for the concept of *exposures*). There is no doubt that the minimum order quantities become larger as the replenishment period increases. For example, if the replenishment period were increased from one to three weeks, the smallest reasonable order quantity would be equivalent to a three-week supply (the order quantity in a periodic review system is equivalent to the usage during the review period). In the case of a periodically-replenished inventory, however, this is much more a theoretical than an actual consideration.

In Chapter 5, while discussing statistical measures of customer service, it was pointed out that counting stockouts alone neglects the *duration* of a stockout. In a continuous review system, the length of time that an item is out of stock is not likely to change as the order quantities are increased, so that measuring service by the number of stockouts becomes an effective means of measuring relative performance. This is not true, however, in a periodic review system, since lengthening the replenishment period not only makes the lot sizes larger but also increases the potential duration of any stockout that occurs, and a comparable measure of service no longer exists.

In practice, it is best to ignore the theoretical effect of the increased lot sizes and reduced exposure to stockout that occurs when the replenishment period is increased. Service from the customers' point of view will be poorer because it will take longer to correct an out-of-stock situation with more time between factory shipments.

Reserve stock

Reserve stock for individual items can be calculated using the same statistical techniques described in Chapter 5. With a computer, periodic updating of reserves is thoroughly practical. In many applications (particularly since warehouse inventory control can usually be improved drastically by integrating it with factory control) it is often worthwhile to start out with some fairly simple reserve stock calculations.

These can be handled by sampling some representative items from each of the product groups, picking samples of "A" items, "B" items, and "C" items. Order quantities frequently work out to be nearly equal and may then be standardized in terms of length of supply for all "A" items, all "B" items and all "C" items. For example, in a warehouse inventory that was being replenished every second week, it might be decided to order up to the target inventory level for any "A" or "B" item that was below target and to order any "C" item that was far enough below the target to be shipped in an economical quantity (usually a unit package). Since these order quantities are often similar (with a tendency for the "C" items to have the largest order quantities and the "A" items to have the smallest order quantities) it is sometimes satisfactory as a starting method without computing equipment, to set reserve stocks by category. This might involve, for example, having a three-week reserve stock on all "A" items, four-week on "B" and five-week on "C" items, since the lower-volume items tend to have a greater variation in demand.

In many cases, it actually turns out to be fairly satisfactory to maintain the same level of reserve stock for all classes of items (since the "A" items, while having a more stable demand, also have a higher service requirement). Nevertheless, this conclusion should not be drawn automatically. Even where only manual techniques are available, an analysis of a sample of the inventory items should be made and a series of simple rules should be established for rationally determining reserve stocks. Once the system is operative, further improvements can usually be made by doing a weekly or monthly statistical analysis of incoming business by item, recalculating the standard deviation of forecast error and computing the reserve stock requirements for each item according to this error.

Additional reserve stocks may be required if shipping lead times are unpredictable or if the shipping quantity is limited. For example, a company that uses its own truck to ship to its branch warehouses would normally ship only as much as that truck could hold, so as to avoid using more expensive common carriers for small overages. If the total sales ran higher than anticipated for a number of weeks, there would be a chance of seriously jeopardizing customer service if only one truckload could be shipped during each replenishment period. This can be avoided by scheduling an extra common carrier shipment, by sending an extra shipment via the company truck between regular replenishment periods, or by carrying extra stabilization stock in the warehouse such as would be carried to protect against variations in the total level of incoming business in conjunction with the production plan (see Chapter 8).

Order quantities in a warehouse replenishment system are basically a function of the replenishment period. Standard economic order quantity calculations should almost never be used for a branch warehouse. When the replenishment period has been determined, the minimum order quantity which will probably be used on the majority of items in inventory is automatically determined, since the order quantity can never be less than the average demand during the review period in a periodic review system. Moreover, the items being ordered from the main plant are usually in inventory, all items are included in one order, and the ordering costs are usually very small. There will be no setup cost in the factory directly related to the number of warehouse replenishment orders, the total cost for picking an order will usually vary little with reasonably small changes in the number of pieces of items to be picked, and the cost of putting items away in the warehouse varies little with the number of pieces of each item.

In general, then, the order quantity for all "A" items is usually made equivalent to the demand during the review period, and each "A" item is simply ordered up to the target level and replenished in each shipment made to the warehouse. The "C" items, which also tend to be the slow-moving items, are usually replenished only in reasonable minimum shipping quantities (such as carton quantities). "B" items are frequently treated like "A" items, or some minimum ordering quantity is set for them in order to reduce the number of items that are picked each week. For example, it might be reasonable to set the minimum ordering quantity for a "B" item at a four-week supply when the normal replenishment period is two weeks. This would mean then that "A" items were picked in the main plant warehouse to go with every shipment, that half of the "B" items would normally be picked one time and half the other, and that "C" items would be picked only when it was possible to ship a minimum economical shipping quantity.

While these are broad, common sense rules for determining order quantities in a branch warehouse replenishment operation, there are occasional freight and handling economies available through shipping in pallet loads or other large unit loads which are practical only for the fast moving items and which increase inventories. It is important, when studying such alternatives, for the production and inventory control manager to be capable of showing the added inventory investment that will be required, so that the actual economies involved in shipping in larger quantities can be evaluated objectively.

The calculation of the target inventory for an individual inventory item is shown below:

$$T = DLT + DRP + R$$

Where: T = Target Order Level
DLT = Demand during replenishment lead time
DRP = Demand during review period
R = Reserve Stock

Data for item #114 are:
Lead time = 2 weeks
Review period = 1 week
Reserve = 1.5 weeks
Forecast = 80 units per week
$T = 160 + 80 + 120 = 360$ units

Thus, whenever a replenishment order is being prepared and the inventory for Item #114 is under 360 units, the difference between the actual inventory level and the target will be ordered. The order quantity in a simple periodic review system is equal to the demand during the review period so the *average* order quantity for Item #114 would be 80 units if actual incoming orders were as forecast.

There are circumstances where it is desirable to have a minimum order quantity. If Item #114 were shipped only in cartons of 144 units each, the target inventory would then be calculated:

$$T = DLT + OQ + R$$

Where: OQ = minimum ordering quantity (greater than DRP)
$T = 160 + 144 + 120 = 424$ units

This formula simply reflects the fact that when the minimum order quantity is greater than the demand during review period, the target inventory must be adjusted upward to reflect this. The new order quantity should be as close to a multiple of the usage during the replenishment period as possible so that, on the average, the inventory for this item would be replenished every second, third, or fourth shipment to the warehouse.

The base inventory level for a branch warehouse can be calculated like any other base inventory level and, on the average, will be equal to the sum of one-half the order quantities plus the reserve stocks for all items. If the accounting records charge in-transit inventory to the branch warehouses, these will also have to be added into the base inventory levels.

The sales replacement concept

The basic idea in setting up a warehouse replenishment system is to set the overall levels of inventory and keep them fairly constant and to replace what has been sold. This concept, called *sales replacement,* is utilized in practically every successful warehouse inventory replenishment system and usually takes the following form:

1. Target inventory levels are set for each item.
2. These target inventory levels determine the base inventory level total for the branch warehouse under consideration.
3. Periodically (usually coinciding with the replenishment cycle, although sometimes more frequently), either sales during the past replenishment period or the current inventory situation for each item is reported back to the main plant, all items are reordered up to their target inventory level and shipped to the branch warehouse.

The principal advantage of the sales replacement technique is that it stabilizes warehouse demand and keeps it from amplifying customer demand while, at the same time, it relays the actual requirements and the latest activity at the warehouse, so that this can be fed into the main plant production control system.

Some companies still use the cycle review system. Once every month or two, a physical inventory is taken and replacement stocks are then reordered from the main plant. This type of inventory replenishment system requires very high inventories and usually results in very poor service since it is slow to respond to change.

Branch warehouse stock status reports

Branch warehouse stock status reports can range from very simple manual reports to fairly sophisticated reports turned out on data-processing equipment. Figure VIII-3 shows a basic branch warehouse stock status report. If the target inventory for each item on this report were equal to a six-week's supply, the

Figure VIII-3
Branch Warehouse Stock Status Report
(All figures in units)

					Week #22
Item	Weekly average (W. A.)	Minimum order quantity	On hand (O. H.)	In transit (I. T.)	On order with main plant (O. O.)
#112	200	50	740	200	---
#114	80	10	210	80	180
#116	20	--	90	20	---
#118	90	10	240	100	100
#120	300	50	670	700	200
#124	100	10	250	150	100
#126	150	10	590	100	---
#130	70	10	430	---	---
Totals	1010		3220	1350	580

$$S.Q. = \text{Weekly shipping quantity} = 1000 \text{ units}$$

$$\text{Total available} = (O.H. + I.T. + O.O. + S.Q.) \div W.A.$$

$$= \frac{3220 + 1350 + 580 + 1000}{1010}$$

$$= \frac{6150}{1010}$$

$$= 6.1 \text{ weeks supply}$$

weekly averages could merely be extended by 6 to establish the individual target levels.

For the sake of this example, however, it has been assumed that there is a further complication. In this particular case, a company truck is used to make regular shipments to the branch warehouse, but can hold only approximately 1000 units (this assumes that 1000 units usually comprise about the same volume and weight, which is often true for product families). Because of this limitation, each new order should total approximately 1000 units. The formula for determining the total target level in this case is shown on the bottom of Fig. VIII-3. This formula calculates the total weeks of supply of all inventories available including *on hand, in transit, on order,* and including the *next complete shipment.*

The determination of specific order quantities for each item involves first setting up a *target level,* which should be the same number of weeks of supply as calculated for all items. Thus, all items would run out of stock simultaneously if not replenished, and a balanced inventory results. Figure VIII-4 shows target level inventories for each item and Fig. VIII-5 shows the new order

Figure VIII-4

Branch Warehouse Stock Status Report with Target Level

(All figures in units)

						Week #22
Item	Weekly average (W.A.)	Minimum order quantity	On hand (O.H.)	In transit (I.T.)	On order with main plant (O.O.)	Target level
#112	200	50	740	200	---	1220
#114	80	10	210	80	180	490
#116	20	--	90	20	---	120
#118	90	10	240	100	100	550
#120	300	50	670	700	200	1830
#124	100	10	250	150	100	610
#126	150	10	590	100	---	910
#130	70	10	430	---	---	430
Totals 1010			3220	1350	580	6160

Figure VIII-5

Branch Warehouse Stock Status Report with New Order Quantities

(All figures in units)

						Week #22	
Item	Weekly average (W.A.)	Minimum order quantity	On hand (O.H.)	In transit (I.T.)	On order with main plant (O.O.)	Target level	New order
#112	200	50	740	200	---	1220	280
#114	80	10	210	80	180	490	20
#116	20	--	90	20	---	120	10
#118	90	10	240	100	100	550	110
#120	300	50	670	700	200	1830	260
#124	100	10	250	150	100	610	110
#126	150	10	590	100	---	910	220
#130	70	10	430	---	---	430	---
Totals 1010			3220	1350	580	6160	1010

for each, calculated by subtracting the *on hand, in transit* and *on order* figures from the target level. Note that the total of new orders is approximately 1000 units.

One of the important points to keep in mind if the total shipping quantity is limited is that the total inventory on hand will decrease if total sales exceed this shipping quantity. The ordering technique illustrated by Figs. VIII-3, VIII-4 and VIII-5 will only allocate this shipping quantity, and will not protect against loss of customer service. It is necessary to carry some total reserve stock to guard against variations in demand when shipping restrictions exist. This situation was discussed in this Appendix in the section titled *Establishing target inventory levels.*

There are many other variations possible in branch warehouse stock status reports. One of the simplest approaches is to set an ordering bogey, usually in the form of a minimum weight which will meet an economical shipping quantity using common carriers. An order clerk then reviews the warehouse stock status of all items, orders those he thinks are required, and then compares the shipping weight of this order with the total shipping weight bogey. If he has not ordered enough, he then adds a few items of which there is an adequate supply at the main plant and which would have to be ordered for the branch warehouse within a week or two anyway.

Most companies find that for many product families, average weights are satisfactory for such calculations. When a computer is available, of course, it is quite reasonable to calculate the total from the actual weight of each item on the proposed order. In fact, a computer can be programmed to then reexamine the items in stock and order those that are closest to the target level in any week when the total weight is not reached with the regular order. A computer can also be used to calculate exponential smoothing forecasts for each item, readjust targets, calculate statistical reserve stocks to establish more accurate target levels and set up a replenishment system that will be practically automatic except, of course, for special programs or unusual conditions.

Practical considerations

The following suggestions can help the practitioner solve his warehousing problems:

1. When installing a computer system, particularly one with automatic replenishment, it is important to assign operating responsibility to one person other than the systems engineer. There is a strong temptation for everyone involved to take a "hands-off" approach to the system. Consequently, inaccurate input or circumstances which were unforeseen when the computer system was programmed pass uncorrected until a disaster of major proportions occurs, and the problems are then blamed on the computer system.

2. It is wise not to develop too-sophisticated a branch warehouse replenishment system at first. The important point in developing any system is to improve upon the present situation in the first steps, to do this as quickly as possible, and then to refine the system. Inventory replenishment systems

are frequently so crude that they can be improved substantially with very little sophistication. The practitioner will usually find that he can improve upon his present system readily without starting with a complex set of new techniques.

3. The most serious problem of all will be developing coordination between the main plant and the branch warehouses—this will be a difficult concept to sell. It is important not to oversell it, since even this most necessary step will not cure all of the problems existing in any normal inventory control system. Present performance should be measured—the inventory turnover and the customer service being given at each branch warehouse with the present system—and then the improvement resulting from system changes can be shown clearly. Many of the personnel involved, particularly those not in favor of an integrated warehouse inventory replenishment system, will tend to remember the "good old days" when there was never anything out of stock and everything worked out beautifully! Performance measures provide objective comparisons and goals for everyone.

4. When developing good communications between the main plant and the branch warehouse after ordering targets have been calculated at the main plant, even if done using data-processing equipment, the individual targets should be reviewed by the branch warehouse manager so that he can feel he has had a part in establishing them and, equally important, so that he can adjust the targets for any special circumstances in his territory.

5. The ideal branch warehouse stock status report should be made at the main plant using inventory figures submitted by the branch warehouses and should show on it the inventory stock status for the main plant as well as the branch warehouse. This enables the order clerk to do an effective job of allocating items that are in scarce supply and will also be of great help when he is ordering to a minimum shipping weight bogey. For example, since he can tell which items are and which are not available at the main plant, he is not likely to include on his order critical items that cannot be shipped and which, therefore, would cause his total order to fall below the weight bogey. A copy of this stock status report sent to the branch warehouse will show the branch warehouse manager the details of the order that will be shipped to him subsequently. It will also show him the stock condition at the main plant, to demonstrate that he is getting his fair share of the available inventory. This will help tremendously in developing confidence and a better working relationship between the branch warehouse manager and the main plant.

6. A regular shipping schedule for the branch warehouses (particularly if there are many of them) should be established for the main plant shipping room, and their performance in meeting this shipping schedule as well as shipping customer orders should be measured.

7. One of the frequent complaints heard from production and inventory control people is that things are beyond their control. Management decisions, for example, are made to increase the number of branch warehouses

or to use a cheaper method of shipping that will increase the shipping lead time or will require shipping to the branches at less frequent intervals. Management personnel making this type of decision should be given information as to the effects likely to occur (increased inventory or poorer customer service that will completely or partially offset the advantages of reduced costs or increased sales). Far from being beyond the control of the production and inventory control man, it is his responsibility to assist in formulating these decisions.

In the future, there will be many times in most companies when the management will have to determine whether or not to add warehouses, eliminate warehouses, or use premium shipping methods such as air freight. There are many intangibles involved in this type of decision, but the amount of added inventory investment and the probable changes in the level of customer service are not intangible. These should be pointed out clearly and objectively by the production and inventory control man.

Bibliography

Published material on branch warehouse inventory control is scarce, but the following two references are excellent:

1. Block, Kenneth L., "Effective Inventory Control in National Branch Warehousing Operations," *APICS Annual Conference Proceedings*, pp. 117-129, 1960.

2. Magee, John F., *Production Planning and Inventory Control*, McGraw, New York, pp. 181-197, 1958.

INDEX

EOQ simplified $\sqrt{\dfrac{2AS}{I}} = \sqrt{\dfrac{2S}{I}} \times \sqrt{A}$ or $K\sqrt{A}$ ∴ $K = \sqrt{\dfrac{2S}{I}}$

[handwritten top margin: Aug. inventory = ½ EOQ + Reserve Stock]

[handwritten annotations: "EOQ" next to Economic lot-size; "71 - 76" next to EOQ; near Expediting:]

A - annual demand $
u - " usage in pcs.
S - ordering cost
I - inventory carrying cost as a decimal fraction /A of avg. inventory.

$$ EOQ = \sqrt{\frac{2AS}{I}} $$

Pcs(units) $\sqrt{\dfrac{2uS}{Ic}}$

$$R = \frac{D - S + \Sigma F}{N}$$

Desired fth. inventory "starting" total sales in planning period

N # of weeks

Service Level = Replenishment periods w/no stock-out × 100
per year.